High Society in the Third Reich

High Society in the Third Reich

Fabrice d'Almeida

Translated by Steven Rendall

polity

First published in French as *La vie mondaine sous le nazisme* © Perrin, 2006

This English edition © Polity Press, 2008

Polity Press
65 Bridge Street
Cambridge CB2 1UR, UK

Polity Press
350 Main Street
Malden, MA 02148, USA

This book is supported by the French Ministry of Foreign Affairs as part of the Burgess programme run by the Cultural Department of the French Embassy in London (www.frenchbooknews.com).

This work has been published with the assistance of the Institut d'histoire du temps présent, CNRS, Paris, France.

Cet ouvrage a été publié avec le soutien de l'Institut d'histoire du temps présent, CNRS, Paris, France.

ISBN-13: 978-0-7456-4311-3
ISBN-13: 978-0-7456-4312-0 (pb)

A catalogue record for this book is available from the British Library.

Typeset in 10pt on 11.5pt Palatino
by Servis Filmsetting Ltd, Stockport, Cheshire.
Printed and bound in Great Britain by MPG Books Ltd, Bodmin, Cornwall

The publisher has used its best endeavours to ensure that the URLs for external websites referred to in this book are correct and active at the time of going to press. However, the publisher has no responsibility for the websites and can make no guarantee that a site will remain live or that the content is or will remain appropriate.

Every effort has been made to trace all copyright holders, but if any have been inadvertently overlooked the publishers will be pleased to include any necessary credits in any subsequent reprint or edition.

For further information on Polity, visit our website: www.polity.co.uk

Liberté • Égalité • Fraternité
RÉPUBLIQUE FRANÇAISE

Contents

Acknowledgements

One evening in 1998, I watched *Il Generale della Rovere*, Roberto Rosselini's 1959 film, with Vittorio de Sica in the title role. I told a friend, Fabio Passera, how much I'd enjoyed seeing de Sica's performance as an actor, and he mentioned that de Sica had become famous during Mussolini's Fascist regime by playing the role of a worldly seducer in light comedies. On that day I had the idea of studying high-society life under Fascism and comparing it with that of the Third Reich. I had to go to Berlin to improve my German, which I'd studied in school but which was not very good. Nicolas Beaupré, who was then completing his thesis, encouraged me to contact Professor Étienne François. I did so. This marvellous meeting allowed me to conduct, thanks to an invitation from the Frankreich Zentrum at the Berlin Technische Universität and a three-month Deutscher Akademischer Austausch Dienst fellowship, a preliminary investigation to determine the feasibility of a comparative study. In Germany, no comprehensive work had been published on my topic. I could therefore pursue my project. The opportunity to do so was provided when I met Professors Harmut Kaelble and Jürgen Kocka, along with Arnd Bauerkämper, all of whom agreed to endorse my candidacy for a Humboldt Foundation fellowship. I was able to work with them for six months at the Freie Universität in Berlin, at the Zentrum für vergleichende Geschichte Europas. I later continued my research when the Centre National de la Recherche Scientifique placed me at the Centre Marc-Bloch in Berlin, which was then directed by Catherine Colliot-Thélène, Olivier Beaud, and Pascale Laborier, successively, who offered me assistance and support. Throughout, the University of Paris X-Nanterre showed great understanding and my colleagues there helped me think things through. Annette Becker in particular encouraged me in this project.

In the course of these residences, researchers and friends discussed my hypotheses and the writing options open to me. Stephan Malinowski was the most important of these colleagues; along with Christian Ingrao and Lucas Delattre, he provided a constant intellectual stimulus. Wolfgang

Benz, Laurence Bertrand-Dorléac, Alain Delissen, Claudine Delphis, Christian Delporte, Jacques Ehrenfreund, David El Kenz, Patrick Eveno, Stephen Gundle, Leonhard Horowski, Olivier Janz, Marc Lazar, Charles Maier, Béatrice Malinowski, Peter Mark, Horst Möller, Gaetano Quagliariello, Heinz Reif, Maurizio Ridolfi, Alceo Riosa, Brigitte and Roland Schaeffer, Wolfgang Schieder, Klaus-Peter Schmid, Peter Schöttler, Klaus-Peter Sick, Bernd Sösemann, Florence Tamagne, Cristelle Trouvé, Jakob Vogel, and Guilhem Zumbaum-Tomassi each sparked an idea or a specific line of inquiry.

The librarians and archivists at the Bundesarchiv (Berlin), the Auswärtiges Amt, the Zentrum für Zeitgeschichte (Munich), and the Zentrum für Antisemitismus Forschung (TU-Berlin) gave me considerable aid in understanding their collections.

May all these friends and colleagues find here – along with Anthony Rowley, who has been the attentive companion of this project – my warmest thanks.

We can never swallow as much as we'll have to vomit up.

Max Liebermann, December 1934

List of Abbreviations

AA	Auswärtiges Amt, German ministry of foreign affairs.
AEG	General Electrical Company, an industrial firm founded in 1887.
BAB	Bundesarchiv Berlin. German federal archives.
BBC	British Broadcasting Corporation.
BDM	Bund Deutscher Mädel. National Socialist youth organization for girls.
BMW	Bayerische Motoren Werke AG, a firm founded in 1917 to produce engines; it began mass production of automobiles in 1929.
BSB	Bayerische Staatsbibliothek (Munich). Bavarian State Library.
CIO	International Olympics Committee.
DAG	Deutsche Adelsgenossenschaft. Association of the German nobility.
DAP	Deutsche Arbeiterpartei. German Workers' Party.
DCA	Anti-aircraft defence.
DHK	Deutches Herrenklub. German Gentlemen's Club.
DKW	Dampf Kraft Wagen, automobile firm founded in 1916. Cooperated with Audi and Horsch to create the Auto Union racing team.
DMI	Deutsches Mode Institut, the German Fashion Institute.
DNB	Deutsches Nachrichten Büro. The Third Reich's official press agency, created in 1934.
DNVP	Deutschnationale Volkspartei. German national-conservative party.
HJ	Hitler Jugend. NSDAP group to train young people.
IFZ	Institut für Zeitgeschichte, Munich. Munich Institute for Contemporary History.
IG	Farben Interesen Gemeinschaft Farbenindustrie AG. German chemical firm.

KdF   Kraft durch Freude. Association for the organization of
               leisure activities under the Third Reich.
Korv. kpt.   Korvetten Kapitän, Corvette captain.
KPD   Kommunistische Partei Deutschlands, German Communist
               Party.
MGM   Metro Goldwyn Mayer.
NS   Nationalsozialismus. A series of German national archives
               proceeding from the Nazi party.
NSDAP   Nationalsozialistische deutsche Arbeiterpartei. National
               Socialist Workers' Party (Nazi party).
NSFK   Nationalsozialistisches Fliegerkorps. A group of NSDAP
               aviators who formed the nucleus of the Luftwaffe.
NSKK   Nationalsozialistisches Kraftfahrkorps. Nazi motorized
               group for transportation and highway safety.
PA   Politisches Archiv, the political archives of the German
               foreign ministry.
R   Reich. Series of German national archives proceeding from
               the state.
RAD   Reichsarbeitsdienst. National labour service created in 1935
               to utilize the labour power of young people between
               eighteen and twenty-five and to relieve unemployment.
RSHA   Riechssicherheitshauptamt. Main national security police
               office.
SA   Sturmabteilung der NSDAP. Nazi party's storm troopers.
SD   Sicherheitsdienst. The SS's security service, which func-
               tioned as a secret police.
SS   Schutzstaffel(n) der NSDAP. Nazi party's security services.
T4   'Tiergartenstrasse 4', address of the chancellery of the
               Führer of the NSDAP that administered a euthanasia pro-
               gramme under this abbreviation.
UFA   Universum Film AG, a film company founded in 1917,
               bought in 1927 by Alfred Hugenberg, and nationalized in
               1937.
USHMM   United States Holocaust Memorial Museum.

Introduction

In 1872, when Wilhelm II's empire was still at its height, the Berlin journalists' association organized a Press Ball. It became an annual affair marking the end of the winter social season, but when it resumed after the First World War the social calendar was less strictly regulated than it had been in the old imperial court. In 1933 the ball took place on 28 January in the restaurant at the Berlin Zoo. Everyone who was anyone in the world of the media, art, diplomacy, or, of course, politics, took to the dance floor. Chancellor Kurt von Schleicher, who was on his way out, did not attend. However, several government ministers commented on the news of the day for the benefit of acquaintances they had long associated with on the floor of the Reichstag or in press conferences. They talked in the loges for the guests of honour, located on the second floor of the restaurant so that their discussions might be more private. On the ground floor, the orchestra was playing dance music varying from waltzes to jazz. A state secretary confided to a journalist from the Ullstein group that President Hindenburg was preparing to appoint Adolf Hitler chancellor.[1] This solution would make it possible to end the parliamentary impasse of cabinets supported only by the president, and to put together a government supported by the Nazis, national conservatives, and social democrats. The solution did not please Hindenburg, but politics required it, since Hitler refused to join any government of which he was not the leader.

This small, carefree world looked upon politics without serious concern; it was relatively confident in the wisdom of its elites. It assumed that Hitler would be supervised, that his authoritarian government would be provisional, like von Schleicher's, and would encourage economic recovery and social peace. The Ullstein group, owned by a family of converted Jews, had no idea that this event would mark the beginning of its downfall. Jewish journalists would no longer be able to work and would no longer be received in high society. The Ullstein brothers would have to step down and sell their empire at a loss. Journalists who worked for the other liberal Jewish press group, Mosse, would experience the same fate.

Jews would no longer be able to walk the streets in peace. Few of their acquaintances would greet them any more. Refined society was changing, and in two or three days its foundations were rebuilt from the ground up, in the apparently harmless form of a parliamentary alliance.

Late in the evening the real party animals arrived – the small fry of the spectacle of high society, the indispensable ornaments of a successful evening. Among them was a young continuity-girl from a good family, Sybil Peech, who worked for the film studio UFA. She was amazed to see so many men in Nazi uniforms. This annoyed her, because her sympathies ran to communism. She had the vague feeling that this press ball might well be her last, as she was later to write in her memoirs.[2] She left the party early to go with a few other stage people like Max Reinhardt, his wife Helene Thimig, and Peter Lorre, Fritz Lang's favourite actor, to a bar in the West quarter, 'Chez Lily'. Lorre, who sensed that he would soon be in exile in Hollywood, was furious: 'Always more brown.' The kings of the night finished their walk with a bitter taste in their mouths.

The next day's newspapers did not yet announce that there was to be a new chancellor, but that evening a few privileged persons who were in on the secret discussed it by telephone. Göring, Ribbentrop, and von Papen assured Hitler that everything was set for his appointment. Around noon on 30 January 1933, the future members of Hitler's cabinet were received in the president's office to take the oath of office. After the official announcement of the news, the eminent figures in the National Socialist movement gathered. Hitler's friends jammed into the lobby of his favourite hotel, the Kaiserhof, while under the windows a crowd of supporters, SA members in uniform and party members in civilian clothing, shouted in joy. Hitler acknowledged the ovations and congratulations. He had chosen to wear a morning coat for the occasion, and even donned a top hat to watch the parade of his supporters. The new chancellor of the Reich was not a boor. He knew the ways of high society and would be able to adapt to its forms of civility, whose language he had already mastered in order to make a good impression.

In a few days, the country underwent a strange shift and common sense was metamorphosed. The whole problem of high-society life under National Socialism lies in this fiction of revolutionary change that in a few weeks became a norm so profoundly interiorized that it defined new rules for social competition and the assertion of personal success. Those who were excluded by this mutation hardly had time to mourn their fall before a torrent of violence consumed them and finally resulted in a massacre whose horror could not have then been imagined. Therein resides the greatest enigma of National Socialism: the juxtaposition of a society that believed it was heir to Culture's highest values with the unleashing of genocidal barbarism.

Above all, Germans who belonged to high society manifested the duality of Nazism with regard to its beneficiaries and its victims. The most famous beneficiaries have already been studied: Hitler, Göring, Goebbels, Himmler, et al. Lengthy biographies enable us to highlight a few networks and to identify events that characterized this circle.[3] A few groups have been examined in monographs that provide a wealth of information about the way the regime functioned: members of the SS, of the Reich's security service (Reichssicherheitshauptamt, RSHA) and of the Gestapo, diplomats, officials, and so on.[4] Leaders' wives have also been the subject of numerous publications of varying quality.[5]

For a long time, the quarrel over Marxism led scholars to turn their attention away from institutions and toward large social classes.[6] For communists, the great capitalists and the upper middle class were the ones responsible for the cataclysm. No, liberal historians replied; in fascism they saw the triumph of the middle classes, who were afraid of becoming part of the proletariat. More subtle thinkers such as Franz Neumann conceived of this chaotic regime as a coalition of blocs – the party, the army, the governmental administration, and the great capitalists. The argument turned on the validity of certain major questions: was Nazism a form of totalitarianism or of fascism? Didn't it conform to the theoretical schema of the former while claiming to adopt the style of the latter? Behind these oppositions, readers could discern political choices. Victims of their own presuppositions, many historians failed to examine the actual established groups that helped this strange regime to take and retain power.[7]

Not until the publication in 2003 of Stephan Malinowski's great dissertation could one read an in-depth study of the role played by the nobility in the corridors of power from the birth of the empire in 1871 to the end of the Second World War.[8] With the skill of a watchmaker, Malinowski demonstrates not only the great families' conversion to the new institutions but also the way this milieu served as an intellectual laboratory for the German extreme right, and how the National Socialist idea was still dominant among the eleventh-hour opponents who tried to kill Hitler on 20 July 1944. That is how Malinowski's meticulous research was able to recuperate from the limbo of political and social history a category that had long been considered pre-eminent and indispensable for understanding the way power functions and that has brought about a profound change in the way we see National Socialism.

The enormous body of scholarship on Nazi Germany, the Second World War, and the Shoah may thus have astonishing lacunae that can be understood only in terms of historiography. This is also true for high-society life. The post-war generation of historians, who knew only too well what unheard-of advantages the regime had showered on these prodigal sons, regarded high society as a taboo subject and ignored it. At that time, it was thought more important to deprive the monster of its magic by describing its violence and re-educating Germans in a peaceful, democratic way of life. Competition with communist regimes probably had the effect of preventing too much attention from being given to the continuity linking the elites of the Third Reich and those of the Federal Republic. Was it not East Germany that produced documentaries accusing ministers in the Adenauer governments of having served in the SS? In this context, historians set aside anything that might point to an indulgent attitude toward Nazism. Historians were not unaware, passively at least, of the 'positive' attraction the regime exerted on the elites, but they remained silent about it in order to avoid feeding a nostalgia that was dangerous during the Cold War. For similar reasons, this silence continued over the following decades. The avenues followed by historians ended up by causing them to forget what had formerly been known implicitly. A later, post-war generation of historians did not know at first hand about the advantages and pleasures conferred by Nazism. It took the quarrel between social history and the history of everyday life (*Alltagsgeschichte*) to draw renewed attention to subjects related to cultural history and to raise indirectly the question of the regime's attraction for those who experienced it.[9] Peter Reichel played the role of a catalyst by emphasizing the complexity of the mechanisms employed in order to put the masses under a spell.[10] He broke with an interpretation of the regime strictly in terms of propaganda and manipulation by drawing largely on the perspective opened up by George Mosse's notion of a national pedagogy leading to a political religion.[11] The question of the elites remained. It has been recently raised through the prism of economics by a generation of historians who are as provocative as they are competent, including Frank Bajohr, Götz Aly, and, in the domain of art, Jonathan Petropoulos.[12]

The absence of overall reflection on social relationships no doubt results from another form of resistance among historians:[13] dread and scorn for the '*petite histoire*' that was so beloved of journalists and moralists and that limited itself to small explanations while ignoring great social factors. Discussing political figures in a very intimate way was long considered a matter of mere description that could not explain what was really involved, the main causes. However, in recent years writers have been able to insert this apparently anecdotal material into complex, essential explanations that sometimes fall within the domain of cultural history and sometimes within that of anthropo-history. Even Ian Kershaw's biography of Hitler includes quotations and details whose emblematic dimension the reader appreciates.

The study of high society is one of the ways of renewing the analysis of politics on the basis of questions that are primordial for the study of human organizations: the family, exchange, and, of course, the institutions of power. We thus see that the problem of high society under Nazism is not related solely to a desire to understand how passions were braided together in an age of violence and tensions unlike any other in human history, but also to a desire to outline a few recurrent features of the composition and functioning of political societies. The comparative dimension and *histoire croisée* will thus remain a focal point for grasping the interest of reflecting on Nazism at the beginning of the twenty-first century.[14] National Socialism was part of a process of creating a fascist Europe and overturning democracies through mass politics. It helped generate the extreme political religions that we regard as forms of totalitarianism. Its history brings out enduring features of political and social behaviour. Are not many of the scandalous aspects of this period still found in our advanced democracies?

Nazism was not a regime based on violence alone, far from it.[15] More than its brutality, it was its methods of seduction that allowed it to establish itself and to endure. Without descending into caricature, it has to be asserted clearly that the Shoah would not have been possible without the profound illusion that the regime was doing something good for most of the German population. For this advantage, the elites were prepared to sacrifice a part of the population, the Jews, in whom they saw an obstacle to the realization of the perfect national community. The physical destruction of this obstacle was the price to be paid for the greatest happiness.

Quickly established, functioning in a fluctuating way, Nazi power showed the same flexibility in adapting to conflicts as had earlier regimes in which so many forms of legitimacy intersected. Very disparate groups and administrative departments (the SS, Gestapo, police, Wehrmacht, Reichsbahn, Reichsbank, foreign affairs, supplies and industry) were involved in questions as important as the implementation of genocide. The coherence of these elements was provided only by interpersonal relations and forms of hierarchy that were based chiefly on the reputation an individual enjoyed among his peers.

Hitler played a major role in this system. But today everyone knows that his decisions could not run counter to the will of certain hierarchs who enjoyed, if not great impunity, at least a reciprocal confidence that guaranteed them against third parties. Above all, the Führer could act only insofar as what he did was the object of a consensus within most of the elites and was supported locally. To examine this phenomenon, which was a novelty in the twentieth century, it is useful to compare it with the *ancien régime* French monarchy and to make use of the concept of historical regression. The everyday management of power was greatly influenced by the presence of clienteles and nepotism in a system that paralleled in this respect a court society.[16] Hitler was a sort of Louis XIV without a Versailles. He had the pomp, the courtiers, the quarrels between princes, and the bizarre aspects of a sovereign, even toward the end of his career. His passion for the colossal did not lead him to construct a gigantic court, but instead to transform his whole country into a series of groups of courtiers in which he could navigate at ease, finding everywhere the same obsessive zeal in the crowds and among the local bosses who had embraced his programme as if it was obviously the right one.

High society had, of course, existed long before Hitler's regime. National Socialism was not yet even an idea when the princely courts and great patrician families, the powers in the world of German finance, commerce, and industry, began establishing personal relationships that were the spice of high society. But the Third Reich marked an important change. In this period of uncertainty regarding social classifications, this was the moment that witnessed a true 'descent' of high society.[17] A social descent, first of all, because the intermediate professions and managers, and even certain subaltern elements, henceforth thought of themselves as having a direct or indirect relationship with refined society and adopted high-society manners in many aspects of their lives: cultural practices, the pace of life, and representations. To be sure, literature, cinema, and the press contributed to the broad dissemination of information about high society and produced people who imitated this particular aesthetic. High society was also opened up quantitatively, since with the multiplication of social events and the growing number of guests expected to attend them, the group involved in such social relationships was more numerous than before. High society thus became a plural social laboratory, and this change went along with a form of generalized politicization that was accompanied by an unparalleled concentration of power.

The concept of high society should thus not be understood solely in terms of the tinkling of champagne glasses (Ribbentrop had sold champagne before becoming a diplomat), evening dresses, and dinner jackets, but rather in terms of a series of considerations regarding human destiny and baubles that govern men's hearts, as Napoleon put it. High society shows the ability of a government to live with the elites of its country, to achieve a synthesis of the power principle with the pleasure principle.[18] And there *was* pleasure under Nazism.

Being a member of high society means participating indirectly in power through coalescence, receiving part of its benefits, and taking advantage of its shadow to conceal one's privileges. But the essence of high society does not reside solely in its dealings with the power that shapes its contours. It also has to do with principles of action and life in common. Becoming a socialite means carrying out precise tasks that qualify an individual, in the eyes of others, to enter circles of activity and speech.[19] These rules of selection are not immutable, even if they share characteristics that are a distant legacy from courtly society: politeness and civility. The Nazi socialite therefore did not resemble a socialite under the Weimar Republic. Nonetheless, on closer examination a continuity between the two periods is discernible whose origin is certainly to be found in the fact that both regimes had to deal with the mass culture that was then exploding. Cultural life and collective forms of consumption are in a symbiotic relationship with power both before and after 1933. Thanks to this symbiosis, the commercial successes of actors and the theatre world were amplified by an unprecedented symbolic weight. Stars became moral authorities. Party leaders sought to share in these famous thespians' new legitimacy. The continuities with the Wilhelmine Empire are no less remarkable: the old sovereign courts of the princes federated in 1871 survived despite the Weimar Republic's efforts to prohibit them. The Bavarian royal family continued to determine the way refined society lived in southern Germany. Its marriages and birthdays remained important events to which it invited relatives from all over Europe as well as the crowned heads of the old continent. Aristocratic habits were omnipresent and still fed social life in the 1930s. To put it another way, they constituted the spinal column of social life, along with the chivalric way of thought that was inherited by the National Socialist ideal. The SS in particular claimed to be a new aristocracy and modelled itself on the nobility. In the early 1930s, it created cavalry detachments (Reiter SS) to emphasize this affiliation and recruited heavily in the castles.

However, it cannot be denied that 1933 marked a major turning point.[20] After Hitler came to power, social relationships were rewritten. They were marked by high points explicitly connected with National Socialist ideology, and the cohabitation of elites occurred in new places that were suited to promote the cult of the leader, first of all because this totalitarian regime claimed to realize a fusion of the elites with the masses within a community of the people. The regime tried repeatedly to carry out this programme, in particular by going to war. Did it succeed? That is the first question that confronts the historian.

The break is also discernible in aesthetics and style. After 1933, the colours of public and private life changed. The flag bearing a swastika became Germany's official insignia in 1935 and was seen everywhere, while the black and brown of Nazi party uniforms adorned the streets along with the blue-green of army and diplomatic uniforms that Hitler personally redesigned. Then there spread, in association with a pervasive virility, a curt, brutal style in work relationships and a way of speaking about politics, even in the family, that was marked by unusual violence. This radicalization of language and actions gradually made its way into social codes and authorized modes of behaviour that seemed to represent a regression in comparison to the elegance of the refined society of the Belle Époque. It was ultimately interiorized and indicated by symbols such as the swastika, a sign of the supposed original purity of the ancient Germans. The swastika's omnipresence revealed the amplitude of the change that had occurred. Between historical continuity and radical change, the historian rediscovers here one of the oldest questions in the debate over Nazism and the uniqueness of this regime in the history of the twentieth century.

The present study seeks to deal with this question in a nuanced manner by emphasizing discrepancies and occasionally pointing to the continuation of older practices. It challenges general categories and classifications (the bourgeoisie, the middle classes, etc.) because social history has nothing to gain from being reductive. By basing everything on definitions and taxonomies, the historian risks losing sight of the central events and ways of being that are fundamental for understanding what happened in Germany between 1933 and 1945.

This perspective is no doubt related to the fact that I am not German, and that I was trained in a historiography in which the question of high society and private life has occupied a fundamental place ever since the work of Philippe Ariès and Georges Duby.[21] High society (*la vie mondaine*) is not in fact a German historical concept. The German word *Mondän* is, moreover, rather pejorative. It connotes a lamentable frivolity. The word is understood, but leaves the impression that it can refer only to an uninterrupted series of trivial festivities. In speaking of these groups and their activities, Germans more often use the expressions 'high society' (*hohe Gesellschaft*) or 'refined society' (*feine Gesellschaft*), and, to refer to people who belong to this group, the term 'society'. In the inter-war period, the term frequently used, with a negative connotation, to designate this group was 'the prominent' (*Prominenten*, abbreviated to '*Promi*', literally 'those on top'; it might be better translated as 'the powerful'). The term '*Bonze*' (bigwig), which was frequently used by the far right before it was applied to the far right itself once the latter came to power, had a strong critical connotation. Another, humorous, expression used to designate party big shots whose breasts were covered with decorations and medals was *Goldfasan* (golden pheasant). 'Sociability' could be an alternative concept, because two words approximate this meaning in German. One is directly derived from the same root (*Sociabilität*), while the other is older and alludes to polished manners (*Geselligkeit*). In addition, to indicate a rather retrograde attitude, people used the term '*k.u.k.*' (*Kaiser und König*, an expression referring to the pre-1914 period). The idea of a 'court' does not suffice to account for the peculiar nature of relationships within high society under National Socialism. Using this term would lead us to focus excessively on the study of the structures Hitler set up to govern his entourage. It puts too little emphasis on the heart of the problem: indirect subordination and interpersonal relations.

In France, the expression '*vie mondaine*' (high-society life) derives from the distinction between clergy and laymen. Those who were attached to worldly goods ended up being those who could cultivate their lives by regularly attending events at the court and in high society. Thus high-society life could now be defined as a set of places, moments, events, practices, and representations not exclusively connected with a certain vocational activity and shared by members of high society. To live exclusively in high society's perspective is to become a socialite, and this in turn implies neglecting certain important things, those that require work and moral rigour. Life in high society can therefore not be reduced to cultural life, even if they sometimes intersect.

In its complexity and ambiguity, the concept of high-society life has the advantage of emphasizing the importance of human relationships and their determining effect on individuals. It presupposes events that bring men and women together; it implies material infrastructures and cultural practices; and it draws a dividing line between members of high society and other citizens. Above all, it allows us to reflect on the borders between the spheres of public life and private life, without presuppositions, because it is a question of seeing what role one sphere plays in the other. Thus we can delimit an area where humans and institutions evolve and, consequently, hierarchies and complicities come into being. The idea of high society life also assumes that what binds its actors together is neither simple nor unambiguous. Hitler knew this better than most; he used all sorts of means to ensure loyalty to him.

Several factors seem to have forged durable solidarities and structured the links between high society and the state. First, there was self-interest, particularly when conceived in material terms. The quest for money and the accumulation of goods led many people to follow the Nazi regime, which rewarded them so generously. This argument has often been made, and the rewards in question will be illustrated here by gifts,[22] tax reductions, and a way of life. Second, there was ideological passion, which has also been extensively studied.[23] It is very pertinent for decoding the motivation of certain actors operating in the grip of genuine belief.[24] Two additional factors are less often mentioned, but emerge clearly if one takes affects into account. First, there are collective emotions, structuring phenomena that elicit common reactions to an event and that are inscribed on people's memories and socialize their minds. Collective emotion and memory create group and generational identities. The defeat of Germany in 1918 and the revolutions and repression that followed it exercised considerable influence on whole areas of German society, as did Hitler's successes in the area of foreign policy. The range of emotions to be taken into consideration is not limited to joy and fear, but also includes disgust, anger, astonishment, and sadness, whose manifestations witnesses did not find ambiguous.[25] Finally, there were personal affections, whose importance is shown by couples or friendships that were not betrayed despite the obvious material competition at stake. Here Hitler's often-mentioned charisma has to be taken into account:[26] Hitler and Göring knew how to elicit real feelings of gratitude and desire, as well as the genuine affection felt by their contemporaries.

This book studies Nazi power in its apparent ceremonious solemnity, but from the point of view of those who experienced these events, and evaluates their emotions. Thus we shall look at the operation of power behind the scenes, where conversations were prepared and negotiations among members of the elites were organized in order to divide up offices and benefits.

Our project is thus to return to a kind of history that draws attention to phenomena that are small but nonetheless very revealing and examines and describes them in detail, a kind of history that remains curious and does not draw conclusions and lessons when the reader can draw them him- or herself. What is needed is a new way of seeing transversally events that have too often been cut off from the sequence to which they belong, although it is clear that they contain a portion of the truth that is indispensable for formulating an interpretation. Since the establishment of micro-history, historians are well aware that the detail has become the minimal unit on the basis of which a period can be understood.[27] In the cinema, close-ups reveal personal tragedy and a scene's complexity.[28] In a painting, Daniel Arasse said, an inconspicuous detail sometimes indicates the work's deepest meaning.[29] Description is therefore not a neutral tool. It activates a theory of the social, as the anthropologist Clifford Geertz has shown by creating the concept of 'thick description'.[30] In order to understand Nazism, we have to exhume details, singular facts, and particular cases that have been too long neglected, obscured by the dense shadow cast by political, military, and criminal events.

In order to exhume these details, I have used original documents, often lying unpublished and neglected in archives that are nonetheless frequently consulted. These are the archives of the Third Reich, those of the German minister of foreign affairs, those of the Nazi party, and the complex archives on de-Nazification, along with collections of images and contemporary newspapers. These sources are not neutral. The very fact that they were preserved already raises a question: why, despite the massive destruction of archives resulting from the war, did so many letters, postcards, plans for seating arrangements, lists of participants, and invitations to things as trivial as dinner parties, breakfasts, or film premières come down to us? Why were the little booklets describing the clothes and decorations that guests were to wear not thrown away? Why were the lists kept indicating which guest was going to travel in which car in the convoys of cars leaving for vacations at Hitler's mountain retreat? Simply because for the Nazi regime these events were not insignificant or negligible. On these occasions, the alliance among the different groups that were involved in power relationships and that declared themselves to be dominant was reaffirmed and strengthened. For the most part, public testimony given after the war complements this view. It is a rich source of details on the evolution of manners. It provides the historian with startling evidence regarding the mentality before the Shoah, at a time when people could calmly close their eyes to massive despoliation and liquidation because they accepted the persecution of Jews and Gypsies, scorn for Poles and Czechs, sterilization of the handicapped, and the placement in concentration camps of homosexuals, political opponents, marginal people, and delinquents.

The definition of Nazism needs to be shifted toward high society. And what is in question here is indeed 'high society', an expression whose contours are vague but which takes on substance when connected with specific objects such as guest lists and defined by measuring the frequency of parties, concerts, theatrical performances, or premières, seeing who is corresponding with whom, and evaluating the density of interpersonal networks. Thus emerges a vast group of men and women who participated in society life more or less constantly and regularly. It was they who constituted high society under the Third Reich.

A word concerning the term 'elite', which is so often used in the plural in this study. Here, the word does not have a normative or positive value. It does not signify an obscure class that has been arbitrarily created by liberal scholars in order to defy Marxist interpretations. The elites represent something more concrete: all those who succeeded professionally and socially and who, by virtue of their success, contributed directly or indirectly to the exercise of power. This view was more or less that of Vilfredo Pareto, an Italian-Swiss sociologist who found fascism so much in accord with his theories that he ended up endorsing it.[31] He was therefore well qualified to describe the social mechanisms that allowed its victory. For Pareto, all these professional elites were in competition for access to the government. A regime was defined by a certain coalition of elites that, taken together, constituted the political class. If a new elite emerged, the coalition and form of the government changed. In its mechanist dimension, this circulation of elites has its limits for the sociologist. It remains more a descriptive than a predictive model. But it has the advantage of breaking with generalities and encouraging the historian to look closely at who does what, how, and where.

A different history of Nazism thus appears whose essential anthropological dimension explains in part its development. It complements the anthropological history of Nazism that has so carefully studied the paradigms of race and blood, as well as paradigms of violence.[32] In short, we are called upon to examine a banquet. This banquet lasted twelve years, almost a generation, but it was the counterpart of the murder that took place over a relatively short time and is known under the name of genocide. What is high-society life if not the gigantic feast of savage sacrifice that the Nazis made of so many people, and primarily the Jews? In saying this, I am not proposing to return to the already ancient theory of the scapegoat, whose limits were shown by Hannah Arendt,[33] but instead suggesting that the festive aspects are intrinsically linked to the perpetration of the mass crime. Ethnologists have long debated the relationship between banquet and sacrifice, and my work owes a great deal to Maurice Bloch, who sees these two phenomena as instances of a ritual whose objective was to found the human community.[34] Seen up close, high-society life welded together German high society as much as did its willing or tacit participation in crimes that would, it was thought, guarantee its perpetuation.

To study life in high society is thus also to reflect on the crime from another point of view, that of the murderer. This exercise is indispensable for taking the measure of his act and understanding how he could be indifferent to the suffering of others. The strange connection between feast and sacrifice, feast and massacre, explains in part this attitude. In the 1930s, people were inspired by this kind of belief. They were immersed in a composite mythology glorified by National Socialist leaders. Nordic divinities, for example, invited deceased warriors to a vast banquet presided over by Odin. Didn't Nazism claim to bring heaven down to earth? In Christian lands, didn't the Last Supper remind people of the death that was necessary in order to achieve the community? Finally, weren't the Spartans' sacrifices in battle with the Persians or the Carthaginians examples that had been taught in secondary schools since the end of the nineteenth century? Didn't Gebhard Himmler, who was the father of Heinrich Himmler (the head of the SS), a great Hellenist, and still director of the best secondary school in Munich in the 1920s, tell his students about the sacrifice – described by Polybius – made by Hasdrubal's wife, who strangled her children, threw them into the flames, and then leapt into the fire herself in order to wipe out her husband's treachery?[35] The feast, the massacre of others, and self-immolation are parts of an eschatological conception of the world that assumed that pleasure was to be found in victory and the destruction of adversaries, and if this was not possible, then in perishing oneself to keep a principle alive.[36]

These ponderous ideas were implicit in high-society life. They delimited its sphere, which stopped where one began to get blood on one's own hands.[37] However, those officiating sometimes forgot their obligation to purify themselves, to wash away the traces of the crime, to destroy the remains of the victims, or to take off their high-society clothing, and then they created confusions, overlaps between one sphere and the other. As a result, we can now see how the two phenomena were intertwined and fed each other, how the very contours of festive activity depended on the cruelty of the National Socialists' choices.

The reader has no doubt understood that while National Socialism was indeed a product of a powerful machine for mobilizing the masses, making them accomplices in its crimes, and rewarding them, it was due above all to the elites. Without the latter's cynicism, history would not have been so tragic. The fantasy of unlimited pleasure would have collided with the domesticated frameworks of a democratic power. The banquet would have been more modest, and the gods' cuisine would not have led to so many human sacrifices.

The tragedy began in 1933, but the theatre was older. Here is the plot, which is reflected in the organization of this book. Immediately after the Great War, socialites received the turbulent members of the NSDAP in their salons (chapter 1), and were very taken with their provocative style. They supported this party which, for a time, seemed to be calling for a restoration of the monarchy, and which seemed to them well suited to defend their ideals. The Nazis' accession to power seems to have emerged directly from this muffled world that gave them a human face (chapter 2).

After 1933, a system of gifts and exchanges was set up that created a genuine high society that was soon deeply penetrated by a bureaucracy whose goal was to manage displays of adherence and to determine what symbolic or material rewards, if any, should be granted those who sought their recognition (chapter 3). Thus we can see how three sets of social relationships were structured concentrically around the centre of political power represented by the Reich chancellery. The destruction of Jewish high society was the corollary of this mutation. It reveals the coherence between the Nazis' ideological project and their social action. The spoliation of Jewish property provided a durable foundation for Hitler's pets (chapter 4), who sought a luxurious life in conformity with their aesthetic sense and their doctrine (chapter 5). Under the impact of totalitarianism, they modified their habits and relied on the NSDAP especially to create signs of excellence and distinction that would show everyone how the regime had evolved (chapter 6). Diplomacy was also affected by this movement (chapter 7). It was the object of a strategy of seduction whose goal was to mask the Reich's imperial ambitions and to establish abroad groups that were sympathetic to its cause and would provide the starting point for a fifth column at the highest level. Finally, the Second World War amplified and imperilled the project of fusing the elites (chapter 8). It left in place a high society that was marked by the experience of defeat in 1945 but had never truly analysed its dark side.

1

The Birth of Nazi High Society

Growing agitation and febrile political activity overtook Germany at the end of the Great War. The defeat was followed by revolutionary uprisings that were put down with much bloodshed. A climate of civil war lurked just beneath the surface. In Berlin, the minister of the interior, Noske, saw to it that public meetings were subjected to rigorous surveillance after the repression of the Spartakist communist revolution of January 1919. In Munich, the atmosphere was explosive: since the end of the monarchy, partisans of order and reaction had been battling each other as well as the communists.[1]

This political effervescence did not escape the notice of Bavaria's government officials, who had just taken over after the demise of the short-lived soviet republic set up by Bavarian Marxists. An extensive system of espionage and surveillance was established to identify possible adversaries or allies of the new authorities. In this context, the army played an autonomous role, backing the social democrats in the central government so far as they were useful to it. The army was observing political developments before deciding whom to support. In Munich, the General Staff assigned Captain Ernst Röhm to maintain paramilitary networks. One of his close associates who was responsible for propaganda and intelligence, Captain Karl Mayr, recruited a corporal with good nationalist inclinations: the thirty-year-old Adolf Hitler.[2] Hitler had not, however, fought the Reds, instead remaining obediently in his barracks. However, later on he had made tough-sounding remarks that had drawn attention to him, and he then was able to play a role as an anticommunist indoctrinator in the service of the army. In September 1919 Mayr assigned Hitler to spy on the Deutsche Arbeiterpartei (DAP), and then authorized him to join it and try to influence it. Finally, Hitler's brilliant rhetoric convinced Anton Drexler, the founder of this small party, to appoint him to an important office in its organization.

When Hitler joined the DAP in the autumn of 1919, the party had about five hundred members. In November 1923, at the time of the putsch, membership had risen to almost fifty thousand. This success was due in part to Hitler's seductive power over wealthy milieus, a power made easier by his frequenting of the fashionable salons of Munich and Berlin, where he found financing and connections. From this grew a complex relationship between high society and the Nazi movement that was characterized by mutual influence.

Is Hitler *Salonfähig*?

Hitler was the obscure son of a bureaucrat and had not reached high rank in the army; he thus had hardly any qualifications for access to high society. In early twentieth-century Germany, society was divided according to wealth and birth.[3] Fashionable groups were open to noble and rich families. Occasionally, someone who had achieved a remarkable exploit, mainly in the military or artistic realm, might be admitted to high society, like the composer Richard Wagner. In addition to talent, the newcomer had to have a sufficient sense of social conventions and find friends and family members who would agree to act as mediators. On these conditions alone, an individual could become *salonfähig*, that is, worthy of being received in a fashionable salon. In 1919, salons were still the main form of social relationships among members of the elite. Often hosted by a woman who set their tone, salons brought together, on a daily or weekly basis, groups of acquaintances varying in size from about a dozen for intimate meetings to several hundred on the occasion of the great parties of the season.

In Munich, one of the most important salons was hosted by Elsa Bruckmann, a princess of Romanian origin born in 1865; her father, Prince Theodore Cantacuzino, served at the court of the King of Bavaria. She was the wife of Hugo Bruckmann, a rich publisher who had embraced the nationalist cause in the 1880s. This lady, who was elegant despite her heavy body and square jaw, organized afternoon and evening meetings in her vast home at 10 Leopoldstrasse, where the old and the new artistic and literary generations of Munich met. However, her salon was not open to Jews, no matter what their merits, for the Bruckmanns thought, like Richard Wagner and his son-in-law Houston Stewart Chamberlain, that the struggle between the races was more important than that between classes, and that Jews were corrupting the original vitality of Germans, of Aryans.[4] Would Adolf Hitler have been qualified to frequent the Bruckmanns' house?

Descriptions of Hitler at this time vary. For some people, he was leading a bohemian life and the main features of his character were already present. For others, he was rather organized and routine-bound, spending his days moving between his room and the cafés where he pursued his political activities. Interpretations also vary regarding his relationship to modernity, and even to good manners. A French observer, Robert Bouchez, a former French diplomatic attaché in Munich, has left us a belated account of the man that is as amusing as it is implausible: 'I also remember one day when we were sitting at the same table, on the rough wooden benches at the Hofbräu beer hall. Hermann Kriebel sat next to me. Hitler was drinking coffee, a "Mokka," as they said over there. He lifted his pinky when he held his cup . . . Obviously he was not a gentleman.'[5] If Bouchez puts so much stress on Hitler's vulgarity, he does so in order to draw attention to his brutality and mediocrity. In France, lifting the pinky was the sign of the pretentious, lower middle-class social climber ignorant of the simplicity of good manners. In Germany, this gesture was considered simply crude.

No similar observation is to be found in other testimonies. Otto Strasser, who was at first a supporter and then a resolute adversary of Hitler's, mentions different things. His book, written after the war, never fails to point out anything unfavourable to the Nazi leader. However, Strasser does not mention either Hitler's lack of breeding or his affected manners, although he dined with him when they first met in October 1920. Strasser's brother Gregor had organized this meeting, which was also attended, notably, by Marshal Ludendorff, the hero of the First World War. To be sure, Otto Strasser describes Hitler as eccentric, already a vegetarian (this is denied by other witnesses) and refusing to drink alcoholic beverages. However, Hitler did agree to eat the luncheon served by his hostess, Else Strasser, even though it included meat. According to Otto Strasser, Hitler was excited, impatient and behaved with obsequious hypocrisy toward Ludendorff. He describes Hitler's rather brusque gestures, but nothing that denotes ill breeding. How could the pharmacist Gregor Strasser, a notable of Landshut, the Bavarian town where this dinner took place, have agreed to receive a boor in his home, especially in the presence of such an august figure as Ludendorff? Strasser's testimony thus suggests that in the domain of politeness, at this time, Hitler's behaviour was not peculiar.

Ernst Hanfstaengl is more ambiguous in discussing this matter. To be sure, Hanfstaengl, a publisher of art books who came from an old, wealthy Munich family, was trying to make himself look good in his memoirs, and precisely in the area of social life. He presents himself as the person who introduced Hitler into refined society and tried to hone his taste in art. His meeting with Hitler took place later than Strasser's, on 22 November 1922. At the urging of an American military attaché, Hanfstaengl had gone to hear Hitler speak in another Munich beer hall, the Kindlkeller. Seduced by Hitler's rhetoric, he decided to make his acquaintance, and became his friend. Soon, Hanfstaengl invited Hitler to his elegant home, where his wife Helene was also taken with the rising leader. 'Stories are sometimes told,' Hanfstaengl explains, 'that we were the people who taught Hitler table-manners. That's not so. He was not so uncouth as that. But he did have some curious tastes. He had the most incredible sweet tooth of any man I have ever met.'[6]

These contradictory views manifest a hypothetical distance between the elites and Hitler, in which what is at stake is the construction of an image of the leader as a revolutionary more or less close to the people. In reality, Hitler was brought up in the family of an authoritarian bureaucrat.[7] His father, Aloïs Hitler, was a sort of minor notable. He was the director of the customs office in Linz, and thus held a relatively high rank in the Austrian bureaucratic hierarchy. Despite a tendency to alcoholism and brutality at home, Aloïs, whose parents were peasants, learned good manners and, as Joachim Fest explains,[8] changed his name in order to have a more honourable patronymic. In this household, table manners were not so different from those in great houses. Certainly the quality of the food and the value of the tableware were inferior. But the refinement of customs and manuals of etiquette imposed their rules on this social stratum, because subaltern bureaucrats underwent the influence of the elite of the educated bourgeoisie (*Bildungsburgertum*) that they aspired to join. This middle-class education was all the less distant from the criteria of behaviour among the national elite because several events had changed the level of requirements for behaviour at the summit of society.

First of all, the First World War had resulted in a vast intermingling of social levels. Soldiers and officers from the upper classes made the mutual discovery of their common humanity and the possibility of acting in concert, despite a few differences in manners. Thus people agreed, in order to ensure the success of important undertakings, to frequent persons from different social milieus. Veterans belonging to high society brought back from the front a crude and violent way of speaking that they used to let off steam in private and in public. They no longer hesitated to act brusquely or to wear casual clothes if doing so made them seem more manly.[9] Members of the middle class of all ages who had avoided the war but had fought in the Freikorps adopted similar modes of behaviour.[10] And then after the socialists gained power part of the ritual of government was upset and simplified. For several years, people hesitated between simply returning to the old etiquette and choosing to adopt new rules. For example, President Ebert changed the way state dinners were organized and tried to temper the authoritarian image of the head of state created by Wilhelm II. Moreover, Ebert preferred small committees to large receptions and proved very persuasive during working breakfasts with colleagues, journalists, and leaders.

Thus, given the change in customs, Hitler was *salonfähig*, worthy of being received in the salon of a good family, as early as 1920–2. As his role as a political leader was confirmed, his social value also increased. However, it is not clear whether the Bruckmanns had already received him in their home at that time. But other fashionable people got used to the style of this man who won the affections of those he wanted to seduce.

1920–2: The First Triumphs in High Society

Hitler's social network grew gradually, though it is not easy to chart its development precisely. His first relationships were connected chiefly with his political commitment. His meeting with members of the Thule Society in early 1920 filled out the group of friends he had made in the army and the DAP. Several of these nationalists fascinated by esotericism were rich and cultivated, like Dietrich Eckart. The son of a notary, Eckart had pursued a career in literature and journalism in pre-war Berlin. Having consumed his father's fortune, he married a woman from a wealthy family and was thus able to lead a comfortable life, while his works for the theatre, such as his *Heinrich der Hohenstaufe* and his translation of Ibsen's *Peer Gynt*, allowed him to make the acquaintance of the capital's celebrities. After the death of his wife, he decided in 1915, at the age of forty-seven, to move to Munich. His anti-Semitism brought him into contact with the nationalists and permitted him to meet leading figures and journalists; he joined the Fichte-Bund and then wrote for the newspaper *Unser Vaterland*. He helped finance the very nationalist *Münchner Beobachter*. In 1920, thanks to his mediation, the NSDAP was able to buy the old *Münchner Beobachter*, whose national edition had taken the name of *Völkischer Beobachter*, and make it a sort of official organ of the NSDAP. Moreover, Eckart kept up his relationships in the theatrical world. He had an incontestable *savoir-faire* and his literary work allowed him to enjoy a good reputation in the Bavarian capital. After the war, his nationalist commitment was radicalized. Although he had not fought during the Great War, he now was eager to see action. As a widower, he had time for political activity. He met Hitler through the DAP toward the end of 1919, and became his friend and almost his tutor. It was Eckart who constructed Hitler's first high-society network. On 16 March 1920, Eckart took his protégé on a Berlin jaunt in an aeroplane piloted by his friend Ritter von Greim, a military man who had recently been ennobled. He introduced Hitler to all sorts of people, most of whom were patriots and anti-Semites: Major Albrecht von Gaefe-Goldebee; the writer Ernst Graf zu Reventlow, whose French wife, Marie-Gabrielle, a former cabaret dancer, had taken the title of Countess of Allemont;[11] Maria Walter Stennes, the head of the Freikorps; and others. During the same trip to Berlin, Hitler met General Erich Ludendorff for the first time in the salon hosted by the widow of the industrialist Carl Albrecht Heckmann.[12] He was so intoxicated by these encounters that he did not want to return immediately to Munich, despite his friend's admonitions.

Was it at this point or a little later on that Eckart took Hitler to the home of the Bechsteins? In any case, by 1922 they had already developed a close relationship. The Bechsteins hosted a rather prestigious salon. Edwin Bechstein ran a piano company that had been founded by his father in 1853. He was born in 1859 and had met and married his wife, née Caito, in

London. Frau Bechstein, whose first name was Helene, was swept away by the energy of Hitler, who was thirteen years younger than her. She decided to speak to her husband on his behalf, and soon Bechstein and Hitler became friends. With the Bechsteins, Hitler gained access to the very high society of wealthy industrialists. When the Bechsteins came to Munich for the winter, they lived in the Vier Jahrezeiten hotel, close to the old Royal Palace. They invited their political protégé to visit them there, and gave him useful gifts, as one might support an artist. The couple also acquired a fine house in Obersalzberg where they could enjoy the mountain air. Hitler was welcome there. Helene Bechstein bought him his first luxury car, a red Mercedes worth twenty-six thousand marks.[13]

It is unlikely that Eckart was the one who introduced Hitler, around the same time, to the publisher Bruckmann, the head of the book publishing confederation in Munich. The views of this industrialist, who made his anti-Semitism and ultra-nationalism evident early on, corresponded very closely to those of the rising Führer. Elsa Bruckmann may have become Hitler's friend at this time, and he may have occasionally frequented her salon without already being as close to her as he later became. According to legend, Elsa gave Hitler his first riding whip (*Peitschl*). Since his days in Vienna, Hitler had often carried a cane, as a way of asserting his superiority over mere proletarians. With the whip, his style changed. He became less bourgeois and more brutal. Was it in order to defend himself in the fights and shoving matches that were so common during his meetings? That is not at all clear. Hitler is said to have had three riding whips given him by his high-society connections: one by Elsa Bruckmann, another by Helene Bechstein, and a third, the one he carried for the longest time, by Frau Büchner, the proprietress of the Moritz pension in Obersalzberg, whose establishment was soon thereafter converted into a luxurious hotel called the Platterhof. Like Hitler's moustache, the whip was thus more a trademark than a means of defence. Today, the whip seems connected with some fantasy, whereas at that time it was still a common object, since horses were still everywhere, even in urban environments. The riding whip lent an air of authority. However that may be, at the Bruckmanns' home Hitler not only received gifts but also met people like Gertrud von Seidlitz, the widow of the painter Friedrich Wilhelm von Seidlitz, who came from a noble family. Taken with Hitler, his widow, who was nearing fifty, joined the party in May 1921.

Hitler's other high-society acquaintances at this time did not go so far as the widow von Seidlitz. Neither the Bruckmanns nor the Bechsteins joined the NSDAP. However, Eckart and Max-Erwin Scheubner-Richter, another party member who had access to Bavarian social circles, must have suggested that they do so. Nonetheless, what is important is that these refined people lent their influence and also their money. For the party was in desperate financial straits. It was once again Eckart who introduced Hitler to a few Berlin industrialists such as the Borsigs, the locomotive manufacturers, and Emil Gansser of the Siemens firm. Other lenders were contacted through the efforts of a few tenacious fellow travellers.

1923: Danger and Notoriety

At this time, Hitler maintained many relationships with groups that were not acquainted with each other. From 1922 on, Hanfstaengl provided a way to penetrate high-ranking Munich families. In order to make the party seem socially acceptable, he organized dinners with well-known figures such as William Bayard Hale, William Randolph Hurst's Berlin correspondent; a German-American painter, Wilhelm Funk; the wife of Fritz-August von Kaulbach, who was also a painter who came from a great family of Bavarian artists; Olaf Gulbransson, a cartoonist for the satirical magazine *Simplicissimus*; and Prince Henckel-Donnersmarck.[14] The examples Hanfstaengl gives in his memoirs obviously reflect his desire to broaden Hitler's geopolitical vision, to get his friend to pay more attention to the United States, and to diversify his palette.

Was it Hanfstaengl's influence and the work of groups close to Eckart or the logic of Nazi mobilization that in the course of 1923 finally made Hitler a central figure in Munich life? He was received by General von Lossow, then a minister, and by the leading figure in Bavaria, Gustav Ritter von Kahr, the head of the conservative government. He began to frequent the great houses and good tables, while at the same time pursuing his activities as a speaker in beer halls, an indication that his situation was improving.

These large beer halls should not deceive the observer. They are too often presented as popular or even working-men's taverns. In fact, they permitted an intermingling of different social classes. Workers were less at ease there than white-collar employees who came with their families to eat full-course meals at reasonable prices. Occasionally, well-off families went slumming at the better beer halls like the Hofbräukeller. These places were vast, with several large, high-ceilinged rooms. In them the air was smoky and they were lively on weekends or during political meetings and musical performances, when the customers were more numerous. Initially, the Nazis could not fill one of these halls; they met there because it was cheaper. Being short of money, they quickly changed their format, renting the hall and then charging an admission fee. That was what they did at the beer halls and especially for the great Krone Circus, which could hold between three and five thousand people. To profit by renting it, you had to be sure of success. Therefore Hitler decided to advertise his meetings; he put up posters to bring in customers. He used red, both to compete with the communists for the workers and to provoke the authorities. Simple line drawings represented marches and combats. The swastika became the party's emblem, in opposition to the hammer and sickle. The slogans were curt, like shouts. Hitler took care with his speeches in order to make them an attractive and impressive spectacle. He became a kind of stage performer as well as a prophet.

Hitler's importance in the party also reflected in his ability to attract audiences and thus bring in money. His influence on a few well-off people can be gauged by their donations. In June 1923, when the movement was trying to shift into high gear, he sounded the call to arms. Gertrud von Seidlitz, for example, donated thirty thousand goldmarks to support the newspaper and the party. Hanfstaengl gave an additional thousand gold-marks for the newspaper, despite the fact that he was not yet a member of the party; even though he participated in numerous meetings of the party's leaders and officials, he was reluctant to take a party card. At that time, high-society companionship did not give rise to a stereotyped atti-tude or formal support for the party organization. What counted more was the relationship with a leader.

Alfred Rosenberg, who had also been in contact with the Nazi move-ment through the Thule Society, used his contacts with Russian refugees in Munich to get access to high society. Thus, without having established a relationship with Hitler, he managed to get into the Bruckmanns' salon. He also approached honourable Russian widows to ask them to finance the party. In his memoirs, Hanfstaengl, who hated Rosenberg, says that he decided to break with the Bruckmanns because of their unsuitable acquaintances.[15]

This political craft aimed at securing financing should not be taken to suggest that Hitler's sole activity consisted in frequenting the powerful in order to raise money. He was genuinely attracted by luxury and brilliance, and this attraction was partly aesthetic. Thus he liked his friend Helene Bechstein because she seemed a true Wagnerian. And it was she who inter-vened on his behalf on 30 September 1923 in order that he might be allowed to visit the Villa Wahnfried, which had been built by Richard Wagner. That evening, at the Anker, one of Bayreuth's luxury hotels, Helene Bechstein held a reception. Among the guests was Winifred Wagner,[16] who was intro-duced to Hitler. This was the beginning of a long-standing relationship with the couple, who were heirs to the composer's work. Siegfried Wagner, Richard's son, received Hitler in the monumental villa.

To understand the attraction of this milieu for Hitler and other Nazi leaders, we have to return to the enormous revolution brought about by Richard Wagner. The Bayreuth Festival was no doubt one of the first signs of an international social season. It drew music lovers from France, England, and Italy. But above all it became the Mecca of the national con-servative aristocracy. Wagner had been able to complete the construction of his theatre, starting in 1872, with the help of the king of Bavaria. The composer wanted to provide people of taste with a moment of relaxation far from the great cities, during the fine weather. Little Bayreuth seemed just right. It was a sign of the times that at the first of the *Festspiele*, in

August 1876, there was a single large loge for the princes, whereas all the other spectators sat on benches affixed to bleachers: it was the symbol of the *Volksgemeinschaft*, the community of the people, realized thanks to the love of music. Only the stage was lit, because the composer knew all too well that by illuminating the auditorium he would have reduced the music to a secondary social event, condemned to hopeless competition with the beautiful, elegant women spectators: the social would have triumphed over art. Wagner wanted to spread the ideal of a German people united and triumphant. The mythology of his operas fed National Socialist culture because party members and theorists thought they found in them the proof that a divine, heroic race of supermen existed. The Nazis also admired Wagner's anti-Semitism, which confirmed their prejudices, and in their view he was not only a musical genius but also a teacher about life and a political philosopher.

Hitler was convinced of this. His Wagnerian passion led him to listen to the Master's works in a kind of trance, as described by his boyhood friend August Kubizek.[17] In his adolescence, both in Linz and in Vienna, his ardour did not flag: he returned several evenings in a row to hear *Tristan und Isolde*, *Götterdämmerung*, and other works. Going to the opera did not make him a socialite. He was still too young and had too little access to refined society. But there he no doubt learned a certain way of presenting himself. Hitler surely observed the poses and attitudes of the women, the great bourgeois and the nobles who regularly attended these performances.[18] His Wagnerianism probably taught him about aesthetics and manners, thus supplementing the secondary education he had received at the Linz Realschule. He therefore made Bayreuth a leading cultural centre under the Third Reich and made possible an unprecedented diffusion of the composer's works, which were also played during the NSDAP's large meetings, framing the humble marches composed by Ernst Hanfstaengl. The whole political liturgy of Nazism rings with echoes of this grandiose musicality. Going to the opera was no longer a simple cultural activity; it became an act of faith in the abilities of the Führer, who made his tastes known and encouraged Germans to imitate them: *Tristan und Isolde* is the great masterpiece, the *Ring des Niebelungen* a magisterial lesson in idealism, and *Götterdämmerung* gives expression to the power of destiny.

For members of the Wagner family, whom he finally met in 1923, Hitler pretended to be naïve, listening to anecdotes with the feeling that he was entering a sanctuary. From that time on, Bayreuth was a city on which Nazism put its stamp. It had a branch of the NSDAP, and Hitler often went there to rest and to escape the violence of the Munich atmosphere. His encounter with the Wagners increased his attraction to the city. Henceforth, he stopped there on every car trip to Berlin. However, the *Festspiel* had not taken place since 1914. The Wagners' ambition was to re-launch this tradition. Hitler encouraged them, all the more because from that point on the whole clan seemed to grow fond of him. The husband of Wagner's eldest daughter, Eva, who had made a name for herself as a philosopher and the biographer of her father-in-law, Houston Stewart Chamberlain, even went so far as to claim that she found it reassuring that Germany had been able to produce such a marvellous person as Hitler in these difficult times. It has to be said that Hitler repeated many of the ideas Chamberlain had set forth in his books, notably *The Foundations of the Nineteenth Century*, which Hitler had read and integrated into his own ideology. We can easily imagine how much the two men's conversations must have resembled less a critical exercise than a celebration of their common convictions.

The Wagner family – which had grown smaller after the deaths of Chamberlain (1927) and Siegfried (1930), nonetheless remained a formidable lever for gaining access to high society, since many Wagnerians saw each other as members of a kind of sect that had its own celebrations and rituals. The successful revival of the Bayreuth Festival in 1924 provided a unique opportunity for Hitler to rub shoulders with an intellectual high society that recognized him as a political adept and one of its own in matters of aesthetics and, soon, in manners as well. He was in prison during the 1924 festival, but eagerly attended the following season at the invitation of the Wagners. However, he afterward forewent the festival until 1933, fearing that he might compromise its political neutrality at a time of major party manoeuvres. Wagnerism – its milieu, ideas, and myths – thus explains in part the survival of Hitler's social connections after his imprisonment and his semi-withdrawal from the party between 1924 and 1926.

In terms of Hannah Arendt's analysis of the composition of nationalist and anti-Semitic movements, we can say that Hitler's social connections constitute a mixture more complex than the convergence between 'the masses', 'all the *déclassés* of capitalist society',[19] on the one hand, and a segment of the avant-garde elite in Austria and Germany around 1920, on the other. There are indeed '*déclassés*' and failed writers like Eckart, as well as disappointed people from an earlier world, like the Count zu Reventlow, who had been driven out of the navy because of his marriage to a French woman, but there were also incontestably successful figures like Bruckmann, who was the leader of the Bavarian book industry, and the very wealthy Bechstein; these latter in no way constituted an avant-garde. A conquering dynamics was developing that would be echoed by rapidly ascending families like the Himmlers, who produced a government minister in only three generations.

The revanchist and even reactionary rage of some of these people should thus not mask the constructive ardour of other segments of the elite, whose faith in the fatherland led them to resolutely commit themselves to the struggle against Bolshevist subversion, superimposing religion on political engagement. The example of Julius Lehmann, an old nationalist and anti-Semitic publisher and also a leading figure in Bavarian Protestant circles who had joined the Freikorps in 1919 in order to liberate

Munich, whereas he had avoided fighting in the First World War because of his advanced age, shows the spiritual dimension of National Socialism that upset the strict logic of social attraction.[20] Lehmann, after passing through the Thule Society, joined Hitler's DAP, to which he lent his financial support. In order to more clearly determine the nature of this milieu, we need to broaden our perspective to include the circles frequented by other National Socialist leaders.

The Elegant Hermann Göring

Before the beer hall putsch in November 1923, other party leaders already occupied a special place in the composition of a high society that was favourable to Hitler and saw in his ideology a reflection of its own convictions. Göring was the first of these. For an observer of high society, the significance of the two men's meeting on 12 October 1922, a 'day of destiny in the life of Hermann Göring',[21] cannot be reduced to political passion alone. Göring had all the qualities necessary for integration into the movement's elite at the highest level, qualities that were to be strengths in action. In order to understand his rapid ascension to a primordial position – head of the SA – among the Nazis, we have to examine his past. Göring was of partially noble descent on his mother's side, and he had been brought up as the heir of a good family. He spent his childhood in a castle and frequented the aristocracy at the schools he attended, including the academy where he received his military training. He chose aviation as his field of activity, one that was also highly prized by nobles.

Göring was above all a hero of the Great War, in which he was a fighter pilot. He was the last commander of the squadron formerly headed by Manfred von Richthofen, the 'Red Baron', the famous air ace who had been shot down during an aerial duel on 21 April 1918. Göring's bravery and his influence over his men allowed him to obtain the highest distinctions as well. Thus he was praised in the press and was quite well known by the end of the war. After the armistice, he was hired as a pilot by airlines serving Scandinavia; once again, he demonstrated his courage by carrying out a dangerous air-taxi flight, on 20 February 1920, in the service of Erich Graf von Rosen, an explorer who was also the brother-in-law of a young Swedish woman, Karin von Kantzow, née Fock. This aristocratic woman, who was married and the mother of a little boy, was seduced by Göring's adventurousness and left her husband in order to follow Göring to Munich, where she married him in February 1923. On that day, the veterans of the Richthofen squadron formed an honour guard, and the wedding guests included several Nazi leaders. This already colourful marriage clearly revealed the connections between the military and the Nazis.

Through Karin, Göring entered very high Swedish society and experienced a confirmation, indeed an improvement, of his social level that was advantageous for his incipient political career. His wife gave this enterprise her complete support, for she was a fervent believer in the NSDAP and its Führer. She went so far as to say: 'Hermann and I would gladly die for this cause.'[22] Göring had met Hitler the previous October, and the two men were getting along so well that Göring had been given the responsibility for training the storm troopers (*Sturmabteilung*, SA), Hitler's personal guard, which was composed of veterans, especially from the Freikorps, and young daredevils from the universities or unemployment offices. They were assigned the task of keeping order during Nazi meetings and street demonstrations or parades. Above all, they received training by the Wehrmacht, whose leaders thought it necessary to help what might become an auxiliary, anticommunist force. There again, Göring's military prestige helped him succeed and reassured the representatives of the General Staff. But he also had other reasons. Just outside Munich, not far from Nymphenburg, he had a fine house with a domestic staff in Obermenzing, a small town. He received everyone who mattered, and knew how to use his wealth to make himself liked, not only by socialites but also by leaders of more modest origins, who were flattered to be invited to his home. Ernst Hanfstaengl described him as the only elegant figure in the party.[23] He even mentioned Göring's car, a Mercedes that he used for making his rounds and for excursions. But what no one knew at the time was that all this was due solely to the generosity of Karin's ex-husband, whose love for her led him to put his fortune at her service.

This first circle of social relations was shaken up by the Beer Hall Putsch. On 9 November 1923, when troops fired on the Nazi procession and caused the death of fourteen men, including two of the movement's leaders, Scheubner-Richter (killed on the spot by a bullet) and Eckart (who died somewhat later of a heart attack), when Göring, wounded by a bullet in the leg, had to escape to Austria, and when Hitler had to flee and was then arrested, a dream slipped away. Those who supported the putsch suddenly had to enter a phase of discretion, an internal or external exile. The government intended to prosecute the dissidents. Fearful, Hanfstaengl left for Vienna.[24] There he found Göring, and they became closer friends. He tried to find out more about Hitler's past and wanted to meet his family. He also took advantage of the opportunity to establish new professional and artistic relationships.

When Prison Becomes a Holiday

At this time, a strange episode was taking place in Landsberg. In the prison where all those sentenced in connection with the putsch were held, the relationships that grew up were characterized by the forced intermingling typical of the military institutions that most of them had known as well as by a form of political hierarchy. The large number of visitors received by the prisoners, and by Hitler in particular, introduced high society into this place where well-known figures met anonymous friends of the prisoners or ordinary party members. The prison register shows that between 3 April and 27 August, there were four hundred and eighty-two visitors.[25] Political men, former party members, and friends hurried to the leader's bedside. The conditions under which he was held were, moreover, less rigorous than they might at first appear. He had a large room next to that of Rudolf Hess, who served as his secretary. He was allowed two walks a day, during which he could talk to anyone, and even go to a common room where men were playing cards or reading the newspapers. Otto Strasser claims that the prisoners, one of whom was his brother Gregor, grew tired of Hitler's incessant political sermons. But the prison warden partially contradicts these claims.[26] These advantages were connected with his status as a political prisoner and especially with his reputation, which distinguished him, in the eyes of the warden and the guards, from the run-of-the-mill detainee. Visitors could thus come in one after the other and bring him mail, sweets, and the cakes he loved so much.

Among the visitors were whole families such as the Bechsteins and the Bruckmanns. For a few early, fanatical supporters, these visits became regular pilgrimages. Elsa Bruckmann in particular has left a document testifying to this devotion. This document, written for the tenth anniversary of Hitler's imprisonment, is not without a certain grandiloquence. She declares that it was at this time that she really came to know Hitler, although he had already visited her home before he was imprisoned. She wants to stress the fact that she went to him, as is indicated by her title: 'My First Journey to the Führer' (*Meine erste Fahrt zum Führer*):[27]

It was in May 1924 that I went to see the Führer in the Landsberg prison, that I went toward the man whose name I had so often, so many times, heard, and whose speeches had given me the faith, had urged me to construct a new Germany; to shake his hand for the first time, to bring to his attention my devotion to his person and to his work. [. . .][28]

Was Landsberg to be the end?

I knew it with certitude, pride and clarity, with the light that gives us indubitable knowledge. Whether he was free or in prison, whether he resumed his course quickly or slowly and with difficulty, he remained the Führer, and thanks to his will the people would grow greater and would realize itself, the truth would win out. [. . .] This instant of the first meeting was for me decisive, for I saw in the man facing me the same simple grandeur, the same enhanced authenticity rooted in life itself, that I had experienced earlier in the presence of the great Führer, of the orator, with the distance of common experiences and gatherings.[29]

Elsa Bruckmann refers to the difficult conditions under which these interviews took place and mentions a certain rudeness on the part of the jailers. But nothing could spoil her happiness, because she brought Hitler the assurance of other supporters. She conveyed Houston Stewart Chamberlain's greetings as well as those of student members of the movement. She offers a conventional, sentimental image of the Führer: he was wearing Bavarian lederhosen and a yellow linen coat. It was his 'bright, simple, gallant eyes' that exercised the greatest attraction on this mature woman. The meeting ended with a certitude: 'However, he himself, the Führer, seemed simple and calm, direct and clairvoyant, courageous and infallible. The duty imposed on him by destiny – he wanted to fulfil it, would fulfil it, because it resided in his breast and in his will. We both knew that when we separated.'[30]

This document indicates how the connection with Hitler was conceived temporally. The Führer is the depository of a future that members of high society were counting on. When Elsa Bruckmann composed her eulogy in April 1933 (for Hitler's birthday, on 20 April?) she knew that she had been right to wait, and her compliment sounds like a reminder to the Führer not to forget his early supporters. By 1933, Hitler had entered into another dimension and no longer needed his old friends in the same way. But the Führer hadn't forgotten Elsa Bruckmann. His response? A Mercedes, which he sent along with a note, in the autumn of 1934. Hugo Bruckmann then took up his pen to pour out his feelings as well: 'I needed some time to completely appreciate this bit of good fortune: first of all that the gift was chosen by you and that you decided, with so much affection, to give your greeting this travelling form; and then the car itself.' Hugo describes it as a 'dancer full of spirit', but 'with an elegant discretion'. Elsa took advantage of her husband's thank-you letter to ask the Führer once again to decorate their old friend, councillor Kirdorf, who had begun financing the movement in 1927. Hitler did not forget his old friends, even if other people seemed closer to him now; he retained the certitude that his old guard would serve him to the end.

Success Makes One Acceptable

In the late 1920s, another generation came to the fore. For the pre-putsch group, Hitler's attractiveness had to do with his coarse, even brutal style. His taste in ties was not found comic; on the contrary, it put the final touch on the image of a warrior. Several witnesses describe him in Bavarian costume – lederhosen and brightly coloured coats that made a vivid contrast with the formal wear normally required at parties. Hanfstaengl's humorous description of Hitler's sole blue suit, in 1920, illustrates a similar discrepancy.[31] Similarly, when the Bechsteins gave him a dinner jacket and patent-leather shoes, Hitler understood that despite his desire to improve his appearance, he couldn't wear them, because the leader of a populist movement could not afford to be suspected of going middle class. Better yet: the head of the NSDAP went about with bodyguards and weapons that he left at the door when he entered a salon.[32] The aroma of adventure that accompanied him was part of his image. It guaranteed his authenticity. Can anyone dressed so simply be lying? However, it does seem that Hitler thought up this look and deliberately adopted it in 1921–2 in order to emphasize, in wealthy milieus, the distance that separated him from other nationalist organizations, his ability to deal directly with reality. This way of presenting himself went along with a change in his behaviour that was increasingly accentuated from this time on, and whose goal was to strengthen his prestige. He began striking poses and making ceremonious gestures. He avoided blunders such as dancing with the wives of party members. Joachim Fest sees this distance as the first step in the construction of Hitler's personal myth.[33] To judge by what Elsa Bruckmann says about him, this strategy seemed to work in high society.

When he set out to take power in 1925, and especially after 1927, Hitler's new partners viewed his brutality more ambivalently. They didn't think it was a structural part of Nazism and, worse yet, they persuaded themselves that the leader's politeness in private was a sign of a certain wisdom in the movement itself. Moreover, his sense of humour attenuated the distance between the orator and the salon conversationalist. On stage, he wielded a mordant irony, whereas in private he played on words and imitations to win people's good will before making a few serious statements.[34] The indulgence shown by Hitler's high-society friends was neither naïve nor disinterested. One observation can be made without going into the strict chronology of events: as the party won votes and elections, it became more respectable and acceptable for those who were trying to get closer to power. Nazi leaders who early on occupied eligible positions therefore had great advantages in the competition to establish relationships, and were thereby able to change their place in the organization. Those who most frequented high society were ultimately the ones who succeeded best in this political balancing act.

Hermann Göring was clearly a past master at this subtle game. After he was granted amnesty, he returned to Munich to pledge his allegiance to Hitler. He was back in the saddle to the point that the Führer put him at the top of the party's list in Berlin. However, in the 1928 legislative elections the NSDAP did very poorly, receiving only 2.6 per cent of the vote. But twelve legislators were elected, including Göring, Gregor Strasser, Gottfried Feder, Wilhelm Frick (who presided over the parliamentary group), and a man who was a newcomer in the party compared to these old stars: Joseph Goebbels. Hitler had not been able to stand for election because he was considered stateless.[35] In this little group, Göring gained a larger voice. To be sure, Goebbels knew how to make sensational declarations and push the SA to engage in agitation. But the former aviator had a greater power of seduction for the establishment. Karin, who was gravely ill, joined him and continued her work as a propagandist in fashionable circles. Thus the little flat the couple had rented at number 7 Badensche Strasse became the centre of an active social life. The flat consisted of only a large drawing room and a bedroom, but it was tastefully decorated and hung with a few paintings by old masters. It was at this period that Göring was friends with Prince August-Wilhelm von Preussen (called Auwi), who had been drawn to Nazism ever since the meeting in Bamberg in 1926 and who entered the SA in the spring of 1930. Auwi soon introduced Göring to Crown Prince Wilhelm von Preussen, as well as to Prince Christoph von Hessen and his brother Philipp. Göring's personality kindled their desire to meet Hitler, for whom they decided to work more or less openly. Berlin life gradually began to take on the colour of Nazi uniforms, especially after the elections held on 14 September 1930. The NSDAP's representatives in the Reichstag, who now numbered one hundred and seven, took advantage of parliamentary indemnity to defy the Prussian government's prohibition on wearing brown shirts. During the inaugural session of the new assembly, on 13 October 1930, they even wore their uniforms in the Reichstag itself.

Toward a Nazi High Society

This change in the atmosphere surrounding the party struck observers and increased their curiosity with regard to this rising power. Among the female socialites, Magda Quandt (the ex-wife of the banker Günther Quandt, one of the wealthiest men in Germany), idle and slightly depressed after two recent failed love affairs, decided to go to a campaign meeting at the Berlin Sportpalast toward the end of the summer of 1930.[36] The preparations for the general elections to be held in September led to a genuine glut of political meetings. This time, the Nazis wanted to put on a major show for fifteen thousand spectators, and the Gauleiter gave a passionate and ironic speech modelled on those of his master, Adolf Hitler. The speaker was one of the party's youngest leaders, only thirty-three years old, Dr Joseph Goebbels. His performance filled Magda with enthusiasm. Her background did not predestine her, however, to embrace racist ideas.[37] She was an illegitimate child who had not at first been recognized by her father. Later, she was adopted by a Jewish businessman who had become her mother's lover, and who remained attached to her. Disappointed by her marriage, she carried on an affair with a militant Zionist that brought her marriage with Quandt to an end. After her conversion, owing to Goebbels's oratorical talent, she took out a party card and worked on the party's behalf in Westend, a chic new neighbourhood in Berlin that combined huge villas and English-style gardens. She was soon put in charge of the women's organization and worked as a volunteer for the party's local office. In particular, she classified the Gauleiter's archives. Goebbels noticed her and took her to opening nights at the cinema, to which he was invited by his artist friends. This was the beginning of an idyll that culminated in an elaborate wedding performed on 19 December 1931.

The wedding ceremony bore all the marks of Nazi social life. The Berlin storm troopers – in shirtsleeves and caps, because they were not allowed to wear their uniforms – formed an honour guard. Harald, Magda's first son with Günther Quandt, wore the uniform of the Hitler Jugend, which was permitted. In the mayor's office, Adolf Hitler sat at the couple's left: he was a witness. He even took Goebbels to the ceremony in his car, along with his assistant, Wilhelm Brückner, and Julius Schreck at the wheel. Magda rode with the actress-director Leni Riefenstahl in a second chauffeur-driven car. They were followed by the cortège of guests. The ceremony was depicted and commented upon in the press, as a pleasant high-society event.

The National Socialist party had become essential in the everyday life of its members, especially the most important among them, to the point that not a single important act of their existence escaped its influence. The frequency with which the organization met explains this hold on their lives. The basic groups were supposed to meet at least once a week, and the specialized ones as well. Nazi storm troopers had to attend training sessions at least three times a week. Between 1920 and 1923, they even had to take part in long manoeuvres and be constantly at the call of the party's leadership. At the beginning of the 1930s, this demanding system was relaxed. But the storm troopers remained political semi-professionals while waiting for the party's electoral successes to bring about a re-evaluation of their incomes. Contrary to what Goebbels and Hitler said at the time, their violent acts were part of a strategy of agitation. Sven Reichardt has shown that despite the rebellions and tensions of 1931, the organization was following the party hierarchy's orders when Nazi members of the Reichstag and Hitler pretended to be imposing a legalistic pace.[38]

When the emblematic names of princes or famous actors who henceforth committed themselves to the cause of National Socialism were mentioned in the press, this had a powerful effect and encouraged large segments of the middle classes to forget their concerns about this extremist movement. For party members who came from the lower classes or from the petite bourgeoisie, joining the NSDAP amounted to finding common leisure activities and amusements, a frame of reference that went beyond work and family. Within the party, the fraternal ties between members were almost those of a sect, given the devotion that was expected after joining. Picnics, group parades, dances, and songs to the sound of fanfares, and all this under the sign of the swastika. There you have forms of social relationships in which many young Germans participated. Almost 40 per cent of party members were less than thirty years old.

The Nazi party functioned as a community in which an individual could invest all his time and his emotions. However, it did not constitute a counter-society. It claimed to renew politics and purge it of factors that it found harmful.

Seen from a foreign point of view, this political phenomenon seems surprising, since the Weimar Republic was exceptionally open intellectually. Wasn't this the time of Bertolt Brecht, Thomas, Mann and Kurt Tucholsky? Weren't there more music-halls and cafés frequented by homosexuals in Berlin than in Paris? Wasn't it in this city that women writers praised free love, and the works of Swedish authors lauding nudism and a life in accord with nature were received with enthusiasm? Wasn't it in 'red' Berlin that Jews settled, ardently working to support German culture, some in publishing, like the Mosse family, and others, like Fritz Lang, in the cinema? Wasn't Germany as a whole in the van of the liberating modernity of the roaring twenties? Everything was on the boil in the 1920s. In Frankfurt, a school of Marxist philosophy was overturning the frameworks of European thought. In Dessau, the Bauhaus was becoming a unique point of reference in art and architecture. In Weimar, Hamburg, and Dresden, theatre was innovative, provoking and following the revolutionary trends. This wave of creation is striking for a present-day observer studying Germany between the two wars.

The emergence of Nazism seems obscene and out of place in such a context. However, it wasn't simply the old-fashioned or abnormal who lined up behind Hitler. For a whole group of nobles, industrialists, bankers, military men, employees, peasants, workers, and government bureaucrats who were obsessed by the authoritarian, reassuring grandeur of their childhoods and rejected the new developments of their time, the Weimar Republic and the hint of sulphur in its brilliant intellectual and artistic life constituted an anomaly. Nostalgic, they drew from their memories ideas for changing the regime and the course of modernity.

There was an immense gap between the rich, colourful, and open social life under the Weimar Republic and the nationalist groups among the elites that sought power and showed a great collective intolerance. The republic had become a political foil encouraging a reactionary mentality that in its radicalness and brutality could be considered revolutionary. The odd thing is that the Nazis, who began from what seemed to be a minority position, won over vast areas of public opinion, and that by 1930 their views had become an ideological consensus.

Without the solidarity that resulted from nationalism and the war, without the gamble made by a few visionaries, without the adaptation to the traditional mores of high society, this rise would not have been possible. All the time and money that had been bet on Hitler during the years of weakness and growth must also be seen as an investment. On the eve of the shocks produced by the 1932 elections, Nazism certainly did not command a majority of public opinion. Its strength lay elsewhere, in control over future development it had acquired by convincing the elites that the Nazis would inevitably have to be given a chance to run the country. In this sense, an explanation in Arendt's terms, connecting the rise of Nazism with declines in social status resulting from the development of capitalism, seems still less convincing when we examine the groups that were about to bring the NSDAP and its parliamentary coalition to power. Such an explanation would be acceptable only if we thought that all the traditional elites were incapable of evolving in order to preserve their position in a social universe that was being reconstructed. However, the nobility, while it was no longer by itself a dominant political force, was still able, thanks to clever alliances, to increase its influence on society as a whole. Still less convincing is the interpretation exclusively in terms of the middle classes or capitalist bourgeoisie, because even the traditional elites were converging toward Nazism. This conglomerate of groups emanating from all areas of social life explains the existence of vertical solidarities during the Third Reich. Corporatism did not function solely as an alternative to syndicalism. It was already present in the kinds of relationships the different elites entertained with other citizens, including the lower classes. Thus for the alliance Hannah Arendt supposes between *déclassés* and the populace we could substitute two terms more adequate to the circulation of information at this time: socialites and conformists. They shared the same desire to see their hero rise to power and they were convinced that he would soon do so.

Private Homes and Public Action

On 16 December 1932, The Deutscher Herrenklub (DHK) organized a solemn reception at its Berlin offices at 2–3 Jägerstrasse in Mitte, the centre of the city, near the Gendarmenmarkt. The Deutscher Herrenklub was elitist. At its apogee in the early 1930s, it had fewer than five thousand members in all of Germany, and in Berlin, about three hundred. It was founded in 1924 by former members of the Juni-Klub, whose ambition was to form an active conservative elite. Its name referred to the lords of the earth, for only socialites distinguished by their wealth and connections could join. They were not all nobles, but they shared a political ideal.[39] Famous names appear on the roster of members for 1931. Paul von Hindenburg, the president of the Weimar Republic and former Chief of Staff, was the honorary president. Oswald Spengler joined in 1926. Albrecht von Hohenzollern was on the roster, as were various members of the von Trotha family, including the admiral. General Mackensen, the last survivor of the General Staff during the Franco-Prussian war of 1870, was also on it. Jurists and military men were over-represented in the club. To grasp the contours of this milieu, we should note a few absences: there are no Krupps, no Porsches, no Siemens, and of course the names of the highest Nazi leaders – Hitler, Goebbels, Strasser, Himmler, and Rosenberg – are also missing.

Among the founders of the DHK, the former chancellor Franz von Papen, a member of the Catholic Centre Party, was prominent. On 16 December 1932 he was to deliver a speech on 'The New State'. Three hundred people in the audience heard him say that politics required an authoritarian governing principle and a figure who embodied this principle; that von Schleicher's government could not carry out a reform programme that would suffice to rebuild the economy; that therefore a broad coalition had to be envisaged in order to restore authority. No doubt he was thinking of himself in developing an argument that pointed toward dictatorship.

No one was shocked by von Papen's remarks. Since the end of the 1920s, conservatives had been obsessed with a military and hierarchical regulation of society. If political extremists like Hugenberg and Hitler did not enjoy unanimous support, their speeches struck a responsive note in the hearts of these representatives of German high society, and in those of their wives as well. Most of the latter belonged to an organization founded in tandem with the Herrenklub, the Deutscher Damenklub. These ladies accompanied their husbands when they went to official parties and gala dinners. The seating arrangements for the annual banquets were characterized by an alternation of men and women that reminds us of those drawn up by attentive mistresses of the household.[40] The Herrenklub was thus not a political organization of the partisan type; instead, its function was to promote social relationships among the members of high society. At the Berlin club, for instance, there was a fine restaurant where members could dine together and even receive guests. On that particular December evening, Kurt Freiherr von Schröder was among those present.

Von Schröder, who was forty-three, belonged to one of the most powerful families in the Cologne region. His father, Arthur, had gone into finance, as had his brother Heinrich. Kurt, after studying law, also turned to finance, and went to work for the J. H. Stein bank, where his father-in-law, Georg von Schnitzler, was a stockholder. While he was studying law, von Schröder had belonged to one of the most fashionable youth organizations, the Burschenschaft Saxo Borussia. His address book was full of aristocratic addresses. He fought in the Great War, ending up holding the rank of Commander. In 1928, he joined the Deutsche Volkspartei. His work and his conservative leanings brought him into contact with Hjalmar Schacht, and, through the latter's mediation, with Fritz Thyssen. On the basis of these relationships, in November 1932 he decided to write to President Hindenburg to ask that 'the leader [Führer] of the greatest nationalist movement be named chancellor of the Reich'.[41] Thus he openly supported Hitler without, however, being a member of his party. Von Schröder belonged to the group of businessmen organized by Wilhelm Keppler (the Keppler Circle) that believed that a radical change in politics could bring about an economic recovery. He had already met the Führer on several occasions and had established ties with Heinrich Himmler.

After von Papen's speech at the Herrenklub, that pinnacle of high society, on 16 December 1932 – a speech that lasted almost two hours – von Schröder went to congratulate him. The two men spoke privately for a few moments. The details of their conversation are not known, but they agreed that von Papen had to meet with Hitler in order to consider the NSDAP's participation in the government. The banker was to set up a discreet meeting between von Papen and Hitler.

The meeting was set for 4 January 1933, at von Schröder's home. He lived in a fashionable suburb of Cologne, near a lovely wooded park with a pond, at 35 Stadtwaldgürtel. His house, which von Papen entered by the front door and Hitler by a side door, represented in concentrated form the great capitalist bourgeoisie, banking, and the old aristocracy. Hess and Himmler, who had accompanied the Führer, remained in the living room, while von Papen and Hitler withdrew into the study with von Schröder.

During the Weimar Republic, it was relatively common to conduct discreet political negotiations in a private home. In August, Hitler had negotiated with von Schleicher in a villa in Fürstenberg, eighty kilometres north of Berlin. In the context of parliamentary and political crises, this practice became the only way to pursue informal relationships and to keep several doors open. At Kurt von Schröder's home, despite the initial tension that characterized their discussions, Hitler and von Papen agreed on the necessity of working together, but the hierarchical relationships between national conservatives and National Socialists remained in suspense.

New meetings were necessary. This time a more discreet site was chosen, because news of the meeting in Cologne had got out and several articles about it had appeared in the papers, forcing everyone involved to deny that it had taken place. Three meetings were held on 10, 18, and 21 January at the home of a wealthy man who had joined the NSDAP in May 1932, Joachim von Ribbentrop. Ribbentrop, a true man of the world, had spent most of his youth outside Germany, notably in Canada. He spoke perfect English. After the First World War, in which he served in the cavalry with such courage that he was awarded the Iron Cross, he was attached to the German military mission in Constantinople, where he stayed for a year. He chose to be politically active within the Deutsche Volkspartei, but supported von Papen against von Schleicher during the 1932 crisis. Since 1920, Ribbentrop had resided in Dalhem, a commune recently annexed to the capital. There he owned a large villa bought in part with money provided by his wife, Annelies Henkell, the heiress of one of the greatest families of sparkling wine (*Sekt*) makers.

The German love of sparkling wines is too often forgotten. One need only recall that it was Germans who gave their names to champagnes as prestigious as Krug, Heidsieck, Mumm, and Roederer, and that wine makers on the other side of the Rhine helped improve vinification techniques at the end of the nineteenth century. Ribbentrop knew all this; he had established a firm that exported spirits and its success was based on the sale of champagne, particularly Taittinger, in Germany. He was one of the government's regular suppliers and his customers included especially Berlin's great hotels and restaurants. He was thus a member of high society by his way of life as well as by his sources of income.

The decisive step was taken on 22 January when Hitler, who had gradually convinced von Papen to yield him the chancellor's office, met Oskar von Hindenburg at Ribbentrop's home. Von Hindenburg, the president's son, arrived about 10 p.m. and talked privately with Hitler for two hours, while the other guests waited – these included, in addition to Ribbentrop, Frick, and Göring for the Nazis, Otto Meissner, President Hindenburg's state secretary. This close proximity deserves to be emphasized, since Meissner had repeatedly communicated to Hitler the president's refusal to appoint him chancellor, in particular in a letter of November 1932 in which, in veiled terms, he accused the Nazi party of inciting civil war. However, after this evening, Meissner supported Hitler's candidacy. The content of the private conversation with Oskar von Hindenburg is not known. The historian can conjecture that Hitler must have used his classic methods of manipulation: aggressiveness and threats, then an outline of a common project and the promise of a reward. In fact, both Oskar von Hindenburg and Otto Meissner benefited from their alliance. So did Hitler; the two president's men became loyal supporters. They were of particular service to him in gaining power and they remained devoted to him.

The three voices that were most important in changing the old president's mind were those of von Papen, Otto Meissner, and Oskar von Hindenburg. These new-style sirens caused the president to forget his promise never to call Hitler to the chancellery. In considering the combination of factors that produced this event, how can we overlook the fact that it took place behind closed doors and involved powerful political, economic, and aristocratic actors? These leaders were convinced that their calculations were more reliable than new elections whose results remained uncertain. Finally, Hitler's accession to power resulted from his old relationship with German high society. Thanks to his tactical ability and his networks of friends, the NSDAP was able to give a new form to the elites' profoundest desire: to make an apparent revolution so that nothing would change.

The presence of all sorts of individuals in and around the party forces us to be very prudent in characterizing this group socially. There were certainly *déclassés*, but alongside them there were also businessmen and parvenus. The old and the new aristocracy also played important roles, because until 1932 Hitler was seen as a monarchist. The 'middle classes' – understood in the strict sense of the term, excluding families belonging to

the nobility, the *haute bourgeoisie*, and the *Bildungsburgertum* – were not ideologically dominant in the movement, and were far from holding all the
strategic party positions. They also lacked the cohesion necessary to take
power. National Socialism thus did not have a coherent social identity. As
Karl Dietrich Bracher pointed out as early as 1955,[42] it represented a sort
of coalition of several areas of competency and centres of social resources
(industry, the army, the government bureaucracy, etc.). But what held
these together was not solely a sense of self-interest and a doctrinal racial
programme. Their solidarity and their mutual confidence proceeded from
a long-standing association and intermingling that welded them together
into a leadership group prepared to make decisive choices for the country
and convinced that it alone could act on them effectively. It was not a
matter of an alliance between classes, but rather of the entry onto the scene
of high-performance adepts in mass politics. In this sense, Hannah Arendt
is right to point out the way European high society, faced with the challenges of modernity, took refuge in an intense social life and an exacer-
bated sense of distinction.[43] Radical nationalism had proliferated in it like
bacteria in a Petri dish, overcoming worries and fears, glorifying adven-
turers, and forging a new form of social transcendence. Hitler understood
this very well; he was to perpetuate this system of management by
socialites and sycophants, influencing the forms of social relations and
putting the state in its service.

2

The Great Pleasures and Small Benefits of Nazi High Society

To celebrate the inauguration of the new era, Rudolf Hess bought himself a watch. He told his wife Ilse about it in a letter dated 1 February 1933. Still moved by the triumphs of the day he had just experienced, he asked: 'Did I dream all this or am I awake?' The preceding day, Hitler, just named Reichskanzler, had called Hess to his room at the Kaiserhof hotel, which had for several years served as his residence in Berlin, in order to share in his victory. Hess congratulated him, but feared that something might at the last minute prevent the transfer of power. As they left the hotel, party members in mufti and storm troopers in uniform cheered the Führer. Then the planned parade took place in front of the chancellery and the residence of the president of the Republic, stretching down the most famous avenue in Berlin, Unter den Linden, and into the Tiergarten, that forest at the heart of the city.

Hess's letter to his wife is astonishing because his vocabulary is not stereotypical. The labels are flattering; one senses the sycophant's way of speaking of the new rulers, but the Nazi phraseology remains a little uncertain. How much should one colour one's language with ideology in order to be politically correct? For example, in his letter Hess speaks several times of the 'Chief (*chef*)', but he puts 'Führer' between quotation marks, as if the word were still a little too big for the man.

Things moved very quickly. The use of the term 'Führer', which had been tried out by Hess himself as early as 1922, exclusively to designate Hitler became current in the party by 1928. Beginning in 1930, the press adopted it when referring to the head of the NSDAP. In 1932, the term appears in the letters the Keppler group sent to Hindenburg. When Hitler was made chancellor, the designations 'Herr Reichskanzler' and 'Hochverehrter Herr Reichskanzler' were used along with 'Führer'; then, gradually, and especially after Hitler was promoted to the presidency of the Republic in August 1934, the expression 'Führer und Reichskanzler' became usual. Nevertheless, party members and many Germans used an expression with religious and military connotations: 'Mein Führer'.

Behind this terminology, which was only partly dictated by the law, were strategies intended to create support for Hitler and to draw attention to him. Only a few months after he took office, people were already conforming to the new regime and regarding it as normal. 'The new Germany' was a phrase that found its way into every discussion, designating the changes taking place and marking the break with the Weimar regime, which was discredited more than ever. In a few quick steps, German public opinion turned around. After the Reichstag fire and the investigation that followed it, the communist party was outlawed and all its associated organizations and newspapers were destroyed. The government proceeded to make massive preventative arrests. In the new elections held in March, the party's candidates won more than 40 per cent of the vote. After 1 April 1933, boycotting Jewish shops and ostracizing of this part of the population provided another way of welding together the national community. Finally, on 23 March 1933, Hitler was given full powers by the vote of a very large majority in the Reichstag, including members of the Centre Party. Thereafter it was no longer necessary for the Reichstag to meet, although it continued to subsist officially. Thus within six months the map of German values and powers had been redrawn in accord with National Socialist and racist notions. The enthusiasm for the new regime was such that everyday objects and advertisements were covered with swastikas and political slogans. Hitler's secondary residence in the Obersalzberg became, as early as the summer of 1932, the goal of mass pilgrimages.

The few opponents chose to flee the country, twenty thousand of them going quickly into exile for political reasons. Soon socialists and syndicalists were also subjected to harassment and brutality. Those who remained had to be discreet, and even then many were arrested. They were interned along with communists in the first concentration camps, for which Dachau served as the model. In all, two hundred thousand Germans who opposed the Nazi regime spent time in prison or in these new camps along with persons identified as abnormal, deaf-mutes, or manic-depressives. Jews soon experienced a still more terrible fate that was the subject of specific legislation. But for the time being the seventy million Germans living in the Reich began to indulge in what was to become their favourite sport under the Nazi regime, getting into the good graces of the powerful and acquiring advantages in the new context of reform.

The country as a whole seems to have been eager to grovel before the new masters. Demonstrations of support and acts of allegiance and respect multiplied. All Germany entered into a state of vassalage and transformed itself into a gigantic royal court. Everyone sought to gain the notice of those in power and to serve them in order to rise or distinguish themselves on the social scale. They all knew that Hitler was at the centre of a vast culture of clientelism that extended even to the humblest Kreisleiter (district chief).

The Nazi Restoration of High Society's Values

Hitler carefully prepared his entrance into the Berlin social world. His experience in Munich had been complemented by the respectability conferred on him, starting in 1929, by the establishment of an extreme right-wing alliance with veterans of the very reactionary paramilitary Stahlhelm group, the DNVP, and radical peasant parties. Henceforth regularly in Berlin, he lived at the Kaiserhof hotel, which also served as his office and his meeting room: he took advantage of teas and luncheons to deal with business in the hotel's large restaurant. In this palatial hotel, which boasted fine cuisine, he met with the group that had gathered around one of his muses, Countess Viktoria von Dirksen. On Thursday evening, this plump, energetic woman with a strong jaw was joined by her friends to discuss all sorts of subjects while enjoying the refreshments served in the hotel's lounges. The hotel's name already implied a programme by its reference to the emperor, the Kaiser. In a second marriage, Viktoria von Dirksen, who came from a noble family (she was a Laffert), had wedded in 1918 Willibald von Dirksen, himself the scion of a family that had been ennobled in 1887. Like Elsa Bruckmann and Helene Bechstein, she was older than Hitler, whom she met for the first time on the evening of 29 May 1922, when he came to present his programme before the Berliner Nationalklub 1919, of which she was one of the founders.[1] She was convinced that the nationalist prophet would restore the empire she had known in her youth. Therefore she frequently invited Hitler to her evening parties, attended by high officials such as Hans Heinrich Lammers, magnates like Hugenberg, and members of the imperial family, such as Prince Eitel Friedrich von Preussen, the brother of the heir to the throne. Starting in 1930, Viktoria von Dirksen introduced Hitler and other members of the NSDAP into fashionable Berlin salons. She became friends with Magda Quandt, who had returned to Berlin, and then with Joseph Goebbels. After the triumph of January 1933, she went daily to the Goebbels' apartment, proud to have helped ensure the victory of a movement that could lead to the restoration of the monarchy. Didn't the new chancellor's conformism seem to suggest that possibility?

As soon as he took power, Hitler adopted the existing protocol. His ambition was clearly to reconcile high society with political power in order to put an end to the intellectual independence of the avant-garde and to the reservations of a certain number of conservatives' reluctant to accept institutions based on popular elections. He also received with elegance the good wishes of important state officials. Then, on 24 February, Hindenburg invited him to a magnificent formal dinner. This was his true entry into the great world of high society. By his easy manners and the good impression he made on other guests, Hitler overcame the old president's remaining doubts about him. From then on, he went from one social occasion to another orchestrated by Goebbels and Viktoria von Dirksen, and used this channel to consolidate support for his policies. He always knew what to say to make himself liked, and even accidentally kissed the hands of several Jewish socialites, as was pointed out, not without irony, by the chronicler Bella Fromm.[2] Neither did he hesitate to invite members of his cabinet and their wives to ensure amicable cohesion in his government. In a few weeks, Hitler had succeeded in establishing his image as a pleasant man who was entirely acceptable in high society.

Curiously, Hitler's attitude and his brutal speeches following the Reichstag fire (28 February 1933) did not affect this image. Probably the upper class regarded his imprecations against communists, Marxists, and Jews as propaganda, and it was certainly in basic, visceral agreement with them. It must have seen in them a demagogic ardour that proved Hitler's sincerity. It was all a matter of politics, that is, of energy. The success of the operation obliterated the feeling that the Nazi reaction was excessive. Nobles and high officials felt reassured by the impression of continuity, and even of a return to old ways, that characterized the new functioning of the state. Rarely has a regime worked so hard in the domain of etiquette or made such punctilious use of protocol. The clearest manifestation of this occurred on 21 March 1933, dubbed the 'Day of National Recovery'.

Accounts of this event in the press and in the propaganda film shown along with regular newsreels allow us to describe the system of precedence set up by Hitler at the beginning.[3] Let us recall that this political ceremony had a special character: the constitution did not provide for it. It brought together prominent people, some of these occupied political offices and some did not. The old imperial family participated in it, without in theory lending it any institutional character. However, the crown prince was seated just behind the royal throne, left empty, in the military church in Potsdam, the former capital of Frederick the Great.

Those who conceived this demonstration sought to inculcate a mythical connection between the old German Empire and the Third Reich, and consequently adopted imperial customs. Hitler's speech paid explicit homage to the kings of Prussia and the former empire. Bouquets of flowers and wreaths were laid upon the tomb of Frederick II. Hindenburg was the first to do so, thereby closing a ceremony that he had opened by saluting the vacant royal throne with his marshal's baton. All the witnesses, whether direct or indirect, saw in this a symbolic transfer of authority, discipline, and traditional hierarchies to the new national empire, the Third Reich.

One image is symbolic of this day: Hitler, wearing a suit and holding a black hat, bowing and shaking Hindenburg's hand as he greeted him in front of the church door. Distributed in thousands of copies, this image showed Hitler's respect for legitimate military, aristocratic, and institutional authority. It was modelled on a photograph of Mussolini, in civilian clothes, bowing before Victor Emmanuel III, in uniform, just after the March on Rome, as the two men prepared to honour the flame on the altar

of the fatherland. Mussolini is said to have been amused by this plagia-
rism, to the point that in diplomatic circles the rumour circulated that
when they first met, Mussolini greeted Hitler with the words, 'Ave,
Imitator'. Both men had built their authority on the values and traditional
structures of the nobility, and the latter was to play an important role in
the definition of the elites and social relationships promoted by their
regimes. Politeness and noble manners were in fact imposed on this
Germany shaped by courtliness, at the centre of which stood a strange
regent for a dead monarchy: Adolf Hitler.

The Three Spheres of the Conviviality of Power and the Socialite Reservoir

In January 1933, members of the new regime issued many invitations and
attended many private parties. After 1934, two events accelerated this systematic conviviality. The first of these was the elimination, in June 1934, of
Ernst Röhm, the leaders of the SA, and a few conservative opponents. This
liquidation, known today as 'The Night of Long Knives', was described in
the German press of the time as the legitimate repression of 'Röhm's
putsch'. However, few people were deceived by this phraseology, and this
political crime had great influence on the elites. It demonstrated that from
now on the regime was strong and firm, that it had the support of the army,
and that it was going to stay in power. There again, the official treatment
of the event played down the radicalness of the regime's act. At the very
time that Röhm was being liquidated in the Licherfelde SS barracks in
Berlin, Hitler was organizing a tea party in the chancellery's garden, to
which members of his government, their wives, and their children would
be invited – a way of giving the impression that putting down a group of
dangerous, marginal evil-doers was an ordinary, everyday matter. On the
one hand, the state and the legitimate family; on the other, political and
sexual deviants.

This argument had its limits, but it spared people's consciences and promoted the resumption of the old talk about the serious work that had to be
done rather than the nasty political battles that were weakening the
country. When at last Hindenburg died at his home in Neudeck on 2
August 1934 and Hitler was able, by means of a constitutional decree, to
become both chancellor and president of the Reich, nothing any longer
prevented the National Socialists from strongly influencing high-society
life. Thus it is not surprising that the correspondence, invitations, and
exchanges of good wishes and gifts addressed to the head of state and government officials increased enormously. Henceforth a whole staff was necessary to deal with this nationwide grovelling.

Bureaucrats produced mountains of paper that are today preserved in
archives: invitations, announcements, lists of guests and recipients of gifts

or advantages, and lists of petitioners as well; receipts, bills, and so on.[4] The regime, which was very fond of statistics, recorded all contacts between individuals and the leaders. The documents were probably intended to serve as an aid to organization and were useful in a world in which punctiliousness became an obsession. But the compulsive archiving of these repetitive pieces, of which copies were made for all the offices concerned (sometimes more than forty of them), was to be used in another, less noble context: proving that individuals were present at certain places and times, demonstrating their consent or adherence, providing a basis for gratitude or blame. And – who knows? – for preparing the judgement of history. Despite the destruction resulting from the war, many invitations and lists of congratulations were preserved, and these allow us to gauge how opinion was manipulated and to evaluate the types of relationships high society entertained with government.

A first sphere of high society was very close to the government and, one is tempted to say, to ardent support for National Socialism. It was composed of a small number of men and women, between two hundred and two hundred and fifty, who were systematically invited to official dinners, who on their birthdays received telegrams and gifts from the highest Nazi leaders, and who themselves addressed ardent eulogies to other dignitaries. This group included chiefly ministers and state secretaries (but not all of them), important officials of the party, the SS, and a few other influential organizations such as the SA, as well as adjutants and advisers with strong personalities. This political elite was very mixed, socially speaking. But through the positions of certain high-ranking government ministers and the distribution of pre-eminent military offices to certain members of the nobility, it was undeniably coloured by high-society culture and even by snobbism. This group regularly met and recognized that it was part of a small elite of individuals with power. To adopt the vocabulary the philosopher Antonio Gramsci forged to describe Italian Fascism, this group formed an 'organic' elite that abandoned its social origins and old solidarities in order to enter as completely as possible into the Third Reich's ideological hegemony.[5] This dimension explains the relative stability of its composition, which was renewed at its margins only by deaths and infrequent new selections based on favour or the exercise of a specific function.

Contrary to a too widespread presupposition of impotence and innocence, women and wives who were part of this group adhered fully to the ambitions of the National Socialist programme. As is shown by the memoirs of several of them, notably those of Henriette Hoffmann and Emmy Göring, they were kept informed of the evolution of the regime and of important decisions. Moreover, they used their celebrity to petition their husbands' colleagues for advantages or help for their friends. Thus at this social level, women were in the political background only in appearance. In a sense, the fact that decision-makers were not much concerned about being re-elected favoured other forms of influence that worked to the advantage of family and clientele relationships.

The regularity of meetings and the high level of responsibility of members of this first group facilitated the circulation of information about the group itself and its collective action. Each individual could guess what advantages and privileges other members of the group enjoyed by reference to his or her own. Similarly, there can be no doubt that they knew about the crimes committed by the Nazis, whatever they claimed after the war in order to escape being sentenced to death or imprisonment and to de-Nazification.

The second sphere was broader. It was characterized by regular relationships in which occasions for correspondence and meeting were still numerous but not systematic. Evidently, the protocol services of the different ministries or the adjutants' offices convened this group only in relation to a specific event and to the sector in which they were active. Individuals in this group were thus picked out or mentioned in general correspondence because of their personal relationships with Nazi leaders. These celebrities, who were involved in the regime and recognized as such, did not have complete power, even if their presence was what gave many official meetings a high-society flavour. They were delighted to receive special invitations to attend the party congress in Nuremberg and were provided with cars or buses specially fitted out for their comfort in the city, whereas ordinary people had to walk. Some of them even enjoyed the privilege of a reservation in the hotel where Hitler himself was staying. Here people in theatre and the arts showed themselves off. Actresses were particularly prominent ornaments for the great demonstrations, as were musicians. They helped organize parties by arranging for entertainment. In this sphere appeared a few diplomats who, without always sharing the opinions of their interlocutors, were supposed to gain the latter's confidence in order to get them to reveal their secrets. The Hendersons, the François-Poncets, the Cerrutis, and the Attolicos were good guests. This Berlin high society was relatively aware of its importance but pledged itself to the leaders in the hope of gaining some advantage. Between six and eight hundred persons participated in these events, depending on the period and the affinities involved. Moreover, the press amply reported on their activities, which exemplified the Nazi way of life.

The third sphere brought together persons who were occasionally invited to major state events or to parties sponsored by dignitaries of the regime such as Göring or Goebbels. There were between four and five thousand of these, who felt that they were admitted to the Reich's high society but sensed that they were not an essential part of history. They consented to the regime for ideological and practical reasons. They included nobles, high officials, and agents of the party at the regional level, most of the famous artists, star athletes, heads of associations, mayors of major cities, businessmen, and so on – in short, the true socialites, who maintained a functional solidarity. They obtained the audiences they requested. To do so, they adopted the Nazi rhetoric and were able to produce the purest Aryan style on demand. They might even innovate when they had to make a compliment or deliver an encomium. They made a large contribution to the spread of Hitlerian ideology among the masses and to its constitution as a set of general principles. Indifferent to the brutal logic it entailed, they thought only about their own social success. As geographical relay points, they also ensured Nazism's grip on the territory and supported local activism. They brought an aroma of the capital into other regions of Germany and repeated rumours and witticisms, thus proving that they had the ear of people in high places. It was they who talked with feigned dismay about Robert Ley's alcoholism, who knew the name of Martin Bormann's mistress, and who followed Goebbels' love affairs in the hope of being able to derive some advantage from them. In this sphere the Führer and Göring had true friends whom they very rarely saw because of their busy schedules.

Then there was the immense reservoir constituted by the dominant classes of wealth, birth, and nobility. These were men and women who moved in high society and who would bridle a bit at being described as socialites because they regarded this term as degrading a 'natural' distinction they had so dearly acquired over time. During the inter-war period, after the blood-letting of the First World War, the nobility represented less than 0.2 per cent of the population, as did the upper middle class consisting of the families of Mark-millionaires whose income fluctuated with the financial markets but whose ranks remained stable. To this may be added the upper stratum of the *Bildungsburgertum*, which constituted less than 2 per cent of the total population. All together, between three and four million privileged Germans frequented more or less refined social circles. The collective characteristics of this social elite were chiefly ideological. The nobility became the element that structured the group's identity. Financiers and businessmen claimed connections with it through alliances or associations. They saw the Third Reich as an opportunity to correct the nobility of birth through an aristocracy of action, and fully recognized their own views in the Nazis' pseudo-Darwinian discourse on the victory and success of the strongest. It was not surprising that these wealthy families rapidly decided to join the NSDAP, and that the men began to wear a uniform whose martial appearance confirmed them in their supposed virility. These families understood the rallying that was going on and rushed toward the party, whose members numbered two and a half million when Hitler decided to put an end to new memberships in June 1933, in order to keep the party apparatus, which he pretended to believe was 'popular', from becoming too bourgeois.

However, we have to note the division that originally characterized this group. The nobility and the upper bourgeoisie started out from conservative positions. Before the 1930s, few members of these groups defended Nazism. They were first led to support an alliance between Nazism and conservatism, and then allowed themselves to be infected by an ideological radicalization. The rising curve of their coming into phase with the regime also corresponds to belief in a perpetuation of Nazism in the form of a revisited national culture. The pace of their allegiance to Nazism therefore accelerated between 1932 and 1934, the period that concludes the experimental cycle of Hitlerism in power. Between the destruction of the SA's opposition and the conservative alternative (assassinations of close collaborators of von Papen and General von Schleicher and his wife), these leaders understood that they had to hurry to occupy the last vacant positions and to take advantage of the new opportunities offered by the Waffen SS and the Wehrmacht in the following years. Far from displaying a reserved scepticism with regard to the new regime, the elites that emerged from the transformations of the Second Reich ended up enthusiastically supporting it when they saw that officer positions had multiplied tenfold and that a simple recommendation would allow them to avoid competing with lower middle-class candidates, and when they saw that the annexation and conquest of Austria and Czechoslovakia provided opportunities for a colonial career. Basically, Nazism confirmed their position as notables. These 'traditional' elites, Gramsci would say, were grateful to the Third Reich.[6]

Great events brought together men and women belonging to these different spheres and very occasionally popular figures, heroes for a day. The latter knew nothing of the rules of high society, but they were proud to enter into the ceremonial and to be in proximity to the master who fascinated them.[7] They gave him bouquets, embroidered cushions, beer steins, and flags. They could hardly be distinguished from the masses they represented. Their enjoyment remained essentially spiritual.

The case was very different for socialites. During semi-public events, they fulfilled a specific social function in an order constructed as much for their use as to make a certain impression on the masses and on foreign countries. Nonetheless, the comedy played out before the cameras did not prevent the creation of personal ties, a mixture of affinity, self-interest, and militant ardour.

An Outline of Official Conviviality

On 10 April 1935, Berlin rejoiced in the marriage of Hermann Göring and Emmy Sonneman. The event had international scope and examining it allows us to offer a concrete illustration of the way in which different spheres of social relationships that animate high society can intersect in a single encounter and how political ideas and anodyne remarks, public and private life, can intermingle.

Preparations for the wedding ceremony, which was a true affair of state, occupied the party and city for nearly three months. The date originally set had been changed because it corresponded to the anniversary of the death of the former empress. On the evening preceding the wedding, a ceremonial outing at the Opera was organized, and for the first time, the bride's bedroom was guarded by a soldier.[8] Was it still necessary to protect her long-since lost virginity, or was it a matter of emphasizing that she now had an official status? In the morning, the guests met before the burgomaster to sign the marriage registers. Adolf Hitler was once again a witness, as he was in all chic marriages. He had been a witness at the weddings of Goebbels, Schirach, and even the Gauleiter Terboven, in Essen, on 28 June 1934, when the arrest of Röhm was being prepared. In this specific case, it was whispered in diplomatic circles, Hitler had ordered his paladin to marry his mistress in order to conform to morality.

Hermann Göring was a widower. Karin, his first wife and a fervent admirer of Adolf Hitler, had succumbed to illness in 1932. The former head of the SA had consoled himself by attending the theatre and electoral meetings. While passing through Weimar with his friend Paul Körner, Göring met an actress who was already middle-aged, and also a divorcee: Emmy Sonneman. She came from Hamburg. Her profession and her patrician birth were symbolic of the Third Reich's synthesis of notoriety and notability.

Thus the wedding was very media-conscious and recalled the pomp of princely marriages.[9] After the ceremony at the burgomaster's office, the couple returned for a short time to their flat in the Leipzigerstrasse to put on their splendid wedding clothes. A dazzling white dress for the bride, set off by a sprig of white flowers on the veil. The bridegroom wore a gala dress uniform with medals and a sash. The city streets were decorated with flowers and hung with flags. The couple was greeted by the prelates on the steps of the cathedral. Adolf Hitler, who followed at a relatively discreet distance, shook hands with the prelates and with Himmler, who came up to greet him. Then the cortège entered the church. Flowers were strewn around the benches onto which officials and the press crowded. The bishop's sermon lasted seven minutes. Singers from the Opera lent their voices to the ceremony. The wedding vows were pronounced and then the cortège left the church as professional photographers snapped pictures. A military honour guard, their sabres bared, were framed by another line of party dignitaries giving the German salute and murmuring 'Heil Hitler'. Smiling, Emmy Göring came out on her husband's arm. They were now to go to the Kaiserhof hotel, where the wedding luncheon and reception were to take place. After a final salute to Hitler, who returned it, the members of the honour guard sheathed their swords. The guests got into their cars. During the short trip, the Führer greeted expertly the crowd that cheered him, distracting attention from the heroes of the day.

The luncheon was attended by three hundred and sixteen guests sitting in a large U framing seven long, parallel tables. Emmy Göring was seated between Hitler and her husband. On the seating plan we find figures from the high German nobility: Prince Philipp von Hessen, his brother Christoph, Prince zu Wied and their wives, the Duke of Sachsen-Coburg und Gotha and Prince August Wilhelm von Preussen. Marshal Mackensen was seated across from the bride. Göring's sister-in-law, Countess von Rosen, was seated next to the Führer. About 20 per cent of the guests were connected with noble families, that is, they were over-represented with respect to the national average of about 0.2 per cent. Businessmen were less numerous, but Fritz Thyssen, the steel-works heir, was among them. Members of the government constituted a large contingent, and included figures such as Hess, von Neurath, Lammers, Meissner, and Schacht, as well as party officials such as Heinrich Himmler, the head of the SS, and Viktor Lutze, the head of the SA, who owed his promotion to his betrayal of Röhm the year before. The rising political stars were there, notably Heydrich and Bouhler. The historian notes the absence of Albert Speer, who had not yet boldly asserted himself. All these men were accompanied by their wives. There were many military men, headed by the Chief of the General Staff, General von Blomberg. Artists were also represented, of course, in view of Emmy Sonneman's profession. The soprano Ursuleac and the tenor Bockelmann, from the Opera, had participated in the ceremony, but remained discreet at table. The superintendent general of the theatres, Dr Franz Ludwig Ulbrich, was present. From the National Theatre of Berlin came the bride's colleagues Hermine Körner and Eugen Klöpfer. The director Gustav Gründgens, appointed by Hermann Göring and Emmy's partner, was seated in a good place, not far from Wilhelm Brückner. With Brückner, Schaub, and Otto Dietrich, the press attaché, there were three members of Adolf Hitler's personal staff in the room. Göring's adjutants, Körner and Bodenschatz, also took part in the celebrations. Bodenschatz was seated across from Dr Brandt, who had been Hitler's personal physician since 1933. Brandt had met the Führer because during the past summer he had treated Brückner, who had had an accident at Obersalzberg and had been helped by the Görings. Hitler made him an adviser for medical affairs.

At the table of honour, did Mafalda de Savoie, princess and wife of Philipp von Hessen, talk with Göring about her native Italy in the course of the meal? The wedding trip might have provided her with a pretext for doing so had the couple not chosen to spend a few days resting at the homes of Hermann's brothers rather than undertake the already arranged journey to Venice. As for the Italian orange-tree blossoms that had been intended for the bridal crown, they had arrived already faded, and had to be replaced. The superstitious Frau Göring might have seen in this a sign.

There was a tinkling sound and a man stood up. Everyone fell silent. The speeches began as the guests were finishing their meal. The first speaker was Adolf Hitler, the 'Führer und Reichskanzler'. To relax people a bit, he began by declaring that he had given many speeches, but was a terrible banquet speaker. When the laughter subsided, he expressed his affection for Göring and his wife and his belief that the most stable couples were those who fought together for a cause. And he congratulated himself on having had Göring as a battle companion: a mixture of feelings connected with both private and public life. Applauded, Hitler sat down satisfied. The second witness to the marriage, Hans Kerrl, minister of religion, then humorously congratulated the couple and expressed a few moving good wishes. General von Blomberg gave a brief eulogy in the name of the army. Count Erik Rosen's remarks were more intimate. He spoke on behalf of the family of Göring's first wife, whose brother-in-law he was. He referred to the deceased Karin and the good luck they had all had, in Sweden, to have met Hermann, so that they were proud to celebrate with him on that day the birth of the new Germany.

Carl Vincent Krogmann, the mayor of Hamburg, concluded by giving a brief speech. He had been invited along with his wife because Emmy Sonneman's family was from Hamburg, and he took advantage of this opportunity to draw attention to himself, although he certainly did not belong to the first or even the second circle of Third Reich high society. 'As a mayor,' he said,

> I have the right to speak, indeed, I have a duty to do so in order to register a complaint and not only for the reason that everyone has been able to see, namely the presence on the menu of an ice cream made in the Bremen fashion, but a complaint because the minister-president of Prussia has modified, despite our Führer's contrary opinion, an important part of the reform of the Reich by annexing a precious part of Hamburg, a precious part of Hamburg in honour of which I lift my glass, Frau Göring.[10]

Such a speech might have been found annoying, since Hitler had just rejected Göring's proposal for administrative reform. People in the first sphere knew about this tension at the top. Krogmann had learned about it shortly before, from the State Secretary Pfundtner. But the sally succeeded. The Führer laughed, and the rest of the audience joined him. After the meal, Hitler said a word of congratulation to Krogmann. So Krogmann, like his father before him, now had direct access to the ear of the leaders.

When they left the table, Emmy Göring withdrew into a suite at the Kaiserhof with a few close friends. Hitler soon joined her in order to discuss the new situation created by her marriage. From now on, he told her, she would be the Reich's First Lady. No official event would take place without her being present. Indirectly, this meant that this role would no longer be played by Magda Goebbels, who had found it difficult because of her psychological fragility. She must have been grinding her teeth as she sat that day at the table of a couple who were rumoured to be her rivals.

The success of Göring's marriage strengthened his social and political position as the second most important figure in the government. He had proved to everyone the princely grandeur of the regime and demonstrated the consensus that reigned within the leading groups. This event also provided an opportunity for people belonging to distinct social spheres to intermingle. It inaugurated a period of increasingly frequent social events. In fact, elitist social relationships became a way of deepening ideological agreement within high society. They complemented the party's mass meetings, whose objectives were to win the support of the people and to strengthen the National Socialist political religion. Over the months and years that followed, Göring engaged in feverish activity on the terrain of the political apparatus. He competed with other members of the hierarchy who were aware that munificence was an incomparable instrument for constituting a clientele and for obtaining confidential information. Goebbels was not far behind him in this area. For him, much was at stake: he wanted to retain his status as the organizer of the regime's ceremonies. But Göring's power took him by surprise, for as president of Prussia, minister of the air force, general of the army, master of the hunt and of the German forests and the Führer's designated successor, Göring had access to enormous resources.

On 11 January 1936, Göring displayed this power by inviting two thousand and ten guests to join in the celebration of his birthday and to attend a gala dinner he was giving at the Berlin Opera, which had been redecorated for the occasion. The walls and stairways had been specially hung with cream-coloured satin; artificial fountains had been set up in each corner of the hall. Musicians of the National Orchestra played the repertory of waltzes and classical music. The stage was connected with the hall by a floor in order to obtain enough space for the tables. Valets in red livery led the guests to their seats, lighting the way with lanterns held above their heads to create an intimate atmosphere. The admission tickets that were sold to aid the poor, as in the great charity balls, cost fifty marks, or ten times the price of a ticket to an ordinary charity ball. The programme included a show, followed by the ball and a tombola. This event had such an impact on public opinion that Klaus Mann made it the point of departure for his novel *Mephisto*. Mann describes the guests' servility with striking realism. Hitler did not show up that evening, saying that he was ill.

Goebbels found it hard to accept this brilliant success. Seeing the reaction of the foreign press, which was stunned by this degree of luxury, he used it as a pretext for an effort to discredit Göring. To inform the Führer of what the press was saying about his rival, he sent Fritz Wiedemann, in an envelope marked 'confidential', a translation of a very hostile article that had appeared in a Dutch newspaper, *De Masbode,* and also quoted the *London News Chronicle.*[11] The author of the article wondered how Germany could afford to spend such large sums when millions of workers were living in a precarious situation and 'are not sleeping on roses' (*sic*). He wrote that in this there was 'nothing socialist, whether it's called national or not'. Evidently the manoeuvre failed: in the summer of 1936 high officials were competing in the display of luxury in order to seduce high society. On 30 July Goebbels convened representatives of the foreign press in the marble hall of the Berlin Zoo, and the president of the International Olympic Committee, Julius Lippert, invited members of the committee to a small luncheon at Berlin's city hall. These official events became less formally connected with the Olympic Games when at the end of the day Göring received more than two thousand guests at a garden party held in the grounds of his new ministry of aviation. Joachim von Ribbentrop entered this festive competition by celebrating his appointment on 11 August as German ambassador in London. He invited seven hundred guests to his villa in Dahlem. A gigantic tent was set up for the dinner. The champagne was a fine vintage Pommery, a sign that when Ribbentrop entered politics he did not lose his professional contacts. His superior, the minister Konstantin von Neurath, also organized a reception. On the pretext of inviting the Olympic committee, he invited all the German statesmen to his castle in Charlottenburg for a sumptuous soirée. Hitler, for his part, invited almost six hundred athletes and leaders to the chancellery, and organized intimate dinners with officials involved in sporting politics.

Going a step further, Goebbels concluded the series of events with a dinner and ball on the last day of the Olympic Games. All the guests went to Peacock Island, on the Havel River. Among them were members of the Olympic committee, diplomats, and German statesmen, as well as outstanding athletes and members of the Führer's Adjudantur, including Fritz Wiedemann and his wife, who thanked the minister of propaganda for this invitation.[12] Motorboats manned by crews in livery ferried people back and forth from the island. Since the day had been rainy, at the last minute lanterns had to be found to replace those that had been damaged, so that the trees might be transformed into fountains of light. Staff was in short supply, so the minister called upon extras whose manners left much to be desired. It seems that the surrounding thickets were used for relations far more intimate than propriety demanded. The foreign press spoke of an orgy. The culmination of the evening, Goebbels had said, would make people lift their eyes to the heavens. At midnight there were amazing fireworks whose glow could be seen from the Potsdamer Platz, several kilometres away, and thus the parties given by the Goebbels, unlike those given by other leaders, also provided amusement for the common people.

Basically, these expensive pleasures were impressive but not necessarily the ones most sought by those with access to the highest circles. It was good to be invited to these events, but it was more important to gain access to the relatively restricted circle of top leaders. Goebbels, whose power was based on Hitler's confidence in his ability to handle propaganda, understood this. To manage the theatrical world, he had to meet frequently with the Führer. In this way he compensated for the fact that his access to Hitler was less regular than that of Himmler, for example. Thus he organized receptions reserved for celebrities who he knew were likely to attract his patron.

Uncertain until the last moment whether Hitler would appear, Goebbels worked hard on the programmes. Then he sent his proposals to Hitler's staff. On 29 October 1937, for instance, he gave a reception in honour of artists at the ministry of propaganda.[13] If Hitler came, the seating plan at the table would be changed. Seats would be added for him and for Julius Schaub. Would another one be needed for Fritz Wiedemann? The guest list was a mixture of old acquaintances and stars who enjoyed the favour of the Führer, who loved the cinema. At table were found, for the old guard, Heinrich Hoffmann, Philipp Bouhler, Count Helldorf, the head of the Prussian police, and Funk, the finance minister, all accompanied by their wives. Among the close but more recent associates were the Speers. They kept Eugen Klöpfer company; Klöpfer had become the manager of several German theatres after a difficult showdown between Goebbels and Göring. The Berlin theatres remained under the authority of the minister-president of Prussia, whereas other artistic and cultural domains, as indeed elsewhere in Germany, were put under the control of the ministry of propaganda. As an accomplished host, Goebbels received guests in company with his wife and eldest daughter. Among the film directors, the most famous was Veit Harlan. In the course of 1937 he directed two films that won him prizes: *Die Kreutzer* and *Der Herrscher*. At the Venice festival, Emil Jannings, who starred in *Der Herrscher*, received the prize for best male actor, and the film was awarded the national prize. Hilde Körber, his wife, an almost platinum blonde who was thirty-one years old, was in the cast. She was, of course, invited to the dinner and seated across from Julius Schaub, who liked pretty actresses, while Veit Harlan sat opposite Ilse Mangel, a budding actress who two years earlier had played with Lil Dagover in a light film made by the UFA.

Lil Dagover was the most famous actress seated at the table. She began her career in silent films, under the direction of Fritz Lang. After the Great War, she worked with Murnau. In 1931, she went to Hollywood, like her compatriot Marlene Dietrich. But she was not successful there and returned to Germany. She adapted well to the new regime, which offered her roles in its big productions such as *Fredericus*, made in 1936. Did this older star disdain the young actresses promoted by the minister of propaganda, like Lida Baarova, who was seated not far away on her left?[14] A starlet of Czech origin, Baarova had arrived in Berlin two years earlier, and had won her first role when she was barely twenty. She met Goebbels at a high-society party, and became his mistress shortly afterward. Magda Goebbels, who was supposed to sit opposite the Führer, at the other end of the table, knew about her husband's mistress. She tolerated his affairs so long as they did not perturb her own life too much. Nevertheless, she ended up being affected by this liaison, and complained about it to Emmy Göring and Adolf Hitler. Gustav Fröhlich, Lida's official lover, also was offended by this affair, to the point of wanting to challenge Goebbels to a duel. Hitler intervened at that point to avoid a scandal that might compromise the image of his entourage's exemplary morality that he wanted to establish. He forced his minister of propaganda to break with Lida. She fled to Prague in the autumn of 1938.

On that evening in 1937, however, like the other guests, Lida Baarova took advantage of this dinner, which was set to begin at precisely 8:20 p.m. Ten minutes were to be devoted to the crabe royal à la mayonnaise with asparagus; seven to the clear soup; eighteen to the young goose served with browned potatoes and a salad of cucumber and lettuce; eight to dessert; seven to the 'pieces of cheese' and radishes; ten to a piece of fruit. Then came a quarter of an hour for leaving the table and moving into the reception room, where coffee, little cakes, pastries, liqueurs, and cigars were waiting. At 9:40, the programme planned an hour-long song concert. Other guests, eminent singers, performed: Irma Beilke, who after singing in *The Marriage of Figaro* triumphed in the role of Papagena in *The Magic Flute*, was accompanied by Hans Reinmar, who had already been her partner, as well as by Tresi Rudolf. Konstanze Nettesheim, Wilhelm Schirp, and Karl Schmitt-Walter completed this fine group. They sang lieder by Schumann, Richard Strauss, and Schubert, and even Johann Strauss's *An der schönen blauen Donau* ('The Blue Danube'). A deliberately German programme.

After the meal, other guests joined those already present. These included the singers who had not taken part in the dinner and a few people well known to Hitler and Goebbels: the Höpfner sisters, Flokina von Platen, Olga Chekhova, Jenny Jugo. These were all figures in the theatre world, and at least one of them, Olga Chekhova, tried to seduce Hitler.[15] Thus this dinner was less about managing the arts than about encouraging informal relationships.

There was nothing about this event that violated the rules that had governed soirées in Berlin high society for more than a century. Even the ménage à trois involving Goebbels seems to have been taken from a boulevard comedy of the kind that Berliners had been enjoying since the days of the Kaiser. The evening's originality lay elsewhere, in what all the guests thought but did not say. They considered themselves members of a superior group that alone could enjoy special pleasures from which the masses, and *a fortiori* those banned by the regime, were excluded. The example of the artists shows that the host, the minister, could exercise a subtle form of sexual pressure, but always gave something in exchange. A reading of the fiscal files shows that the minister proved generous with these theatre friends, who were rarely members of the party.

Lightening the Burden of the State on the Pleasures of Life

All the names of actresses on the guest list for 27 October 1937 are also found in a summary document drawn up by the ministry of finance and dated 18 June 1938. Fritz Reinhardt, state secretary for finance, prepared it and sent it to the chancellery of the Reich, that is, to Hans Heinrich Lammers.[16] Reinhardt was a party veteran who had joined the NSDAP in 1923. He had had painful experiences in the Great War, having been taken prisoner on the Eastern Front. He had advanced training in management and before the Nazis took power he became a specialist for fiscal affairs attached to the Führer's personal office. On 1 April 1933 he was appointed state secretary and assigned primarily to keep an eye on fiscal policies. He did not really belong to the highest sphere of power, but he had an important backer in Funk, his supervising minister. The document he sent to Lammers dealt with a request from the minister of propaganda that had been forwarded to him by the Führer. Goebbels was asking for a special tax reduction for artists.

The subject had been under discussion for several months. In December 1937 Goebbels had already proposed that artists involved in the cinema (directors and actors) be given a reduction of 20 per cent corresponding in theory to their publicity costs. Evidently little known, this reduction favouring one profession did not satisfy the tax office, or, to be sure, the central offices of the Hitlerian state. This kind of advantage seemed minimal, but nonetheless gave rise to an inequality that might be detrimental to the government. Goebbels' people tried again, this time asking the chancellery to accord a reduction of 40 per cent for artists on a list to be gradually drawn up.[17] The minister of propaganda would subsequently decide whether it was opportune to set a general rule for all artists. The project was clearly submitted to Hitler, since a letter from Lammers's office sent to the finance ministry on 3 June 1938 states that

> The Führer and Chancellor of the Reich has granted Minister Dr Goebbels a tax reduction for artists, 40% of whose income should be exempted from taxes. A list of prominent figure who are to benefit from this exemption proposed by the minister named below is enclosed so that you can act on it. I must moreover note that Minister Dr Goebbels attaches great importance to the rapid adoption of a special rule.[18]

Reinhardt was ultimately assigned to deal with this matter.

The analysis Reinhardt proposed in a document dated 18 June was not a simple executive act. The state secretary sought to ensure that Hitler was in full agreement with the project. He asked for a tactical confirmation, doing everything he could to see to it that his interlocutors re-evaluated the advantage granted by their protégés. His letter is quite explicit on this point:

Before I transmit the directive in question to the ministry, I would be grateful if you were to communicate to the Führer the following facts: the list that has been transmitted to me grants the exceptional reduction to 253 selected persons. According to tax returns filed by these persons in past years, it appears that their costs for publicity were less than 20 per cent.[19]

Reinhardt gave a series of examples. In 1937, Albrecht Schoenhals declared only 14 per cent (out of a total income of 162,720 marks) for publicity costs. Paul Hartmann declared 18 per cent (out of a total of 113,490 marks). The more famous actors Karl Ludwig Diehl (total 173,107 marks) and Gustav Fröhlich (total 178,118 marks) did in fact declare publicity costs of 20 per cent. But Diehl and Fröhlich took advantage of the law authorizing great musicians to declare 20 per cent of their total fees under this rubric, whereas in reality their actual expenses for publicity were 8 per cent and 15 per cent, respectively. Secretary of State Reinhardt nonetheless recognized that a few darlings of the theatre world had publicity costs in excess of the 20 per cent accepted by the finance ministry. Wilhelm Furtwängler, one of the most famous German orchestra directors who also held the office of Staatskapellmeister, received 117,000 marks in 1936, but deducted 39,600 marks, or 35 per cent, for publicity costs. In the same year, Käthe Dorsch reduced her tax base by 25 per cent of the 152,700 marks she had earned. The apparent record-holder in absolute numbers was Hans Albers, who for an income of 562,000 marks obtained a reduction, without further explanation, of 100,000 marks. Behind each of these cases we can divine a discreet intervention on the part of the chancellery or the minister of propaganda.

Moreover, Reinhardt took pleasure in complicating things, the better to emphasize the strange and even indecent aspect of the sums involved when compared with a worker's salary (200 to 300 marks per month), or even that of a state secretary, who at that point earned no more than 1,500 marks per month. He asks whether he ought to take into account the actors' investment income (from stocks or bonds), because Diehl received 27,985 marks in royalties in 1937, and Hans Albers received 9,800 marks in royalties. He goes on to remind his reader that a few artists on the list were not residents of Germany for tax purposes, and that in such cases the 1936 law authorizes a flat payment of 4 per cent on the sums received in Germany. In these cases should he also deduct the costs of publicity?

The two questions that were really bothering Reinhardt were in fact of greater consequence: should this reduction be made automatically or only when justified by documented expenses? Wasn't there a risk that other artists would demand similar advantages? He therefore urged that the list be re-examined with a view to reducing it and adopting a simple rule: a 20 per cent automatic reduction and an additional 20 per cent if the expenses are documented. The last sentence of his conclusion leaves no doubt about how little influence Goebbels had: 'I request that you inform me of the Führer's decision and I shall immediately take the necessary steps.'

Reinhardt's reaction must not be interpreted solely in terms of jealousy or bitterness. It also reflected his structural role as guardian of the state's resources. His objective was to guarantee the largest possible tax base. That is simply good policy for a minister of finance.

Hitler's logic was different. In order to govern, one must be generous and know how to give. Lammers wrote on 7 July 1938: 'Dear Mr Reinhardt, yesterday I showed the Führer your letter and I saw that the Führer does not desire that this matter of 40 per cent for artists' complete publicity costs be dealt with in a rigid fashion, but rather on an individual basis.'[20] He added that he had tried to reach Reinhardt by telephone and that they had to discuss a few details. In view of all this Reinhardt could hardly have failed to understand that the goal of this operation was purely clientelist in nature. Henceforth he knew that his office would have to treat with kid gloves the artists listed in this document and even ask the chancellery's advice case by case.

The names on this list allow us to make two immediate observations. The first concerns the professional distribution of the beneficiaries. Among the women artists, only actresses were selected. No woman writer, painter, sculptor, or dancer is mentioned in the document. On the other hand, singers such as Irma Beilke or Konstanze Nettesheim are on the list. This quite clearly delineates the fields in which women artists were recognized under Nazism. On the contrary, the variety is greater among men: sculptors like Thorak, composers and orchestra directors like Furtwängler, famous actors like Heinrich George, or theatre managers like Eugen Klöpfer found a place on the list.

Among the musicians, several names are lacking, and this shows the differential role that favour could play at this time. For instance, Herbert von Karajan, who was still in Aachen, had not attained the status of one of the Führer's favourite orchestra directors. He did not threaten the position of Furtwängler, who enjoyed all the support of Hitler and Goebbels. The latter even wrote in his journal in 1936 how much he liked Furtwängler, and how devoted the musician was to their cause.[21] Inversely, the absence of Richard Strauss is a sign of his disgrace.

The second observation has to do with institutional position. Most of the people mentioned did not occupy an eminent place in cultural institutions. To be sure, some of the directors of the Reichstheaterkammer were on the list, but that kind of anchorage did not justify the tax reduction for most of the persons cited. Similarly, many of those on the list were not members of the NSDAP. Among the actresses in particular, the rate of membership was very low. Neither did the choice depend on celebrity, since among the persons listed were secondary figures in the theatre world. Thus one can deduce that the favour of the minister or the dictator alone explains inscription on the list for tax reductions, and that this favour was based on personal relationships with the beneficiaries. By granting these tax advantages, Goebbels and Hitler showed their fidelity.

At the same time the desire to grant advantages to individuals rather than adopt a rule concerning a professional category indicates that the state was not corporatist but had instead constructed a system of subjection maintained by a series of rewards. This also explains why artistic couples benefited separately from these personal advantages. Thus, to limit ourselves to legitimate liaisons alone, Hilde Körber and Veit Harlan were each listed separately, as were Frita Benkhoff and Paul Kemp.

Finally, the process of elaborating this tax reduction shows how the regime functioned. A guideline was traced on the basis of a pseudo-legal justification (the reduction was for publicity expenses). The legal qualification simultaneously masked the fact that the group to receive this advantage was selected on the basis of utility and affinity. The necessity of conveying certain information solely by telephone indicates that these acts were confidential. What mattered was that from the outside the system appeared to function in accord with rigorous rules. Hitler claimed to be defending the law the better to establish his own dominion. By holding several offices at once, he had become the incarnation of juridical legitimacy. Thus he played on habits and normative constraints in order to impose on others a framework that he himself did not hesitate to ignore. This affair also shows that the subaltern levels of government did not know how far they should go in corrupting regulations in order to satisfy the hierarchy. In this case, State Secretary Reinhardt, on the last rung of the political apparatus just above the bureaucracy, made sure he knew what his superiors wanted before having the measure carried out by his office.

This was not the first time the state secretary had been faced with requests for tax exemptions emanating from the chancellery. Shortly after he had taken office, he had had to deal with an unusual case, that of the painter Ernst Vollbehr. The latter, a veteran Nazi hand who was one of the first members of the Stahlhelm, had got the NSDAP to buy part of his collection and received a very nice tax exemption.[22] Vollbehr took advantage of his old friends' accession to power to enter, with fanfare, into the artistic establishment.

On 23 February 1933, in fact, Vollbehr had written to the chancellery to promote his series of paintings on the Great War. Hitler responded and visited the exposition of his works at the National Library in Berlin on 1 June 1933, accompanied by the painter and State Secretary Lammers. Hitler had agreed to have the party buy the paintings, in view of the fact that the ministry of propaganda and the army could not find the money to do so. At the time, the operation had been justified on propaganda grounds. The tax exemption was granted on the pretext that the twenty-eight thousand marks paid barely covered the painter's costs for these thousand paintings, which had at the time been financed by the army General Staff, for which Vollbehr had been the official painter during the First World War.

Hitler's decision to support prominent figures in public professions was strategic. He wanted to establish a close connection with the elite of a profession, for the latter set the tone and exercised an influence. Artists were not the only ones to benefit from fiscal or other advantages. The same can be said for certain high-ranking officers. For example, Marshal von Mackensen obtained an exception to the inheritance law and had his lands classified as inalienable and transmissible to his sole designated heir.[23]

The Führer's fiscal gifts to his favourites were ultimately not gratuitous. Through them, he demonstrated his omnipotence, put his stamp on people's minds (because in order to receive one had to accept), and won people's fidelity while at the same time contributing to the construction of his own myth, that of a generous man of culture, which he intended to spread.

Little Gifts Maintain Loyalty

Often it is asked whether one should really give gifts. Quite a few people say one should not. They are right. The problem is not so much what one gives but how one gives it. [. . .] Unfortunately, today the art of giving has become a matter of convention. Old, beautiful customs that gave gifts their meaning are becoming, through a mad transmutation, something determined by the calendar alone. [. . .] Giving ought to come first of all from the heart. Otherwise it is basically nothing but corruption Just corruption.

Hans Martin[24]

The privileged members of the first two power groups received not only regular invitations to official events and favoured treatment at them, but also frequent small gifts, as did the personal friends of the most powerful leaders. This strange practice became a veritable institution that had its own conventions and its own calendar. Did it constitute a form of bribery, as Hans Martin suggests in the text quoted above? Martin, a German specialist in good manners whose book was a best-seller that ran through ten editions in the inter-war period, denounced the utilitarian aspect of gift-giving. In this he was following the traditional view set forth in the *Knigge*, the eighteenth-century classic manual of good breeding that sustained the elegance of the following century. To be sure, other regimes had known such practices, but Nazism exploited them massively and systematically. The Nazis' gifts were sometimes paid for with public funds and benefited from state infrastructures.

These gifts were given in accord with a conventional calendar. The holiday universally celebrated by the Nazis was Christmas. The Führer had got into the habit of giving Christmas gifts toward the end of the 1920s, a sign that his financial situation had improved. From 1925 on, royalties on *Mein Kampf* had provided him with several thousand marks a year, and by 1931 he had become a millionaire.[25] He gave gifts to so many people that procuring them cost him a great deal of time. According to Julius Schaub, Hitler started looking several weeks in advance, shopping the stores for the right gift for the persons he wanted to honour.[26] His gifts were not in any way unusual: vases, porcelain tea or coffee services, sweets, lamps, books, cigars. He was also fond of giving pictures – paintings, sometimes old ones, but also his own watercolours, like the one he gave Heinrich Hoffmann, mentioned in the lists for 1935–6 drawn up by Julius Schaub and Christa Schröder.[27] Schaub himself received a watch in 1935, but lists nothing for 1936. Christa Schröder received money, along with cups, in 1936. The mention of these cash payments is surprising; they look very much like bonuses. The two secretaries mentioned on the list also received cash payments. As for Hitler's personal physicians, Brandt and Haase, they were not forgotten. Other servants were rewarded in the same way. Frau Hammitsch pocketed three thousand marks in 1936. Let us recall that the salary of an unskilled worker was then about two hundred marks a month.

Carefully examined, the list can be broken down into various groups. Real friends and veterans who had been with Hitler from the beginning, like Max Amann, the party's faithful publisher who owed his fortune to the Führer's victory, Ulrich Graf, or Wagner. Then come the old and strong supporters, particularly the Bruckmanns, the Bechsteins, and Frau von Dirksen. Then those important and powerful individuals who were the regime's leading figures, Göring, Himmler, Funk, and Hess, with whom Hitler's relationship oscillated between genuine affection and a strategy of power. Göring, who received a painting by Adolf Ziegler in 1935 and in 1936 a souvenir from the Feldherrnhalle, leaves the historian perplexed. Ziegler's status as an artist was middling and his taste was often decried, but he was one of the painters most active in the struggle to develop a Nazi, anti-modernist art. Among other recipients of Christmas gifts, Magda Goebbels got wine glasses, 'a picture' (a landscape by Hitler), silverware; in 1935, Joseph Goebbels got a stereophonic record player, the pride of Third Reich technology, and in 1936 he got a watch. The Goebbels' children each received gifts as well: perfume, handbags, make-up kits, or books. A few fashionable acquaintances also shared the Führer's favours, such as the actresses Jenny Jugo and Marianne Hoppe. Finally, the lists mention, without any particular distinction, gifts made to Fräulein Braun, the Führer's mistress, who was at that time living in total anonymity. In addition, these gifts were not presented at a great reception. Frequently, they were delivered by a porter and accompanied by a note.

The calendar was then systematically reviewed by secretaries to ensure that birthdays were not missed. A 'List of birth-dates' was drawn up by Hitler's staff in 1939.[28] This list was composed in part of information taken from an appointment calendar, indicating that the objective was to send a note or a gift on the person's birthday. The document in the German federal archives is obviously a duplicate. A few copies of this list must have been circulated in the offices in order to complete it. The list was corrected by hand. A few notable additions are visible, such as the birthday of Paul Wernicke, one of Hitler's adjutants. Above all, several sheets mention those who are to receive a telegram or other mark of personal attention. Himmler, for instance, gets the notation 'pers.': he was to be called in person, which is not surprising, since he was the Reichsführer SS. Old Hugo Bruckmann had to be satisfied with a telegram, like most people on the list.

The list includes the titles of the persons appearing on it. In the German context, the celebration of a birthday involves the glorification of the individual's achievements more than his or her personal qualities.[29] The office held thus takes on great importance, since it is a sign of success. The birthday wishes, even more than the presents, showed Hitler's gratitude for the work done by the person who received them. The birthday list, unlike that for Christmas gifts, contains the names of all the high dignitaries. This time, the state secretaries are better represented (Fritz Reinhardt, for example, appears on it), and all the ministers are on the list alongside the names of long-standing friends and staff members who were close to Hitler. Married women are listed by their husband's names preceded by 'Frau'. Women's first names are not given except when there is a risk of confusion, as in the case of little Helga Goebbels, who had two sisters, or Margot Höpfner, for the same reason. Nonetheless, behind the names of Frau Göring or Frau Goebbels great influence was hidden. As a mark of their distinction and particular dignity, at Christmastime Hitler had the great ladies of the regime (and them alone) wear orchids, at that time a rare and precious flower that throve on shade and humidity.[30] This way of celebrating friends, partners, and colleagues was not limited to National Socialism. At the same period, Roosevelt practised it as well, and more recently, Helmut Kohl's chancellery sent out notes and sometimes gifts on the occasion of birthdays; but in Hitler's case the phenomenon was made systematic and rationalized to a previously unknown extent. Hence the necessity of creating instruments that would make it easier to carry out of this task.

For their part, Himmler's assistants made file cards bearing the names of about eighty dignitaries of the SS.[31] Only one woman had a card, the wife of Obergruppenführer Otto Hoffmann. Other women's names sometimes appeared on their husband's cards when the birth of a child was recorded. These cards are very precise and indicate, by year, three categories of gifts: Christmas presents, birthday presents, and presents given for special reasons (illness, marriage, the birth of a child). A kind of curve of the practice of gift-giving in the SS emerges. In 1933, a single person, Obergruppenführer Prützmann, received a Christmas gift (a portrait of Himmler). Starting in 1934, on the other hand, several dignitaries were given presents for Christmas and also on their birthdays. This phenomenon became more widespread in 1935 and then became routine. From that date onward, a picture representing the taking of the SS oath often served as an initial birthday gift and reminded the recipient of his link with the organization. The SS's strong involvement in the government after 1934, and still more after 1938, was thus accompanied by an effort to increase the cohesion and loyalty of its leaders, and gifts played a major role in this effort. Himmler, by personalizing his presents, humanized the relationship in a situation where the hierarchy and the government were likely to incite brutal competition.

Among the gifts, books predominated. Some of these were freely handed out all through the year. Schäfer's *Berge, Buddhas und Bären* in 1936, or his *Unbekanntes Tibet* in 1942, illustrate this practice. Schäfer, an ornithologist, had visited the Himalayas in 1930 and written several studies on them. Having become a member of the SS with the rank of Hauptsturmführer, in 1938–9 he led an expedition to the Himalayas that was wholly financed by Himmler's organization and whose objective was to look for traces of the origins of the Aryan race. His accounts conformed to National Socialist doctrine, and must have confirmed the executives in their beliefs. Just as 'educational' were the books on Napoleon, Genghis Khan, and Cromwell given to other party members. By distributing them, the Reichsführer SS was carrying out his work as a propagandist. Was that why he gave Obergruppenführer Friedrich Jeckeln, on the occasion of the latter's birthday in 1942, a pocket edition of *Mein Kampf* along with a bottle of liquor for good measure? The fact that one of the chief architects of the mass liquidation of the Jews in the Soviet Union in 1941 should be given a copy of this book at such a late date is already singular, to say the least. The preceding Christmas Jeckeln had been given a book on the Incas, like many of his colleagues. Should we conclude from this that Jeckeln had not yet read *Mein Kampf*, despite the high offices he had held in Brunswick before the war? Or was Himmler, in giving this present, referring to a particular event or conversation? Among the presents, some did refer precisely to a personal relationship between Himmler and a member of the SS. Thus he gave Fritz Sauckel a souvenir of the day they had spent together in his fief of Weimar on 4 April 1940.

The particular gifts mentioned on the cards of Himmler's assistants often corresponded to a social obligation. This was the case for presents given on the occasion of weddings or the birth of a child, all of them illustrating family morality and in accord with conventions. Tea or coffee services were obligatory here, like the silverware valued at five hundred marks that Himmler gave Gruppenführer Pancke in 1935. The same year, Walter Darré received two silver pots as a wedding present, and later on, *Genghis Khan*, in two volumes. When they were ill, members of the SS could count on receiving something to read or to drink: red wine, cognac, or Sekt in reasonable quantities, usually one bottle, sometimes two. Obergruppenführer von Bach was privileged to receive without an express reason an 'old wine from Godesberg'. On the occasion of births, Himmler preferred to give candlesticks. Among the rarities, a few leaders received toys for their children. Berkelmann, in Posen, was rewarded with a teddy-bear 'for Renate', while Freiherr von Eberstein, in Munich, received a toy fire truck 'for his boys'.

These objects strike a different note from most SS gifts. Military objects in bronze were distributed in large quantities: busts of the Führer, 'steel helmets', flag-holders engraved with the SS emblem. Also pictures of hunting scenes and sculptures of stags or foxes. In 1942, it was porcelain figurines of horsemen for Christmas. All this in the style of German realism.

Obviously, photographs of the Reichsführer SS bearing his personal dedication were always greatly appreciated. For particularly meritorious persons or on ceremonial occasions, they were framed in silver. Their symbolic value was thus enhanced by the value of the worked metal. This is an indication of a form of devotion to the strange figure of Himmler, who was at the time already described as cold and calculating. We have to imagine that these portraits were not to adorn only the homes of high-ranking officials of the SS; they were hung in the office, while the portrait of the Führer remained in the living room – unless the portraits of the leaders were lined up on top of the piano.

Hitler also used signed photographs as a way of rewarding a good companion. The ambassador Hans Georg von Mackensen, who had been assigned to Rome since 1938 and had helped draw up the treaty of alliance with Italy, was recompensed with a photograph of the Führer adorned with a luxurious frame made of silver and jewels, valued at eight thousand marks, and bearing the date of the treaty (22 May 1939) and Hitler's signed dedication.[32] Under Neurath, von Mackensen had been state secretary for foreign affairs, and he was also the son of Marshal August von Mackensen. For his ninetieth birthday in 1939, the latter received a giant portrait of the Führer. The presentation of this gift was accompanied by great publicity. The reward given the son was situated in the context of a family allied with the regime and to which Hitler was loyal.

Interior decoration was changed by these presents. The gifts were displayed. They served a function that went beyond the pleasure of giving and receiving. It was a question of making clear to everyone the place that one occupied in the regime, which varied with the quantity and the quality of the objects displayed. The donor and the recipient were both quite aware of this phenomenon completely characteristic of high society in the twentieth century, which signifies that values and superior beliefs are shared and puts a lien on the future.[33] Emmy Göring's description of wedding presents received in 1935 bears witness to this:

> The day before the ceremony, we were able to gauge the extent of the reaction it had elicited: the gifts already received filled two enormous rooms.

They had come from all over, each more magnificent than the last. For example, the king of Bulgaria awarded Hermann his country's highest distinction and sent me a lovely bracelet set with sapphires. Hamburg gave me a sailing ship in silver that I had always admired at the city hall. That gave me special pleasure. IG Farben sent two extraordinary specimens of precious gems made by synthetic processes. Many, many people sent objects of all kinds and presents are still coming in.[34]

Frau Krogmann added to Hamburg's official present a little painting and a flag of the city. Her husband brought an enormous bouquet of flowers in the municipal colours. It was important that the city obtain ceremonies and official visits in order to maintain the National Socialist faith. These gestures made it easier to do that. IG Farben soon received special advantages in Göring's four-year plan, and starting in 1936 it made huge profits. As for the royal couple of Bulgaria, Göring did a great deal to enhance their official journeys and to support their position.

3

Managing Hitler's Court

Hindenburg, the lame duck president of a dying republic, decided to show his admiration of Hitler by means of a small gesture. On 20 April 1934, Hitler's birthday, Hindenburg sent him a bouquet of flowers accompanied by a note of congratulations. Hitler's response lets us glimpse his pleasure in seeing the old warrior's pride finally acknowledge his success.

> Your letter expressing good wishes and the flowers you were good enough to send me, Herr President, on the occasion of my very happy birthday, deeply moved me. I add to my thanks the assurance that I am delighted to be able to contribute as I have wished to the reconstruction of the Reich in the service of the old marshal of the world war now in peace.[1]

This exchange is not merely a matter of courteous attention without implications. It signifies a recognition of an old conservative's act, and is an expression of the admiration that the traditional elites would henceforth overtly show for Hitler. A similar value accompanies the good wishes for the New Year addressed to the chancellor.

As it happens, such messages acquired singular prominence on the ideological terrain. Many correspondents were moved to express their support, and even their enthusiasm, for the Nazi leaders, their decisions, and their beliefs. They inserted phrases that objectified their implication in the regime. This in turn helped gain the attention of the leaders, who rewarded the writers with symbolic or material advantages. The heart of the Nazi court lies right there, in the curious interval bounded by personal attraction, social conventions, and activist commitment. A whole department proved necessary to optimize the effects of exchanges of correspondence and gradually to modulate subjection to the Führer. It was involved in activities similar to those of other chancelleries of the period. But in democracies this department was not connected with the person of the leader and did not federate a series of offices that were funded by the state and the ruling party. It was part of the foreign office. Before studying its composition and functioning, we must first examine Hitler's letter-writing habits.

Epistles at Hitler's Court

Hitler maintained an ample correspondence whose goal was to show attention to his close associates and thereby increase their loyalty. In December 1933, almost a year after his accession to power, he decided to use this tool in a remarkable way: he sent letters of congratulation to certain leaders. Thus the regime's most influential figures were identified at the outset.[2] These letters were probably not a sufficient reward for most people's efforts, but they constituted a kind of recognition of an implicit debt while at the same time setting the Führer above the ordinary.

Among the beneficiaries were the old companions who had played a special role in Hitler's accession to power: Amann, Bouhler, Buch, Darré, Goebbels, Göring, Hess, Himmler, Ley, Röhm, Rosenberg, Schirach, and Schwartz. The list is surprising because of the absence of certain major figures such as Funk and Frick among the ministers and Hoffmann among the friends. The little group of men designated here thus takes on strategic importance. Hitler expected that they would serve him zealously. In each case, he emphasized long involvement in the service of the cause and a character trait or competence that indicated the individual's personal value. In the case of Amann, Hitler praised the success of the party's central publishing house. In that of Goebbels, he declared that the latter's 'brilliant propaganda' was able to shake the foundations of the old system. In that of Göring, he expressed his gratitude for all he had accomplished since 1923 and declared him the most 'reliable' comrade in battle. The note addressed to Hess puts great stress on his personal relationship with a man who has been his 'closest confidant' and who had followed his 'joys and sufferings even in prison'. The head of the SA, Ernst Röhm, enjoyed a special privilege. He was the only one addressed with the familiar 'Du' in these notes. Even Amann, Hitler's old companion from the trenches of the Great War, did not enjoy that favour. Like Hess, who had nonetheless shared Hitler's cell in the Landsberg prison, he is addressed with the formal 'Sie'. Here we sense that political distance is being put to strategic ends, in order to arouse a devotion whose nature differed according to personal character.

The chancellor's marks of attention soon became part of an economy of symbolic retribution. They were sought after as true rewards. The letters expressing good wishes were meant for semi-public use. Like the telegrams of congratulation, they could be read aloud at a reception or later displayed. Soon this practice led people to ask for this privilege when they enjoyed favour. For example, the consul Wilhelm Wessel wrote to the chancellery – in this case, to Wilhelm Brückner – on 4 April 1934 to remind his correspondent of the birthday of his father-in-law, the old Emil Kirdorf.

> I should be very grateful if you would be so good as to bring to the Führer's notice that my father-in-law, Herr Geheimrat Dr E. Kirdorf, Müllheim/Ruhr-Spieldorf, will celebrate his eighty-seventh birthday on 8 April. After the long relationship that my father-in-law has maintained with the Führer and in view of his advanced age, I am sure that some sort of sign from the Führer on 8 April would make him very happy.[3]

The letter Hitler sent by porter the same day is a model of the care the chancellery took with its communications when it wished to gratify an ally: 'Please accept my sincere wishes for happiness on your birthday. It happens that work allows me to visit you personally in Streithof in the course of the coming months in order to tell you how delighted I am that fate has allowed you to see the rebirth of our people and of the German Empire.' At the end of the letter, Hitler did not fail to send his greetings to Kirdorf's wife, a way of emphasizing his intimate friendship with the former head of the mining syndicate.

In 1933, individuals were still making use of epistolary celebration to show their adherence to the regime. Thus in early October 1933 a certain Frau Meyer sent, through Göring's mediation, a letter containing a poem praising the Führer.[4] The reply she received from a member of Hitler's staff was not enough for her. She sent another hand-written letter accompanied by three roses to express her ardour, and on 28 October she obtained another reply accompanied by a photograph bearing a dedication and a facsimile of Hitler's signature. Apparently, she must have asked for a new picture with an original signature, because the following February she was still waiting for a document signed by the Führer's own hand. In April 1934 she was at it again for the chancellor's birthday: a letter and three roses. This time, the reply was a simple note from a staff member. These humble signs of support for the project of German rebirth and the Nazification of Germany were gradually organized and finally codified.

Although unclear at the outset, after 1935 the dates for sending the Führer one's good wishes became more precise. Hitler was to be wished well on his birthday, at Christmas, on New Year's Day, on 30 January (the date he took office as chancellor), and on the occasion of his major political and military successes. The greatest influx of congratulatory messages was connected with his birthday. A whole series of birthday cards, preserved in the presidential archives of the Reich,[5] concerns this event. Hitler's forty-ninth and fiftieth birthdays (1938 and 1939) in particular are documented in this way. A whole sociology emerges from these letters, which were sent by all kinds of people who – let us stress this fact – were under no obligation to write to the head of state. Then there were the messages from collective entities, the Protestant church, for instance, with its seventy thousand clergy, its deaconesses, and its youth organizations; sporting associations, schools, municipalities, business firms, social or charitable organizations, orchestras, and so on. And then there were always individuals whose letters show the variety of writing styles and choices of illustrations. For example, children accompanied their notes with drawings in which slightly tremulous swastikas have obviously been retraced several times in order to produce a fine effect of relief.[6]

Let us recall that this practice of sending messages of good wishes was symptomatic of the customs of high society. It presupposed that the great exchange greetings and are emulated by their subordinates or clients. This mechanism was involved in all the elites' correspondence. Among many others, this telegram, sent on 19 April 1939 at 2:20 p.m. to the presidential chancellery, illuminates the style of these collective efforts to celebrate Hitler's personality cult:

> We, members of conventual communities, ministers, pastors, candidates, vicars, deaconesses, and assistants in the community of the ecclesiastical circle of Kölln-III, one of the largest ecclesiastical circles in the Brandenburg marches, commemorate our beloved Führer and chancellor Adolf Hitler on the occasion of his fiftieth birthday, with pride, joy, and loyalty, and with our deep gratitude to our lord and saviour, and we implore the blessing of the Almighty for our incomparable Führer, for our country, and for the renascent German people.[7]

This message is signed by all the ecclesiastics in south Berlin and the surrounding area – Kölln was originally one of the two adjoining villages out of which the city grew. The confusion of religious and political values is clearly not accidental. It indicates that the act was perhaps not so routine as the repetitive nature of this document might suggest. This style expresses the transfer of the sacred from the churches to the National Socialist movement.[8] Belief in the myth of collective salvation through participation in political rituals had insinuated itself everywhere. By becoming an actor in this profane religion, the clergy expressed its adherence to the national idea as much as it drew attention to itself.

It is difficult to determine the number of signatories of these affected eulogies. Does a rector who sends good wishes on behalf of his university, or a Gauleiter who officially assures Hitler of the support of the inhabitants of his region, speak only for himself or is he really communicating a collective confidence? What weight should we give to the direct and indirect writers? The mass of these documents and their concentration at fixed dates leaves the impression that there was a consensus among the elites and a large part of the population. This also testifies to the generalization of the high-society practice of writing letters expressing good wishes and congratulations, which had now spread to the middle and lower classes. The Great War was probably still influencing this development, because correspondence back and forth from the front had become so common, leading soldiers with little writing skill to express in this way their affection for their loved ones. Henceforth this instrument of communication functioned as a way of entering the political world and helped popularize the cult of the Führer.

The Führer's Offices

Administrative officials were struck by the volume of mail that confronted them. They gradually set up structures for dealing with it and, more generally, with the flood of information reaching the highest level of the state. Hitler held three conjoined offices that gave him full powers: he was the head of state, the chancellor of the Reich, and the Führer of the NSDAP. He was first of all the head of state. As president, he had a presidential chancellery (Presidentialkanzlei), whose main coordinator was the same as under the Weimar Republic: Otto Meissner. A jurist, Meissner had been named to this post in 1923. He was able to adapt to the 'new Germany' and continued to hold his office after Hitler became chancellor. He dealt in particular with relations with eminent personages and the old glories of the Reich. He also handled correspondence with the great foreign chancelleries. His work was very much concerned with protocol. His zeal won him a promotion in 1937: he was made a state minister and kept his post until the end of the Second World War.

From November 1934 on, the responsible official in the Führer's chancellery at the NSDAP was Philipp Bouhler. Bouhler had been trained as a military man and had worked as a journalist; he also dealt with personal aspects of Hitler's correspondence, particularly individual complaints and appeals. But the tasks assigned him gradually became more political, and he took part in many decisions relating to repression. In the archives of his organization we find documents connected with the T4 euthanasia programme (which often used poison gas) for the mentally ill and handicapped. Almost 100,000 persons were killed in this way. Bouhler reported on his activities directly to the Führer.

Bouhler's direct rival at the Reich chancellery – but one who in fact acted in a distinct way, as super-head of the cabinet with the rank of state secretary and then in 1937 minister – remained throughout the regime Hans Heinrich Lammers. He held several titles and positions. Lammers was chiefly concerned with preparing legislation. His influence on the elites' social relationships was relatively small because he did not control Hitler's calendar and in these matters had to refer to the chancellor's personal adjutants, who were better informed. Moreover, he suffered from not having more frequent access to Hitler and mentioned this problem to other ministers, who tried through his mediation to obtain or force a decision by the Führer. However, we should not underestimate his influence, because

he met with the Führer at least once a month. He also got a residence in
Obersalzberg after Hitler made it an annexe of the state's central offices in
1938.

As founder and leader of the NSDAP, Hitler created his own administrative office (Stellvertretung des Führers). Rudolf Hess was its director.
His superior was Martin Bormann. Their job for the party was to examine
the correspondence addressed to the leadership, especially requests for
membership or decorations, not to mention appointments to positions of
responsibility within the NSDAP, which from 1933 on constituted a powerful parallel administration. The small group that Hitler had joined in
1919 had five hundred members. At its apogee during the Second World
War, the party had thirteen million members after it was reopened to those
who had come up through youth organizations and other Nazi groups.
Bormann dealt with more everyday matters, and even Hitler's personal
affairs. Hess dealt with the party's representation in public and within the
state, since he was given the rank of minister.

Adolf Hitler's Personal Staff

We come finally to the main tool for filtering and promoting a strategy for
seducing the political, economic, and cultural elites: Hitler's personal
chancellery, or rather, as he calls it, his 'Adjudantur', his staff. At first, the
latter operated out of the Reich chancellery, and then obtained a whole
building on the grounds of the new chancellery. Wilhelm Brückner was the
one who initially set up Hitler's staff, but it was Fritz Wiedemann who was
its real organizer. It was entirely devoted to handling Hitler's personal
affairs, managing his schedule, his travel arrangements, his wardrobe, his
errands, his invitations – in short, everything from his socks to relations
with the king of Italy and the emperor of China.

Such an organ required unfailing energy and perfect health. But members
of Hitler's staff enjoyed an enormous advantage in the regime. They were
the only ones who saw Hitler every day, and who were therefore able to
obtain from him a decision or a punishment. They thus enjoyed an audience
and an immense influence in all the other administrative offices, and were
envied for their position. They make us think of the officers of the court in
the Versailles of Louis XIV or Louis XV who had come from high aristocracy
and whose pure blood and the services they had rendered guaranteed that
they would be granted the privilege of handing the king his dressing gown
or of opening his curtains, and who, thanks to this daily contact with the
monarch, obtained sinecures and honours for their families or their
clienteles. Two men in particular stood out in this microcosm in which
hierarchies were gauged by rank in the SS or the SA.

The head of Hitler's personal staff was, as we have said, Wilhelm
Brückner. The son of a musician, as a young man just out of school he had

fought in France during the First World War, then studied engineering. He joined the SA in 1922. He was sentenced to eighteen months in prison for his share in the putsch of November 1923; after he was freed he headed an SA regiment, resumed his studies, and worked on nationalist propaganda abroad until Hitler appointed him to his staff in August 1930. Brückner had risen to the rank of SA Obergruppenführer, the equivalent of a general. He was the highest-ranking member of Hitler's personal staff. He remained in his position until 1940, then joined the Wehrmacht with the rank of major. The reason for his departure was a disagreement within the staff. Disowned, he had to leave and thus lost the master's favour. All his influence passed to the second strong man: Julius Schaub.

Schaub had survived all the conspiracies and had finally eliminated all his serious rivals for the position of confidant. Luck helped him do so, especially the death of the former chauffeur, Julius Schreck, who had occupied a position similar to his in 1936. Schreck had reached the rank of Brigadeführer (brigadier) in the SS. He was preparing to rejoin the leadership of the SS and to become its head when he was killed in a car accident.

Schaub's other potential rival, Fritz Wiedemann, was eliminated for a different reason: he no longer enjoyed Hitler's affection. He had been Hitler's adjutant and then his lieutenant during the Great War and had joined Hess's office in 1934, before moving to Hitler's personal staff in 1935 and finally asking to be appointed consul general in San Francisco in 1939.[9] Hitler granted him this form of retirement. In 1941, Hitler transferred Wiedemann to Tientsin, in China, when Germany declared war on the United States, a sign that he preferred to keep him at a distance.

Schaub thus remained on Hitler's personal staff from 1933 to 1945, functioning as a confidant, secretary, chauffeur, and zealous enforcer. In 1932, he had been named Sturmführer in the SS. Hitler rewarded his obedience by making him a member of the Reichstag in 1936. This was a nice sinecure because after that date the Reichstag practically never met. During its sessions the role of the deputies was to listen to the Führer's speeches and to applaud as loudly as possible. Finally, in 1943, Schaub was promoted to a very high rank in the SS: Obergruppenführer. A pharmacist who had joined the party in 1925 and had been privately employed by Hitler as early as 1925, Schaub was not working for an ingrate. Some people whispered that his master knew secrets about his first marriage with a woman who had been prosecuted for prostitution and that his devotion to Hitler was therefore based less on conviction than on coercion. Reading his testimony before the prosecutors at the Nuremberg trials, one is permitted to doubt this theory.[10] He still defended Hitler's memory and didn't use this kind of argument to cloud the issue; instead, his intention was to try to clear his master of accusations – indeed, he still sought to defend Nazism as an ethic.

Schaub has too often been seen as a simple valet or chauffeur, as if these tasks exempted him from any responsibility for the conduct of political affairs. It is clear that the matters Schaub dealt with concerned important personages and the highpoints of Hitler's life. It has been shown that he was present when Hitler gave the order to assassinate Röhm and when decisions about the war were made. Testifying before American prosecutors, he claimed that he had always withdrawn after introducing visitors into Hitler's presence, but in a number of photographs his silhouette can be seen in the background. With his wife he even attended official dinners; his place at table was reserved. And he was neither stupid nor deaf. It is possible that Hitler did not always discuss political questions with him. But because he was constantly present at the highest level of the state, was able to listen and to see documents passing through the office, and even presented many texts for Hitler's signature, he was informed about everything that was going on in the Reich. Moreover, he admitted that he had been at the crisis meeting preceding Kristallnacht, the gigantic pogrom directed against German Jews in November 1938.

Among the members of this elite was Albert Bormann. He was Martin Bormann's brother, and he ran the NSDAP for Hitler, along with Rudolf Hess. Because of his complicity with his brother, Albert had a good deal of influence, despite the fact that his rank was inferior to that of Brückner and Schaub. He was an NSKK-Brigadeführer, the equivalent of a brigadier, and served as the 'head of [Hitler's] private chancellery'. He often went over certain matters directly with the Führer without consulting other adjutants.

A few women also worked in this inner sanctum of Hitlerism. They were chiefly secretaries. They took down messages in shorthand and typed them up. They enjoyed the Führer's confidence to a fairly large extent and also received marks of his affection. Among them were Christa Schröder and Traudl Junge, each of whom published a book about life in proximity to Hitler.[11] Their testimony after the war sometimes gives a distorted view of the adjutants and secretaries, especially that of Traudl Junge (née Humps). She entered the story of Hitler's personal staff only in 1942 and was to marry one of Hitler's aides-de-camp, the adjutant Hans Hermann Junge. Centred on Hitler, her description of life in this little world neglects the role played by the shadowy men who were the adjutants, and sticks to the naïve interpretation typical of the mass media. Traudl Junge was fascinated by big names and couldn't get over the fact that she had been close to history in the making. Did she have any doubts before the final defeat? That is unlikely. All the secretaries were very loyal to the regime, as much for economic as for ideological reasons. Economic reasons because, like all Hitler's staff, they were extremely well paid, between two and three thousand marks, whereas a state secretary earned fifteen hundred to two thousand marks. Johanna Wolf, the eldest of the private secretaries, who entered Hitler's service in 1929, probably earned more. In addition, they all got bonuses and special gifts, in particular when they married. And ideological reasons because each of them had got her job with the help of a sponsor. Johanna Wolf was a member of the party before she was hired. Traudl Junge joined the group on the recommendation of Albert Bormann, one of whose close relatives worked with Traudl's sister in the German Dance Company (Deutsche Tanzbühne) in Berlin. She had been well indoctrinated by her father, a small-town party boss. She had spent several years in Munich, and that was also an advantage in this milieu. Finally, let us recall that these secretaries, and in particular Christa Schröder, Gerda Daranowski, and Johanna Wolf, were the neighbours and confidantes of Eva Braun, who had been put in this office so that she could be near Hitler. The Führer wanted to maintain the fiction that he was celibate, and thus to make people believe that Germany was his only mistress. He concealed his liaison with Eva Braun from the public at large and kept people guessing about his love life right up until he finally married her, a few hours before he committed suicide in April 1945.

The Social Functions of Hitler's Personal Staff

Always wary, Hitler's personal staff tried to reduce the number of petitioners and scroungers. Its members were well acquainted with their superior and his weaknesses and manias. If a girl approached him, he would soon be asking his adjutants to give her a sum of money or some present as a sign of his generosity.[12] In Munich, girls hung around outside his flat in Prinzregentenstrasse in order to see him and talk with him. Sometimes they had to be forced to go away, because for many women Hitler was a mythic figure, an object of fantasy and desire: they wrote ardent love letters and even committed suicide for him.[13] If the admirer was a child, he or she had to be given the Führer's photograph with a dedication. If they were out of photographs, the staff had to take down the child's address and send him or her the picture that had been awaited.[14] Hitler's adjutants selected the visitors who would be allowed to see the Führer. Occasionally, they prepared notes to facilitate the interview. Thus they frequently called upon other ministries to provide them with the information they used to write up biographical notices or summaries of the proposals that the Führer was to discuss with a newcomer. They were the great organizers of social relationships with the centre of power and the very high society of the Third Reich.

An ocean of correspondence, often concerning minute details, thus occupied Hitler's personal staff, which rapidly came to seem the supreme ministry. Everything having to do with Hitler personally passed through his staff. However, quickly realizing the actual role of this informal council, ministers and the heads of the major Nazi organizations also tried to use this channel to accelerate procedures. The advantage was so clear that every powerful figure in the regime tried to get his own man on the staff. Wiedemann evidently maintained particular ties with Göring regarding relations with intelligence and the secret service. That was why superior officers, notably Admiral Canaris, the head of the Abwehr (military intelligence), tried to establish closer relations with Wiedemann. Himmler and Bormann were counting on Albert Bormann's presence on the staff. Himmler also relied on Hans Junge and Hermann Fegelein, who, thanks to his marriage with Gretl, Eva Braun's sister, was often allowed to see the Führer after June 1941. Starting in 1938, Ambassador Hewel, who officially joined Hitler's personal staff in 1940, promoted the foreign ministry's interests. Lammers and Meissner relied on Brückner's help. Thus they saw their influence wane after the latter's departure.

Hitler's adjutants had special powers, their own official cars, drivers, and escorts, and they were authorized to carry weapons. They travelled at high speed all over Germany aboard their BMWs and Mercedes, coupés or four-door saloons, paid for by the state; when necessary, they requisitioned military aeroplanes. Captain Bauer, Hitler's pilot, helped them out in an emergency, as did Erich Kempka, who took over as Hitler's chauffeur after the departure of the scandalous Emil Maurice (who was fired for having maintained too close a relationship with Hitler's niece and mistress, Geli Raubal) and of his successor, Julius Schreck. They all acquired a taste for luxury. While on assignment, they slept in sumptuous hotels and had Brückner pay the bills; they liked fine restaurants and invited their friends to them at government expense. Incidentally, they also served, as did Julius Schaub, as talent scouts and discoverers of amusements for Hitler.

Two situations favoured the entrance of Hitler's adjutants into high society. The first was that they followed him like his shadow. They were invited everywhere with him and, unlike servants, they ate at the table of the masters even when the number of guests was not very large. The adjutants also served as fillers at evening parties. On the occasion of a diplomatic dinner in 1939, they were invited with their wives.[15] However, Brückner dined at a separate table, near the entrance, ready to hurry off to do Hitler's bidding if he was needed.

The adjutants' access to high society is explained by a second reason: they received invitations to the theatre through the chancellery's mediation. Since Hitler was not able to go everywhere himself, his staff substituted for him. Even his secretaries received special seats at the theatre or the opera. This advantage allowed Julius Schaub to identify young talents or entertaining women to present to the Führer – or to seduce himself.

The filtering carried out by Hitler's staff was not at all systematic or objective. It depended on a subtle evaluation of the petitioner, in terms of power, notoriety, utility, or pleasure. The simplest method was still to have contacts. Messages from unknown individuals were dealt with in bulk or simply ignored. As is shown by the example of the letters of good wishes addressed to the Führer, personal acquaintances were given priority. For this reason, the adjutants' presence in respected groups facilitated access to the Führer. Socialites were aware of the implicit hierarchies and first used the telephone to ask for a meeting and then confirmed their request by letter. The Kirdorf family, for example, had no difficulty in getting the Führer to join in paying homage to old Emil, who had died a year before. The adjutants arranged Hitler's schedule so that he could make a last-minute decision to participate.[16] Having been on the front cover of a magazine also helped distinguish one from the crowd. Notoriety or personal acquaintance were important even for party members. It was not sufficient to appeal to long-standing membership in order to get what one wanted. It was better to meet with one of the leaders in order to present one's request. The Führer himself could be asked once this first hurdle had been cleared.

In some cases, perseverance led to admission to the Führer's presence. Friedl Haerlin, a Berlin actress approaching forty, blonde and curvy, did not hesitate to make her request repeatedly.[17] Was she trying to jump-start her career? In April 1938 she had tried unsuccessfully to be directly invited to the reception given by the Führer in honour of actors. Learning the lesson of this failure, she adopted an indirect strategy. First she sent Hitler, at Christmas 1938, a collection of poems she had written, accompanied by a list of her principal roles and two photographs. In her letter, she makes it clear where she is playing and the name of the play, adding that 'my dearest wish is that you might attend a performance, my Führer'.[18] Wilhelm Brückner wrote her a letter of thanks on the Führer's behalf and wished her a happy '1938' (*sic*). She was not satisfied. In March 1939 she tried again, expressing her surprise at not having received an invitation to the Führer's reception. Brückner pretended that he couldn't help her; according to him, the lists had been drawn up exclusively by the ministry of propaganda. One suspects that in case of need the chancellery would have had no difficulty in requesting an additional invitation.

Friedl Haerlin didn't give up. She had sent her book of poems not only to Hitler and Brückner, but also to Julius Schaub, in December 1938, and she had spoken with Schaub on the telephone. Afterward, she met with him. Did she know he had a weakness for actresses? Had she heard rumours to that effect? In any case, Schaub got her an invitation to the reception held in Munich on 14 July 1939. The most amusing thing is that her letter of thanks is transformed into a new request that 'the man whom I love and whom I am going to marry in a few days' be allowed to meet the Führer as well. One question hangs over these documents: what did the adjutant get out of all this? Was it the pleasure of double-crossing his personal rival on Hitler's personal staff?

Brückner also knew how to please. He sent bouquets of flowers to artists whose performances he liked, as he did to Hilde Hildebrand, a classic beauty who had made a hit in *Die grosse Komödiantin* ('The Great Comedienne')[19] at the Renaissance Theater (Berlin) in 1939, and who the preceding year had played in a film whose title was symbolic of the time:

Tanz auf dem Volkan ('Dance on the Volcano'). He probably knew personally this star who made almost fifty films between 1933 and 1945. The note from Brückner accompanying the flowers mentioned his office, a sign of his power.

Basically, the members of Hitler's personal staff, and especially the adjutants, were bit-players in a high society part of whose codes and whose keys they had learned by frequenting it, but whose functioning and customs they did not control. Gossips ended up noticing them and from that time onward their names appeared in the papers and in illustrated books devoted to the Führer.

The role of the civilian adjutants did not stop there. They all had permission to carry a weapon. In order to serve Hitler, one had to be prepared to kill and to be killed. Even when they were posted abroad, they requested the authorizations necessary to keep their weapons, on the pretext that they had to be ready to defend themselves. In 1934, for instance, Julius Schaub left for a vacation in Italy carrying his automatic pistol.[20] For his part, Julius Schreck had two Walther pistols, a 6.35 Model 8 with a magazine and a 7.65 Model PP like James Bond's.[21] The Walther firm, which was proud of this publicity, had given them to Schreck free of charge, along with extra magazines and a leather holster. In 1939 all his colleagues were provided with weapons and also gas masks.

All Hitler's adjutants were combat veterans and could if necessary supplement his personal guard, which was commanded by Sepp Dietrich and equipped with submachine guns and handguns. They were SS men who wore, depending on the situation, formal uniforms or battle dress. They were taller than average, in order to impress visitors and illustrate German virility. They were responsible for protecting and watching over the Führer's residences. Sepp Dietrich was not, however, a simple bodyguard. He was a farmer's son; after the war, in which he had fought as an artilleryman, he was tempted by the republic of soviets in Bavaria before becoming a policeman. He came late to the NSDAP, in 1928, and thanks to his activity as an informer he was able to rise rapidly in the ranks of the SS. For that reason he was recruited for Hitler's personal guard in 1933. In June 1934, he led the massacre of the leaders of the SA in Stadelheim. Nonetheless, he enjoyed a reputation as an agreeable fellow. Within Hitler's personal staff, he obviously carried out other tasks than those inherent in the direct protection of the Führer. He seems to have run a network of informers and travelled a great deal around Germany, independently of travel in company with Hitler. He seems also to have provided the link between the criminal police (Kripo) and the military part of the personal staff. The criminal police was deeply involved in information-gathering and protecting the Führer, his residences, and his trips. Two police superintendents and police officers were detached for this purpose.

About a dozen men also served as orderlies, aides-de-camp, and secretaries specializing in matters concerning the Wehrmacht, the navy, and the air force. They constituted the military Adjudantur. Their role was not very great in social and high-society life in time of peace, except for the officer in charge of relations with the navy, Lieutenant Commander von Puttkamer. On the other hand, they were omnipresent in relations with high-ranking officers and the General Staff. Above all, after 1939 these men were constantly with Hitler and followed him around the head-quarters. They then became responsible for protecting him and carrying out his directives. The most famous of these aides-de-camp is von Below, who published memoirs marked by a disturbing nostalgia.[22]

So many administrative, hierarchical, and professional strata character-ize the Adjudantur that the motivations of its members varied, oscillating between obsessive devotion to the cause and intense competition, not to mention jealousy. The stake in disputes within the Adjudantur was often some trivial detail, but this proves the clientelist, or even mafia-like, way in which the regime managed things. The axiom was simple: the closer one was to Hitler, the longer one supported him, the greater the privileges and advantages to be gained. In order to justify not taking this or that person along on a trip, Brückner repeatedly had to claim that the decision had been made personally by the Führer. Who sat in which vehicle in official convoys was a matter to which the adjutants lent particular attention, because that was how they could tell where they stood in their leader's affections.

Seen from our own perspective, these disputes seem anodyne. Nonetheless, they indicate the ambivalent feeling in this little milieu: power with regard to the public, and dependency with regard to the sov-ereign. These influential people had only delegated power that was con-ditional on retaining the confidence of a man whose mood-swings affected the whole of their everyday existence, especially after 1942, when his health began to deteriorate. They could not completely control the course of events and direct the government's social relationships. The heavy social structures of Germany were imposed on them. They did not create high society, but selected from it the best elements, accumulating money, adventures, and privileges when the opportunity arose. The flow of social events did not depend on them. But the presence of Hitler at these events sometimes depended on their way of interpreting things. In this sense, Hitler's adjutants constituted a sort of organic elite within high society, a way of giving a Nazi colouring to a deeper social process whose contours had been determined by the traditional elites.

The SS Clientelist Bureaucracy

The clientelist logic served by Hitler's personal staff is found in precisely the same form behind the other major Nazi leaders. Himmler, Göring,

Goebbels, and even Rosenberg had their own private staffs that managed their vast networks of relationships. These structures did not all have the same name and did not carry out exactly the same tasks. Nevertheless they also filtered and organized clienteles. They managed the phenomenal growth of the leaders' power. Their history reveals the complexity of the relationships between the state, high society, and organs connected with the NSDAP. A true socialite knew these offices and was aware of their importance in public life.

The example of Himmler's adjutants is revelatory of the process through which these originally informal structures were institutionalized. Himmler himself was initially an adjutant. In November 1923, he helped Röhm at the time of the Putsch. Then he joined the refounded NSDAP in 1925, rapidly becoming the officer responsible for propaganda (1926–30). At that time his task consisted in organizing the tours of Adolf Hitler, the party's best orator, the one who filled vast halls and thus the coffers of an organization perennially short of money. Himmler accompanied Hitler on great occasions and took advantage of these trips to gain his boss's favour. His appointment as head of the SS in 1929 was largely the result of his bond with the Führer. It was probably he who convinced Hitler that it was necessary to make the SS independent of the SA. At that time he had a secretariat. His election as a deputy in 1930 allowed him to finance an initial, autonomous administrative structure for his own affairs. In 1933, he became the head of the Munich police while retaining his other functions. In this position, he set up the Dachau concentration camp. The 'success' of this experiment led Göring to name him head of the Prussian secret police (the Geheime Staatspolizei, best known as the Gestapo). With the Gestapo and the SS, he directed the destruction of the SA, which was his adversary, in 1934. Finally, he got himself promoted to the rank of Reichsführer SS and had the Gestapo and SS grouped together in a state secretariat in the ministry of the interior. Thus he became the Third Reich's police chief. His accumulation of powers did not stop there. The SS created its military divisions in 1940 (the Waffen SS) under his direction. In addition, the criminal police and the internal intelligence services were entrusted to him to be regrouped within the Reichssicherheitshauptamt (RSHA), a gigantic security office. Finally, in August 1943, he was named Reichsinnenminister and controlled the SS, all the police and security forces, and his private army, the Waffen SS.

Himmler's functions formed a kind of amorphous structure whose contours were perceived only by himself and by Hitler, to whom he submitted reports at least once a week in the course of long lunches or work sessions. To judge by Himmler's appointment calendar, he and Hitler were so close that it is difficult to tell who proposed or who adopted a given idea.

Himmler's personal team sought above all to serve its direct boss. Its initial organizer was Karl Wolff. Wolff had volunteered for military service during the Great War and had been awarded the Iron Cross; after the war he served in the Freikorps and the army, finally ending up as a salesman in a shop in Munich. In 1931, he joined the NSDAP and was admitted into the SS. In June 1933, Himmler made him the head of his personal staff, a post that he held until 1939. Wolff reorganized the staff several times as promotions and honours continued to be given to his superior. In 1936 the workload became so heavy that a complete reorganization and the creation of an official service – the Persönlichen Stab Reichsführer SS – proved necessary.

On 2 June 1938 a written proposal was submitted to Himmler, the purpose of which was to improve the efficiency of the ' personal office and the Adjudantur of the Reichsführer SS'.[23] The Chefadjudantur, that is, the office of the top officials of Himmler's personal staff, which had been operating for the past year and a half, was to be reorganized in accord with the police adjutants. The Chefadjudantur's mission was to deal with 'the Reichsführer SS's personal lists of people who travel with the Reichsführer and in whom he has confidence, to arrange meetings, send out invitations, dispatch greetings and gifts, make travel reservations, keep the diary, etc.'. The enormous importance accorded to managing Himmler's friends and relations, with regard both to seeing them (invitations) and to honouring them (gifts, greeting cards), is striking.

Himmler's two personal adjutants, Obersturmführers Wild and von Hadeln, agreed to redistribute their functions.[24] Wild was made responsible for travel arrangements, selecting visitors and those who were to accompany the Reichsführer, and keeping his diary. Von Hadeln was to deal with invitations, gifts, the selection of Gruppenführer Wolff's visitors, and keeping Wolff's diary. By 1938, Wolff, as the head of the personnel office, had thus become a sufficiently important figure for his activities to be supported and included in the process of bureaucratizing personal tasks. The Chefadjutant charged with administrative matters was Ludolf von Alvensleben, an impoverished noble landowner who, after having been member of the Stahlhelm between 1923 and 1929, had finally entered the NSDAP. He served in the SA for a time before switching over to the SS in April 1934 with the rank of Obersturmbahnführer. He worked in the police side of the organization and thus attracted the attention of its head, who recruited him at a time when the Nazis were tightening their grip on society in preparation for their great international offensives.

This institutionalization of the personal offices of the powerful finally produced a parasitical exploitation of state services. It gave rise to clienteles and relations of subordination subjected to the power accumulated by the SS and the party, which were institutions parallel to the state. For this reason, Himmler set up systems of solidarity and reward for SS members and their families. They all had to be personally indebted to him. When they had babies, Himmler's adjutants sent them milk and vitamins; for marriages and great occasions, they sent a little gift; and when there was a death, they sent a letter of condolence. They even cared about medical matters. The SS order was thus transformed into a kind of patriarchy attentive to its subjects so long as they carried out their duties diligently. Was this so far from classical civility and upbringing?

This may be explained by Himmler's social origins. His father, a language and literature teacher, had before 1914 been for a time the tutor of the children of the Bavarian royal family. Afterward he taught Latin in Munich's largest secondary school, which catered chiefly to the middle classes and the wealthy, and became its director. One of his students was Ernst Hanfstaengl. Heinrich Himmler was thus an heir of the *Bildungsburgertum*. However, in practice the conduct of Himmler's office differed from Hitler's only on certain specific points. For example, Hitler loathed and avoided hunting, whereas Himmler loved it and invited guests to accompany him on his hunting expeditions. In general, the Nazi bureaucracy respected high society's rules of etiquette and politeness and reproduced them in the service of the new leaders in order to give the latter an equivalent influence, social veneer, and respect.

When Himmler rejected requests, he always had a reason and gave excuses for the rejection.[25] Although after 1935 his personal staff used a system of fixed formulas, they never went so far as to use pre-printed rejection slips. The routine character of these rejection letters suggests that many requests never went beyond the lower levels of triage. The secretariat, which opened the letters, must have made a cursory selection that took some of the load off the adjutants. The secretary in Himmler's personal office, Erika Lorenz, was very efficient and ended up making decisions on subjects that were apparently benign but had to do with the organization's functioning. She performed administrative tasks for the adjutants, dealt with Himmler's requests, particularly regarding books, paid bills, and so on. She also occasionally intervened to resolve certain SS families' problems. Finally, Himmler had a personal secretary in the person of Rudolf Brandt, who helped him handle general and public matters. Brandt signed several of the orders issued by the Reichsführer SS, which is why he was sentenced to be hanged after the fall of the Nazi regime.

Always in the Service of the Powerful

Following Himmler's example, all the major ministers created similar organizations. Göring's services, which were very developed, fulfilled analogous functions. At their head was Karl Bodenschatz, who had met Göring when he was twenty-five, during the Great War, in which he served as Göring's adjutant in von Richthofen's squadron. Bodenschatz remained in the army and continued fraternal contacts with Göring, whom he addressed with the familiar 'Du' form. In 1933, Göring appointed him as his personal adviser and first adjutant, as part of the development of the new Luftwaffe. In 1936, Bodenschatz organized Göring's personal office; Göring had by that time become the minister-president of Prussia. Bodenschatz's promotion in 1941 to the rank of general did not prevent him from loyally serving his superior and even representing him in the Führer's headquarters. He briefed Göring daily on military developments. However, during the war he could no longer deal with Göring's immense network of relations that had allowed him to conduct a kind of parallel diplomacy. For that purpose, Göring had another colleague, Paul Körner. Körner, a combat veteran and former jurist, had entered Göring's service in 1928, at the age of thirty-five, followed him to the Prussian interior ministry, and finally represented him in the management of the four-year plan starting in 1936. Thus Körner knew all about the movements of money and became the key player in Göring's group in matters of finance and information.

Rosenberg shared in Himmler's and Göring's centralizing logic. A great creator of institutions and little offices, Rosenberg, whose intellectual vacuity was equalled only by his ideological ardour and his taste for pillage, had a personal office from which he coordinated diverse operations. Nonetheless, in Rosenberg's case the personal aspect of the documents has obviously been largely destroyed.

On the other hand, Goebbels left a massive paper trail behind him. The ministry of propaganda evidently practised a policy of archiving and remembering virtually everything. It took a large view to the point of setting up a foundation, the PK-Stiftung, whose role was to provide financial support for journalists and personages from whom it commissioned articles and propaganda. Among them were acquaintances made at the parties Goebbels organized to rub shoulders with theatre people and journalists. Goebbels' power was based on his ability to organize a set of festivities that maintained the illusory brilliance of an active nightlife while at the same time using it to keep acts and actors within the strictest Nazi orthodoxy. It was he who sponsored and encouraged the press ball held after 1933, a tangible sign of the way German journalists were kept under his heel. His political power had little influence on the government's decisions, but it dominated symbolic matters. Hitler protected him because he was better able than others to attend to the form.

The intellectual elites understood early on the necessity of becoming involved in the network of personal relationships. They followed high society in rallying to Nazism and, in the course of the 1920s, personages close to the Conservative Revolution and elitist associations – such as the heirs of the Juni-Klub founded by Moeller van den Bruck or the Nationalklub of 1919 – turned toward the NSDAP to find in it a sounding board. This was the case, for instance, of Hans Grimm, the author of a best-seller, *Volk ohne Raum* ('People without Space'), published in 1927.[26] In this novel, Grimm emphasized the right of the young German nation to conquer territory proportional to its vigour and population. He was thinking chiefly of Africa. Hitler understood this message and projected it onto Europe, quoting Grimm, whom he met in 1928. Grimm was especially fascinated by Goebbels, whose oratorical qualities, energy, and friendship he admired. This companionship led him to support the NSDAP and to join the newly founded Reichsschrifttumskammer (Chamber of Writers of the Reich). In return, in 1934 the film rights to his book were bought by two prominent figures in the National Socialist movement: Robert Ley and Ernst Hanfstaengl. Grimm's status as an official writer also allowed him to organize remunerative literary meetings in the course of which he acted as a propagandist. Other, better known examples, such as Ernst Jünger, Martin Heidegger, and Carl Schmitt, reflect this great drift toward clientelism among the intellectual elites, who moved from traditional salons to those of the Nazis, embracing the new ideology in both its radicalness and its anti-Semitism. They became part of the new cultural life of which Goebbels and Rosenberg were the masters. Thus they were confirmed in their status as organic intellectuals of the new regime and received the funds and the posts they wanted. They placed their students and their friends. Ten years after the Nazis came to power, when the war was at its height, Ernst Jünger had very harsh things to say about these 'veritable pimps, the low catamites of today's powerful' – a wretched company to which he himself had belonged:

> They lack the slightest intellectual sense of shame: they can't blush unless they are slapped. So now they're going to start remodelling themselves in new positions, and maybe they'll work for men and powers that we find just and that we place very high. We shall then have the special bitterness of hearing this rabble preach the truth out of simple opportunism.[27]

Basically, the multiplication of adjutants and aides reflected the transformation of social life under the Third Reich. Earlier, what had been viewed as belonging strictly to private life – weddings, mourning, the birth of children – was taken into consideration socially only in connection with ceremonies that were still strongly shaped by an intimacy necessary for self-control. Henceforth these events belonged to the public sphere for anyone who adhered to the logic of high society. All these leaders had finally diverted these civil customs in order to make them instruments of seduction, psychological pressure, and attraction. Thus they created networks of dependency that gave them influence, a sign of the favour they enjoyed among other high officials and of the citizens' respect for them. The conflation of tasks is flagrant. It was the leaders' personal offices (their private space) that organized their receptions and their social life in the name of their (public) positions. From that point on, the state apparatus and all the great social institutions conformed to this relational mould and reproduced its ambiguities. The office and the administrative service were henceforth less important than the clientele relationship, and mafias were able to enter the salons with a clear conscience and take the best advantage they could of the unprecedented situation in Germany, in which political power pillaged and prostituted itself in order to exist. In order to exist, one has to give. And to give, one has to take.

The Game of Favour and Zeal

The bureaucratic logic put in the service of clientele relationships ended up becoming invasive and occupied a central place in the activities of state organs. Everyone sought to oblige his superior and to win his approval, to move beyond the framework of professional relationships and to play on feelings in order to obtain a positive decision. Evidence of this slippage is found in the relationships between the propaganda and intelligence services and Joseph Goebbels, their supervising minister. They owed him their salaries and working conditions, which had significantly improved since the Nazis came to power. That was why they undertook to honour him particularly on the occasion of his birthdays. Here again, the mixture of private with public life is flagrant.

Thus several documentary films were made without the knowledge of the minister of propaganda and popular education, with the amiable complicity of his family, so that they could be given to him as a surprise on his birthday, 29 October. The first of these documentaries, and probably the one most full of feeling, was produced in 1940.[28] It described a quiet day at home in the Goebbels' household in Schwannenwerder. It begins with a walk taken in the Grunewald forest. The children soon stop and, facing the camera, recite a compliment for their father. Later on, the two little girls play on a swing while Helmut, the only son of Magda and Joseph Goebbels, plays at attacking a castle with a little cannon. Shortly afterward his sisters call him and they all go together to see the rabbits. This and other playlets compose a documentary indulgent toward the pretty little family. This reassuring view illustrated remarkably well the Third Reich's family morality. Apparently it was a success, because two years later the same team made another documentary for Goebbels' birthday.

To vary the themes, this time the technicians chose to begin the film in Berlin and then to continue it in the luxurious country house in Oberau that the people of Berlin had given to their Gauleiter.[29] Viewing the bucolic pleasures depicted in it, one would never guess that a war was going on. Games on the grounds, a ride in a little cart, making a bouquet, and comical chases after animals are among the insouciant images confected for the boss's delight. However, one passage jars: it shows a child wearing a Mickey Mouse mask and swimming in a pond, at the end of the day, shortly before the film shows them all singing 'Happy Birthday'. The fact that these ultra-nationalists did not blot out the American symbol of

Walt Disney's little mouse shows that the film was not censored as carefully as the rigid propaganda productions – one reflection among others
of the hypocrisy of the public rejection of foreign productions and their
private use.

Suddenly a sequence in the film plunges the spectators into actuality.
General Erwin Rommel, passing through Berlin, comes to visit the
Goebbels at their home: the children, standing at attention, wait to greet
him. He comes in with his aides-de-camp, and the commentary emphasizes that he has come there to rest, far from the battlefield. The general
holds the children by the hand and looks on as they play under the fond
gaze of his aides-de-camp. There again, insouciance sweeps away the
context and the film goes on, changing the atmosphere.

Now it's time to take little Helmut Goebbels to school. He sits in the first
row. His teacher constantly asks him questions and congratulates him on
his good replies, punctuating everything with 'gut' and 'richtig'. Finally
the whole class sings (close-up of Helmut) and the film ends. Through the
indulgence shown by the teacher is projected the indulgence of all those
who have to do with the powerful. It's not a question of fear, but rather of
zeal and ideological adherence.

Everyone hopes to derive direct advantages from obedient conduct.
This reasoning holds for those in the highest places as well as for those in
the lowest. Adolf Hitler understood this very well, and used gifts as so
many favours. He granted important deals to his protégés, such as those
he gave the film-maker Leni Riefenstahl, whose work and personality he
admired.[30] The films of the NSDAP congresses that he commissioned from
her, before making her the official film-maker for the Olympic Games,
were generously financed and benefited from exceptional technical
means. Riefenstahl's grandiose aesthetics, her way of viewing bodies, of
placing the cameras to anticipate movements and to show their continuity
from different angles, is perfectly melded with her conception of art. Her
work also moved the Führer because she drew on other creators dear to
him: in directing *Triumph des Willens* she relied on the advice of her friend
Albert Speer, who designed the sets and the way in which the ceremonies
took place, and she asked Herbert Windt, the composer of several official
songs for the NSDAP, to direct the music. Favours were showered on her
and others, weaving a web of solidarity within the cultural and artistic
world that tended to promote a single worldview.

Hitler also knew how to make marvellous gifts that deeply and permanently indebted a friend. For instance, on 26 June 1940 Hitler's SS adjutant
Wünsche was working on the thorny question of what to give the sculptor Arno Breker for his fortieth birthday on 19 July.[31] Hitler wanted to
please Breker, and since April he had been wondering how to reward this
loyal aesthete of the colossal in a way that would be in conformity with
National Socialist ideology. He spoke about it with Professor Albert Speer,
the inspector general for construction in the Reich's capital, who gave him

a good idea: give Breker a studio in the countryside, since Breker was talking about buying a second residence near Linz.[32] The Führer had already rewarded his sculptor friend with public commissions. This time it was not a question of recompensing him for a specific work, but of honouring a man, an oeuvre, and, still more, *the* sculptor of the Third Reich, the man who since 1933 had always responded favourably to the regime's requests and whose aesthetics was in accord with the Reich's ideals. A handsome official document would enhance the value of the gift. Hitler asked the studio of Professor Paul Ludwig Troost, who had remodelled the head offices of the Nazi party, to design a certificate suitable for the future gift. Hitler wrote the words that were to appear on the certificate:

> To Professor Arno Breker, sculptor, by this certificate on the occasion of his fortieth birthday, I give into his sole ownership the Jäckelsbruch house near Wriezen, its grounds and the newly constructed studio that stands on them. I here express my grateful thanks for his creative work in the service of German art and I add my sincere good wishes for the pursuit of his work. Berlin, 19 July 1940. The Führer.[33]

The fortunate recipient of Hitler's gift could thus create and relax in the same place. Hadn't Hitler proclaimed loud and strong that German artists should live like princes and not like homeless persons? Associating with artists and supporting them financially were part of the National Socialist cultural programme and helped legitimate the clientelist system. Other personages would have to make room for them, so that friendly passions might be fully satisfied through an abundance of goods.

A Disgrace

In 1922, after the death of his librettist, Hugo von Hofmannsthal, Richard Strauss began to work with the writer Stefan Zweig. Strauss, who was considered the greatest living German composer (Jews like Alban Berg, Anton Webern, and Arnold Schönberg were not considered), then enjoyed immense prestige. His daughter-in-law, Alice, was of Jewish origin, and consequently so were her grandchildren. In 1933, Strauss was sixty-five years old. He understood that the arrival of Hitler marked an important turning point in the history of Germany and convinced himself that a 'new Germany' was in fact about to be born. Stefan Zweig thought that Strauss's decision to support the new regime was as much the result of careerist calculation as of a desire to be on good terms with the new masters in order to spare his loved ones any possible problems.[34] However that may be, Strauss rallied to the regime in February 1933. He praised the Führer's musical penchants and offered his services for organizing prestigious musical events. When Bruno Walter was dismissed from his orchestra because of his Jewish origins, Richard Strauss replaced him for a concert. When Toscanini decided to leave Germany and give up the Bayreuth Festival, Strauss once again took over. This early support for the regime and these actions brought him to the particular attention of Hitler and Goebbels, who asked him to direct the Reichsmusikkammer (Reich Chamber of Music) within the corporate institutions that were being set up. Strauss did not intend to sacrifice his collaboration with Zweig on the altar of the new regime. But the situation of an author reputed to be subversive, decadent, and, above all, Jewish became more difficult. The works of the Viennese writer, despite their success, were put on the index, and he had the great honour of being among the authors whose works were burned during the *auto-da-fé* of 10 May 1933. On that day, thousands of students emptied the libraries of books they considered decadent and committed them to the flames.

Despite this known collaboration with a Jew, Strauss was named to head the Reichsmusikkammer in 1934. There, he directed German official music like a potentate, placing his friends in other prestigious directorships and advancing his pawns. He collided with other potentates, including Rosenberg, who found him too fond of Jews and complained about it to Goebbels. The latter defended the composer this first time, in 1934, by arguing that he had confused Zweig with a social-democrat who had fled to Austria, Arnold Zweig.

Strauss wasn't worried by this episode. With Stefan Zweig, he based *Die Schweigsame Frau* ('The Silent Woman') on a story by the classic English writer Ben Jonson. The work was supposed to be performed in Dresden in the summer of 1935. The ancient Saxon capital was not fond of Jews. The orchestra director Fritz Busch had already been the object of a boycott in Dresden so intense that he had been fired. *Die Schweigsame Frau* did not have much success there. According to the prefect, 'at the première, the hall was full, thanks to five hundred invited guests, but the second performance was so meagrely attended that the superintendant general distributed free tickets, and the third performance was cancelled because the soprano who sang the main role was ill'.[35]

Zweig was concerned about the future and had been wondering, even before the opera's première, whether he should continue to work for Germany. On 15 June 1935, he wrote a letter to Strauss in which he expressed his doubts. Some of his friends urged him to break with Strauss, reproaching him for having allowed his name to be soiled by operating under Nazism. Moreover, the authorities were as bothered as was the writer. They wanted his name taken off the playbills. Strauss resisted this pressure and saw to it that Zweig's name was not removed. Zweig, to spare Strauss, proposed that they continue to work together secretly, giving all the necessary instructions to an 'Aryan' writer. In this way, Zweig thought, the composer's work would not be hampered. Strauss replied on 17 June, shortly before the première, in an irritated letter that he knew would be read by the Gestapo, which was watching him, probably at the instigation of Goebbels, who had had his fingers burned by the quarrel with Rosenberg and by the rumours circulating in Berlin. Zweig himself never received the letter. Months later he learned what was in it and its effect on Strauss's career. Strauss thought he was at the zenith and that he enjoyed an invulnerability conferred on him by the regime's complete recognition of his art. His letter was imbued with this ambiguity.[36]

Strauss began by reproaching Zweig for his 'Jewish stubbornness' and his 'racial pride', 'as if one shouldn't be anti-Semitic'. He went on to say that he had never acted 'as a German', but always in the interest of art. If he had replaced Toscanini, it was out of love for Bayreuth, and if he had replaced Walter, it was also out of love for the orchestra. 'That had nothing to do with politics.' Moreover, he had 'mimed' his function as president of the Reichsmusikkammer; he had served in this capacity only out of his 'awareness of his artistic duty'. Strauss continued: 'Under every regime, I should have held this very difficult office. But neither Kaiser Wilhelm nor Herr Rathenau offered it to me.' Thus he asks Zweig to forget his political grievances and to continue working on their next production. He signed the letter 'Your just as stubborn Richard Strauss' and did not forget to take the opportunity to send his good wishes to Zweig's family.

Strauss's letter was intercepted and forwarded to Goebbels, who confronted Strauss with it. Strauss had to resign. He had fallen into disgrace. Nothing could prevent his dismissal from a position that was, moreover, so fiercely sought. He tried to intercede with Hitler in order to prevent his fall from turning into an infernal persecution.[37] With this end in mind, he emphasized his nationalist feeling and his concern for his work as a whole. He told the Führer that he had acted in a fit of anger and because there were no good librettists in Germany. He recited the complaints made about this letter: it lacked anti-Semitism, it scorned the community of the people, it made light of his presidency of the Reichsmusikkammer. He rejected these complaints, arguing in particular that the improvised phrases of this letter did not truly express his worldview. He explained that his whole life was devoted to German music, and he had bent all his efforts toward 'the recovery of German culture'. Flattery required that he ask 'the greatest German creator' to understand that his resignation was motivated by the desire to use what little time was left to him to pursue his ideal. Finally, he requested a personal interview with 'mein Führer' in order to make his farewell.

Strauss had no idea how right he was. His disgrace was almost complete. The Führer refused to postpone his departure. Henceforth, he was forbidden any engagement in Germany. He was allowed to continue to live in Germany, however, and his friends and relations were not bothered. Moreover, he was authorized to leave the country. Because of his international audience, he survived, by composing and directing prestigious orchestras. The man who had looked down on Toscanini now found himself in a more uncertain position with regard to the great Italian director. Like so many others, Strauss had believed he could turn Nazism to his own ends. His support for the regime, like that of the writer Gottfried Benn, played on ambiguities. After 1935, these men struggled to keep their positions. Even the respite provided by the Olympic Games did not change the tendency toward radicalization that characterized a highly ideological regime convinced that the country was to achieve greatness through a series of tests, the first and most important of which were the systematic elimination of the Jews and the war against communism. Disgrace was therefore not the simple result of a blunder; it revealed a state of Germany society that called for total allegiance to the government. Inversely, cases like those of Strauss and Benn show that holding a position in the regime provided limited protection for those who did not wholeheartedly support its development. They were less violently dismissed and even enjoyed a strange sort of tolerance at a time when outsiders were really beginning to be hunted down.

4

The Destruction of Jewish High Society

In 1882, a wealthy Berlin businessman, Friedrich Wilhelm Wessel, bought, for twenty-seven thousand marks, a small island in the Havel River almost twenty kilometres south-west of the capital. Sandwerder ('sandbank') was located a few hundred metres from the *Pfaueninsel* ('Peacock Island'), of which the German emperors were so fond. Its twenty-five hectares were wooded and rather wild. Wessel decided to make it into a park and then sell parcels for the construction of country houses. The site is quite close to Wannsee, where Berliners already went in the summer to bathe. Well-off families had large villas on the island's shores and held regattas there.

Germany as an Island for Millionaires

In 1901, Wessel had the name of his property changed to Schwannenwerder ('Swan Island').[1] The Wessel family had a small castle – 'Schwannenhof' – at number 37 that can still be seen today. Equipped with a tennis court in 1889, it also had running water. It was soon connected with the riverbank by motorboat, and later by a wooden bridge. Schwannenwerder became a summer retreat for the upper stratum of the Berlin bourgeoisie. Its layout was simple: a road running around the centre of the island served the forty lots put on sale, which thus had direct access to the water and to the park, with nothing to block the view in either direction. Enough to charm the most exigent buyers. The great shop-owners such as Berthold Israel and Rudolf Karstadt, bank presidents such as Schlitter, Goldschmidt, Salomonsohn, and Solmssen; the proprietor of the Schultheiss brewery, Walter Sobernheim; and the owner of the Trumpf chocolate factory, Richard Monheim, all bought lots on Schwannenwerder. This little colony of millionaires modelled its mores on those of its Wannsee neighbours. They spent weekends and part of the summer season there, and finally began to live there year round after the car made it easier to commute daily to the capital.

With the war and the economic crisis that followed it, a few new names replaced those of investors who had lost their money. Speculators like Max Klante, financiers like Julius and Henry Barmat now put the mark of their luxury on the place. In 1924, the Barmat firm was involved in a financial scandal that tainted the island, which was given the nickname 'Barmatwerder'.[2] A muted hostility to this resort grew up; it was reputed to be a refuge for millionaires of the 'Jewish Republic', an expression coined by the nationalists in order to discredit the Weimar regime. This anti-Semitism is also found among the people who lived in the nearby suburb of Zehlendorf, which was at that time divided into a zone of large, patrician villas and a workingmen's quarter full of small houses built by the government for low-income residents. The Nazis cheerfully established themselves there.

After the victory in the March 1933 elections, men from the SA branch in Zehlendorf invaded the island and symbolically raised the NSDAP flag over the water tower. The police did not intervene, and in this climate began the forced sales, at low prices, of the properties held by Jews. In a few years, Schwannenwerder became the symbol of the Nazi establishment's success. The best known of the parvenus was Joseph Goebbels, who in 1935 bought at a very modest price lot 8–10, owned by the Jewish banker Schlitter. Three years later, he appropriated the neighbouring lot, which had been owned by Samuel Goldschmidt, who had been forced to emigrate. The actor Gustav Fröhlich became his neighbour in 1936; he soon shared his house with Lida Baarova. In 1937, Gertrud Scholtz-Klink, the head of the Reich's women's organizations, decided to establish a school for the Reich's girls at number 38, in the former home of an industrialist who had been forced to leave. Lot 20–2, the Salomonsohns' villa, was taken over by the chancellery in 1939 and reserved for Hitler's personal use. He did not reside there, but the possibility remained open. In the same year Hitler's physician, Dr Theo Morell, obtained an 'Aryanized' lot that had belonged to Georg Solmssen. As for Albert Speer, he bought for one hundred and fifty thousand marks Baroness Goldschmidt-Rothschild's property at number 7. Ultimately he preferred to reside in his flat in the Lindenallee in Charlottenburg, and in 1942 he resold his land at a great profit to the German Railway Company. In 1936, in order to ensure the residents' tranquillity, a guard was ensconced in a small house at the entrance to the island. That was the smallest and the last parcel created. It measures three hundred square metres.

Within six years, all the Jews had been driven out. Most of them left the country. Schwannenwerder was absolutely *Judenrein*, that is, 'cleansed' of its Jews. This place is emblematic of what took place in German society, and particularly in high society, during the 1930s. In a very short time, men and women who had lived in the country for centuries found themselves banished from society. Despite their profound integration and intimate knowledge of German culture, they were considered revolting creatures whose elimination was the necessary condition for establishing collective happiness.[3] Anti-Semitism was no longer the ideology of those on the margins of society. It had become the official doctrine of the National Socialist state and constituted the heart of the Third Reich's ideology.

However, what is most surprising about Schwannenwerder is the way the Nazis often made use of the Jews' property without changing it, at the risk of taking over a culture and a way of life that Hitler's speeches had declared to be noxious. The meticulous, obsessive character of the eviction, spoliation, and then extermination of the Jews nonetheless followed a logic that was far from being solely material.

The pleasure and enjoyment the German elites derived from this was rooted in a self-esteem heightened by the simple fact that they felt that they belonged to a superior species. In his novel *Mephisto*, Klaus Mann has admirably described the suddenness and power of this feeling. His protagonist, Hendrik Höfgen, was largely inspired by the actor Gustaf Gründgens, the author's former brother-in-law. Worried about what will become of him after the Nazis seized power, Höfgen finds reassurance in recalling his Germannness:

> He belonged to no party. And he wasn't a Jew. This fact above all others – that he was not a Jew – struck Hendrik all of a sudden as immensely comforting and important. He had never in the past estimated the true worth of this considerable and unsuspected advantage. He wasn't a Jew, and so everything could be forgiven him [. . .].
> 'I am a blond Rheinlander,' exulted Hendrik Höfgen, revived by champagne and his optimistic reflections on the political scene. It was in the best of spirits that he went to bed.[4]

German high society was flattered by the idea of race and cultural racism, in which it saw an application of its own beliefs regarding the hereditary transmission of qualities of command and distinction.[5] By excluding Jews, it shifted the social barrier that separated it from the masses and strengthened the mirage of a *Volksgemeinschaft* that broke with class divisions. High society opened its doors to those it had previously regarded as contemptible. Thus a man of obscure birth and middling fortune was seized by a feeling of having acquired a new dignity, for he was aware, as Klaus Mann writes, that '[i]n the Berlin drawing rooms anyone was welcome who either had money or whose name appeared constantly in the popular press.'[6] Mann adds: 'In the fashionable quarters of the Tiergarten and Grunewald black marketeers mixed with racing drivers, boxers and well-known actors.' Social ascension ended up being conflated with belief in the efficacy of the Nazis' racial policies.

The Rise of a Climate of Anti-Semitism

Grunewald is one of the fashionable quarters of Berlin, built almost in the middle of the woods in the early twentieth century. Around 1930, a large Jewish minority resided there, as well as in the Bayerischesviertel and around the Kürfurstendamm. There were gathered old Jewish-German families who had been emancipated and had passionately embraced the cause of German unity. Some of them had converted to Protestantism, occasionally under the Wilhelmine empire, but also during the First World War and during the 1920s. These families were well integrated into society. In early 1933, Jewish children and adolescents living in Grunewald got along well with their schoolmates, to judge by the testimony of one of the latter.[7] The same seems to have been true for the young people living around the Kürfurstendamm.[8] These wealthy families tried to play down the impact of the political break in January 1933, which they hoped would be temporary. For a few weeks, they allowed themselves to be soothed by a feeling of normality, because they were not immediately confronted by the fact that racism was becoming banal. It must be noted that despite their extensive social integration, German Jews often frequented circles that were parallel to and even competed with those of the ultra-nationalist elites, less because of direct discrimination than because of differences in taste and sensibility.

The social circle of the old painter Max Liebermann, who was eighty-four years old in 1933, illustrates this gap. Liebermann had helped found the art movement known as the 'Berliner Sezession' after a battle with conservatives in the Academy. In 1920, he became president of the Prussian Fine Arts Academy, and was made its honorary president in 1932. Among his friends were both liberals and conservatives. Liebermann knew the writer Theodor Fontane and Admiral Tirpitz, whose portrait he painted. He also painted President Hindenburg and the socialist sculptor Käthe Kollwitz. The mathematician Albert Einstein frequented his house, as did Walter Rathenau. Rathenau, a businessman of Jewish origin, had entered public life and had a fine career. His moderate policies and his role as foreign minister had won him a ferocious hatred, to the point that he was finally assassinated by a group of extreme right-wing fanatics, members of the terrorist organization Consul, on 24 June 1922. His funeral was the occasion of the only large-scale national protest against anti-Semitic political violence. Ten years later, such an event had become unthinkable.

On the eve of Hitler's accession to power, members of Jewish high society were suffering from the economic crisis, like everyone else, and were hoping for a turnaround. They were concerned about immigrants coming from Eastern Europe, on which the most violent anti-Semitic diatribes concentrated. Few Judaeo-Germans discerned the true importance of 30 January 1933. They thought the adversary would attack only the newcomers, if it had the time even to do that. Their illusion regarding the regime's fragility persisted for a few months, and even a few years for those who went into exile. Nonetheless, from the outset brutal and sudden moves were made against all Jews.

The first massive aggression occurred on 1 April 1933. The government decided to carry out a boycott of Jewish shops and businesses, and its harshness was lost on no one.[9] The SA played a pivotal role in this event. In each city, storm troopers gathered activists and posted sentinels in front of Jewish businesses. Symbolically, the organizers of this boycott, notably Goebbels and Julius Streicher, the Gauleiter of Franconia who presided over the central committee assigned to coordinate the activities of the local committees, declared that the date chosen corresponded to the birthday of Otto von Bismarck, who was born in 1815. According to them, the persecution of Jews was a patriotic duty.

For Jewish shop-owners, the boycott meant that they lost their customers, and sometimes had their windows broken or were beaten. Shops selling luxury goods did not long suffer from the boycott if what they sold could not be found elsewhere. Thus fashion designers kept their rich customers. However, the pressure to 'Aryanize' lucrative economic sectors, such as furs, increased over the years. More modest shop-owners suffered seriously from this change in attitude toward them.

For the Judaeo-German world, the boycott marked a rupture that was all the deeper because the discriminatory measures increased in number from that time on. The goal was to isolate Jews and destroy everything that could provide them with dignity and income. By attacking a few key sectors, the NSDAP and the government thought they could reduce the role of Jews within the elites. On 7 April 1933, Jewish government officials who had begun their careers since 9 November 1918 were automatically dismissed. Only a few combat veterans avoided this elimination that deprived its victims of their right to their pensions or to request indemnification. On the same day, new appointments of Jewish lawyers were forbidden. Jewish physicians were next; they were gradually excluded from social security reimbursements. Then they were forbidden to treat Aryans; they could treat only other Jews. This explains why a few Jewish students were still able to pursue medical studies. With the creation of the Reichskulturkammer on 22 September 1933, it was Jewish intellectuals who were cut out. Other professions, such as tax advisers or dentists, met the same fate.

To all this was added the introduction of a *numerus clausus* in secondary schools. Thus the Jewish students at the Grunewald *Gymnasium* were gradually excluded and marginalized. The school's administration forgot the generous donations these families had made to the community – and also dismissed the teachers of Hebrew. These decisions put Jewish children in a painful position. Most of them were driven away and had to pursue private studies under the auspices of the Jewish community. Those whose academic excellence allowed them to remain in the framework of the classical *Gymnasium* were subject to humiliating behaviour on the part of their classmates. The questionable legality of these measures shocked a minority of Germans; the majority of public opinion approved this policy of segregation. Oddly, a number of Jews still refused to see what was happening, not daring to acknowledge the reign of terror under which they now lived. They tried to find in blindness the energy to survive.

The journalist Bella Fromm, whose private diary describes with meticulous rage the way social life functioned at this time, describes the insouciance of many of her 'Aryan' acquaintances. Frau von Neurath, who had a salon, sent her a message through Mammi von Carnap, one of her great friends, in November 1933.[10] Frau von Neurath, the wife of the foreign minister, believed she could shelter her old friend under her wing if she would convert. She seemed unaware that Jews who had converted to Protestantism were subject to the same prohibitions. As if it were simply a question of religion. No, everything was a matter of 'race'.

The enterprising Bella Fromm, who had long frequented the salons, continued to be welcomed in them thanks especially to the foreign diplomats who had taken a liking to her. The French ambassador, André François-Poncet, and the American ambassador, William Dodd, were very friendly with her, as was the Italian ambassador, Vittorio Cerrutti, whose wife came from an upper-class Jewish family. Bella Fromm was soon forbidden to pursue her activity as a journalist. She, too, had to give up writing for the German press. She obtained permission to work as a correspondent for an Austrian daily and for a few American papers. The writer who had formerly been the arbiter of distinction and elegance, whom Frau Goebbels hoped would write nice things about her, whose article appeared in the columns of the great popular daily papers, the *Berliner Zeitung* and the *Vossische Zeitung*, who sang the praises of the women of high society, now found herself in the position of the poor relation, a sort of Christmas beggar eating at the table of a right-thinking family. She describes the distress of those who, like herself, struggled to earn a living though they had long lived very well. Bella Fromm refused to leave Germany, because she thought her position would allow her to help the less fortunate. She intervened on their behalf at the consulates, worked to get visas for the critical cases that came to her and helped them leave.

One of Fromm's colleagues, Max Reiner, was no better off.[11] In 1933 he was fifty years old and at the summit of his fame. He enjoyed a good income (forty-two thousand marks a year). His speciality was writing columns on political life and the Reichstag. For twenty-five years, he had been working for the Ullstein group. He wrote especially for the *Vossische Zeitung* and the *Berliner Zeitung*. He had a broad knowledge of Berlin life, because he wrote both the crime column and the society column. He loved the opera and the Philharmonic orchestra. He applauded *Die lustige Witwe* (*The Merry Widow*), Hitler's favourite operetta. He attended the opening night for the revue season, which was generally held at the Metropoltheater. An assiduous theatre-goer, he was a connoisseur of the works of Gerhart Hauptmann and Hendrik Ibsen. He was personally acquainted with Reinhardt, the manager of the Deutsches Theater. He had been allowed to join the theatre people's club, the Deutschen Bühnenklub. There he regularly met Richard Strauss, the great composer, with whom he had been friends for over twenty years. After a night on the town, about three a.m., Reiner sometimes took a last walk down Friedrichstrasse at the hour when 'the bourgeois allow themselves to be swindled by tarts'.[12]

Reiner had observed from close up the beginnings of the Weimar Republic, and when President Ebert died, he provided support for his widow, using his influence to obtain subsidies for her. He often attended honorary dinners in the company of von Bülow's and Stresemann's former ministers. Reiner thought that the danger would come chiefly from Alfred Hugenberg, an extreme right-wing magnate. He was slow to recognize the threat posed by the Nazis.

Like Bella Fromm, in 1930 he abruptly discovered the place the NSDAP had taken. The deterioration of the situation quickly began to worry him. After the attack on Jewish passers-by on the Kürfurstendamm in September 1931, he saw a climate of terror spreading and wondered why the police were doing nothing to stop it. His conception of the time was changed by Hitler's accession to power on 30 January 1933. A new age was beginning. That very evening the city remained calm despite a gigantic Nazi victory parade. At the editorial offices of his newspaper, Reiner and his colleagues followed the news in a state of despondency, almost on the verge of depression.

Within a few weeks, the new regime put its stamp even on Reiner's newspaper. Swastikas appeared in the buttonholes of employees who up to that point had not indicated that allegiance. Reiner was overcome by dread when his friend Tietjen, the superintendent general of the theatres and the manager of the Bayreuth Festival, was forced by Göring to dismiss all the Opera's Jewish singers; he himself had hired them before the elections. In April, the press was 'cleansed' in its turn. Reiner had to give up his job. Ullstein's board of directors decided to make an exception and give him a large retirement pension.

Out of work, Reiner took long walks. In the Tiergarten, he noticed other victims of the political turnaround who were walking along sombrely to stave off boredom. Occasionally one of them would stop to share his or her dismay. The wife of a social-democratic official told him about her deprivation and the violent treatment she had suffered at the hands of the Gestapo, describing the prison for him. Her mental state worried him; fear had broken the poor woman.

Reiner resisted this pressure. Until 1935, he continued to go to the old Bühnenklub. But then Goebbels decided to dissolve this club, which he regarded as suspect. In the evening, Reiner's last refuge was the bridge club, to which women were not admitted. He decided to leave after the promulgation of the Nuremberg Laws in 1935. A painful and difficult decision. He had to make arrangements for his departure and obtain the passports and administrative authorizations that a touchy and anti-Semitically inclined bureaucracy did not hesitate to delay, for the pure pleasure of doing harm. He was still waiting when he happened to run into Gustav Noske on the Kürfurstendamm. Noske, who was then sixty-seven years old, was the former army minister who had carried out the brutal repression of the Spartakists, and who called himself the republic's 'pit bull'. Here he was, old and complaining about the Nazis' lack of respect for him, because he had not been able to obtain an exit visa to go to a spa to take the waters. He had nonetheless written personally to Frick, the interior minister. Reiner was disgusted by Noske's disgraceful act: begging a Nazi to issue a passport for such a trivial purpose when he was a former socialist minister! And then telling a Jew about it! A short time afterward Reiner managed to get out of Germany and settled in Palestine.

Isolation

The systematic destruction of social life is symptomatic of the project of isolation and imprisonment undertaken by the Nazi regime. Saul Friedländer has termed this situation 'the new ghetto'.[13] Reiner no longer dared go out at night because he was afraid that an SA or SS gang would show up in a restaurant or cabaret and he would be in danger of being insulted and roughed up, if not murdered. High society, more subtle, gave its former friends the cold shoulder. On closer inspection, we see that between January and 1 April 1933 the cleft within German society separating 'Aryans' from supposed 'non-Aryans' had become an abyss.

Singled out for abuse, the children of good Jewish society in Berlin had to be taken out of German schools to avoid constant persecution. Those who remained were mocked by their classmates, who repeated rhymes in the form of the anti-Semitic slogan 'Deutschland erwache, Juda verecke' ('Germany awake, Judas die'). There was even a round in which 'Jude, Jude' ('Jew, Jew') was repeated over and over. Around Bonn, children sang 'Nun geht der Jud endlich kaputt'[14] ('Now the Jew is finally destroyed').

A Jew could no longer find peace even in places devoted to leisure and relaxation. In March 1933 the Berlin golf club informed its Jewish members that they were no longer welcome. The Grunewald Rot-Weiss Klub, where Berlin tennis players gathered, was henceforth closed to Jews. In April 1933, its star, Daniel (Danny) Prenn, who had won the Davis Cup for Germany in 1929 by defeating the British players Fred Perry and Bunny Austin, was abruptly turned away. The German Tennis Federation mentions Prenn by name in the regulations it adopted in order to 'Aryanize' German tennis: 'The player Dr Prenn will not be chosen for the national

Davis Cup team for 1933.' No player of his 'race' could any longer be part of the national tennis team or hold any administrative post in the Federation. Prenn, who was born in Russian Poland in 1904, had been full of hope when he came to live in Germany. He finally left his adopted country for England.

A few persons expressed sympathy or tried to moderate the break by slightly twisting the rules, but the mechanism had been put in operation. Hugo Moses, a Jewish banker who came from a small town in the Rhineland near Bonn, decided on his own to break with all the associations he had supported up to that point, including his tennis club. The president of the club called and told him: 'Your family and your fellow believers are welcome here, you've done so much good that no government or party can change anything whatever. You defended your country for four long years. We ask you to reverse your decision. It would shame us all.'[15] In a secret vote, sixty members had voted to keep Moses in the club and two had voted to exclude him. Despite this expression of friendship, Moses preferred to withdraw from the club.

The sporting way of life, which was one of the main components of high society, was henceforth to be impermeable. Swimming pools were closed to Jews, especially after the 1935 Nuremberg Laws. Leonardo Conti, who was in charge of the NSDAP's public health policy, hung over the Wannsee beach a sign indicating that Jews were not allowed to swim, or even be seen, there. Conti, who was born in 1900 in the Italian-Swiss canton of Ticino, fought on the German side in the Great War and was a fervent Nazi. He joined the party in 1927 and was admitted to the SS in 1930. His public health goal was to limit contacts between Germans and Jews, to avoid a physical proximity considered degrading. In Conti's view, Jews had no sense of modesty and carried diseases. His pseudo-hygiene was inculcated in the Reich's physicians and applied by public health commissions.[16] After the 1936 Olympic Games, his prohibition on Jews in public swimming pools was generalized. The new statutes for athletic associations emphasized in particular the need to construct separate dressing rooms and showers in order to avoid bodily contact with sub-humans.

The prohibition on contact between Aryans and Jews, conceived as an instrument of spiritual redemption, was applied to all leisure activities, including vacations at the seaside.[17] On the North Sea, for instance, the island of Borkum adopted a regulation that prohibited the presence of Jews on the beaches. Several tourists were beaten in order to get them to leave. The common opinion was that anything could happen to a Jew on the island. Everywhere, including in shops, signs warned Jews to keep out. Children learned a ditty that they and their parents spread around: 'Don't let any Jew come here, Borkum must remain free of Jews.'[18] This 'Borkum Song' became a sort of hymn for residents of the island. Between 1935 and 1938 most seaside resorts and spas were gradually emptied of their Jewish population.

Those, like Max Liebermann, who had a house in the Wannsee area had to sell it. Liebermann did not witness this disaster, because he died in 1935. What he thought of the regime can be summed up in a phrase: 'We can never swallow as much as we'll have to vomit up.'[19] After his death, his daughter had to emigrate to the United States after selling the house on the lake whose garden Liebermann had so often painted. Liebermann's wife remained in their apartment on the Pariser Platz in Berlin. In 1943, eighty-five years old and bedridden, she poisoned herself with veronal when a group of SS men came to arrest her and send her to a concentration camp.[20]

Reluctance to apply anti-Semitic rules gradually decreased. In 1935, the Nuremberg Laws finally provided a legal foundation for efforts to denigrate and pillage the Jews. Only a few people did not yield to the ambient climate, especially since the government exerted personal pressure to avoid any weakness with regard to Jews. It was a matter of preserving 'German blood and honour', as it was put in a law of 15 September 1935 that defined 'persons with German blood', first- and second-degree 'mixed-bloods', and Jews.

The Expansion of the Domain of Hatred

The hunt was then expanded to include those who had Jews in their entourage. It was necessary to prevent the birth of children to mixed couples. Early on, women were subjected to humiliation for having frequented a Jew. Testimony given by one of these women, under the name of Hildegarde Bollmann, shows how by April 1933 these practices had become customary.[21] She was forced to walk along the Kürfurstendamm in Berlin with a sign hanging around her neck: 'I am a pig who slept with a Jew.'

Segregation was a 'vital necessity' for doctrinaire National Socialists.[22] Goebbels and Rosenberg put heavy pressure on theatre groups to make them break with Jews. That was what they did in the case of Joachim Gottschalk,[23] an actor whose wife Meta was Jewish. He was so upset by the anti-Semitic laws that he committed suicide along with his wife and their very young son Michael.

Suicide became increasingly common among German Jews. To the journalist Bella Fromm it seemed that it was all around her. Pessimistic about the future, the physician of her best friend – Vera von Huhn, nicknamed 'Poulette' – took an overdose of sleeping pills on 1 June 1933. Poulette herself committed suicide on 25 November 1933 when she learned that everyone holding a press card would have to prove that he or she was of Aryan descent and that government officials had learned that one of her grandmothers was Jewish. This meant that she could no longer go to major receptions and fashionable salons. Her note of farewell poignantly expresses the tragedy that the loss of social relations and work had been for so many men and women:

I can't live anymore because I know they're going to force me to give up my work. You're my best friend, Bella. Please take my papers and use them! I thank you for all the love you've given me. I know you're brave, braver than I am, and that you have to go on living because you have a child and you have to take care of him. I'm convinced that you will fight hard, harder than I could. Your Poulette.[24]

Bella hesitated. Should she run away or fight? She finally decided to stay in order to help the victims of the regime as much as she could. To be able to act more freely, she sent her daughter to the United States.

There was no point in rebelling. Ferocious repression sent those who resisted to concentration camps, where Jews were separated from political detainees and common criminals. They were subjected to extreme violence, beaten half to death and exhausted by mindless work, underfed and insulted. The SS was beginning to experiment with the terrible ways of treating Jews that became systematic after the war began. How could Jews revolt, since they had been totally disarmed? They had been practically forbidden to own weapons since 1933, and after the Nuremberg Laws of 1935, having firearms meant risking twenty years in prison. Hunting licences, which made it easier to buy firearms, were not to be given even to *Mischlinge*, mixed-bloods, though the rigour with which this rule was applied varied from region to region. Seeing acts of violence every day, most Jews understood as early as 1933 that appealing to the authorities could be dangerous. In Munich, the Jewish lawyer Michael Siegel went to the police station on 1 March 1933 to file a complaint against SS and SA activists who were attacking passers-by. This was a serious mistake: his trousers were cut off at the knee, a derisory allusion to Bavarian shorts, and then he was forced to walk barefoot around the city with an explicit sign hanging around his neck: 'I will never complain to the police again.'[25]

The National Socialist regime rearmed the country and strengthened its military forces. Whereas Jews were less and less able to work, or even to find a job, the army and the police were hiring large numbers of people from both the lower and upper middle classes and preparing for the military attacks that began with the Anschluss in March 1938. Thereafter, the hundred and eighty thousand Austrian Jews fell victim to the same fate as their fellow believers in Germany. Even the most eminent among them, such as the Rothschilds, found themselves in difficulty. Baron Louis de Rothschild was arrested on 13 March, not having been able to leave Vienna by plane just before the invasion. He was held prisoner for nine months, subjected to harsh treatment, and isolated from his friends and family. His brothers and his wife were able to avoid the worst thanks to the help of the Duke of Windsor, who was at that time in Austria. Clearly, Hitler's regime intended to be paid for letting him go, just as it allowed German Jews to emigrate if they paid indemnities. To obtain his release, the baron is supposed to have handed over his property and paid an exceptionally high ransom. How could a Rothschild have been captured like that? Perhaps he believed that a class reflex would come into play and that he could move about unimpeded? It is more likely that the attack took him by surprise; like many businessmen, he wanted to hang onto his interests as long as possible.

The gradual isolation of people whom the Nazis identified as Jews accelerated after 1938. Up to that point, the regular attacks on persons and goods had been part of a programme of tormenting Jews whose contours remained vague and that recalled the anti-Semitic fevers of other periods. After the successive crises of the dismantling of Czechoslovakia and the Kristallnacht, the project of evicting Jews from Europe was clearly revealed. Henceforth, it was a question of eliminating the Jewish minority, pillaging its property, and violently forcing it to leave or proceeding to liquidate it. This phase of anti-Semitic radicalization would not have been possible without the diplomatic triumph in Munich in September 1938 and the nation's closing ranks around the triumphant elites.

The Obsession

On 7 November 1938, a young man entered the offices of the German embassy in Paris. The only official on duty that morning, the diplomat Ernst vom Rath, came toward him. Vom Rath had hardly had time to ask what the young man wanted before the latter shot him at point blank range and ran out the door. Caught by the Paris police, who took him to the police station to interrogate him, the assassin identified himself: Herschel Grynszpan, seventeen years old. He was a Jew of Polish and German extraction and was studying in Paris on a scholarship. He stated that his act had been provoked by the expropriation and forced departure of his family for a camp located on the Polish border. He had frequented Zionist associations, but declared that he had acted on his own. While this interrogation was going on, vom Rath was dying. The embassy telegraphed the news to Berlin. Hitler met that same night with Goebbels and other leaders, notably Wagner. They were in Munich to celebrate, as they did every year, the anniversary of the Beer Hall Putsch. They decided to contact immediately the Reich's lawyer, Friedrich Grimm, to tell him to take action in France.[26]

A plan for a generalized pogrom had long since been drawn up. The idea had already been floated when Councillor Gustloff was murdered in Davos, but the proximity of the 1936 Olympic Games and commitments made to international athletic authorities had finally caused it to be rejected.[27] After the Munich Conference and the victory in Czechoslovakia in September, the time seemed ripe for broad action. A pretext was needed and Herschel Grynszpan had provided it, just as the Reichstag fire set by Van der Lube had made it possible to start repressing the communists. Was Grynszpan a provocateur or did he act without being manipulated?

A mere quibble? No, because the notion that this was an operation set up more or less cynically by the regime depends on elucidating this issue. Behind the devastation can be glimpsed a strategy of pillaging Jewish property chiefly for the benefit of the National Socialist elites. In any case, once the mechanism was put in motion, Nazi leaders acted with implacable swiftness. Even before vom Rath died, everything was set for reprisals. When the news of his death finally arrived on 9 November, the order was given to launch an attack on all Jews. The plan concerned the whole of Germany, but Munich wanted to be exemplary because it was the movement's capital.

The Gauleiter of Munich, Adolf Wagner, ordered SA members in civilian clothing to go through the city and locate the shops and individuals who would serve as the best examples.[28] The point was to strike luxury shops and men who remained prominent despite the semi-clandestine way of life that Jews had been forced to maintain since 1935. Twelve Jewish banks still existed, along with shops on the central streets, and these were regarded by the Nazi establishment as a provocation. The great synagogue had already been vandalized and its demolition begun. During the night of 9 November, SA groups were assigned to make a comprehensive sweep that included any and all flats. It seems that Göring had given orders that precious objects be spared a pillaging that might have damaged them and benefited the uncouth mass of the SA members. Their assignment was to bring all the objects seized to depots where they would be sorted. In Munich, the SS was in charge of the looting the luxury shops. For example, they stole precious furniture from Otto Bernheimer's shop, where Himmler and Göring bought Oriental carpets. Forty-six shops were pillaged in this way. The SS didn't stop there. They began a round-up in flats and took men away in trucks bound for Dachau. Several hundred individuals thus spent a few frightening hours in the camp; the goal was to make them understand what awaited them if they complained. It was also hinted that they had not yet finished paying. Then they were taken back to the city, where they could see that the synagogue in Herzog-Rudolph-Strasse had burned to the ground, but that firemen were doing their best to keep the fire from spreading to neighbouring houses.

In Berlin, nine synagogues out of twelve were burned down. In Germany as a whole, according to Heydrich, the head of the Gestapo, about 7,500 shops were destroyed, 101 synagogues burned, and 76 demolished. The toll has since been revised: 267 synagogues are said to have been damaged, with twenty thousand persons, chiefly men, sent to concentration camps over the following weeks, and about a hundred killed. This did not bother most Germans, just as the 1933 boycott had not bothered them. The brutality of this event was put down to excesses committed in the heat of the action.

However, in several cases individuals took a different attitude. Ruth Andreas-Friedrich, a young Berlin journalist who liked to drink late-evening cocktails at the Kaiserhof bar, was one of those stunned by the violence. At seven a.m. on 10 November, she heard someone knock at her door. It was Dr Weissmann, one of her lawyer friends. 'Hide me. They're after me,' he told her. The young woman, who was still half asleep and didn't know what was going on, asked what had happened. 'Are you living on another planet?' Weissmann replied. 'The Devil has come into Berlin. The synagogues are burning, Jewish blood is spurting from knives. The storm troopers are going along striking with the blade. And you're still asking what's happening?'[29] The lawyer was hidden, and the journalist went to her office to find out more. She could only witness the extent of the disaster. Men had been rounded up and struck. As in Munich, the shops had been pillaged. On the Kürfurstendamm, people had been hunted down and beaten. Farewell, quiet walks to forget unemployment. From now on, Jews had to go to ground.

Since 1937, in fact, the political police, the Gestapo, and the Sicherheitsdienst (SD) had been monitoring the activities of Jews. Monthly reports were submitted to the central authorities in which developments in public opinion and the risks of sedition were summarized. The reports on public opinion in countries invaded in 1938 and afterward are particularly important because they show that the goal was to reduce the autonomy of Jewish groups in any way possible.

Confronted by the violence of the persecution, daily harassment, and the increasing restriction of their space, the members of the Jewish bourgeoisie displayed a surprising vitality. Aware that they were involved in an unequal struggle, they took refuge in intensified social activity to withstand the shock. Every time the regime tightened the screws another notch, they responded by trying to preserve their dignity and by continuing to arrange occasions whose gaiety belied the ambient moroseness.

Thus the Gestapo drew attention to the increasingly frequent balls organized between 1934 and 1936. These private events never attracted large crowds, but were nonetheless sometimes attended by several hundred people. Moreover, Aryans were not forbidden to participate in them, as the political police pointed out.[30] Especially since, on the pretext of toasts or welcoming speeches, the organizers made political speeches. For that purpose, they used Yiddish, and even, the police claimed, Hebrew, a language then very little used by German Jews. Behind these reports one can discern the fear of being fooled. Beyond this intrusive aspect we can see the continuing importance of songs and dances belonging to Judaeo-German culture and the activism of Zionist groups that were trying to convince German Jews to go to live in the settlements in Palestine.

Between Morality and Denial

Henriette Hoffmann was young, rich, and curious. One night in 1943, she heard sounds outside, cries and sobs. Leaning out of her window, she saw a convoy of women heading east.[31] Troubled, she sensed that they were not going on a pleasure trip. So she spoke to her husband, Baldur von Schirach, the governor of Austria and the former head of the Hitler Youth organizations. He told her that these women were in fact being transported under abject conditions toward a destination where the fate that awaited them was hardly enviable. Surprised but perspicacious, she then asked if the Führer knew about this. 'You can tell him about it, if he doesn't know,' her husband replied ironically. And that is what she did. Yes, the Führer said, he did know about it, and he made it clear to the young woman that this matter was no concern of hers; that Jews were bad; that they had to be eliminated; and that she ought to hate them. So now she in turn knew what was happening. Would she change her way of life?

Henrietta von Schirach's testimony was published after the genocide. This great lady of German high society acknowledged that she was aware of the systematic destruction of the Jews of Europe, but did not inquire further into their situation before the final massacre. In her book, she seems to have accepted the fact that genocide was the irreducible, specific feature of the National Socialist regime, but this crime itself makes her forget all the other monstrous events of the time. She lived through the boycott, the little pogroms of 1935, the adoption of the Nuremberg Laws, Kristallnacht, the eviction of Jews from the working world, the spoliation of their property, their marginalization. Surely she had heard about the summary liquidations – of Röhm, of communists, socialists, homosexuals. She certainly was aware of the euthanasia of the mentally ill, the T4 programme carried out on the eve of the war, the forced sterilization of mixed-blood children, and the eradication of the German Gypsies. She must have known about the Russian prisoners who were dying of the cold, without shelter, in camps near Berlin during the winter of 1941. But none of this seems to have succeeded in opening her eyes to the regime's nature. Very high society in the Third Reich thus lived in denial when it was not participating in the regime's destructive action.[32]

Hitler's secretary, Traudl Junge, went even further. In her belated testimony given on German television and later used as the conclusion to the film *Der Untergang* (*Downfall*), she said that she had discovered Nazism's crimes only through the Nuremberg Trials and that she had long lived with an easy conscience before she visited the monument to Sophie Scholl in the early 1990s. Thus Hitler's personal secretary supposedly knew nothing about the 'crimes of Nazism' during the war. She must not have read the newspapers, which reported the events of 1938 with pride and discussed at length the theories of the Nazi leaders. She struggled to admit that she was deeply committed to an ideology whose contours and effects she did not question until the defeat and total collapse in 1945. However, she was prepared to give her life for Hitler. She was like the world of socialites who regarded the massacre and the spoliation as something the times required, something that had to be accepted as a matter of fidelity to the Reich.

Moreover, in the government's view, power justified all crimes. Julius Schaub explained this poor man's Machiavellianism to the prosecutor at Nuremberg. Asked about the fact that he had frequented and served murderers, he seemed surprised. He'd learned of the murder of millions of Jews by reading the newspapers during the Nuremberg Trials. Perhaps. But the murder of Röhm? Well, that was not the same thing, he replied. 'That was political.'[33] The rest was just trifles. The usual horrors of war. Except that between 1933 and 1939 Germany was at peace.

Even the military, frequently described in testimony as harbouring many opponents of Nazism, didn't lift a finger to stop the massacre of Jews and Gypsies.[34] The army carried out the genocide in Byelorussia; in Serbia, it liquidated Jews and Gypsies without the SS administration even being present in the area. Military leaders sent out anti-Semitic manifestos. If some of them opposed Hitler, it was really the conduct of the war that they opposed, at the point when defeat was becoming certain, starting in 1943. In the mid-1930s, the army had been Nazified and was glad to receive generous financing, along with individual and collective advantages. The army was so corrupted by ruthless ambition that the Führer never had any shortage of candidates for leading posts. This is shown by the insouciance with which he regarded the eviction of both the Head of the General Staff, General von Blomberg, and his possible successor, Fritsch, on moral grounds. The former was accused of having violated rigorous moral standards by marrying a lower-class woman who was also guilty of having worked in her mother's 'massage parlour'.[35] Hitler and Göring had encouraged this wedding, however, and had taken part in it. Against General von Fritsch, an accusation of homosexuality was involved. The army approved of the Nazis' reaction, which they saw as preserving the honour of the General Staff and public morals. In reality, the army became a key institution in the Third Reich. The fact that for geopolitical reasons it was not collectively implicated in the Nuremberg Trials does not alter its terrible historical responsibility. The historian remains perplexed on reflecting that the Bundeswehr recruited its initial core among these zealous veterans of the Third Reich.

Today, it is difficult to resituate oneself in this strange period's way of thought. The violence of the war and the cruelty of the genocide inaugurated a new phase in the awareness of the crimes of humanity, of crimes against humanity. However, it is necessary to undertake this exercise in order to understand how the destruction of Jewish high society could have been regarded as normal.

Understanding the Spoliations: Between Ideology and Individual Motivations

The minutes of the Nazi leaders' meeting immediately after Kristallnacht help us understand the relationships between anti-Semitic actions, racist beliefs, and the desire to despoil a certain segment of the Reich's population. Göring was interrogated at length regarding this text during his trial at Nuremberg and he authenticated its content, sometimes trying to play on its words in order to exonerate himself.

As head of the four-year plan, Göring presided over this meeting. He therefore invited Funk, the economics minister, Hilgard, the representative of the insurers, and other high officials such as Kurt Daluege, the head of the security forces, and Heydrich, the head of the Gestapo. Along with them, he invited Count Schwerin von Krosigk, the finance minister, and Fischböck, an official in charge of the eastern marches (Austria). According to Göring, Hitler, who was absent, insisted that Goebbels also participate in the meeting. The putative objective was to reconstruct the country after a destructive rampage of unprecedented proportions. But the actual course of the meeting shows that much larger issues were at stake and allows us a glimpse into the ideological functioning typical of the upper spheres.

In reality, the participants in the meeting wanted to 'take revenge' on Jews and prevent them from taking legal action to demand redress. The goal was to settle 'the Jewish question as a whole', as Hitler had Martin Bormann write to the members of the committee.[36] The intention was to drive them out and to annihilate them. Moreover, Göring concluded the meeting by declaring: 'I am going to announce officially that German Jews as a whole must pay, as a punishment, a contribution of one thousand million. [. . .] Those pigs won't kill another one of us any time soon. In short, I have to say it once again: I wouldn't like to be a Jew in Germany.'[37] In fact, all Judaeo-Germans were to be treated as accomplices of von Rath's assassin, without trial, on the basis of a simple declaration. They were to be bled dry, both literally and figuratively.

Earlier, Heydrich explained the logic of the steps already taken to drive out the Jews. The point was to force rich candidates for departure to give money to the Jewish communities and the synagogues in order to facilitate the emigration of the poor. Because, Heydrich added, 'the problem is not how to strike the rich Jews, but how to strike the Jewish rabble'.[38]

This incredible discussion among leaders focused for a time on the idea of starving the Jews, an idea proposed by Funk but rejected by Göring on the ground that it was impractical. Göring emphasized this at his trial in Nuremberg. But his own proposals were hardly less cynical: the Jews had to pay the cost of the pillaging that was occasioned by their presence. They would therefore not be reimbursed by insurance companies, which would transfer to the ministry of finance part of the compensation that would otherwise have been paid to cover the Jews' losses. That would allow insurers to avoid paying enormous sums to replace broken glass, for more than half the Jewish shops were insured against riots. On the other hand, German 'Aryans' would have to be fully reimbursed. Hilgard tried to resist this in the interest of German insurers, even though the measure would have offered them legal protection. Göring comically put him in his place: 'Excuse me! If you're legally forced to pay five million and an angel comes to you in the somewhat corpulent form that is my own and tells you that you can keep a million – for heaven's sake, isn't that an advantage?'[39]

This sleight of hand was still not sufficient. Göring therefore proposed that they make radical decisions to 'Aryanize the economy'. All shops, in particular the large ones, and all factories belonging to Jews would have new owners before 1 January 1939. Jews would have to sell their property at low prices to Germans, and especially to members of the party whose businesses or shops had fallen victim to the economic crisis. Göring added that he didn't want to see any favouritism on the part of party officials in order to avoid scandalous enrichments. If any such favouritism occurred, he would personally tell Hitler who was responsible. The social structure was not to be thrown into turmoil, it was simply a question of eradicating the Jews. As a result, the whole Jewish upper middle class would be deprived of income. By selling its property, it would have just enough to pay for its emigration. At the same time, meritorious 'Aryans' would find themselves in improved conditions and the state would fill its coffers. In other words, the downfall of one group was the condition for the advancement of the others.

Goebbels was still not satisfied. He wanted to adopt symbolic measures. So he suddenly declared that Jews should be forbidden to enter the forests; he'd had enough of seeing all those Jews walking through the Grunewald forest, which was so close to his fine house in Schwannenwerder. Angry at seeing Goebbels infringing on his territory, Göring, who was also the master of the Reich's forests and the hunt, replied sarcastically: 'We're going to designate one part of the forest for Jews, and Alpers [a state secretary] will see to it that only animals that resemble them go there – damn, it's true that the elk has a hooked nose.'[40] To which Goebbels responded that he considered this behaviour provocative ('ich halte dieses Verhalten für provokativ'). In another exchange, they argued over whether Jews should be assigned seats in trains. But this did not distract them from the essential point: money.

Glossing over the thirty-five deaths that had occurred during Kristallnacht, as reported at this time by Heydrich, and over Göring's regret that Jews hadn't been beaten more and their shops protected in order to spare the economy, and then turning to the astoundingly good deals that could be expected from the Aryanization of Austria, these leaders lingered over specific cases. The looting of the Margraf jewellery shop in Unter den Linden produced a sum of one million, seven hundred thousand marks. At that point Göring, who loved precious gems, interrupted and turned to Heydrich and Daluege: 'I want you to get those diamonds back for me.' Defending himself after the war, Göring claimed that this 'me' referred to the ministry of finances. The prosecutor in Nuremberg ironically dismantled these minutes of a meeting that seemed to assemble a gang of crooks around a table.

These minutes show the complexity of the ideological determinants, and in particular the relation between theory and practice, doctrine and action. The participants' zeal manifested itself in financial measures. The looting that had taken place the preceding night was legitimized. It was even increased and systematized on the national scale. The whole German bourgeoisie was going to be able to take over the Jews' property at small cost and thus had an interest in their elimination. This great sell-off included, of course, the Jews' personal belongings – jewels, works of art, and other precious objects. The main German leaders were already beginning their collections: Himmler, Göring, Goebbels, Funk, and Ribbentrop decorated their homes and the state palaces.

This ideal of violent appropriation and the quest for luxury are very characteristic of Nazism, as much in 1938 as later on, when it became increasingly radical. However, the motives for the looting cannot be understood without reference to the violence and murder that accompanied it. The tranquillity and even the pride with which these men envisaged the physical elimination of the Jews, outside of any military context, reflects a mentality that was already deeply rooted in the leadership. This is shown by the complaints about fraternization with Jews that Goebbels echoed during the meeting held on 12 November 1938; Göring was in complete agreement with him on this, and his replies sought only to promote his own provisional solutions involving segregation and expulsion. The incredible consensus that was established regarding violent actions against Jews explains why the German public paid little attention to them. The belief that anti-Semitism was normal was in turn intertwined with pro-Aryan racism and belligerent nationalism. Ultimately, to be anti-Semitic was to participate in a great patriotic battle. That justified receiving a reward. The almost syllogistic conclusion was that getting rich by appropriating Jewish property was a national project.

Though rather limited, these arguments were nonetheless made in German high society. They constituted an ideological rationalization that lumped together all Nazi Germany's enemies: Jews, democrats, and communists. 'Judaeo-Bolshevism' became the magic formula linking adversaries in opprobrium. In word and in spirit, it was developed at length in correspondence and reports. Even a former socialist like Gustav Noske allowed himself to be overcome by this populist ideology and at the end of the Second World War made dark statements against the Jews of Eastern Europe and Marxism.[41]

Basically, the German people set aside its sensitivity in order to take advantage of the opportunities offered by the destruction of Jewish high society. Here Arno Breker provides a perfect example. In June 1939, he moved into his new home in Grunewald, 65 Koenigsallee. This 'Aryanized' house was none other than that of Walter Rathenau, the Jewish foreign minister who had been murdered in 1922. After 1928, an association of his friends had regularly met there to talk about public life. Rathenau's youngest sister lived in the house with her family and held a famous salon there until anti-Semitic laws forced her to flee Germany in early 1939 and sell all her property at a loss. Breker, the Third Reich's official sculptor, received Hitler, Speer, and German high society in this vast mansion, located near the Hubertusee and the Halensee, two small lakes that were charming in the summer.

Anti-Semitism, a Criterion for the Selection of Elites

Constantly reshaped by the growth of prejudices and the power of received ideas, German high society was closely supervised by the authorities. Associations were scrutinized, studied, and supported or condemned depending on their reaction and Nazi leaders' impressions of them. A glance at the associations traditionally devoted to the elites can thus provide a good indicator of the power of conformism in recruiting new members.

Which one was the most conformist? Apart from the NSDAP itself, the Deutsche Adelsgenossenschaft (DAG) was perhaps the group most in symbiosis with Nazism. This organization, created in 1874, resumed its activities after the Great War. It had between twenty and thirty thousand members drawn from the ranks of the lower and middle strata of the nobility, but its audience soon extended to the great families because of its strident monarchism. Its newspaper, the *Deutsches Adelsblatt*, was a weekly of sixteen to twenty-four pages. Modest in appearance, it would now be regarded as the confidential newsletter of an association or club. In addition to articles on politics in general, which are of particular interest to us, it published reports on social life by regional officials, brief family announcements cherished by genealogists, and advertising inserts. The paper's size grew under Nazism because the government published more and more promotional material in it, an infallible sign that its readership's fortunes and power had increased.

Even before 1933 the subjects dealt with by the DAG, the tone of the articles published in its newspaper, and the remarks of its leaders clearly showed its support for the conservative revolution. It wanted a leader who would restore order in Germany. These aristocrats were, of course, monarchists, but they distinguished the desired future leader from the king, for whom they still felt affection. Violently opposed to the Treaty of Versailles, they treated its anniversary as a day of mourning. They wanted a resumption of German imperialism and referred with pleasure and nostalgia to the vigorous pan-Germanism of earlier days. Their anti-communism imbued everything they said. Finally, they had a religious respect for the nobility and for chivalry. A symbolic image often appeared on the cover of their newspaper: a knight in armour standing in front of a tree, sword in hand. In the background are a plough, sheaves of wheat, a scythe, a village with its church spire, a castle, and a river (the Rhine?). The DAG defended the Junkers, that is, the landed nobility, whose slogan remained *Blut und Boden*, blood and soil. Through this association can be glimpsed a whole milieu of country squires who were more or less rich, proud to be Germans, living among themselves, and repeating ancient rituals. They were also anti-Semitic. Speaking for them on 21 January 1933, Friedrich Schinkel endorsed a 'socialist conservatism'[42] that seems very close to National Socialism.

The advent of Nazism was in conformity with these aristocrats' desires because it unified the nationalists. They said so openly and hoped that members of the association would play a social role in promoting and defending the new order. On the occasion of the boycott in April 1933, they stated that the role of the nobility was to counter the lies that 'international Jewry is spreading against the German awakening'[43] and to do its duty. In the autumn of 1933, the DAG undertook to draw up a list of the blueblood nobility, checking the Aryan character of all families since 1750, or more than five generations, when only three sufficed to meet the requirements of the law. The objective of the marshal of the nobility who presided over the association, Prince zu Bentheim-Tecklenburg, was to make his the only organization representing the nobility of blood. The prince soon had cause to complain that only half of the twenty thousand adherents had taken the necessary steps. Never mind; the organization expelled the few Jews who were members. It was pure enough to meet with Hitler and to support his initiatives. The Führer appreciated its vociferous support, but he didn't allow himself to be seduced by the idea of a restored monarchy. The former dynasty had failed. It was not yet time for it to come back. Hitler therefore limited himself to sending them his greetings, which were retransmitted by the newspaper.

One sign of the anti-Semitic obsession was the brief controversy in 1936 between the editors of the *Deutsches Adelsblatt* and a few zealous readers. Under the rubric 'Jewish announcements' appeared the following item: 'The publishers and editors often receive letters from readers claiming that the *Deutsches Adelsblatt* publishes advertisements for Jewish businesses. Appearances are often deceiving.'[44] There follows the example of Johan Morgenschweiß's fur shop in Leipzig. The name might sound Jewish, but it is that of an old Germanic family, the newspaper notes, basing its findings on the municipal archives of Cologne, the city where the earliest bearers of this name contributed to the foundation of its cathedral in the twelfth century. As for the G.E. Hirsch cigarette factory in Berlin, it had indeed belonged to a Jew, but its administration was now 'purely Aryan': it was owned by R.G. Hago, a pure-blood Aryan. Readers might rest assured, and in case of doubt the editors were at their disposal. On the same page was an advertisement for the 1936 edition of the *Almanach de Gotha*, the standard reference work on the German nobility and the most respected social register.

The DAG's activism was representative of the attitude of most members of high society. The genealogical ideal intersected with racism as an assertion of good blood. Under Nazism, this existential dimension was transformed into a programme of action. The regime looked favourably on the nobility precisely because the latter associated excellence with birth as much as with the imperatives of success and efficiency. As conservatives opposed to egalitarian ideas, even in restricted groups, the aristocrats were naturally faithful servants of the Reich during its successful years.

Inversely, Germans who belonged to the Rotary Club found themselves in a delicate position. The first Rotary Clubs were established in Germany in 1927. Munich's Rotary Club was established on 2 October 1928.[45] The seventy-third district of Rotary International, which included all the local clubs in Germany and Austria, was created at the same time. The Berlin and Nuremberg clubs were founded the following year. In Garmisch-Partenkirchen, a club was formed on 16 October 1933, and in Friedrichshafen-Lindau, on 16 June 1934. It is clear that at first the Nazi regime tolerated this organization, in which members of the NSDAP held offices. However, as the Nazis' policies hardened they became less tolerant of it. The federal archives indicate that after 1936 it was closely watched. However, on 20 August 1936 two hundred and fifty members of Rotary met at Bayreuth to attend a performance of *Lohengrin*. This suggests tastes similar to those of the men in power.[46] During the Olympic Games, the Berlin club issued many invitations for luncheons, cocktails, and dinner parties. Therefore it is hard to see the Rotary Club as a den of subversive opponents of the regime. Its social composition included notables, physicians, military officers, and businessmen. A few nobles belonged, as did prominent men such as the head of the La Charité hospital in Berlin, Professor Ferdinand Sauerbruch. The club's monthly periodical, *Der Rotarier*, did not hesitate to quote *Mein Kampf*, for example in February 1937: 'The art of reading and learning is still: retain the essential, forget the useless.'[47]

Nevertheless, the climate was deteriorating. In the spring, articles hostile to the Rotarians were published in *Blitz*, a National Socialist periodical. The clubs were suspected of being nests of opponents and of functioning as did the Freemasons. To prove its good faith, the Rotary Club asked to meet with the Führer. Philipp Bouhler prepared a report that seemed favourable or at least respectful of earlier decisions handed down by the NSDAP court, which had in 1933, 1934, and 1936 issued opinions authorizing members to belong to both the party and the club. However, on 24 June 1937, the minister of the interior forbade officials in the central government and officials exercising authority to be members of the club. Membership in a supranational organization could not be considered appropriate for high officials. Finally, in July 1937 the NSDAP also decided to withdraw the authorization allowing party members to belong to the club, starting on 1 January 1938. This time the argument was based on the German Rotary Club's relationships with Jews outside the country. That sounded the death knell for this association, which prided itself on bringing together eminent figures and notables. More than half its members were also members of the National Socialist party.

The Nazi leaders' attitude was foreseeable, since the Rotary Club was elitist, to be sure, but also humanistic. What was stranger were the Rotarians' efforts to have these restrictions relaxed. The first to react was Dr Grill, the Rotary official for the seventy-third district. In a letter dated 13 August 1937 he asks that the status quo be maintained and tries to show that his organization is in conformity with the regime and necessary to the realization of its goals. In conformity because since July 1936 it had rejected all non-Aryans and promised not to admit any more. In conformity also because Freemasons had been prohibited from joining the club since 1933; it still had only six Freemason members who had joined earlier, out of one thousand, three hundred and fifty members in total; moreover, these six members were not allowed to hold high offices within the organization. And necessary, precisely because of its international network, which exerted an influence in favour of the Reich outside the country's borders. Grill's plea was not heard. For the Nazis, the twofold suspicion of Freemasonry and philo-Semitism was insurmountable.

The leaders of Rotary International subsequently tried to convince the government that they were not a danger to it. They invited the Führer to their international meeting. They wrote letters to assure him that they understood what the Nazi government had done. The letter from Emile Deckers, the Rotary official in charge of the Belgian district, sent on 28 August 1937 to the German ambassador in Brussels for transmission to Walter Buch, the party's judge, regrets the prohibition and says that it produced a bad impression that might damage relations between Germany and Belgium. Deckers emphasizes that one of the main principles of Rotarianism is respect for established authority. 'We find it hard to believe,' he writes, 'that there is in German Rotary a spirit other than that of discipline and respect for the legal authority of the country.'[48] He adds this surprising commentary on Belgium: 'It is true that by the nature of the organization, there are some members of the Jewish religion, but since that is not a legal objection in our country, we cannot fault our clubs on this point. If the situation is different in Germany, I am sure Rotary will accept the government's decisions.' Deckers seems to deplore Belgium's tolerance. His position with regard to Freemasons is equally ambiguous, since he says that his belief as a Catholic, which is shared by the head of Rotary International, is incompatible with Freemasonry. He concludes: 'The present step has been taken only in order to arrive at perfect agreement and friendship in accord with the Rotarian principles, which in this case are so much in harmony with our personal feelings.'

An effort made by an English Rotarian to sway the German government by arguing that it would be impossible to create another organization in Germany that could promote such friendly relationships met with a stinging response. The Third Reich was well aware of how to promote friendly personal relationships: 'In addition to numerous international associations, programmes for the exchange of young people and academics, meetings of veterans' groups and international scientific colloquia are only a few examples of activities materially and financially supported in this area.'[49] The Englishman got nothing for his pains: 'I have a great admiration for the splendid efforts you have made to build up a great German nation,' he writes in his letter to Hitler. This time, flattery didn't work.[50] How far would this readiness to oblige have gone had the Nazis themselves not forced the Rotarians to put an end to their complicity?

The Rotary Club, faced with the German government's inflexibility, chose to dissolve itself. Thus in 1938 the head of Rotary International said bitterly that the two countries that had prohibited Rotary were Germany and the USSR. However, similar developments were to occur in other countries, such as Italy, where despite initial good relations between the club and the Fascist party, Rotary leaders decided to dissolve it at the end of 1938, no doubt foreseeing that international links would be broken.

In Germany, anti-Semitism was one of the main forces driving exclusion. After 1938, there was no longer any association or group in high society that accorded a place to Jews. Better yet, the absolute certainty of the Jews' absence guaranteed the selectivity of the group. The SS became the high-society institution *par excellence*. The conditions set for joining it were very rigorous: impeccable antecedents, no criminal record, no earlier participation in subversive groups, sponsorship, entrance examination . . . And these restrictions only made it the more sought after.

All Germany henceforth paid attention to family lineage and origins. Genealogy was no longer something that concerned only a few noble families. It became a science and was crucial for access to certain positions of responsibility. From then on, a certificate of Aryanness was an administrative document required for marriages or requests for transfer. It ended up becoming common, but also gave its holder a feeling of security. It was so strongly anchored in people's minds that from 1933 on people had nightmares about discovering that they had a non-Aryan ancestor. Among the dreams Charlotte Beradt collected between 1933 and 1937, many express the fear of discovering that one was Jewish or the pleasure of being able to hide it.[51] The Germans' unconscious had clearly grasped the terrible situation.

Such a climate inevitably produced protective reactions. It sharpened the sense of humour. Many jokes of doubtful taste were imagined and widely told. One making the rounds in Berlin in 1938 went like this:

'Do you know who the most sought-after person in Germany is today?'

'The non-Aryan grandmother, so you can finally get your hands on the inheritance.'

'No, the non-Aryan great-grandmother, because you get the inheritance without the problems.'[52]

Common sense summed up the transfer of luxury and power that was going on in Germany, soberly indicating how self-interest slipped in behind ideological requirements and even threatened to outstrip them. The disappearance of Jewish high society, combining eschatology with materialism, threw into turmoil the way society had functioned earlier and created a permanent state of suspicion. But would this result in a new art of living meeting the requirements of socialites?

5

Was There a Nazi Luxury?

In 1919, the situation in Berlin was so desperate that simply drinking a cup of tea or coffee was considered a luxury. Ten years later, when the crash of 1929 struck Germany, there was great concern that a similar scarcity might return. High society had recovered its taste for abundance and consumer pleasures. The Nazi regime, which claimed to provide a response to the social and economic crisis as much as an ideological revolution, could not ignore this desire for luxury. Nonetheless, it wanted to give it a shape in conformity with its political aspirations. Thus certain objects acquired a special role in National Socialist symbolism and a specific place in the life of socialites. The car is the best example because it concentrates the Nazi fantasy of utilitarian modernity. The car gives tangible form to the Nazi cult of the exploit by connecting it with the tradition of virility.[1] Above all, it made it possible to combine an aesthetic, popular participation with a mirroring effect between elites and masses. Suddenly, car manufacturers' advertisements and propaganda converged. Industrial production had anticipated this change.

The Car, a Masculine Luxury

Since 1926, Mercedes-Benz had been producing powerful, fast cars. The firm's objective was to create luxury cars and attract the wealthiest customers. This was a strategy opposite to that of Henry Ford, who was prepared to reduce performance and comfort in order to lower costs and reach a larger number of customers. By 1928, the firm run by Paul Daimler and Ferdinand Porsche was well on the way to winning its gamble. The old heavy, U-shaped chassis was abandoned, allowing an increase in speed. Only the enormous limousine retained it. The Model K, which was sportier, had a 6.25 litre engine producing 160 horsepower, and was the best of the fast touring cars. There was an elegant coupé version (the 'Transformable Torpedo') with side-mounted spare tyres and a retractable top.

Wealthy customers soon came to prefer the 'Grosser Mercedes', first produced in 1930. Its 7.71 litre engine consumed almost thirty litres of petrol for every 100 kilometres in order to haul around its heavy chassis and six-door body. The version with a compressor developed 225 horse-power. The Grosser Mercedes was ordered by bankers and politicians. It was also exported, even if it did not have the luxury features offered by Rolls Royce. It was envied, especially after 1937, when it acquired a lighter chassis and more powerful motor that made it the fastest commercial limousine, capable of speeds as high as 160 kilometres an hour.

The company enjoyed the Nazis' favour. Hitler had hardly taken power before ordering a new Grosser Mercedes. His vehicle had seven seats. The Führer's chauffeur took delivery on 6 June 1933.[2] Its price: twenty-five thousand marks. Göring, who had been buying Mercedes since the 1920s, acquired a sport coupé in 1931. He then bought a Grosser Mercedes, a touring model with six seats. Ribbentrop also liked these cars, as did the Führer's confidant, Heinrich Hoffmann. Himmler was delighted to get his convertible. Old companions like the Bechsteins and the Bruckmanns loved the comfort and styling of these vehicles.

Hitler, who didn't know how to drive and used chauffeurs, paid a great deal of attention to his car fleet. He wanted to be sure that it was not only prestigious but also safe; shortly before taking power he had been involved in an car accident along with Rudolf Hess and Julius Schaub. In 1938, Hitler ordered a new, armoured Mercedes. He chose the interior arrangements and decorations, and inspected it in the late afternoon of 7 July 1938, before taking delivery. Satisfied with this vehicle, the Führer gave one to his ally Marshal Mannerheim, president of the Finnish Republic. This car, which weighed four tons and could reach speeds of 170 kilometres per hour, reached Mannerheim in December 1941. When the marshal decided to reverse his alliance and turn toward Soviet Russia in August 1944, he put the Mercedes in the garage and used an English limousine instead. In passing, we might note that this car was auctioned off in 1973 as having belonged to Adolf Hitler and brought a record price of one hundred and fifty-three thousand dollars. Cruel Finnish journalists disillusioned the buyers: Hitler had never owned the vehicle. In 1940, the Führer bought a more discreet black, armoured sedan for his journeys to the mountains. It was seized in the Obersalzberg in 1945 and ended up in the Canadian War Museum.

The car truly became the symbol of Nazi success and luxury, first of all because in 1933 Hitler had made this sector the flagship of German industrial development. There were then about sixteen manufacturers, including very prestigious firms such as Zeppelin, whose high-end models were intended to compete with Rolls Royce. On 8 March 1933, at the Berlin international car fair, Hitler gave a speech that inaugurated a policy of rapid development in this sector. He promised state subsidies and the establishment of infrastructures favouring this mode of transportation. The construction of the autobahns was part of this policy, which was launched by a law adopted on 23 June 1933. The plan called for a network of fourteen thousand kilometres covering the Great Reich, including Austria; by March 1938, three thousand kilometres had been completed.[3] The autobahns offered an ease of driving unprecedented in Europe, as well as an improved system of road signs. But the Third Reich also modernized the network of national highways, which were for the most part given macadam or other stable surfacing. The more dangerous curves were altered and preceded by warning signs. In Germany, unsurfaced roads were limited to the secondary network, whereas in neighbouring countries they were common everywhere. Thus Germany became the leading European country for cars. This policy was undeniably connected with the way of life of the leaders, who roamed Germany by car. The goal was to make their travels comfortable and rapid.

When Nazi leaders took the plane, cars followed by road in order to provide local transportation. This practice sometimes resulted in comical incidents that revealed certain people's reluctance to accept the privileges enjoyed by the powerful and their servants. Thus in July 1935, the head of a Mercedes workshop, Hermann Bieller, was assigned by Julius Schreck, Hitler's personal adjutant and chauffeur, to convoy two of the Führer's cars to the workshop in Mannheim.[4] He was followed by three rented cars that were to be returned. The convoy stopped for the night in Mainz, then went on to its destination. On arrival, Bieller wanted to take a shower and change his clothes before going to the Mercedes workshop. Probably denounced by his brother-in-law, who he said was a communist, Bieller was questioned by two policemen. They did not believe that he worked for the chancellery and took him to the police station. There he was questioned again by Superintendent Hepp, who didn't believe him either, despite Mercedes' confirmation by telephone. Hepp wanted the direct assurance of the Führer's office that these men were on assignment. In the meantime, he sent Bieller and his assistant to wait at the central police station. During the transfer, a small crowd gathered in front of the door, curious to see who was driving these big official cars. Giving his exit a theatrical air by putting the two men in a lorry occupied by several of his agents, the superintendent shouted ironically, and loudly enough to be heard by all, 'You know, now we're in the Third Reich.' Bieller was convinced that Superintendent Hepp, a former member of the Centre Party, was taking personal vengeance. Finally freed that night, the Führer's men drove the cars to the Mercedes-Benz workshop the following day and then returned to Munich. As soon as they arrived they filed a complaint with the police and demanded sanctions. It is this complaint that informs us about an incident that seems to reflect the tensions between the Reich's *enfants terribles*, who claimed to be all-powerful, and former officials who didn't want to be pushed around. This little anecdote indicates that certain cars immediately attracted attention, for Hitler's vehicles were different from all others: in addition to their size, they had insignia, pennants, and so on. The popular passion for cars, to which both the general press and specialized monthlies bear witness, placed the elites before the attentive eyes of the masses.

Nazi leaders saw that they could use this passion to increase their popularity. Thus in 1934 they adopted Ferdinand Porsche's plan to construct a low-cost car that could be bought by all German workers.[5] The goal was to bring luxury down to the level of modest families by outfitting them with devices that had long been inaccessible to them, such as the radio known as the *Volksempfänger* ('People's Receiver'). This radio was very inexpensive and soon made Germany the second best-equipped European country in this area. Of course, the objective was to increase the audience for propaganda. Radio also broadcast a certain number of concerts and programmes that provided wider access to cultural pleasures while at the same time diverting people's attention from a reality that was often harsh. At home, Germans received news – controlled, of course – as well as complete reporting on sport, and especially auto sport.

For the Nazis, the car was not merely a means of transportation. It reveals to a large extent the regime's relationship to competition and its desire to promote luxury sports. The leaders wanted German car manufacturing to be in the van and its products the best. A policy seeking prestige was adopted as early as 1933. Hitler chose to give priority to the most capable of the manufacturers: Mercedes. Mercedes had, after all, won Grand Prix races in 1932. Manfred von Brauchitsch, the new head of the Wehrmacht's General Staff, was the firm's star driver. In 1933, he challenged the aeroplane pilot Ernst Udet to a race and lost by only a hair. However, the Germans did not win either the German Grand Prix or the Berlin Grand Prix races in 1933. Pressure was put on for a German victory. The following year, the track of the Avus, in Berlin, was resurfaced. Several thousand spectators were expected. Mercedes had forgone the Monaco Grand Prix in order to be ready. Brauchitsch roared off in his 354 horsepower Mercedes, but the motor developed fuel-pump problems. The German driver preferred to drop out rather than be beaten by the Italians. For the German Grand Prix at the Nürburgring, the necessary adjustments were made. The Mercedes engines developed their full power. The firm's two drivers, Brauchitsch and Luigi Fagioli, led the race, with Fagioli in front. The team director, Alfred Neubauer, asked Fagioli to let Brauchitsch pass him so that a German would win the race. The fiery Italian did so, but perhaps because he found it difficult to obey this order, he let an Auto Union driver pass as well.

A second German auto racing team was set up through the combined efforts of Horch, Audi, Wanderer, and DKW. They hired Ferdinand Porsche, the former head of Mercedes. Auto Union had a car with an aerodynamic body and a V-12 engine developing more than 300 horsepower. A German driver, Bernd Rosemeyer, was at the wheel. The Italian star Tazio Nuvolari agreed to leave Alfa Romeo to join the new team. The ferocious competition between German auto manufacturers to win Grand Prix races, along with the regime's orders and favours, led them to surpass the former Italian domination by Alfa Romeo, Maserati, and Bugatti. Every race seemed to be a duel between Auto Union and Mercedes, the former excelling in speed, the latter in manoeuvrability. However, Mercedes broke the world speed records.

The regime staged this competition by giving the track for the Berlin Grand Prix a steeply banked turn that favoured high speeds. In 1936, the race had to be cancelled in order to complete the work; the curve was so difficult to manoeuvre that a line was drawn on the surface to indicate the right trajectory. On 30 May 1937, the drivers began a terrifying struggle. The cars' safety protections had been reduced in order to go faster. Three hundred thousand spectators witnessed the German victory. Hermann Lang, driving for Mercedes, won out over Brauchitsch driving for Auto Union. However, Rosemeyer, also driving for Auto Union, had the fastest lap at 276 kilometres per hour.

Rosemeyer went on to beat the world speed record by reaching 408 kilometres per hour on 26 October 1937. Annoyed, Mercedes soon requested the Führer's authorization to make an attempt. Auto Union countered by demanding the right to reply immediately if the record was broken. Thus a direct confrontation was necessary. The two firms set the site for the duel: the Frankfurt–Darmstadt autobahn, on a straightaway near the 500 kilometre mark. The date was set for the morning of 28 January 1938. Here we can presume that the intention was to make a symbolic birthday gift on the anniversary of Hitler's becoming chancellor, the celebration of which was to take place two days later. The Italian Rodolfo Caracciola, driving for Mercedes, left first, at 9 a.m., and set a new world record of 423 kilometres per hour. Rosemeyer took off shortly before noon. He exceeded 450 kilometres per hour, but a gust of wind caused him to lose control and crash at kilometre 508. This terrible accident killed Rosemeyer, who was not yet thirty years old. The nation went into mourning. The champion's body was buried with military honours in the forest cemetery in Dahlem.[6] The Führer paid him homage, saying that Rosemeyer had sacrificed himself for the greater glory of Germany.

Women drivers do not often appear in images of this Germany. There were female aeroplane pilots whose fame reached outside Germany, such as Hanna Reitsch, who held more than forty world records and in 1942 became the first woman to be awarded the Iron Cross, First Class, and Elly Beinhorn, Bernd Rosemeyer's wife, who was one of the pioneers of air transportation before marrying in 1936 and serving along with her husband as a model couple for propaganda purposes. However, women sometimes showed themselves off by sitting in the back seat with a pure-bred dog during *concours d'élégance*. They might occasionally appear in an advertisement. But in the common view, cars were for men. For women, luxury and fashion took other avenues.

Fashion, a Feminine Luxury

Extremely retrograde and reactionary with respect to advances after the Great War, the status of women's fashions in Nazi Germany must be understood in the framework of an ideology that emphasized virility and valour in combat. Women's domain consisted in household tasks and having children in order to improve the race and increase the number of fighters. These tasks were viewed with a degree of seriousness unparalleled even in the very hygienist democracies of northern Europe at the time. Girls were to receive training in National Socialist organizations, in particular the BDM (Bund Deutscher Mädel).[7] They learned to run a household and got accustomed to discipline and order. The most gifted also learned to give commands. Thus they achieved the dignity of femininity, which was based not on political rights but on social utility. When they became mothers, they were to take care of their children so that they might in their turn become efficient propagators of Germanness. From this ideological programme flowed the principle that a woman should be modest and discreet. Her beauty was all the more praiseworthy when it was natural. Whence many statements made by leaders and zealous followers condemning women who used make-up. The 1920s aesthetic ideal of the 'tomboy' had to be done away with. The modern German woman was set aside in favour of her predecessors. These principles no doubt derive from the proximity of the leaders to older generations who advocated a Belle Époque way of life. Elegance could not consist in innovations, but rather involved the acceptance of the elites' traditional mode of life corrected by a strict racial hygiene. In this sense, Nazism favoured the diffusion of the ways in which bourgeois and aristocrats were brought up.

In this respect, the proliferation of books on good manners referring to the new Germany and viewing women as good housewives is revelatory. What better example of this than the *Hausbuch für die deutsche Familie* given to all young couples married after 1935?[8] It contains advice to mothers regarding sewing and the upbringing and feeding of children. It says nothing about how to reconcile social life with family life. On the other hand, several chapters deal with the Nuremberg Laws and provide a list of forbidden relationships. Miscegenation's degenerative effects on the race are emphasized. The German woman officially corresponds to a physical type, a racial ideal, and activities limited to the home.

Thus the regime's prescriptions with regard to fashion deviate from the classical conception of luxury. A kind of asceticism and gravity were necessary, whereas luxury was supposed to add a touch of eccentricity, frivolousness, and superfluity. The mass organizations followed these prescriptions, asking their members to forgo make-up, jewellery, and expensive clothing in the name of official moral severity. Nationalist ardour led the Nazis to consider harmful the contributions of French fashion, from dress designs to cosmetics, and including the decorative arts. Goebbels overtly encouraged a boycott of French tailors.

German stylists and fashion designers understood the message. A few months after the regime change, the Deutsches Mode Institute (DMI) was created to coordinate industrial production and circulate bulletins on current trends.[9] Its fashion bureau organized a presentation of 'German designs' on 17–19 August 1933, and in 1934 it began to propose athletic outfits because women were supposed to exercise their bodies while at the same time maintaining their dignity and seductiveness.[10] Another of the institute's goals was to help Aryanize high-fashion houses.

Jews in fact largely controlled the clothing industry. More than 70 per cent of Berlin's ready-to-wear clothing was produced by Jewish tailors – Gerson, Mannheimer, and others. In 1937, one of these tailors, Fritz Grünfeld, a fashion designer representing the German textile industry, received a gold medal at the Paris World Fair. Among his customers were great ladies such as Magda Goebbels and Emmy Göring. However, his success was the exception, and should not hide the fact that from 1933 on this sector was subjected to systematic attack and that many clothing shops were forced to sell out at a loss, especially after Kristallnacht. After the Anschluss, Viennese high-fashion companies such as Stone & Blythe were Aryanized and obliged to produce clothing in conformity with the requirements of the Viennese Fashion House.[11] The discrimination was economic and ideological: National Socialism reproached this urban *haute couture* with not respecting German cultural canons. The DMI, despite several reforms carried out in 1936, and then again during the war, never really succeeded in imposing German fashions or in fulfilling its production goals.

Could education make up for this failure? Fashion was taught in three specialized schools in Berlin, Munich, and Frankfurt. The challenge was to train professionals who were supposed to replace the Jews when the latter were driven out and to promote the German fashion tradition. When fashion competitions were held, students from these schools were systematically promoted at the expense of non-Aryans. The objective was to train a generation of designers capable of outclassing even the great Paris houses. This is shown by a 1940 proposal to establish a Meisterschule der Mode in Munich that would provide advanced training in fashion design.[12] It would be for women who were already active in the field and wanted to perfect their artistic technique, as well as for beginners who wanted to pursue a career in fashion design. The goal was to provide creators and managers for the fashion industry. This project was sponsored by Gerdy Troost, the widow of the famous architect who had decorated the NSDAP's head office. She was one of the most important women in the Hitlerian hierarchy, because she served as the Führer's partner at several official dinners and theatrical events. A memorandum defending this project, transmitted by the mayor of Munich to Hitler's personal

Adjudantur, begins with these jubilant words: 'The defeat of France in the present war has had as a notable consequence the collapse of Paris as the centre of world fashion.' It went on to claim that German fashion was finally going to be able to occupy a central place and exercise an enduring influence. Another of the project's ambitions was to confirm Munich as the capital of art under the Third Reich. In this it was in accord with directives issued by Hitler himself insisting that the 'movement's capital' also be 'the capital of the arts'. For the Führer, fashion was a form of artistic creation. Thus students could be trained in the theory and practice of fashion design by studying forty hours a week for four consecutive semesters. They could take specialized courses in modelling, colour, design, jewellery, style, pattern-making, and fashion.[13] In addition, there would be general instruction suited to satisfy the political sponsors: the history of culture and fashion, artistic forms and the artistic perspective, national politics, and gymnastics. When their studies were completed, the students would be certified designers.

This kind of programme for training and urban activity was started in Frankfurt. In 1933, Frankfurt's mayor, Friedrich Krebs, a committed National Socialist, set up a fashion office (Mode Amt) whose objective was both to promote designers already in the city and to organize events to publicize sales and manufacturers and to encourage the press to give the city an aura of elegance.[14] He therefore appointed as head of this new office Margarethe Klimt, a woman of Austrian origin who had directed the vocational training school in Frankfurt since 1929. She undertook this mission with great enthusiasm, organizing large fashion shows featuring clothes designed by several houses. These events were given extensive coverage in the press. In 1938 the fashion office's activity was fully recognized, and it was installed in a new headquarters in the centre of the city. However, economic activity did not meet the mayor's expectations. It is true that rationing, which started in 1939, hobbled development. Krebs bitterly criticized Klimt, blaming her for the failure. She finally fell ill and left for Vienna in 1943. The same year, the Frankfurt school of fashion was destroyed during an aerial bombardment.

How can we fail to deduce from these failures an ambiguity in the regime's voluntarist policy in the domain of fashion? On the one hand, the goal was to reduce German dependency in the areas of textiles and aesthetics in order to limit imports and increase the country's industrial autonomy. In agricultural policy, the emphasis on sheep-raising in order to produce wool was directed towards the same goals, as were customs regulations. On the other hand, we discern a fantasy of aesthetic hegemony that presupposed the production of clothing that was representative of National Socialist ideology and that could attract a vast clientele outside Germany in order to supplant its old French rivals.

For a time, Nazi leaders thought they had found the ideal solution. They promoted traditional German dress and appealed to folklore in order to gain approval. The dirndl, the classic Bavarian and Tyrolean dress for women, is the symbol of this attempt.[15] It was featured on propaganda posters put out by the party and by private enterprises. Their slogans praised the German housewife wearing her traditional costume. Luxurious versions of the dirndl were made for more well-off customers, such as the 'Austrian dirndl' in damasked silk made in Munich in 1938 for the Countess von Weinberg.[16] As proof of their conformism, the regime's great ladies had themselves photographed wearing a dirndl; Emmy Göring and Eva Braun in particular wore them for public appearances. In the case of Eva Braun, who under the Nazi regime lived a semi-clandestine existence sheltered from the public eye, wearing a dirndl indicated that she truly espoused the aesthetics of the leaders of the movement, and of Hitler in particular. Gertrud Scholtz-Klink, who was responsible for Nazi women's organizations, also like to wear this garment. It played a role in the uniform she had designed for young Nazi girls who were members of the BDM. The first version of this uniform was rejected by Hitler, who did not find it sufficiently feminine. In his view, a young German woman ought to be attractive even when wearing work clothes. He therefore proposed changes that distinguished the dress from 'a potato sack', as he put it.[17] It would be a simple dress with an apron that recalled the dirndl.

Great actresses and film directors like Lil Dagover and Leni Riefenstahl did not hesitate to appear in a dirndl, and cinema was soon promoting it abroad. Even an emigrée like Marlene Dietrich wore it in Hollywood and thus encouraged its exportation – to the point that two Parisian designers included one in their 1939 spring collections. Obviously, that summer the dirndl suddenly became unfashionable.

Social life could not limit itself to a bucolic style extolling simple naturalness. High society was too open to foreign styles to be satisfied with small local effects. Western countries' canons of beauty were brought into Germany through embassies, international travellers, and newsreels, and undermined fidelity to Nazi doctrine. In turn, members of German high society travelled abroad for professional reasons, on vacations or to go to spas. On the great ocean liners, in the new airports, or simply in the display windows of chic shops they saw how styles changed and appearance varied. Society ladies had the means to go beyond official prescriptions and indulge their taste for luxury. Eva Braun was a faithful buyer of Elizabeth Arden cosmetics. She also took advantage of the invasion of France to procure French make-up and perfume. Not to mention clothes and furs. All the great ladies were happy about their husbands' trips to Paris, which allowed them to obtain chic designer clothing.

Women's magazines did not present solely the austere aspect of official fashion. They made a few concessions to the regime's prescriptions, but they preferred to give their readers what they all wanted: the great international trends. *Die Dame*, which was the most upper-crust of the fashion magazines and held the German rights for *Vogue,* showed clothes by the great Parisian and American designers, Chanel, Schiaparelli, Molyneux, Mainbocher, Patou, Grès, and Worth. Clearly they did not attempt to eliminate 'Jewish' creations from their pages. It was not merely a question of selling these high-fashion clothes. German women were able to have their dressmakers copy them or draw inspiration from accessories in order to personalize them. These magazines thus conveyed an international style that allowed women not to seem ridiculous at parties attended by members of the diplomatic corps or great foreign visitors who were passing through. Anyway, would these ideologues – who sought the company of the great beauties of the silver screen – have been happy living with ordinary women?

The *femme fatale* in these magazines and in German cinema hardly differed from the *femme fatale* in other countries, including the democracies. The press, despite political surveillance, reflected women's reluctance to be subjected to a policy of sumptuary restrictions. Even Goebbels's popular newspaper, *12 Uhr Blatt,* showed an image of the well-dressed and sensual woman close to international standards. This can be seen in the illustrations accompanying the numerous articles devoted to cinema actresses, and also in more specialized columns. When it first appeared, the newspaper had a women's column that appeared several times a week under the rubric 'I am the housewife'. Its goal was obviously to satisfy and guide the potential female readership. In it we find breathless debates on subjects like this one from April 1934: 'Short or long hair?'[18] This column is illustrated by two photographs comparing short haircuts seen from behind. No preference is finally expressed, except that one must take care of one's hair, 'not solely for others but first of all for oneself'. Short hair was one of the symbols of the modernization of European women's status. The same column also contained a history of the blouse, which mentioned the role it had played in the reign of Louis XIV, its decline during the Revolution, and its current return, which is welcomed by the author, who fears that its admirers might be deprived of it by a new revolution.

A week later the same paper ran a violent attack on Greta Garbo, whose lovely face contradicted it.[19] The critic said he had not seen her latest film, *Queen Christina,* which had just come out in the United States, but he predicted that it would be a failure because the star was getting old, a victim of her marriage with Ruben Mamoulian, and would end up like the Swedish queen, who, having lost her throne, lived in exile far from her home country. Was the 'divine Greta' (*die göttliche Greta*) so distant from the German physical ideal? Far from it, and the paper, like the article, contradicted itself. Discussing women's evening clothes not long afterward, *12 Uhr Blatt* reproduced a full-length portrait of a model wearing make-up and assuming a glamorous pose. On the same page there were pictures of women's bathing suits for the summer. Skimpy clothing, short hair, big smiles, voluptuous figures, and high heels with straps – almost a vision of

Betty Boop. In fact, the illustration was borrowed from MGM with the following commentary: 'American movie stars are also returning to simple styles: their beautiful swimsuits are open to the sun and designed to be functional.' It was as if the paper were Germanizing American styles. The 'Beauty and Health' column dealt with freckles and offered old recipes for herbal teas, particularly ones made with parsley, to protect the skin against sunburn.

This image was, of course, changed by the war. Such frivolous topics appeared less often and were replaced by practical advice for consumers. However, when the war began, clothes still reflected international fashions. For example, a short article on winter wear for 1939,[20] illustrated with a drawing, proposed three short coats with sleek lines and tailored waists.

Thus the regime was caught between its reformist ambitions and detachment from fashions it regarded as expensive to import and ideologically unacceptable, on the one hand, and, on the other, the everyday reality of German women, especially the wealthiest among them, who were willing to make small concessions but did not want to give up their life-style. Party dresses and clothes worn to social events did not differ from those usual in international high society, and were adapted to the season and the event in question.[21] On the occasion of major events at the Opera or the theatre that were covered by the press, such as the Theatre Festival of the Reich (Reichstheaterfestwoche) created in 1934, the stalls were full of women wearing long dresses and pearl or diamond necklaces. The dresses wound around the body in a style very close to that worn by the great socialites of the period such as the Duchess of Windsor, the Duchess of Kent, and the Princess of Greece, to whom *Die Dame* devoted an article entitled 'On the Art of Photographing Women'.[22] Ultimately, luxury consisted in the variety and possibility of moving from one outfit to another, following one's whims, as did Eva Braun, despite her quasi-clandestine position.

Luxury in men's fashions evolved in similar ways. Why would it be otherwise, since wives often helped choose their husband's clothes or tailors? Thus in fashion magazines we find pictures of men's clothing designed to appeal to women. We must remember that this was a time when women needed an escort at high-society evenings, and ideally the couple wore outfits that complemented each other. So we see men in morning coats and white bow ties, very much in fashion in the 1930s. A few young people, particularly military cadets, still wore short jackets. However, the latter were on their way out, as were the long tailcoats worn by some old-school diplomats;[23] a shorter tailcoat was generally worn, and a white shirt with a wing collar. For everyday or morning wear, a man of the world had a suit and tie. For walking about town, suits with wide stripes in the English fashion were fashionable in the late 1930s. This sporting attire was also worn by golf and tennis players.[24] In the latter case, accessories such as caps and towels completed the outfit: tennis shorts that reached below the knee and high stockings (golfers wore long trousers), a striped sweater, and canvas shoes. What is surprising is that this outfit was sometimes combined with a cotton turtleneck that made the wearer look like an invalid.

Whether masculine or feminine, elegance – understood as what is most fashionable – is based largely on one's ability to gauge the event to be attended and to present oneself in the best possible light. The luxury of true socialites intersects with ideology as soon as someone appears in public, for the atmosphere of a social event depends on the cultural climate, in which politics plays a role. Distinguished dress involves both conformity to a collective order and the assertion of the individual's particularity. A provocative garment creates its effect only in relation to a dominant mode of dress. To be in fashion is to follow custom while at the same time introducing a slight deviation. That is how one shows that one is well informed, occupies a certain place in the social order, and has access to a select group. In this sense, the historian notes that Nazism was not always fashionable, even during Hitler's regime. Its aesthetic attraction for high society achieved its acme during the last phase of his rise to power and the very beginning of his rule. At that time, uniforms were particularly trendy among the elite. Later on, the brown of the SA and the black of the SS became very common.

Pure-Bred, Pure Blood, and Noble Pleasures

Despite its democratization in the 1930s, sport was still an area of distinction under Nazism. Soccer and track and field events fascinated the masses and struck deep roots in popular culture. They conveyed an ideal of performance, a fantasy of the strong body, and a desire for collective action that corresponded to the ideal of the 'new man'.[25] Numerous images depicted this group gymnastics, which was exported even to democracies that wanted to improve the training of their young people.

However, the Nazi regime, far from promoting only athletics for the masses, undertook to maintain traditional competitive activities. It did not hesitate to invest in areas in which the social life of the Belle Époque expressed itself, drawing, as in the case of car racing, on the seductive appeal of publicized excellence. Horsemanship and horse racing constituted a test sector for this policy, channelling pleasures that were limited to the elites and conveyed to the masses as spectator sports. No doubt the risks inherent in racing and betting provided an additional adrenalin surge for spectators that helped them forget the insidious frustration caused by the dictatorship's repression of individual freedoms and its moral constraints, particularly in the area of sexuality.

Several reasons led the regime to take an interest in horses. First, there was the symbolic connection between the German nation and the equestrian world. Everyone knew that the creation of equestrian institutions had been the forerunner of Bismarck's determination to federate Germany. On 15 December 1867, soon after the German victory over Austria at Sadowa in 1866, the Union Klub, the German equivalent of the Jockey Club, was founded. It brought together representatives of racing associations from all over Germany, with the exception of Bavaria. The same group of Prussian aristocrats also decided that the Berlin racecourse at Tempelhof was disagreeable for ladies and trainers because it was too sandy, and had a new steeplechase course constructed in Dahlwitz. They wanted the future capital of the Reich to have a large racecourse, which they called the Hoppegarten.

Secondly, Nazi leaders were fascinated by the biological aspect of horse breeding. They wanted to use it as an example of the potential of genetic selection. Work on pure-bred horses was carried out in conformity with hygienic and racial theories.[26] Many breeders sought to obtain a perfect breed on German soil, just as Nazi leaders tried to use eugenic selection to breed fine human models, archetypes of the distant Aryan race whose original purity had to be recovered. The Nazi regime agreed to increase to more than twelve million marks per year its contribution to the improvement of horse breeding. This fantasy led to other measures, such as Göring's decision to reintroduce bison into Germany, or veterinarians' attempts to re-create by interbreeding the original bovine strain that was supposed to have accompanied the conquering hordes of old. Purity of blood and the triumph of the strongest or, in this case, the fastest: that was the National Socialists' dream. Basically, racing fans, horse owners, and trainers spoke the same language as the regime did. They were moved by the nobility of the horseman and saw the horse as a conquest. They shared a rural pseudo-ideal: within a green enclave, they rediscovered an aroma of manure that reminded them of the German soil.

Finally, the racing milieu was in sympathy with the Nazis early on, and in this it was like the reactionaries and conservatives. An American observer, Edna Haynes, the wife of one of the best jockeys of the time, has left us a critical description of this milieu.[27] According to her, members of the Union Klub engaged in plotting, trickery, and corruption, and were rabid patriots who tried to use unprecedented regulations to keep foreign competitors out of races.

The Union Klub was in fact a refuge for aristocrats.[28] Its first president was Count Georg von Helldorf, and all his first thirty-four successors were also nobles. The most active among them – for instance, Heinrich von Treskow-Dahlwitz, who created the Hoppegarten and the association that managed it – were of very high birth. During the 1920s this powerful association was dominated by Baron von Oppenheim, and from 1934 on it was headed by Franz von Papen, the former chancellor. Von Papen had been an uhlan in 1906 and had thus taken part in races among the officers. The latter were the true glory of German horse riding, like the great champion

Otto Suermondt, a lieutenant in the twenty-fourth dragoons who rode in 1,463 races and won 506 before his death in 1941. As president of the Union Klub, von Papen had only nobles, most of them military men, as assistants. The secretary of the presidium was Major General Count von Seherr-Thoss; there were also two cavalry generals, Count von Pogrell and Chevalier von Dalwigk, an army general, Fromm, a lieutenant general, Count von Uthenau-Hohenthurm, and two officers, Major Walther Bresges and Commander Wolff Metternich. Finally, the Berlin police chief, Count Helldorf, a descendant of one of the club's founders who was close to Hitler, completed the team. From 1933 on, the club's secretary general was Rittmeister Châles de Beaulieu. All the other committees – the finance, technical, and disciplinary committees – were made up of aristocrats and figures in the regime, such as State Secretary Grauert. Comfortably installed in the head offices of the Union Klub, which had been located in the Schadowstrasse since 1915, these men reigned over a select group of horse-racing aficionados.

During the Nazi regime, the club's membership was smaller than it had been in the 1920s, dropping from six hundred to about five hundred dues-paying members.[29] The expulsion of Jews partly explains this decline. The generation that followed the Great War was also smaller because so many men had been killed in the fighting. But it is clear that entry into the club was a matter of co-optation among the wealthy, an even more selective elite than that of the Herrenklub, which had also long been headed by von Papen. The clubhouse where members met was constructed in 1882. They could dine there or sit in leather club chairs in the saloons to chat. This very masculine world was based on a love of competition and gambling. Some of those who gathered there were wealthy owners of racing stables or horse-breeding operations that required extensive financial resources. Other members, such as the von Oppenheim family, had invested their private income in banking.

To gauge the elitist character of this microcosm of owners, we have only to note that it controlled, over the whole of the Reich, including Austria after 1938, about two thousand racehorses, including a thousand that trained on the courses of greater Berlin. The Hoppegarten had become the greatest German horse-racing centre. Almost eight hundred horses raced there and took advantage of its veterinary facilities, its horse clinic, and convalescence stalls. Hamburg, which had had the biggest prizes after the war, had been demoted to a distant second place. Munich was even trying to overtake it.

This change was due largely to the state. In 1933, the Nazi regime began intervening in the management of horse racing, since the company that owned the Grunewald racecourse sold it to the Reich. The latter developed pari-mutuel gambling to the point that the Union Klub had to set up the company handling the wagering in a new office in the Hardenbergstrasse. In 1934, the government had the first grandstand at the Hoppegarten enlarged, and in 1937 the main entry was rebuilt by Professor Krüger, the designer of the monument to the battle of Tannenberg that was so venerated by the Nazis.

Aware of the attraction exerted by the world of horse racing, Göring transformed the former Berlin Grand Prix into the Grand Prix of the Capital of the Third Reich. The winner received the largest prize ever awarded at a racecourse: a hundred thousand marks. To regain the initiative, Goebbels launched a press campaign vaunting this event. That was enough to get French and English horse owners to enter the competition in 1937. In particular, the Boussac stable entered its best five-year-old stallion, Corrida. The 2,400-metre race was accompanied by the shouts of spectators who wanted to see Sturmvogel (Storm-Bird) triumph again for the third year running. The last hundred metres were very close. Corrida won by a head before Amerina, an Italian mare. It was the first time since 1897 that a foreign horse had won this derby. The following year, Antonym, another French horse, owned by M. Holdert, stole the victory from the German owners. These two events confirmed the return of Germany to horse racing at the international, high-society level, though it awakened ardent desires for revenge.

In 1938, another grand prix attracted attention. On 15 March, Hitler decided to create a Union Klub Prize of honour worth forty thousand marks. The course was shortened from 3,700 metres to 2,600 metres. To ensure that the race would endure, Hitler created an endowment that was to last a century. He thereby gave von Papen, the president of the Union Klub, a permanent guarantee for his activities, implying that the Reich now conceived itself in a long-term perspective. Hadn't he said the Reich would last a thousand years?

Curiously, the horse that won the Union Klub Prize that year was named Frauenpreis (Women's Prize). We should see in this further evidence that, despite the over-representation of men, women played an indispensable role in these arenas. They came to gamble. They also took part in dressage competitions and international test events. However, true socialites used hippodromes above all as places to show off their luxurious clothes and display their success in front of their friends. Every year great ladies, including Frau von Papen, organized a spring tea. That afternoon, the former chancellor's wife wore a hat with a veil instead of the tiara she preferred for evening events. A special area was reserved for her women guests. Men remained outside the barrier delimiting the women's space. Sitting at large round tables, about a hundred women from high society and the diplomatic corps shared a moment of relaxation before returning to the officials' grandstand and placing their bets. In June, a fashion show was held at the Hoppegarten. Bella Fromm describes this show in her diary, because she was for several years its organizer.[30] From 1935 on, the Munich racecourse held a show of spring fashions.[31] Two-horse carriages set off the models. Thus the capital of National

Socialism acquired a refined air. Obsolescent elites were reinvigorated by the party's will.

The racecourse reproduced in miniature the social distinctions of the Third Reich. It was one of the showplaces for the elites. It gave ordinary people cheap thrills, whereas wealthy owners invested considerable sums in acquiring, maintaining, and training pure-breds. They also recruited at considerable cost jockeys who were subject to increasingly severe conditions regarding weight and physical characteristics. This horse-racing high society spread throughout Germany and organized about a hundred local associations. The latter invited mayors and Gauleiters to the major races they organized, as is shown by Carl Vincent Krogmann's attempt to defend the Hamburg racecourse, which was falling behind. For instance, he invited Göring and his wife as well as General von Blomberg to the Horn racecourse for the 1936 derby.[32] Here we see once again how involvement in high society worked and how attachment to the regime was disseminated by local elites.

Wealthy spectators went to the racecourses the way they went to casinos, and wagered fortunes on a horse or a combination of horses. The pleasure taken in gambling also explains why the great spas and casinos experienced no decline during this period. On the contrary, Nazi hierarchs like Eva Braun, Magda Goebbels, and Heinrich Hoffmann did not hesitate to go out in groups to lose a little money at the gambling tables. This kind of expenditure was, however, less characteristic of very high society under the Third Reich than the accumulation of great art collections.

The Collecting Bug or the Courtly Art of the Third Reich

Hitler set the tone. His established taste for art, and especially for painting, exercised an immense influence on other leaders of the Third Reich. Their penchant was in singular agreement with high-society life, less in their participation in exhibits, ceremonious openings, or the desire to frequent artists than in another respect brought out by the American historian Jonathan Petropoulous,[33] one of the first to suggest that collecting paintings and art objects was a special characteristic of Nazi leaders. By collecting in conjunction with a strict art policy, the Third Reich succeeded in aestheticizing politics and ultimately in disseminating a style that was to become its symbol.

If we except Hitler, who had hung some of his own paintings in his room, most Nazi leaders owned few artworks before coming to power. Göring, for example, had only a small painting by an old master in his Berlin apartment. Ribbentrop could claim to have the beginning of a collection. On the other hand, Goebbels had more paintings, including several modern ones. Nevertheless, imbued with classical culture, the upper strata of the Nazi party had very fixed ideas, like those of Alfred

Rosenberg, who hated contemporary art and abstraction. Not all the Nazis had the same scorn for modern art, however. After taking power and acquiring the financial resources they henceforth enjoyed, the masters of the Third Reich could give their tastes free rein and try to increase their prestige by acquiring artworks and showing them off.

The acquisitions made between 1933 and 1935 varied in nature. The Goebbels, for instance, owned watercolours by the expressionist painter Emil Nolde. They were even alleged to have works by Käthe Kollwitz, the great revolutionary who depicted the suffering of the working class and the atrocities of war, and who was at that time relatively marginalized and no longer received the prestigious commissions she had earlier enjoyed. In addition, Goebbels is said to have had a weakness for Leo von König, an impressionist and especially a secessionist following Max Lieberman. His work should have been rejected because of the Semitic influence it had undergone. However, several important members of the Nazi movement did not hesitate to associate with him and acquire his works. König did a portrait of the minister Bernhard Rust in 1934. In turn, Goebbels commissioned a portrait in 1935 that was hung in the ministry of propaganda until the regime proscribed modern art. The painting ended up in Goebbels' residence on Schwannenwerder.

The condemnation of contemporary art, and especially abstract art, even though it developed gradually, was a decision made at the highest level. Rosenberg and Ley each tried to take the initiative in 1933, but it was actually Hitler who in the autumn of 1935 put the force of law behind this blacklisting. Goebbels and the ministry of propaganda crafted it, and were so convinced that in early 1936 they undertook a vast 'cleansing' operation directed against 'degenerate art' (*Entartete Kunst*) in all the Reich's art galleries and museums.[34] On 19 April 1937 an exhibit bearing this title opened in Munich; it was intended to show the negative character of modern art. Adolf Ziegler, an old friend of Hitler's, became the official responsible for art policy within the Reich's Chamber of the Arts. Jonathan Petropoulos notes that some people called him the painter of 'pubic hair' because of his favourite subject.[35] However that may be, Ziegler, who was henceforth present at all the official openings, promoted a policy that favoured subjects beloved by his friend, the minister of agriculture Walther Darré: *Blut und Boden*. He made official on the political scale the tastes that were henceforth reflected in the National Socialist elite's private art collections.

All the regime's bigwigs – Rosenberg, Ley, Ribbentrop, Göring, Goebbels, Schirach, Speer, Frank, Himmler, Bürckel, Seyss-Inquart, Heydrich, von Papen, Hess – had a collection, and claimed to have an insatiable appetite for painting. Each of them, as he rose in the social and political hierarchy, increased his possessions and gave artworks as presents to his friends. Hitler played a particular role in this. He received a number of gifts from these men, who flattered his historical fancies through works representing great events or famous men in Germany history. Franz

Lenbach's portrait of Bismarck, which Hitler hung in his office in the chancellery, did not have a solely decorative function. The head of state also used it to imply that he had surpassed the Iron Chancellor.[36] In turn, to thank Ribbentrop for his diplomatic work, Hitler gave him Lenbach's portrait of Bismarck wearing a ceremonial dress uniform. He gave classic works to Goebbels and Göring. These exchanges may remind us of children trading cards. But this exchange had a different ambition.

Prestigious art collections were put together. Göring was able to fill with several hundred paintings the gallery he had constructed for that purpose at his Karinhall residence. He was advised in his acquisitions by a professional art dealer, Walther Andreas Hofer. Göring owned works by old German masters like Cranach and Dürer and by eighteenth-century French painters such as Boucher and Fragonard. At the end of the war, the inventory of his collection listed 1,375 paintings, 250 sculptures, and 168 tapestries, including some produced by Gobelins. This enormous collection is not radically different from those of other Nazi hierarchs. In his different residences, Ribbentrop exhibited works from France, such as Derain's portrait of a young woman, in front of which Annelies, Ribbentrop's wife, posed for press photographers. The Ribbentrops liked Courbet, Corot, Moreau, Monet, and the impressionists in general. The occupation allowed Ribbentrop to acquire paintings by Utrillo, Monet, Degas, Bonnard, and Braque – at the risk of not conforming to National Socialist aesthetic orthodoxy. He collected French classical painters like Fragonard, and Italians as well, since he owned a Madonna by Fra Angelico. Ribbentrop also decorated the castles entrusted to his ministry with valuable furniture, old paintings, and Gobelins tapestries. Himmler, who otherwise led a relatively sober life, preferred art objects. He liked Etruscan bronzes, of which he owned several. He also was advised, particularly by Heinrich Hoffmann (who was well aware of the Führer's tastes), and bought masterpieces, including a Bruegel. He met artists close to the regime, like Breker, and accumulated eclectic paintings in his homes. Goebbels did the same, even adding a little modern art to his collection before cultural rigidity set in. Other major figures such as Baldur von Schirach, Martin Bormann, and Hans Frank, following fashion, owned a da Vinci. Speer, who dealt with many artists who decorated the buildings he designed and who grew very wealthy during the war, was in the van of this movement. Breker painted his portrait in his 'colossal' style. Speer also commissioned other works from him that he gave to the 'prominent' ('die Prominenten').

Hitler lived in a virtual museum, whether he was in Berlin or the Obersalzberg. He owned Cranachs, Dürers, and Holbeins. His ambition was to collect around 6,755 paintings, including 5,350 old masters, for the great art museum he intended to establish in Linz, where he had gone to school. For his part, Robert Ley acquired enough art to decorate the sites operated by his leisure organization, Kraft durch Freude (KdF), and his home. Goebbels did the same at the ministry of propaganda.

Far from being reluctant to display their possessions or lend them, all these men used their collections to impress their contemporaries. They invited journalists and photographers when they made official acquisitions or official donations. Everyone knew their artistic tastes; they were described in the press and communicated to German citizens and foreigners. Collecting artworks was thus a public activity that was part of the courtly behaviour and sociability of the regime. Hence we must ask ourselves what functions art and the accumulation of artworks had in Nazi society.

In his *Paris Diary* (*Pariser Tagebuch*), Ernst Jünger mentions the belief in the magical power of art prevalent at this time.[37] Hitler sometimes looked at a painting for hours before making a decision. Evidently, painting compensated for a lack of spirituality, allowing him to believe that National Socialist politics was part of a long aesthetic history and that together they bore the country's future. In this sense, art was the guarantee of the regime's permanence. We can thus better understand the philosopher Eric Michaud's use of the expression 'an art for eternity' to describe the aestheticization of Nazi politics.[38] We can probably agree with the historian George Mosse, who was born in Germany and driven out by Nazism, when he says that through art the latter constructed its political religion and that aesthetics helped establish a religious respect for power that ended in politicians becoming the creators of society.[39] For Jonathan Petropoulos, art served as a common language, channelling rivalries among the leaders and providing a standard for measuring an individual's prestige.[40] To these observations, we must add that through its symbolic dimension art was also a way of disseminating a belief that was fundamental for the regime, namely that what really mattered was spiritual and immaterial in nature. All these committed collectors, taking advantage of public sales of Jewish property, goods seized and sequestered in connection with Aryanization, and, after the war began, looting pure and simple, pretended to be enlightened art lovers and helped establish the myth that Nazism was keen on culture, whereas these objects served them as investments or simply as compensation in kind.

Exchanges of gifts thus were part of a system of reward and corruption that explains why only the regime's 'parvenus and profiteers'[41] participated in this mad competition in art collecting. Only those who had rapidly become rich could quickly come up with the sums necessary to make these stupefying purchases and put together collections of several hundred major paintings. However, both those who gave and those who received were well aware of the financial value of the gifts exchanged and knew that beyond the aesthetic pleasure they provided, they represented considerable financial assets. In their view, this very materialistic accumulation was justified by their status as victors and rulers. When they hung their paintings, they were displaying power on their walls.

A Private Kind of Comfort?

If, as is often said, the true luxury is to have lots of room, the Third Reich's elites were not lacking in this regard. Top-level dignitaries who were among the regime's two or three hundred favourite sons all had gigantic main residences, supplemented by secondary residences and country houses. This was not connected solely with the degree of their wealth. They received official housing in addition to their personal property. Hitler, who was a multi-millionaire, had a second apartment in Berlin, another in Munich, and a mountain retreat in the Obersalzberg, which he at first rented and subsequently bought. Göring also owned a home in Berlin as well as others in Munich, the Obersalzberg, and, of course, Karinhall. He had an apartment in the Reichstag before it burned down, and later had a private apartment within the air ministry. Speer had a Berlin residence, a fine chalet in the Obersalzberg, and a country estate. Martin Bormann had comparable properties. The modest Himmler had a house in Berlin, in the chic Dahlem quarter, and a large residence in Gmund, on the shores of the Tegernsee, not far from the property owned by another of Hitler's friends, Max Amann. As for Ribbentrop, he had immense real estate holdings that included country estates and urban apartment buildings.

The extant photographs of the interiors of these properties usually depict the saloons or vast reception rooms.[42] The decoration seems impersonal because it was usually entrusted to professionals with the goal of making a strong impression on visitors. Curiously, the historian finds it difficult to find in these décors, which resemble those of a luxury hotel, the stamp of a master or mistress. The furniture is in the style of the period, which differed from that of the Bauhaus architects. For Walter Gropius or Mies Van der Rohe, furniture was connected with structure and focused on functionality; it tended to be austere. On the contrary, for interior decorators like Paul Ludwig Troost, who had begun the construction of Hitlerian Munich before his sudden death in 1934, furniture had an ideological dimension. It had to be expressive and figurative. It conveyed a tradition. This explains the ambiguity of Nazi furniture, which was torn between the modernist functionality of the 1920s and a return to a rusticity and massive comfort connected with the assertion of the qualities of the Aryan race. These principles were tempered by the rather classic tastes of the traditional elite and the no less classic tastes of the 'new men'. The latter's wealth allowed them to fill their homes with fine furniture, often signed. Thus, for instance, Goebbels and Ribbentrop owned French furniture in the Louis XIV or Louis XV style. Marquetry is one of the distinctive marks of the Nazi bourgeoisie.

Inventories and photographs also indicate that décors were specialized in accord with the ways residences were used. This practice was common to all the international elites, but we must mention the tendency to

celebrate agrarian life under the Third Reich. Urban dwellings where work
and diplomatic representation took place look less rural than the hunting
lodges that were so much in fashion, or the secondary residences that were
sometimes called country houses and sometimes, more modestly, tea
houses or retreats. In the latter case, guests did not have to put up with the
discomfort of pseudo-rustic wooden benches and tables fresh from the
factory.

Comfort did not depend solely on the decorative arts. The homes of
members of the first and second circles of the elite had an immense advantage with respect to those of ordinary people: they were well heated. This
may now make us smile, but we must remember that in the 1930s, heating
was still inadequate in many homes. Wood and coal were expensive, and
often, even in the homes of wealthy men, efforts were made to economize
in this regard. For example, Professor Ferdinand Sauerbruck was the
regime's chief physician, the director of La Charité, the largest hospital in
Berlin, and a member of the Wednesday Society, but when he received
friends he was able to heat adequately only his dining room.[43] Large coal
stoves had to be fed. They went out at night; the temperature fell in even
the most luxurious homes, and in the morning the fire had to be rekindled.
For this reason dignitaries had their homes equipped with central heating.
Göring chose a state-of-the-art boiler with a pump. His supplier, proud of
this success, offered his services to other leaders, using his prominent customer as a selling point.[44] He was obviously counting on their desire to
emulate Göring, and his strategy worked: the Führer asked him to equip
the Berghof. Nevertheless, very large rooms were so hard to heat that fire-
places had to be used.[45] Hitler, who was rather sensitive to the cold, stayed
close to the fire, according to Traudl Junge.[46] Anyone who wanted to keep
warm therefore had to be near him. From all this emerges an image of a
pleasant way of life, a comfort or *Gemütlichkeit* very different from the fru-
gality and Spartan style so highly praised in speeches.

The specialization of rooms depending on the activities and passions to
be pursued in them was characteristic of the homes of the rich and powerful. Hitler and Ribbentrop both had a billiard room. Göring astonished
his guests by showing them a room entirely devoted to a miniature train
layout that he and his nephews loved to play with. André François-Poncet,
the French ambassador, described this in detail: several tracks, trains, and
tunnels intersected on a vast table covered with little replicas of mountains
and rural areas.[47] Wanting to impress the visitor, one of Göring's nephews
asked Göring to start up 'the French train'. The marshal approached the
table and threw several switches. Then François-Poncet saw an aeroplane
attached to a wire fly over the train and drop a small bomb with an explosive cap that made the train go off the rails.

In his residences in Berlin and Karinhall, Göring had a room where films
could be projected. Hitler and Goebbels also had one. Hitler's, which was
in the Berghof, was specially set up by the UFA, whose engineers installed

the latest equipment and regularly brought it up to date. The Führer was one of the first to see films in colour and hear stereophonic sound. This expensive equipment was far more sophisticated than the little Super 8 devices that the upper middle class was beginning to buy. The latter were silent, whereas the Reich's elite enjoyed both sound and image. Like Eva Braun, they might make amateur films, but they used state-of-the-art professional equipment.[48]

These men's taste for cinema was not a recent fad. During the First World War, Hitler had already taken an interest in the seventh art. He often went to the cinema in the early 1920s, and continued to do so. Walther Darré described how much Hitler, accompanied by his comrades, enjoyed going to the cinema and afterward taking everyone to a beer hall. There was nothing surprising in this, but it helped unite a group that was often divided by bitter power struggles.[49] Apart from the pleasure given by the films, going to the cinema served other ends. Hitler, Göring, Goebbels, and other high dignitaries wanted to preview newsreels and, if necessary, to censor them. Their officials pre-selected questionable scenes and asked their opinions. Commentaries on the news usually lasted about ten minutes. During their vacations at the Berghof, those present were asked to give their opinions to the Führer, who often had clearly defined points of view. In the evenings, home cinema was a means of both relaxation and intelligence gathering.

Experimentation with television began in Germany in the 1930s, and in 1935 came the first broadcasts in black and white for collective viewing. The number of receivers was limited, of course, by their cost. But here again, *'noblesse' oblige*: the most powerful had a television and used it to watch entertainment programmes and political speeches, especially those by Goebbels, who was one of the first to forge a rhetoric suitable to television as a medium. Naturally, the whole of social life cannot be reduced to collective admiration of novelties and the advantages that these modes of communication provided. However, cinemas that could hold several dozen spectators and televisions set up in a saloon where they could be watched by groups provided ways of being near a major figure and observing his reactions during a film or concert.

A description of the homes of members of the Third Reich elites would not be complete without mentioning pets. Dogs are always to be seen in films from the period. Sometimes inside, sometimes outside, they seem to incarnate the obedience expected of visitors and of the people in general. Nonetheless, some leaders went still further in their desire to distinguish themselves. Göring and his wife Emmy had a passion for lion cubs. Seven of them served successively as little Edda's playmates.[50] Sometimes they slept with their masters, who were fond of their silky fur. However, the Görings kept the animals only one year before giving them to the Berlin Zoo. They went there occasionally to pet the older lions that had moved from the living room to the cage. The choice of so famous a feline was obviously not determined by sensual pleasure alone. The marshal must have seen in them a validation of his power and felt himself elevated by such an animal. How could we not recall in this connection the example Victor Klemperer chose to illustrate the ironic inverted commas peculiar to the Third Reich's language: 'there is a difference between German cats and "pedigree" cats'.[51]

The luxury of great houses can thus be gauged by a multitude of little privileges that long made the homes of the rich and powerful appear to be reservoirs of pleasure. So many possibilities remained available to Nazi leaders, as they had to their predecessors, thanks to the proximity of the mountains, a lake, or the sea. Just beyond their doorsteps they could sail or ski, and they could take long walks on their own estates. They had numerous rooms where they could receive their friends and have them served like princes. Even great hotels and restaurants found it difficult to provide this kind of luxury.

The Impoverishment of Taste

'Germany is not only a beautiful country, it is also a hospitable country, whose restaurants and inns offer a rich, multi-faceted culinary culture.' That is how Germany is described in a 1937 reference book on tourism policy.[52] The hospitality shown guests in German hotels and restaurants became a genuine political issue. It was not simply a matter of satisfying a few prominent individuals who knew luxury hotels and conducted their business in them. According to the ministry of economics official concerned with restaurants and hotels, they had to see to it that foreigners who came to Germany left feeling good about the National Socialist regime. Thus the goal was to reshape luxury services in the major establishments and bring them into conformity with the dominant ideology.

A book by Franz Tepel that formulates these principles also sought to draw favourable attention to the work of the 280,000 establishments and 900,000 employees active in this sector. Tepel makes three points. The first is that prices are regulated and reasonable. As a result, the middle classes, which had recently begun to go on group excursions, could frequent these establishments. The second was that the standard of quality had been raised everywhere in Germany, and that attention was given to every detail that could increase the guest's comfort. The third point was that there was now a particular style of decoration and cuisine suitable for all Germans, including the wealthiest. The latter dimension is the most important for students of luxury services under the Nazi regime. The theoretical discourse according to which everyone was supposed to be goose-stepping was, as we shall see, very much moderated in practice.

Publicists understood that they had to praise a certain conception of taste that could pass censorship. Franz Tepel emphasized the 'patriotic style' (*Heimatstil*). The hotel rooms depicted in his book have the faux-antique doors and rusticity typical of Germany in the 1930s. The restaurants whose façades he described were housed in old buildings in 'traditional' settings. This was the case for the sumptuous gate of the Mummehaus in Brunswick, the Bratwurstglöcklein in Nuremberg, which was built against the wall of a church and proudly flew a flag bearing a swastika, the colonnade of the Insel Hotel in Constance, the wooden vaults of Auerbachs Keller in Leipzig, the half-timbered walls of the Hotel Riesen in Miltenberg, which was supposed to be the oldest restaurant in Germany, or the fine Renaissance façade of the Hotel Zum Ritter in Heidelberg, which also had a wine cellar (*Weinstube*). The reference to a tradition of German hospitality was supported by the presentation of German products such as wine, beer, and cider, pictures of which filled the book's pages. Even the men depicted had the large moustaches and beer-bellies (*Bierbäuche*) that were considered a mark of virility.

The ideological dimension does not end there. Tepel's book also tried to get connoisseurs to go to 'the movement's houses'. A whole chapter is devoted to the latter. Obviously, there are pictures of the Burgerbräukeller in Munich where Hitler got started, and the Hofbräuhaus, where he gave many speeches. But there is also a picture of the great room in the Berlin Kaiserhof, not nearly so accessible as a beer hall. Tepel mentions the title of Goebbels' book, which illustrates the close relationship between this prestigious establishment and the Führer's destiny: *From the Kaiserhof to the Chancellery.*[53]

In order not to give an outmoded idea of all these establishments whose glory was connected with history, Tepel's book mentions three more modern aspects. First, he praises National Socialist hygiene and the cleanliness of the kitchens. This was a sensitive issue at a time when sanitary inspections were not rigorous. Second, he tries to show a lighter and more dynamic atmosphere by reproducing photographs taken in the daytime. Finally, he is at pains to insist on Germany's modernity. 'An airport without a restaurant would be unthinkable,'[54] claims a caption for a photograph showing the terrace of an airport set with tables on a sunny day, with passengers disembarking in the background.

'Nothing incompatible with the international character of gastronomy', the book asserts, adding:

> If we're intelligent, we will inform ourselves about the specialities of each cuisine. It would be inappropriate to expect to eat a fried herring on the banks of Lake Constance, where whitefish abound, to ask for a Wienerschnitzel in Hamburg, when the speciality of the house is a spicy eel soup, to fail to eat salmon on the Rhine, or in the Black Forest to ignore the delicate fresh trout that pass immediately from boiling water to the table.[55]

Then Tepel reminds his reader that smoked ham comes from Westphalia. All by itself, German cuisine contains a culture and constitutes a world. Could one desire anything else in Adolf Hitler's Reich?

The Baedeker guide seeks to convince visitors to stay in this haven of culinary delights. The choice of establishments, even in large cities, follows the same line. Few foreign restaurants are recommended. At most we find listed an Italian restaurant (in Berlin, Vienna, and Dresden) or a Russian restaurant. The leading guide to the Germanic world for 1938 mentions one Chinese and one Japanese restaurant in Berlin. Among the hotels we find all the luxury establishments well known in high society, including the Vier Jahrezeiten in Munich, the Atlantic in Hamburg, the Bellevue in Dresden, and the Adlon and Kaiserhof in Berlin. The Baedeker has separate listings for wine restaurants, restaurants that offer gourmet menus, and beer halls where the cuisine is less refined. The guide is dominated by a logic of social partition, people being supposed to choose in accord with their means and, theoretically, to prefer local specialities whenever possible.

In actuality, the attraction to strictly German cuisine was not so clear. The major establishments served French wines and champagne, Scotch whisky, and Italian aperitifs. Dinner menus in the great hotels included exotic fruit and imported products such as caviar. Thus it would be an error to conclude from the general tendencies mentioned above that there was a genuine impoverishment of high society's culinary practices. Socialites made concessions to the new ideological doctrine by playing down their taste for French cuisine. We may note in passing that the Baedeker did not recommend any French restaurant in Berlin, although there were several of them.

There was thus a great gap between the official sources and the everyday practices in luxury restaurants. Nonetheless, the programme of nationalizing cuisine took hold as the months went by. Among other indications, we may mention that the dishes suggested in the *Hausbuch für die deutsche Familie* included all the German classics but very few foreign recipes or luxury dishes. This popular nationalism pursued an objective similar to that of fashion. The goal was to reduce food imports, to move toward self-sufficiency, and to promote Germanness even in what people ate. Quantitatively, the strategy was successful, because German agricultural production increased and was able to provide a large number of calories after 1936, though without achieving independence. Above all, the objective was to increase production of pork and potatoes in order to feed the masses. Pork roasted in beer was, after all, the national dish. Such an orientation could not satisfy high society, which was aware of the criteria of international good taste, if only because of its contacts with the diplomatic world. Distinction thus naturally lay in the choice of less common meats such as beef and especially fowl. For their part, gourmets who came from traditional elites accustomed to hunt were able to offer unusual foods: duck, pheasant, and other game. The regime's men did the same.

However, one fact remains. The movement toward populism and demagoguery led Nazi leaders to urge the consumption of economical dishes. Thus the Bavarian weisswurst and pretzels so beloved by the Führer were praised as never before. In a strange turnaround, people situated themselves among the dominant figures of the day by affecting modest tastes.

Large Domestic Staffs

Service in great hotels and restaurants was modelled on that in elegant homes. A large domestic staff lived in the wake of great men. Servants were not the privilege of only the highest dignitaries. Most families participating in some way in high society had at least a minimal domestic staff. All of them enjoyed the services of an all-purpose maid, often called the 'girl' (*Fräulein*) no matter what her age, and often a cook. The Nazi regime upset old habits by introducing anti-Semitic legislation. Jews were discriminated against both as servants and as employers. If they were servants, they were dismissed by the great houses. If they employed servants, they were forbidden to have Aryan servants less than thirty-eight years old, and in post-Anschluss Austria, less than forty-five years old.[56] In addition, obstacles to hiring servants were intended to dissuade qualified personnel from working for Jews. Losing access to domestic servants became a clear sign of a decline in social standing. Inversely, integration into Nazi high society was accompanied by an expansion of the domestic staff.

Domestic employees fulfilled many functions in the Third Reich, as they did elsewhere: housecleaning, cooking, laundry, polishing the silver, and washing the crockery were among their most common tasks. There were in addition other activities depending on the nature of the house: upkeep of the garden on large estates, caring for ponds, livestock, swimming pools, and cars; supervising repairs and improvements made to buildings, and so on. Depending on the family, there might be a governess entrusted with educating the children or a nurse for infants, and specialized servants to care for pets. The leaders themselves required intensive care: their valets prepared their clothes, chambermaids made the beds and cleaned the bathrooms. Their entourage also included servants who could serve a dinner for thirty-eight guests and eminent cooks for evening receptions. Not to mention the guards who protected not only the people involved but also the house and grounds. All these tasks were doubled or tripled when a leader occupied several residences and estates.

Hitler was served royally. In 1939, for his Obersalzberg residence alone sixteen women and one man were employed as 'kitchen employees or chambermaids'. Among them were the Döhrings, a couple who served as veritable managers at Obersalzberg.[57] There were in addition eleven servants (*Diener*). The Führer's personal guard (*Begleitkommando*), his drivers and specialized employees (his projectionist, for instance) added another thirty-two persons to his staff. All these servants did not have the same importance or the same relation to the Führer. The four oldest of them – Vater, Wiebezeck, Horst Seidel and Heinz Sander[58] – were like companions. Things were organized so that each of them had a day off. Two of them were always present to serve at table or carry out orders. A team of servants stayed up until the Führer went to bed. They were on duty between ten and eleven hours a day. Their status differed. Some servants were military men on leave from the army or navy. Others came from the SS or were personally recruited by Hitler, like Kannenberg, who had run a beer hall before being hired along with his wife as a steward at the Berlin chancellery.

One man was always at Hitler's side, his personal valet. The first to have really occupied this office was Karl Wilhelm Krause. He published a report on his activities in 1949. His memoirs make explicit what Hitler expected of his closest servants. First of all, confidentiality. When Krause first began to work for Hitler in July 1934, after he had served coffee in the garden of the chancellery the Führer took him aside and told him to sit down. Then Hitler told him, 'No one must know what you see and hear here. You are under my personal command. It may happen that you will receive an order from me through my adjutants. Otherwise, you are to take orders from no one else.'[59]

Discretion was of fundamental importance to the regime. Wanting to construct his image as a political genius, Hitler gave the press an extremely controlled and totally artificial impression of his private life. The information that filtered out regarding his simplicity, his love of walking, and the pleasure he took in eating popular dishes was carefully chosen to influence public opinion. On the other hand, the Führer concealed his innermost experience, his sex life, as well as that of his collaborators. People guessed at Goebbels' affairs or Martin Bormann's double life, but nothing ever came out because censorship was tight and Hitler personally intervened when one of his intimates was not sufficiently prudent. In all these matters, his staff never betrayed its promise to be discreet. This fidelity was not based solely on fear. It also came from a profound empathy between masters and servants.

Krause was a young sailor when he began his job. He was moved by the concern his boss showed in personally arranging his room in the chancellery and making sure that his bed was long enough for him (Krause was 6 feet 4 inches tall).[60] He had to pay attention to details and anticipate all his master's whims. He knew when to add a spoonful of caviar to liven up a lunch consisting of simple eggs. Hitler regularly gave him bonuses and showed him consideration in countless ways. However, he was disgraced for a rather odd reason, almost on impulse, to judge by his account. During an inspection of the Polish front in 1939, he failed to put enough

Fachinger-brand mineral water in the car. Hitler, exhausted by the trip and the heat, rejected the ordinary water his entourage had been drinking for the past three days. Hitler never forgave Krause this lapse. He refused to see him again, forcing him into a kind of internal exile at the chancellery for more than four months until he finally asked to be allowed to resume active service in the navy. Heinz Linge, already one of Hitler's personal servants, took over Krause's job and stayed with Hitler until the latter's suicide, which he was the first to report.[61]

One point in Krause's testimony is perplexing. According to him, he was one of several sailors proposed as servants for the Führer, who selected him. However, the reasons he mentions for his selection are rather obscure. What particular sensitivity led him to be chosen? Other servants came through the classic channels under Nazism, recommended by close associates or chosen for the zeal they showed in their work. Thus in the case of the Mittlstrassers, serving Hitler was a family matter. Willi and his wife Gretel were porters at the Berghof.[62] Willi, who came from Munich, had joined the NSDAP and met Hitler in 1929. Gretel, who helped him, supervised the chambermaids from 1940 on. She brought in one of her cousins, Anna Plaim. Anna became a confidante of Eva Braun, acting as her personal servant. But in the letters she sent to her parents, she never mentions Eva's name, writing simply 'a lady' ('eine gnädige Frau'), the only authorized formula for referring to the Führer's mistress. Another woman who was a servant at the Platterhof hotel, Therese Linke, soon learned of the secret relationship between Hitler and Eva Braun.[63] Therese had been in Eva's service before the latter was allowed to enter the Berghof and had to make do with a room at the Platterhof. Frau Linke, who soon became a cook, won the confidence of the Nazi leaders and recommended her sister for a chambermaid's position at the Bechstein house. This young woman thus occasionally served Goebbels, the Speers, Hoffmann, and Göring. Göring had a personal valet, Robert Kropp, who accompanied him everywhere, even on walks with his family.[64] Reliable individuals thus made careers in the service of the regime's great men.

At the foreign ministry, Ribbentrop worked out a system to recruit specialists whom he placed in expropriated properties, particularly in the former Czechoslovakia. He had soldiers detached from the army and gave them complementary specialized staffs with certificates provided by their former employers. Most of them had worked in noble houses. At the Schönhof castle, an estate of eight thousand hectares, a veritable administration of ten people managed the forest, the game, and the gardens. An equivalent domestic staff lined up in uniform to salute Ribbentrop on his arrivals and departures, their arms extended in the proper Nazi fashion. At Puste Pole, a hunting lodge in Slovakia, it was also German masters of the hunt who officiated. However, some of the women servants seem to have been recruited locally.

The political distance between the masters of the Nazi regime and their servants seems to have been non-existent. The latter resemble the butler imagined by Kazuo Ishiguro in his novel *The Remains of the Day*. Knowing their master's tastes and desires, the servants acted in such a way as to satisfy them. Thus every week Lilli, the cook at Obersalzberg, made her famous cheesecake and sent it to the Führer, whether he was in Berlin or, later on, at German army headquarters.[65] Krause also explains that when Hitler dined away from home, his task consisted of seeing to it that no bit of meat soiled the Führer's plate. He also had to respect the Führer's ideologico-culinary ukases. After the 'guns or butter' propaganda campaign began, butter could no longer appear on tables at the chancellery. Servants were all the more inclined to respect these wishes because reprimands could be brutal.

A paternalistic relationship grew up. The masters did not limit themselves to giving their attentive servants money. They also gave them birthday and Christmas presents. They helped their families when necessary. Above all, they gave their servants a feeling of participating in history, of being its menials.

Servants were thus put in a peculiar situation under Nazism. As faithful retainers, they were privy to secrets whose importance they did not always realize. Krause was on duty at the Berghof when Chamberlain came to visit and heard what everyone said, particularly about the 'Jewish question'. He declares that his knowledge of the Final Solution was not complete and even repeats the claim made by former Nazis to escape any blame: not Hitler but Bormann and Himmler were responsible for the crime.[66] One might almost think that Hitler liked Jews.

The situation of domestic servants improved during the 1930s. They benefited from the regime's populist moves and from the easing of household chores provided by modern technology – gas cookers, vacuum cleaners, dumbwaiters, steam tables, and so on. They were well fed, because the storerooms of the great houses were never threatened by food shortages. Their working conditions were less demanding, given the possibility of adding additional helpers diverted from public service jobs. Nazism made excellent use of fictitious jobs. Servants were the first to benefit from the luxury and opulence that was experienced in Germany and enjoyed in particular by its dignitaries and elites.

The relationship that bound servants to their masters and to the regime was not ultimately based on their jobs alone. They were like the people of the Reich who were fascinated by what was happening before their eyes and wanted to share in it. Almost forty years later, Heinz Linge still idolized the Führer. Right up to the end, he wrote, he believed in Hitler's genius,[67] thus disproving Napoleon's adage that no one is a great man in the eyes of his servant.

6

Sociabilities in a Totalitarian State

From 1936 on, National Socialism had a firm grip on power. People became aware of this and conceived their social activities accordingly. For high society, the economic situation had improved. The fear of a depression nonetheless remained within the small circle of leaders who had been marked by the First World War. They were convinced that they had to guarantee an abundant food supply for the masses or else subsidize the purchase of foodstuffs in order to be sure that order would be preserved in the great cities. Nonetheless, the elites were imbued with a certain confidence. Hadn't the Olympic Games given the world a favourable image of Germany? Weren't indications of approval flowing in from all sides? The government's strategy of remaining calm seemed to have worked. During the Olympics, Hitler had hypocritically had anti-Semitic signs removed from the streets and advised the more violent periodicals, such as the *Stürmer*, to tone down their polemics. He gave the International Olympic Committee guarantees that didn't last beyond the duration of the games themselves. Diplomats serving in Berlin allowed themselves to be taken in by this seductive torpor. If a few of them had no illusions regarding the regime, they all thought that at least the Nazis knew how to throw a party.

Political adversaries and marginal people were seen from the new National Socialist perspective. These sources of national weakness had to be eliminated. To get rid of them, the concentration camps seemed to the elites a simple solution. These places, it was often thought, were no different from the penal colonies to which the French relegated gangsters and repeat offenders. In their ignorance, people imagined that the camps were less violent than their Soviet analogues in the Gulag. A naïve but widespread view supposed that the 'new Germany' had managed to restore the old order and improve it.

This feeling of the situation's normality and even banality was reinforced by the pursuit of routine activities in well-off groups. The latter provided, along with a large number of merchants, employees, and workers, the fertile basis of Hitler's support. For them, Germany was defending a way of life, a culture (one could no longer speak of a 'civilization' since the NSDAP's savage attacks on that idea during its rise to power), an art of living, and a courtesy inherited from the age of Bismarck. However, the practices that had been the glory of German culture were in decline. New civil relationships were emerging that strengthened the impact of politics on social relations and changed the contours of high society.

The Eclipse of the Salons

Nicolaus Sombart was born on 10 May 1923. His father, the private adviser Werner Sombart, was a professor at the Friedrich-Wilhelm Universität, the great Berlin university now known under the name of Humboldt. The Sombarts were of noble descent. Nicolaus's mother, Corina Sombart, came from a German-Romanian aristocratic family. She held a salon that her son observed while still young. He remembered what he saw and in 1983 published a book in praise of it.[1] This inside account through the eyes of a child who became an adult full of nostalgia nonetheless lucidly underlines the ephemeral character of this world.

According to Nicolaus Sombart, a salon presupposes an intelligent woman who gathers around herself a group in which each member tries to seduce the hostess as part of a noble intellectual joust. Naturally, this requires culture and the art of conversation. Young Nicolaus saw this when his mother sent out invitations. One of the saloons in Corina Sombart's home was green and rather large, while the other was red and might have been her boudoir, thus allowing her to manipulate the number of guests in order to create a certain atmosphere. The expanded circle of those who regularly frequented this house numbered about a hundred. There were rich travellers like André Germain, the heir of the founder of the Crédit Lyonnais bank; the director of the Berlin Cultural Institute, Eugène Susini; ambassadors like Pierre de Margerie, his wife Ysabelle, and later his successor, André François-Poncet; the Cerrutis (Elisabetta, Cerruti's wife, showed Nicolaus around the brand new Italian legation); the Comnène-Petrescus from Romania; university colleagues like Carl Schmitt (the director of the association of National Socialist jurists), Jens Jessen, and Karl August Emge (whom Sombart describes as a socialite because he was welcome in all the academies); Russian refugees, who were sometimes impoverished and received aid from the Sombarts; anti-Stalinist Georgians like Gigol Robakidse, who supported Hitler; Chinese nationalists; and figures in classical Berlin such as Helene von Nostiz, Hindenburg's niece. Before 1933, the house also received Jews, including Fritz Andreae, who had married Edith Rathenau. After the Nazis took power, Jews were seen less often and finally disappeared into emigration, clandestinity, or death.

Salon life took place chiefly in the afternoon, which did not prevent the Sombarts from inviting people to dinner in the evening. Tea was the usual beverage, often drunk with a shot of rum as it was in Russia before 1917. No cocktails were served, Nicolaus Sombart explains, until his mother decided to add one she had discovered at the Romanian embassy: gin, champagne, and grapefruit juice in equal quantities.

These get-togethers made it possible to discuss matters both as a group and separately. The subjects of these discussions included the theatre, literature, history, and politics. Regarding Hitler, the opinion expressed by André Germain, who was nonetheless a fanatical admirer of the SS, made a strong impression on the young Sombart:

> He hated Hitler, about whom he could tell the craziest stories, things that seemed at the time completely incredible, and that research on Hitler has still not totally utilized. But he had good sources (his chauffeur knew the chauffeur of a Nazi dignitary, who in turn, etc.). He claimed that Hitler had male lovers (which Rauschning also says), urinated in women's mouths, had killed his niece, and that other women, including Unity Mitford, had committed suicide because they couldn't bear his perversity . . . *Et j'en passe* [and I could go on].[2]

Germain redeemed his gossiping by reading to the group poems by Baudelaire, Verlaine, and Heredia.

Poetry and the arts were in fact at the heart of the passions of this period. The Sombarts lived on the border between an old world in which government was imbued with culture through the salons, on the one hand, and the National Socialist period, in which culture affected the state directly and the state supported it so long as it corresponded to its ideological objectives. Corina Sombart's salon did not attract the masters of the Third Reich, but those who had governed a decade earlier met there, and Professor Sombart maintained respectful relationships with foreign leaders such as Mussolini.

The salon milieu had lost its political function. Moreover, the youth activities imposed by the regime with increasing insistence deprived it of opportunities for recruitment and socialization. In many cases, mobilization around the party led men to prefer places that might more directly affect their advancement. Above all, none of the great ladies of the Nazi regime really held a salon – not Emmy Göring, not Magda Goebbels, and especially not Frau Bormann. In the Goebbels family Joseph set the tone and issued invitations. Frau von Papen and Frau von Neurath tried their hands at being the queen of a salon, but the changes in their husbands' political fortunes put an end to these attempts. Other wives held parties, organized dinners and balls, staged shows, and participated in charitable activities. However, afternoons were no longer used for the earlier friendly get-togethers and noble verbal jousting. The international dimension of salon culture probably conflicted with Nazi supervision of knowledge and relationships. But more fundamentally their diminished visibility proceeded from a gradual shift towards public action that hobbled private sociabilities.

Barbara de Sevin, a young woman whose grandfather was the Duke of Baden, analysed this development on the basis of Hindenburg's case.[3] Her account, written in 1940, won a Harvard University prize for the quality of its research and the acuity of its comments on everyday life. She was seventeen years old when she began her studies in Heidelberg; she lived with an aunt in a large house across the river from the castle. Her aunt regularly received a small group of young people among whom Barbara met Nazi enthusiasts who wore uniforms and sabres as if they were embracing a military career or wanted to show that they belonged to a student club that still practised duels. However, her family, including her aunt (who happened, ironically, to also bear the name Hess), were democrats attached to the republic. The young Nazis were not taken seriously. They were seen chiefly as boys who liked to be active and engage in sports. Barbara was more impressed by the relationships she formed in cafés, where professors and students mingled and continued discussions begun in seminars. She made fun of teachers who found it natural that female students serve tables in order to prepare for their future lives as mothers.[4] There she also met Professor Hecker, who was developing a theory attacking Freemasons, and Professor von Weizsäcker, whose psychology courses she had attended. Barbara liked student sociability and group get-togethers in cafes. In them she saw the two dimensions of social life – feelings and a sense of intimacy trying to find its way in the group, on the one hand, and, on the other, indoctrination, which she considered rather crude.

Then, like many young people of her generation, she joined a party association, the BDM. This was the NSDAP's youth organization for girls, and the obligations membership entailed led her to put her studies on the back burner and pursue a course of quasi-military training, along with all its vexations, rivalries, and humiliations. She noted the enthusiasm of a few ambitious girls and her fellow students' self-sacrifice. She also saw that the model proposed by the BDM's leaders was that of the elegant wife. Moreover, the Nazi leaders she met, Gisela Brettschneider and Gertrud Scholtz-Klink, seemed to her elegant and well groomed. Boys, on the other hand, joined organizations intended for students or entered the armed forces.

Heidelberg thus lost its scholarly air and quiet relationships in middle-class homes and cafés. Social life in the city was regulated by leaves and school holidays. During vacations, it became a little more lively. However, students usually had to go away with their organizations to prepare themselves for a struggle whose importance they sensed. Intellectual, vital Heidelberg waited dejectedly for them to return. Then the city's streets were suddenly filled with young people in uniform who had come back from their youthful labours and who found it difficult to mix with older relatives and property owners. Barbara could not long endure this atmosphere. She took advantage of an opportunity to study abroad that allowed her to emigrate, first to England and then to the United States.

Many German cities experienced similar changes. In the Weimar of the early days of Nazism, the symbolic confrontation between an old world of notables exercising quiet influence and a new Germany with its excited manners and collective dramas is perceptible. As the capital of Thuringia, Weimar, with its fifty-six thousand inhabitants, was less provincial than might be thought. Emmy Sonneman, Göring's future wife, had been recruited by the national theatre in 1930. She shared her dressing room with an actress of Austrian Slavic origin, Franziska Schubert. Franziska later described the social relationships one could establish in Weimar.[5] Although they were rivals, the two actresses often went with their theatre friends to have a drink at the Goldenen Adler after performances. Hans Severus Ziegler, who had been named director of the theatre and was such a close friend of Hitler's that he accompanied him on his escapes to Bayreuth, sometimes took part in these outings. Franziska Schubert was present when Emmy Sonneman and Hermann Göring met in 1932. She talked with Göring when he went to see Emmy in her dressing room and found him likeable and open. She describes Emmy herself as 'sentimental and a salon lady'.[6] As Göring's fiancée, Emmy was finally engaged by a theatre in Berlin.

Franziska Schubert remained in Weimar, where she moved into a new apartment near the park. One of her neighbours was the old Princess zu Wied, who took a liking to her. Franziska henceforth frequented the Princess's salon, where Spanish grapes were served under the trees in the garden and local personages such as Professor Deetjen were received. She also visited Baroness Münchhausen, who was over eighty years old and whose late husband had been a diplomat. This delicious old lady lived in a little house full of antique furniture and paintings by old masters hung at random and without any particular taste: portraits, landscapes, oriental genre scenes. In this overloaded atmosphere guests talked for hours. This circle of old Weimarians who lived like villagers is sufficiently representative of declining salon life. This is indicated by Franziska's account, which accents the most powerful aspects of her relationships: being invited to great events by Berlin businessmen, organizing shows with the Society of the Friends of Shakespeare. Her participation in the local scene and her friendships at the national level[7] did not, however, allow her to escape her status as a Slav. Soon she was obliged to leave the stage. She first went to Austria and then took refuge in Switzerland in 1939.

Cosmopolitan society, which was tolerant and generous, was broken up under Nazism. The salons, youth groups such as the Burschenschaften and the Schlagende Verbindungen, fraternities that served to give structure to networks of influence in universities before 1914, lost their sway.

Substitutes for them persisted as sources more of pleasure than of power and were in addition subject to prohibitions intended to favour Nazi youth organizations. Even duelling suffered from the regime's grip. Hitler took several steps that proscribed it in the SS, the SA, the NSDAP, and soon the army, unless he had given his express permission. Thus duels became rarer. A similar trend can be observed in other European countries, such a practice seeming absurd after the bloody fighting of the Great War. However, all modes of social relationship did not meet with the same fate. Peaceful events connected with groups essential for the regime such as the nobility retained an advantageous situation until the Second World War – no doubt because a nationalist conception of social life was imposed through the aristocracy.

The Nobility's Social Life Goes On

On close inspection, we see that the nobility's organizations were hardly affected by the Nazi regime, far from it.[8] If the Herrenklub lost its political function, the Union Klub and the Deutsche Adelsgenossenschaft (DAG) prospered. The latter organization, converted to racism and the National Socialist brand of nationalism, saw its periodical, the *Deutsches Adelsblatt*, swell with increased advertising after 1935. Its members continued their social life with regularity between 1933 and 1940 and did not change their habits.

The DAG's most important event was the annual meeting in each regional headquarters. The club's local official presented a report on activities, the state of the club's finances, and the prospects for expansion. New members were appointed to the board. Associative life seems to have been fairly consensual. Afterward, those present attended a dinner and danced. There was something ritualistic about this unchangeable organization that recalled the old order.

The reports published in the *Deutsches Adelsblatt* illustrate the persistence of aristocratic festive customs. In each issue, a dozen events were announced or described. In the number for 1 January 1933, which came out just before the Nazis took power, the club official for the Kurmark district reported on a social event and expressed 'the joy and honour' that it took place in the presence of 'Her Royal Majesty the Crown Princess'.[9] This event, which had been held on 9 December 1932 at Berlin's Esplanade Hotel, which was often used on such occasions, had been attended not only by various representatives of the royal family, but also by descendants of the princely families of Weimar, Meinigen, Lippe, and Rudolfstadt. The marshal of the nobility (the president of the DAG), Prince Bentheim-Tecklenburg, and his wife were present; the prince had just been appointed to this post, and the event allowed him to assert his new role. He probably wrote the report, which went on to say: 'After dinner, the dancing began. It could be noted that the waltz was once again danced with pleasure, even by young people, and that the difficult figures of the old quadrilles were dominant: a conscious resumption of the forms adopted in pre-war polite society.'

A tombola followed, for which the prizes had been donated by owners of vineyards on the Rhine as well as by owners of large farms in Brandenburg and Hesse. The sugar industries, the wine-makers' association, and the Schultheiss brewery were thanked, as were all those throughout Germany who had bought tickets to increase the funds available to the DAG's office of social aid. The success of the event was assured by the participation of more than the five hundred noble families in the Kurmark district.

This traditional organization's attachment to National Socialism came out at times, to judge by Baroness von Bibra's account of the event held on the evening of 7 March 1936 at Weimar's Fürstenhof Hotel. The Thuringian branch expressed its satisfaction with the re-established independence of the German army and at the invitation of Herr von Brietenbuch gave three 'Sieg Heil!' cheers for the Führer. Appointments followed, notably that of Marshal von Trotha as head of the local branch. This part of the programme was enlivened by Count Dürkheim-Jassen's report entitled 'The German Nobility's Thoughts about the New Germany'.[10] The emphasis put on the political dimension was explicit, whereas before the Nazis came to power positions were less clear-cut. Following dinner, about two hundred people stayed for a long time talking and dancing. As was often the case, the invitation recommended that cars pick up the guests at about 1 a.m.

In 1939, the nobles of the Schleswig-Holstein district gathered on 13 January for a party held at the Kiel yacht club. Kiel was a port heavily used by the navy and the site of an association that brought together nobles from northern Germany. That evening, about eighty men and women from the local aristocracy joyously celebrated this occasion and danced to 'true classical music',[11] as the official in charge, von Ruhmohr-Rundhof, put it. A few days later, in the Wurtemberg-Hohenzollern district, a party was organized by the crown prince of Hohenlohe at the Maquardt Hotel that was attended by 'a large number of officers in the Wehrmacht'. These comments on participants are scarcely incompatible with what aristocratic families might have written some time earlier, or even a few years later. During these events limited to their own group and imbued with nostalgia, they continued to reject a certain form of modernity. Outside them, the association's doctrine followed the evolution of the regime quite closely, bearing witness to the symbiotic relation between this traditional elite and Nazism.

Surprisingly, the DAG did not explicitly emphasize its dependency, apart from its open letters to Hitler and its addresses to the government, notably on the occasion of 'Green Week', a sort of agricultural show that was held every year at Berlin's fairgrounds. Its participation in the regime was shown only by theoretical articles and tacit signs of agreement. One might have expected membership in the SS or the SA to be mentioned more often in a milieu where it was frequent.

Among other activities, we should examine 'tea parties', because they show how much this custom had entered into German habits. They involved first of all ladies like those in the Silesian city of Breslau who regularly met for exclusively feminine tea parties that were announced in the *Deutsches Adelsblatt*.[12] A few gentlemen also used the term 'teas' in referring to meetings set up for the purpose of listening to lecturers. Lectures were in fact the DAG's main intellectual activity. Every year it organized a colloquium on subjects relating to social and aristocratic life. This national event was one of the relatively rare occasions on which members from all over Germany gathered together. However, reports do not describe in detail the entertainments that must have accompanied them.

Each district arranged its own talks. On 14 March 1936, the Magdeburg-Anhalt office held a meeting in Wenigrode's 'House of God' at which the main attraction was a talk by Dr Schöning on tombs and monuments to the dead throughout the world. People attending the lecture were expected to wear morning dress or dark suits. The lecture was accompanied by slides showing 'the monument in Tannenberg, our imperial monument, and the Niederwald monument – the dramatic symbol of German unity and power that has such special meaning in these days of great historical events'.[13]

The German nobility thus showed no ideological divergence from the regime, whose racism, militarism, bellicosity, and imperial nostalgia it shared, as we have seen, but it cultivated its own peculiar sphere. On certain occasions this slight discrepancy manifested itself. Thus when the Bavarian crown prince married, he invited the entire European aristocracy to the wedding, which was held in the Nymphenburg castle. Dethroned sovereigns such as the Count of Paris and his wife attended this ceremony, which lasted three days. King Alfonso XIII of Spain mischievously took his European nieces and cousins to the cinema.[14] The Count of Paris angered his hosts by making fun of the little paper napkins printed with the arms of the Bavarian royal family. In this good-natured atmosphere – where competition to distinguish oneself nonetheless broke through, as we see – no one mentioned any high Nazi dignitaries. It was as if there were a gap between this old world and current politics.

However, Hitler personally entertained close relations with German royalty. The emperor's wife, 'Empress' Hermine, corresponded with him, writing to tell him, for instance, about her youngest daughter Henriette's engagement.[15] For his part the emperor sent Hitler letters congratulating him on his successes. The crown prince, not to be outdone, visited Hitler and wished him well. The Führer's staff also supported the Princess of

Brunswick's idyll with the Greek crown prince.[16] In addition, noble families asked Hitler to be their children's godfather. There was, for example, Count von der Goltz, who asked Hitler to hold his eighth child at the baptismal font.[17] Here as elsewhere under Nazism, personal connections upset the general tendencies. The nobility preserved its specificity while at the same time supporting the regime, but many of its members entertained close relationships with men who had risen through political activity alone. The Nazis received them indulgently because they planned to inherit the chivalric experience and transform it in accord with their own views. Thus they emphasised this form of distinction in order to show off the regime's new elites.

The Transfer of Signs of Distinction

Access to knightly orders had been blocked by the official abolition of the empire and the nobility. Nonetheless, some had continued their activity. Thus the order of Saxe-Coburg Gotha, which had admitted Adolf Hitler, could no longer accept new members,[18] but it was not considered subversive and was not persecuted. On the contrary, the model of knightly orders flourished in one of the regime's key institutions, the SS. Himmler wanted to make the latter a new nobility, a modern knighthood, and modelled it on what he imagined to be the ancient military-religious orders.[19] In the propaganda he sent out, the SS was associated with medieval symbolism and the heavy combat sword. He thought membership in the SS should be granted as a distinction as one moved up the administrative ladder, and in 1938 he persuaded Ribbentrop, who was very keen on this order, to make it the framework for the theoretical training of German diplomats. It was not a matter of creating a kind of Iron Cross for civilians, but rather of bringing the most valiant men in the society into a single large elite. This message went over so well that some of Himmler's political friends were prepared to pay large sums for an important position in the SS. This was the case for Kurt Freiherr von Schröder.[20] One of those who supported Hitler's rise to power, he then organized the whole system of covert financing for the SS; in particular, he came up with the idea of creating a special account managed by Reichsführer Himmler alone, to which the great German banks made annual contributions and provided exceptional funds when needed. In 1936, he was appointed to the highest rank in the SS as a reward for his loyal service.

The taste for honours was such that the Nazi party also created its own badge that could be attached to one's coat like a military decoration: the golden insignia of the Nazi party. The latter was awarded on the basis of the candidate's dossier. He had to prove that he had been a member of the party for at least ten years. The hundred thousand who had joined first automatically received the badge. This insignia played an important role in social relationships. It inspired respect, rather as did the Legion of Honour medal at the same period. One had to pay for one's insignias. Julius Schaub, who ordered four, had to pay six marks. He lost one on a trip, but got it back when a zealous comrade returned it to the NSDAP secretariat.[21] The photographer Heinrich Hoffmann, the only man who it was said could always make the Führer laugh, also lost his insignia and also got it back.[22] One can imagine that anyone who stole this little insignia was risking severe punishment.

The Bruckmanns were not forgotten when these party honours were handed out. Their membership in the party was backdated to 1925 and they were given a membership number below 100 (the number of members when the party was refounded in 1925) so that they could be automatically awarded the party insignia. The Bechsteins were obliged to intrigue in order to acquire this mark of membership in the elite. Not having ever previously been members of the party, they had no right to it. But Hitler was their personal friend and big Liselotte, their daughter, had not flirted with him in vain. In 1935, the family requested this honour.[23] After Hitler intervened, claiming that they had paid him their membership fees personally, the party was forced to give them a card with an old number so that they could be awarded the insignia. Better yet, a letter explained that they were to be exempted from the obligation to make contributions corresponding to the repurchase of annuities connected with party membership.[24] This document indicates the clear existence of a trade in decorations in exchange for a payment made to the party.[25] This makes us wonder about the role of the party as a central element of the National Socialist government in terms of totalitarian theory. The latter requires qualification, since what seems the determining factor in this competition for honours is more the clientelist and ideological relationship with the leaders than the structure of the party itself. The latter is one instrument among others and throws light on social relationships. Other old friends of Hitler benefited from similar signs of recognition, as did the Baron Kirdorf before his death.

On the other hand, the party's younger members had to wait until they had really proven themselves before acquiring their decorations. Although he was one of Hitler's adjutants, Albert Bormann didn't get his until 1938.[26] Wilhelm Schaub (unrelated to Julius Schaub) couldn't even present his claim.[27] He fought with the party secretariat, providing certificates and letters of recommendation to win his case. Julius Schaub's wife also tried to have the insignia awarded to her.[28] She didn't get it until the Gauleiter of Saxony intervened on her behalf. He reminded party officials that she was married to Julius Schaub, and that made everything easier. Having become the object of intrigues and desires, the insignia was no longer reserved for party receptions. It was worn everywhere, even on suits and evening clothes. It ended up interfering with civilian relationships, perhaps even more than uniforms, on which the rank displayed

Group photo, New Year's Eve, 1938. Hitler is surrounded by his friends. From left to right in the first row we see Heinrich Hoffmann, Hitler's accomplice and friend, Gretl Braun, who in 1934 married Hitler's SS aide-de-camp Hermann Fegelein, Karl Brandt, the Führer's primary personal physician (the other personal physician, Theo Morell, is standing with his wife just behind Hitler), Anni Brandt, Philipp Bouhler, Gerda Bormann, Adolf Hitler, Eva Braun, Martin Bormann, holding the arm of one of the Führer's personal secretaries, Gerda Christian. In the second row, third from left Albert Speer, then rising fast; at the right end of the row, Karl Krause, Hitler's valet and behind him, the steward at the chancellery, the former restaurateur Willy Kannenberg. The group is posing on the steps of the main drawing room at the Berghof. © Collection Roger-Viollet

Hitler's meetings with the diplomatic corps were given particular attention. Here, at the chancellery in 1934, just behind the Führer, who is reading his speech, which was translated and distributed in English, French, and Spanish, we see the minister for foreign affairs, von Neurath, also wearing a suit, and sporting his decorations. To his left, his portfolio in his hand, the presidency's state secretary, Otto Meissner, one of those who played a major role in personalizing the Reich's diplomatic messages. With them, the bureau chiefs at the foreign ministry. © Collection Roger-Viollet

Adolf Hitler receives the Duke and Duchess of Windsor at the Berghof, during their official visit to Germany in 1937. The Reich's most important figures used these famous travellers to promote their doctrine. Göring received them at Karinhall, his residence in the forest. © Collection Roger-Viollet

Reception at the home of the minister of foreign affairs, Joachim von Ribbentrop, 22 May 1939. During the show given in the garden, Hitler is seated in the centre. In the first row, from left to right, we see Göring, Annelies von Ribbentrop, the minister's wife, then, next to Hitler, the actress Olga Chekhova. Behind Göring, the Japanese ambassador, Hiroshi Oshima, and behind Hitler, Gertrud Scholtz-Klink, the head of the women's organizations, and General Wilhelm Keitel of the General Staff, nicknamed Lakeitel (the lackey) by his subordinates because of his obsequiousness. © akg-images/Ullstein Bild

25 August 1938, during the state visit by Admiral Horthy, the leader of Hungary, and his wife (standing to Hitler's left). The evening was devoted to Wagner's *Lohengrin*. In the lobby of the Berlin State Opera, a space set off by chairs and servants in livery was reserved for VIPs. Here, Frau Göring, wrapped in her stole, fulfils her function as the Reich's first lady, while Frau Ribbentrop remains in the background, behind Hitler. © Collection of the Auswärtiges Amt (Berlin)

Hitler enters his loge at the Opera and the audience salutes him. In the loge of honour, Emmy Göring and her husband Hermann are surrounded by other dignitaries. On the occasion of the second annual German Theatre Festival, Hitler decided to go to Hamburg to hear Wilhelm Furtwängler's interpretation of Wagner's *Die Meistersinger*, presented on 23 June, 1935.
© Hulton-Deutsch collection / Corbis

Four loci of modernity under the Third Reich: top, two celebrities at the diplomatic parties held in the ballroom at the Rot-Weiss, the oldest and most fashionable of the tennis clubs, Fernanda, Duchess of Villarosa, and Count Hermann Metternich, in 1934; centre-left, the Opera Ball (11 January 1936), with tables in the loges of honour; centre-right, the Press Ball (February 1938), in the marble hall at the Zoo; and bottom, the Golf Ball, held at the Hotel Esplanade near the Potsdamer Platz, not far from the chancellery. © Ullstein Bild/Roger-Viollet

Hitler at Grevenburg Castle, 15 January 1936, on the occasion of the elections in the Länder. To the right of Hitler, from back to front, Hitler's host, Baron von Oeynhausen, Julius Schaub, Hitler's adjutant, Heinrich Hoffmann., and Otto Dietrich (seated). To the left of Hitler, the baron's mother, seated with her back to the camera, the group leader Heinrich Sauer, the head of Hitler's Adjudantur, Wilhelm Brückner, the Baroness von Oeynhausen (seated), and Julius Schreck, Hitler's driver, next to the fireplace. © Ullstein Bild/Roger-Viollet

The foreign minister, Joachim von Ribbentrop, leaving one of his hunting estates. The servants have come to salute him. Note, to the right, behind the Mercedes, the two officials responsible for the estate and for the game.
© Collection of the Auswärtiges Amt (Berlin)

During a hunting party, the head of protocol, Alexander von Dörnberg, takes a rest. Dörnberg managed all the foreign minister's hunting parties, and sometimes used them to private ends. More often, his role consisted in seeing to it that foreign guests, such as Count Ciano, were able to indulge in their passion.
© Collection of the Auswärtiges Amt (Berlin)

A moment of relaxation on the Chiemsee, during a trip to Bavaria in the summer of 1934. Among the nymphs, wearing a jacket over her shoulders, Eva Braun.
© Collection Roger-Viollet

A typical table set for a gala dinner. Here, the official dinner following the signature of the Munich accords in 1938. The room was dominated by a huge chandelier. The document is included in the albums of the head of protocol. Was it to preserve a souvenir of a diplomatic triumph or to serve as a model for other events?

impressed chiefly other members of the same corps. For that very reason, high officials in the SS didn't care a fig about it.[29]

The distinction provided by this insignia can be seen in official photographs. It accompanies other accessories bearing the party's initials: belts, ties, scarves, hats, and watches. It therefore overqualified an individual, as if there were no limit to zeal and one always had to mark one's commitment in order to be a true Nazi. As we shall see, even places traditionally considered marginal did not escape the ardour of some individuals who were eager to establish the new moral order everywhere.

The Margins, Night, and Pleasure

So many post-war films have shown the Nazis' perversity through their sex lives and the depravity of their private lives that an erroneous image of the regime has been created. If we think of Visconti's *The Damned*, we immediately remember the storm troopers on the shores of the Tegernsee and their bacchanalia. In 1973, Liliana Cavani's *The Night Porter* created a scandal because it posited the existence of an erotic connection between tormentor and victim. The success of this film kindled the imagination of other filmmakers. Don Edmonds took up the idea of an erotic relation in a concentration camp, attributing the sadist's role to a woman in the film he directed the following year, *Ilsa – She-Wolf of the SS*. This gave rise to a cinematic genre known as 'Nazi porn'. A dozen Italian productions, widely shown in Europe and the United States, mined this vein: *SS Experiment Camp* (Sergio Garone, 1976), *L'ultima orgia del Terzo Reich* (Cesare Canevari, 1977), *La bestia in calore* (Luigi Batzella, 1977), also distributed under the title *SS Hell Camp*, and so on. The best known of these films was adapted from an English novel by Tino Brass, *Salon Kitty* (1977). The result of all this was an image of Nazism as a regime in which sexual relations were unrestrained, general, obsessive, and had a sado-masochistic aspect.

Studies using poorly understood psychology have supported this common idea,[30] notably those by Wilhelm Reich, who based his analysis, however, on sexual repression in bourgeois societies.[31] The question of sex was at the heart of some historical inquiries of varying quality written after the war.[32] Great scholars debated the number of Hitler's testicles.[33] Some claimed that he had only one, and that this was the source of his violence and political madness. Humorously, Hans-Ulrich Wehler, one of the leading German social historians, wrote that even if Hitler had had three testicles that would not have changed the general course of events.[34] He thus rejected this kind of ridiculous biological and sexual monocausality and its narrow perspective on society. Moreover, the diaries of Hitler's four physicians contradict hypotheses regarding Hitler's morphological abnormality.[35]

Other historians or writers of memoirs have sought in homosexuality the source of German society's malaise in the early twentieth century.[36] According to these authors, the bellicose and masculine ideas that emerged from nationalism suggested that warriors could get along without women except for purposes of reproduction. The language of extremist groups in the second half of the twentieth century is in fact already found in the Nazi theory of the division of labour: men produce and fight, women have children and serve. This ideology explained the priority given to relations between men that oscillated between friendship and love. The male elites are supposed to have been largely imbued with this notion. This claim is partly justified, but does not really explain either the structure of power imagined by the Nazis, or their maniacal anti-Semitism, or especially their brutal repression of homosexuality – unless we limit ourselves to debatable psychological theories and assume that all the elites lived with a deep self-hatred. In a curious book, Lothar Machtan attempted an even more personalized interpretation, arguing that Hitler was a homosexual right to the end and that he had never had a real relationship with a woman.[37] The extravagance of this claim did a disservice to a book that in other respects threw new light on blackmail in the Third Reich. Machtan's argument fails precisely on the question whether a head of state's conjectured private life produces major effects on the conduct of political affairs: in his view the deportation of homosexuals is explained by Hitler's desire to do away with witnesses to his perversions. In short, Machtan's thesis subscribes to the notion that Nazism was a period of excess and sexual deviancy.[38]

The truth is quite the opposite. Under National Socialism, Germany experienced a harsh era of moral order. The leaders' ambition was to purge the country of everyone who did not conform to an ideal hammered upon by propaganda: Aryan, healthy, fanatical, and useful to society. All those who did not meet these requirements were considered parasites: non-Aryans, the infirm, the half-hearted, the useless. As Florence Tamagne has shown, many European scientists, and especially German scientists, regarded homosexuality as a biological illness.[39] It threatened to weaken the race; therefore it had to be fought. This widespread conception led the regime to change the Weimar Republic's tolerant legislation (paragraph 175 of the penal code), creating in 1935 a special group within the vice squad charged with tracking down homosexuals, prosecuting those who were denounced or caught in the act, and sending them to prison or, later, to concentration camps. Even Nazi leaders who were homosexuals had to be very discreet. Despite their power, they could not get away with scandalous behaviour in public. A leader who was caught in the act or denounced by one of his subordinates, which happened even in the SS, might be deported or, if he had solid backing and was useful to the regime, at least sidelined. From this time on began a zealous competition to conform that caused homosexuals to retreat into secrecy.

This change had a considerable impact on life in high society. Under the Weimar Republic, Berlin had become a kind of refuge for homosexuals from all over the world. Restaurants, nightclubs, and cabarets sometimes catered exclusively to customers from this milieu. By 1937, guides to Berlin nightlife no longer listed a single gay establishment. No mention of the subject filtered out. Everyone who might be subject to the legislation retreated into obscurity.

At the end of the 1920s, lesbians could safely go out in public and began to attract the attention of a well-developed popular press. Several theatre personalities were known for their sexual tastes. The most famous of the German female cabaret performers, Claire Waldoff, whose career had taken off during the First World War because of her troop songs, lived with her female lover Olly. In the music hall milieu, this was known and the period was so tolerant that it bothered no one. Famous for her mordant irony and her criticism of politicians, in 1933 she included in her repertory a song called the 'Hermannlied'. One of its verses mocked medals and decorations that looked like Christmas garlands, Hermann's bedecked belly always being the most prominent:

A garland on the left, a garland on the right
And his belly's so big his belt is tight
Of Prussia he's the boss
And Hermann is his name[40]

Audiences had no difficulty in recognizing Hermann Göring in this ironic portrait. The song made Waldoff's tour in the spring of 1933 a triumph, audiences seeing it as a sign of opposition. She was frightened by this popularity, and to pre-empt a violent reaction she wrote to Göring to ask if the song was a problem. He replied with a short note saying that there was no reason why she shouldn't continue to perform her ritornello. Thus Waldoff kept the song in her repertory, but prudently added a verse to the refrain that alluded to the minister's career: 'And for aeroplanes, he's the champ / Hermann is his name.'[41]

Under the impetus of this success, her tour returned to old hits and military marches that had become popular again. Waldoff was the object of several attacks and official complaints filed by officials of the Kampfbundes für deutsche Kultur (Battle League for German culture) founded by Rosenberg in January 1934, whose goal was to strengthen the Nazis' control over culture. German theatrical authorities under the direction of State Commissioner Hans Hinkel, who had been appointed by Goebbels, had been granted full powers by the law of May 1934. However, they did not prevent Waldoff from performing, probably in part to show Rosenberg that his power was limited, but also because she was very popular. Nonetheless, Waldoff had to stop using works written by Jewish authors or composers and she could no longer employ non-Aryan musicians. She took greater care to conceal her private life for fear that some zealous party member, appalled by her daring songs, might look into her love relationships. On tour, she and her lover reserved separate rooms at hotels, and forced themselves to eat their breakfasts separately, one in the hotel restaurant, the other in her room. Waldoff also toned down the sexual allusions in her songs and relied on different comic effects. The moral pressure took the edge off her ability to resist. As Hannah Arendt explained, the homosexual 'vice' that aroused curiosity under the Weimar Republic was now considered a scourge from which high society wanted to free itself.[42] While remaining a celebrity, Waldoff was marginalized and obliged to live in a strange affective secrecy.

The cabaret milieu was not the only one suspected of sexual deviation. The politics of decency also attacked pornography, which was vaguely defined. Berlin establishments like the Katakombe in the Lutherstrasse and the Tingel-Tangel in the Kantstrasse were closed in 1935, having been judged licentious and seditious. Artists such as Heinrich Giessen and Rudolf Platte were arrested and put in camps because they were considered indecent. Some places changed owners and switched over, like the Künstlerspiel in Uhlandstrasse, which was redecorated in black and brown.

Music hall numbers had henceforth to pass before a censorship committee. This affected all kinds of performances, of course, but especially the world of evening parties and the night. The Baedeker guide devotes a section to 'Places for dancing and entertainment' in the capital. It mentions the Haus Vaterland, located in the Kempinski Hotel near the Potsdamer Platz, praising its saloons, its Far West Bar, and its Rhineland Terrace. It also mentions the Atlantis in the Behrenstrasse and the Altbayern in the Friedrichstrasse for their cabarets. In the West quarter, the great Femina dance hall is listed.

Next to the Zoo railway station, the Baedeker recommends the Germaniahaus and the Wilhelmshaven for their coffee and their cabaret. Next comes the Frasquita, which had been designed by the architect Fritz Gaulke, with a parquet dance floor in the middle of the main hall surrounded by tables.[43] This hall had a magnificent decorated glass ceiling. Two smaller wings could hold additional customers who flocked to this well-known establishment. In the evening there was entertainment, usually a show featuring scantily clad dancers. On the eve of the war and at its beginning, the dances performed by couples displeased the authorities. Nude dancing was supposed to be strictly individual, and in June 1940 the show was prohibited after complaints were filed.[44] Here decency intersects with the fear of homosexuality. Months earlier, a woman spectator had complained about the excessively large number of women who frequented this *Berlin mondän* (in German *mondän* is very pejorative). According to the complainant, these idle people ought to be put to work in munitions factories. Why had she gone to such a place? War and hardline propaganda were obviously upsetting people's minds. In March 1940, the star attraction at the Frasquita, the couple Florence and Ben Roger, was the object of dangerous criticism: 'The man dances naked, and the woman in an evening gown. They both produce an unspeakable impression of decadence and are undoubtedly addicted to morphine and cocaine. Moreover, the man looks like a homosexual.'[45] The ministry of propaganda saw to it that their contract was not renewed the following month.

Other establishments were criticized for reasons that now seem to us futile but that were taken very seriously under Nazism. For instance, a courier denounced the Arcadia Club in Würzburg to the ministry of propaganda on the basis of an advertisement for its orchestra praising its dance tune 'Unter dem Kastanienbaum', which was simply a German version of the song 'Under the Chestnut Tree'.[46] The back of the advertisement recommended a dance figure whose steps were illustrated by a drawing to make them easier to learn. The dance looks very much like an adaptation of the Lambeth walk, a dance invented in England. According to the denunciation, by playing such a tune the orchestra was corrupting German youth and violating the law of 29 March 1938 regarding the preservation of the Reich's music.

At the end of the 1920s the Nazis were already issuing harsh judgements on music that seemed to them symbolic of the 'degeneration of the race'.[47] Jazz, considered to be 'Negro music' (*Negermusik*), was the main target. Wilhelm Frick managed to get it prohibited in Thuringia in 1931. Nevertheless, when they came to national power, the zealots had to change their strategy, because the minister of propaganda, Goebbels, wanted to rely on persuasion and avoid creating a category of prohibitions that would be too easily flouted. However, this policy never got off the ground, and Nazi strategy became authoritarian again. In 1935 the government acted against 'degenerate kinds of music'. Jazz, seen as the symbol of black savagery and the perverse tastes of American Jews, was theoretically forbidden on the radio. Songs that adapted and Germanized this kind of music survived, but pure jazz, and especially 'hot jazz' was definitively buried. Briefly suspended during the Olympic Games, this battle resumed in 1937 with one prohibition after another being enforced regionally. From early 1939 on, the border areas that had still been able to receive foreign jazz broadcasts could no longer do so because the latter were jammed. In 1940, a law prohibiting a new musical genre, swing, was adopted. The general goal was to Aryanize music and to put an end to dependency on other countries.

Similar measures regarding dance reinforced the effects of prohibitions on certain kinds of music. After a period of hesitation, vigorous action in the area of dance began in 1936. The objective was to eliminate Jewish influences on modern dance.[48] Karl Laban, a very innovative ballet director, was violently criticized by members of the Chamber of Theatre who thought his art too greatly influenced by Jews. At the same time, Goebbels had the tempos of popular, folk, and social dances examined with a view to formulating precise prohibitions. In 1937, dancing schools were ordered to cease teaching dances derived from jazz and the Lambeth walk. The prohibition was to be clearly set forth, and even posted, in dance halls. In addition, teachers of dance saw their profession reshaped by an examination and more precise training. Once again, the various regions adopted the interdictions. The logic of these prohibitions was clarified at the highest levels. When the Gauleiter of Munich complained about the difficulties of enforcing them, Martin Bormann wrote to Goebbels to ask that the ministry of propaganda take the necessary steps:

> The Führer said some time ago that it would be completely wrong on our part to import dances from our worst enemies, whether English or American. These dances have no doubt prospered in our country, and precisely for that reason they should not retain foreign names. Consequently, it is our opinion that the good old German dances should be developed far beyond the old folk dances and that it must be possible to connect them with new German dances and promote them through the theatre, cinema, etc.[49]

Thuringia strengthened such measures by making the motivations explicit: foreign influences had to be combated in order to protect young people and attack 'degenerate habits'. Therefore what made German collapse possible, namely 'the Jewish dances known as jazz and rumba', had to be prohibited.[50] On 10 March 1939 Westphalia added a ban on swing.

In Pomerania the situation required serious action, according to a local official who recommended in July 1938 that when it was not clear whether music came 'from Germany or from Africa', it should be not be played, and who was scandalized to see German girls dancing like Africans to music heard on the radio in their homes.[51] Radio Hamburg should broadcast good music issuing from German culture, like 'Strauss waltzes and the Blue Danube'. Measures affecting not listeners but producers were taken in October 1938. They were repealed in 1939, a sign of how difficult it was to enforce them. Their precision allows us to get an idea of what kinds of sociabilities were targeted and their relationships to morality: bands and orchestras were no longer to play foreign music; the English or American rhythm known as 'hot' was banned, and German rhythms could not be played in the American style (that is, with solos and improvisations, as in jazz); musicians were forbidden to wear costumes and false beards or wigs; it was still possible to play softly; the owners of dance halls assumed responsibility for seeing to it that there was no forbidden dance or music; in particular, they had to take care that no one danced to swing.

In the end, all the regions adopted this legislation. However, they found it difficult to enforce, because some Nazis themselves were not very aware of what the new laws covered. In February 1939, one of the Nazi newspapers, the *Hakenkreuzbanner*, published an article virtually promoting the big apple, a dance that came from New York and was related to swing. The article even explained how to dance the Lambeth walk, providing illustrations, so that one might wonder how such things were able to appear in a periodical calling for the Aryanization of culture.[52] Naturally, the goal was to attract activists, but the journalists' descriptive enthusiasm threatened to produce effects contrary to the ones expected.

A few weeks earlier, the head of the Gestapo in Kiel had complained about American dances being danced and sung in public. A demand that they be prohibited had been filed with the president of Schleswig, who had not responded. But the Gestapo man did not stop there. He explained that he had asked the leaders of the Wehrmacht to stop playing these kinds of music, which 'are not military dances'.[53] He thought it necessary to remind the ministry of propaganda that Reichsführer Himmler and the police had banned swing. Following this report, the president of Schleswig questioned the ministry in order to find out how the prohibition should be made and with what limits: should swing, hot, the big apple, and the Lambeth walk all be prohibited?[54] His doubts show that in 1939 the prohibition was still not self-evident.

The difficulty of making these dances and kinds of music disappear entirely annoyed a local official, the head of Silesia's propaganda office, who had read the article in the *Hakenkreuzbanner* in February 1939. Confronted with the reactions of the local elite, which resisted the ban on foreign dances, he was looking for a solution. His interpretation shows the strong tensions that persisted under Nazism and how conformism was seen as a propaganda weapon. According to this official, certain circles in 'society' and 'the elegant world' felt frustrated by the ban on English dances, because they scorned German folk dances and especially the Bavarian waltz. Couldn't they be led to believe that the German repertory consists of English dances imported long ago, this argument to be supported with a scholarly, ethnological study restoring their reputation? In this way, these socialites would no longer feel harmed by not being able to play English dances and would cease to say that 'morning coats and evening dresses are not suitable for dancing the Bavarian waltz'. They would happily adopt this fashion 'if they saw high dignitaries in the state and the party openly dancing to this music during great social events in Berlin'.[55]

The events organized by the state and the party could more or less respond to the wish expressed by this Machiavellian propaganda official. The grandiose nature of these events impressed people. However, their function did not consist solely in deceiving and manipulating those who belonged to 'the elegant world' and society.

Great State and Party Events

In the party's great assemblies, the kind of music played was not the only thing at issue. The instruments themselves were strictly regulated. The regime had a refined ear. It could not bear the wind instruments that were the musical mark of its adversaries. The jazz trumpet was therefore not allowed in party groups or in the SS. The Schallmaien, the famous trumpets invented by Max B. Martin, were hated above all. The instrument itself would not have frightened anyone. It was invented in 1905 by a musician who had the idea of welding several brass trumpets together, each one producing a different tone; a system of valves allowed the player to sound one or the other of the bells. The instrument was not expensive because its simple technology and inexpensive metal made assembly-line production possible. Depending on their size, these instruments could play a very wide range of notes.

Martin trumpets have a ringing, sharp sound easily distinguishable from other wind instruments in an orchestra, which are generally made from copper. This booming sound quickly attracted the popular brass bands, especially the socialist ones, which used it for marches, demonstrations, and celebrations.

Certain harmonies consist only of Martin trumpets. Just after the Great War, the communists began using it again. The musical colouration of the Red Front came largely from this instrument. The local Nazi brass bands, which sometimes emerged from working-class milieus, did not hesitate to use it to ensure that their music was as loud as that of their adversaries. However, because they had adopted this instrument later, they were not able to compete in the great urban centres, especially in working-class neighbourhoods. Above all, groups of Nazi activists in the SA and then in the SS were composed of fighters more used to singing a cappella than to playing the role of a symphonic choir. At first tacitly abandoned and then banned by the SA and party organs in the late 1920s, the Martin trumpet was officially prohibited in official events in 1935. Its use by the communists was the origin of this ban; the fear was that its sound might remind people of an enemy that was to be entirely forgotten.[56]

Music was present in all kinds of events, and primarily at official balls. By appropriating cultural institutions, Nazi leaders had also taken possession of the social events that were connected with them. The Opera Ball, started up again in 1920, became a regular event to which dignitaries were automatically invited and at which they appeared. It often served as an occasion for the coming-out of debutantes, and was also attended by young cadets from the military academies. The Berliner Staatstheater Ball never failed to invite its great protector, Hermann Göring, the minister-president of Prussia. In the tombola held in 1935, he held the winning ticket and was awarded a motorcycle.

In taking control of the sector of information and propaganda, Goebbels reigned over two central events in the Berlin social season. The first was the Press Ball. For a long time, this had been the key event that really opened the season. In 1933, many people – especially Jews and communists, who sensed Nazism's violence – experienced it as the last happy episode before the tragedy began. It continued to take place every year, with official speeches given by the minister of propaganda, who used it as a showcase for his plans or to create attractions. In 1938, for example, Goebbels had a television camera and a receiver installed in the two halls at the Zoopalast, where the ball was to take place, so that in one room it was possible to know what was happening in the other. He took the opportunity to predict that this means of communication would prove very successful, and even suggested that it might soon replace the postal service. At this event, journalists met officials of the regime, who were more accessible inside the hall than outside, where a formidable security force was set up.

Later that season, Goebbels also determined the fate of the ball given by the UFA, the film production trust formerly run by Hugenberg that had been taken over by the state. The ball was held at the UFA Palast. Here it was cinema stars who attracted attention and met with the leaders, whom they generally knew quite well. In 1939, Carola Höhn, Anny Ondra, Dorothea Wieck, Berta Drews, Kristina Söderbaum, Heinrich George, Paul Klinger, and Max Schmeling posed for a group photo. Of all these figures, Heinrich George was the most famous.[57] He had already been acclaimed under the Weimar Republic. He was a great success both on the stage and in the cinema. He flirted with the communist avant-garde. Almost his only friend among the Nazi leaders was Walther Funk, whom he had met during long nights spent drinking and who soon became Goebbels' adjutant at the propaganda ministry and a state secretary. Not in good odour with most of the Nazis when they took power, George came around to the new Germany and in 1933 agreed to make a propaganda film for the general public, *Hitler Jugend Quex*. He is far from brilliant in this film, which claims to show how conversion to Nazism makes men better and destroys vices, but it allowed him to provide evidence of his support for those in charge of culture. Afterward, he continued his career without much difficulty; he obtained a juicy contract with Tobis Film and directed the Schiller Theater. He was even hired for major productions, and was quite far up on the salary scale. Received at the propaganda ministry for private parties, he met Hitler, who in 1937 granted him the title of superintendent. He had been integrated into the high society of the Reich.

The presence of the boxer Max Schmeling is not surprising. He had been part of high-society life for a long time.[58] In the 1920s, when he won the German and then the European championships and came to live in the capital, he had been the idol of journalists, artists, and the patrons of cabarets. He became a friend of the painter George Grosz (who painted his portrait), met the sculptor Rudolf Belling (whom he inspired), associated with Bertolt Brecht, Kurt Tucholsky, and others. He allowed his friend Michael Bohnen, a singer, to take him to upper-crust haunts such as the Romanischen Café, where he saw the star strip-tease dancer of the time, Jana.[59] His headquarters was located at the Roxy Sportbar. There he met the pilots Manfred von Brauchitsch and Rudolf Caracciola, as well as figures in the cinema such as Hans Albers. After he won the world championship in the fourth round of a bout with Jack Scharkey, he was a genuine star. His marriage to the actress Anny Ondra, a great comedienne, increased public enthusiasm for him.

He did not support the rise of the NSDAP, which disapproved of his love for America and his politically questionable friends, not to mention his Jewish manager. He was regarded with scepticism after he defeated Scharkey in 1932. Following Hitler's accession to power, Schmeling returned to Germany, settled in Berlin's chic neighbourhood of Dahlem, and praised the boycott, without, however, firing his manager. Moreover, Hans von Tschammer und Osten, the official in charge of Nazi sports, told Schmeling he should fight more often in Germany, no doubt for propaganda reasons. Schmeling complied. That sufficed to put him in the Nazis' good books. Hitler invited him and his wife to tea and treated him like a friend. Thus he was on his way in the new Germany. In 1936 he defeated Joe Louis, and received congratulatory telegrams from his friends Hitler and Goebbels. He was invited to official dinners, to balls, and to the private homes of the masters of the country, while boxing was promoted as the German sport *par excellence*. According to his account, it was his loss to Louis in 1938 that caused his disgrace. In reality, he remained an establishment figure and tried to begin a new career in the cinema while at the same time continuing his career as a boxer.

All these figures on the Berlin night scene and at official parties constitute a group whose image was largely constructed by the press and by newsreels. They displayed a certain kind of opulence that propagandists and journalists thought would establish in people's minds an image of Germanic prosperity. In order to promote projection onto the elites and a feeling of belonging together, the regime's officials also organized thematic meetings to which specialists were invited.

Thus delegations of German business leaders were invited to the chancellery for breakfast meetings or dinners. They regularly saw high state officials at the openings of the international trade fairs that flourished under the Third Reich. They sometimes accompanied delegations of foreign businessmen who were part of the entourage of official representatives of Italy and other countries. In this world of business, the striking event is the departure of Fritz Thyssen after 1939. Thyssen, who had helped the Nazis take power and supported the government with his money, fled the country. He was concerned about the development of Germany policy regarding Jews and religion, and went into exile, first in

Switzerland and then in France. The man who succeeded him in the role of the great business leader supporting the regime was Gustav Krupp von Bohlen und Halbach. Krupp had backed the Nazi party in the spring of 1933. The following year, he was appointed president of the association of German industrialists, and in 1937 he became one of the pivotal figures in political economics. His eldest son, Alfried, helped him by taking over the direction of the heavy industries owners' association and joined the NSDAP the next year. In a sign of the family's integration into the Nazi regime, Gustav obtained the party's gold medal in August 1940. Hitler celebrated his birthday, received him, and visited him in Essen on several occasions.[60] They also exchanged gifts when they met privately in the hotel that served as the Führer's residence during the party congress in Nuremberg. Krupp's wife accompanied them when they took walks. Other industrialists, such as Porsche, Heinkel, and Messerschmidt, were honoured by the regime, which awarded them the German National Prize, the highest national distinction, whose role was to replace the Nobel Prize after the Swedish academy suspended Germany's participation in the competition in 1936.[61]

Everyone important to the Reich's economy assembled once a year at the chancellery for the great reception to raise money for winter aid for the poor. In 1938, it took place on Thursday 17 February, at 8 p.m.[62] The Krupps and the Schröders brought with them men as powerful as Robert Allers (president of the car industry association), Hugo Henkel (laundry soap and other products), Max Ligner (IG Farben), Hermann Bücher (AEG), Eduard Hilmgard (Allianz), Wilhelm Kissel (Daimler-Benz), P.F. Reemtsma (cigarettes), Ludwig von Winterfeld (Siemens), and others. In all, about three hundred leaders, accompanied by their wives, crowded into the great gallery. There they met not only the Führer, his adjutants, and their wives, but also main figures in the regime, accompanied by their wives. One of those present was Göring, whom they knew well through their dealings in connection with the four-year plan. He helped them increase their profits through complicated systems of reciprocal contributions and government commissions, thus attaching them still more closely to the regime. At the party that followed, there was an operatic entertainment.

Artists were received on German Art Day, celebrated in Munich. On 14 July 1939, six hundred and fifty artists attended at the Führer's invitation.[63] The next day, they observed demonstrations by special groups from the HJ, the BDM, and the security forces, visited art exhibits, and attended a philharmonic concert. On 16 July, they went to pay their respects at the tomb of Professor Troost, and then the festivities continued until the official programme ended at 9:50 p.m. Hitler briefly returned to his home in the Prinzregentenstrasse before leaving at 10:10 to go to the Gärtnerplatz theatre, where he listened to songs from the *Merry Widow* and enjoyed a variety show featuring the dancers Lyse Maja and Valivo, the Höpfner sisters, Myriam Werne, two jugglers, the Rays, and a pair of comedians known as the 'Two Californians'.

The Nazi party increased efforts to make the elites more cohesive, and this was reflected in the state's activities. The great public demonstrations were not staged solely for the benefit of the masses. They also brought together national officials, more or less behind the scenes. The Nuremberg party congresses, for instance, were not limited to the meetings with cohorts from the SA, the SS, the HJ, and the BDM that were painted by Vollbehr. The schedule also included dinners, luncheons, military parades, and private meetings that allowed people to see the Führer or discuss matters with party officials. They were one of the occasions – like the anniversary of the 1923 Putsch celebrated every year in the temple the regime had constructed in Munich – on which people met old comrades or ran into their widows, with whom they had sometimes maintained relationships.[64] The Nazi elite, like any human group, recovered its sense of humour, and even its banter, once the ceremonies were over and a small band gathered around the Führer in his apartment or went to a beer hall. Some photographs show a smiling Göring awaiting the beginning of the official events. Goebbels' diary is fairly reliable on this point and helps us understand that amiability and kindness (Goebbels often uses the German word *nett*) helped relieve the underlying rivalry and latent aggressiveness of the party. A joke told at the time nonetheless reveals the ambition and dishonesty within the NSDAP: 'What's a Marxist? One of your comrades who's above you in the party hierarchy.'

The politics of celebrations was therefore carefully regulated. It was the object of a genuine public policy, as is shown by the work of officials responsible for propaganda and for specific party organizations. Often individual initiatives also promoted its development. In Munich, one of the figures known for such initiatives was Christian Weber. Ruddy, heavy-set, and brimming with vitality, Weber had been a soldier, a stable groom, and a petrol pump attendant. He had met Hitler in 1920 and served as his bodyguard for almost two years. He joined the NSDAP in 1921, got involved in local politics, and in 1926 won a seat on the municipal council. His career followed that of the party. In 1934 he became assistant to the mayor and was soon put in charge of the city's office of public events. In this post he soon showed his poor taste, so much in accord with the cheap flashiness of the time. He created his horse race, the Braune Band von Deutschland, endowed with a hundred thousand marks, in 1934. To make this event more attractive, he organized a large evening party on the grounds of the Nymphenburg castle called 'The Night of the Amazons'; its theme was '2,000 years of German culture'. There was a parade of cars and tableaux vivants featuring beautiful nude women covered with sparkles who were supposed to evoke the glorious past. Afterward, there was a ball. In order to win the leaders' favour, the sly Weber had arranged a party reserved for officials where they could get acquainted with the nude dancers. Gossips said that they were prostitutes who worked for Weber on a regular basis.[65]

In 1935, Weber took over the Munich carnival, providing ample resources to make it the biggest in Germany. The parade stretched over eight kilometres and included a hundred and fifty-six automobiles. Weber followed this up by taking on the Oktoberfest beer festival. He set aside a gigantic area for the event and brought in new fairground people. For the Oktoberfest's one hundred and twenty-fifth anniversary, he organized a parade in traditional costumes. Never had so many tents surrounded the Oktoberfest palace, on which he had inscribed the slogan 'Proud City – Happy Land'.[66] A newsreel report on the 1939 Oktoberfest shows the desire to make it the symbol of a generous, saucy Bavarian hospitality.[67] The report is constructed around the plump image of a tourist attending the festival for the first time. This neophyte tries to seduce a girl wearing a dirndl. They try out all the games in this huge carnival, drinking glass after glass of beer as they go.

At the same time, Weber was making another fortune by taking advantage of the Aryanization of Jewish real estate. In this way he profited from his efforts to promote anti-Semitic policies and simultaneously made Munich more attractive. To promote tourism, in 1936 Weber had supported the organization of the winter Olympic Games in Garmisch. Upper Bavaria was his favourite area as well as that of many of the leaders, primarily Adolf Hitler.

The Berghof's Functions

On 28 April 1923, Weber took Hitler for the first time to the Obersalzberg, a magnificent mountain in the heart of the Bavarian Alps with rich deposits of salt and gems. They went to the Moritz pension (later transformed into the Platterhof Hotel, and taken over by the NSDAP), which had been recommended to them by Dietrich Eckart. Their goal was to rest and go for walks. The following Saturday, Emil Maurice, then Hitler's chauffeur, was to bring along Paula Hitler, Adolf's sister. This brief escape delighted Hitler. He began regularly to visit this pension owned by the Büchner family, who became fond of their customer. It was in this retreat, after his release from prison in 1925, that the Führer completed the dictation of *Mein Kampf*. A small wooden house separate from the pension's main building was fixed up for him. In 1927, the Bechsteins invited him to their new mountain residence in the same village. The Obersalzberg thus became for him synonymous with relaxation and solitude far from the tensions of politics and the city. He decided to rent a village house that had reverted to the government for lack of an heir, the Haus-am-Wachenfeld, which was located high above the road. It was an old farmhouse, a mere shell that had been partly renovated. In June 1932, thanks to the colossal royalties he had received from the publication of *Mein Kampf*, he bought this small property for forty thousand goldmarks and enlarged it by acquiring a neighbouring parcel after having driven out the owners. Not a very accommodating neighbour, Hitler took control of the little town, which was gradually transformed from a plain mountain resort into a second capital.[68]

By the summer of 1933, everything was ready to receive him after his political triumphs. Angela Raubal, his half-sister and the mother of his late cousin Geli, who had been his mistress, served as his housekeeper and saw to maintenance. The bills submitted by the Munich caterer Dallmayr show that she took good care of her brother. Camembert, brie, and other cheeses he liked are on the delivery lists.[69] Large quantities of fruit and preserves reflect his taste for sweets. Meat also figures on these lists; this may seem surprising, since Hitler had become a strict vegetarian in the early 1930s. But he always had something on hand for guests who felt like eating meat. For the same reason we also find alcoholic beverages (Cinzano red and white, Malaga, etc.). It is clear that from that time on Hitler did not come alone to his mountain retreat. His house was intended to receive large numbers of visitors.

Two wings were added, along with an annexe behind the original house, for the staff and for guests. The construction went on over several years and required hundreds of workers in various trades. In the summer of 1936, the above-ground part of the house was available for use and completely decorated. The cellars remained to be converted; they eventually consisted of a vast network of tunnels and bunkers communicating with other structures housing the NSDAP administration under the direction of Albert Bormann, part of the chancellery (Lammers sometimes resided there for months), and, later on, offices of the foreign ministry and the Wehrmacht. A guard corps received the SS men of the Führer's personal bodyguard. For his own comfort, Hitler also had a tea house retreat built farther up the mountain (at 1,830 metres), to which he took relaxing hikes with his friends.

The leisure function was thus coupled with the functions of command and administration. For this reason, an airport was constructed nearby to facilitate travel for officials and Hitler's adjutants. The road network was improved to make it possible to reach Munich and Berlin quickly. A new centralization developed from this point, a sign that the Führer was indeed at the heart of the regime and that his person determined the political organization of Germany.

The fame of the Wachenfeld house was such that in 1932 it became the focal point toward which Hitler's admirers converged. This pilgrimage grew larger from year to year and eventually had to be channelled. From 1936 on, organized tours passed in front of this house, which everyone knew as the Berghof. The Baedeker guide for 1938 even lists this site in its description of the environs of Berchtesgaden. In the summer, the KDF

(Kraft durch Freude, 'strength through joy'), the Third Reich's leisure organization, sent meritorious workers to stand before the gate, where they sometimes had a chance to glimpse the head of state's silhouette. Hitler occasionally went down to see such visitors, handing out a few autographs and making brief speeches. Some of the visitors had the exceptional opportunity to shake the Führer's hand or be received in the house, as was little Bernile, who came there specially from Munich in the summer of 1933. This popular ceremony was publicized in propaganda.

A few insiders understood the advantage to be gained from being near Hitler during these periods of relaxation. On 17 August 1933, Göring looked at a parcel of one thousand square metres[70] that belonged to the Bavarian forest estate. He easily acquired this property and had a house constructed on it by Alois Degano, who also worked for Hitler. Göring generally spent part of the summer there with his family. Sometimes his wife and daughter stayed there alone while he was travelling around Germany. Curiously, he seems not to have used this house for work or negotiations, as he did Karinhall. It was, of course, also mentioned in the guidebooks, but more anecdotally, as if to emphasize the marshal's allegiance to the Führer.[71]

Martin Bormann and Albert Speer also had houses in the Obersalzberg. Speer's was connected with his work as an architect and decorator, which required frequent meetings with Hitler. Bormann, who played an increasingly important role after 1938, also met frequently with the Führer. Both of them benefited from working on site. Speer had an office permanently occupied by two of his collaborators; Bormann had a small party staff at his disposal. Bormann also intervened in the domestic affairs of the Berghof when Hitler was absent. His authority was imposed on the minor staff members and exceeded that of Döhring and Kannenberg (in Berlin) in matters of political discipline. Thus Bormann represented a sort of Nazi political commissar in the palace that Obersalzberg became.

The limitation on the space available to accompany Hitler to the mountains leads us to wonder whether this resort area did not allow a further selection to be made within high society. Clearly, all the personages Hitler saw in Berlin were not invited to the Obersalzberg. Some of the ministers and state secretaries were seldom invited. It is as if this place had been constructed with a view to allowing Hitler to concentrate on work and avoid petitioners. In this respect it might be compared to Louis XIV's and Louis XV's secondary residences, which they used to restrict their entourages and escape scroungers. The setting up of a second administration supports that hypothesis. The head of state took long vacations so that he could work more effectively. A glance at his appointment book confirms this. During 1938, Hitler moved about a great deal, and as soon as he left his retreat, he had to take part in ceremonial events that tired him.[72] Inversely, when he was in the mountains he limited visitors and resumed a healthier way of life. He stayed home under the attentive care of his physicians and took a daily hike up to his tea house. This habit became more marked as the years went by and his health deteriorated.

However, the Berghof was never empty. Selected friends and collaborators were received there: adjutants, ministers, family members, friends like Hoffmann, and visitors like the Duke and Duchess of Windsor and Lord Rothermere. A dozen rooms were at their disposal. Some even stayed there when the Führer was away travelling or when he was residing in Berlin.

After 1938, Eva Braun spent long months alone in the Obersalzberg with the staff, sometimes under Martin Bormann's oppressive gaze. Hers was, moreover, a special case. So long as Angela Raubal was managing the house, Eva had to live at the Platterhof. Hitler went to see her there or had her brought to spend the day with him. She never slept at the Berghof. Her affair with Hitler, consolidated after Geli Raubal's death in 1932, gave her no right to join his court. However, in 1935 she was hired as a paid secretary by the Adjudantur to justify her presence near the Führer. After the summer of 1936, the situation changed. 'Fräulein Braun', as Hitler called her in public, was authorized to live at the Berghof. Her bedroom had a door communicating with Hitler's. From 1938 on, it was clear to the staff that Fräulein Braun was the 'lady of the household'.[73] But she was not in charge of its organization; Döhring and Bormann made the decisions. In addition, she got on very poorly with some of the older servants, such as Krause. Her position gradually grew stronger. She could invite her own friends to the Obersalzberg and was no longer systematically hidden during official visits, even if she was not allowed to play the role of first lady. Hitler denied her the opportunity to meet certain important women associated with the regime – Emmy Göring was never introduced to her – though Magda Goebbels knew her and the Hoffmann family invited her to their home, and Eva Braun had met Hitler through them. The Führer thought it necessary for his personality cult that he enter history as a 'great loner'[74] and never marry. Like the Portuguese dictator Salazar, he pretended that his only bride was his country: 'Mein Braut ist Deutschland', one of his slogans went. The ambiguity of Eva Braun's position thus explains why she had so much less influence than court favourites had had. She nonetheless brought a touch of imagination into a world that witnesses generally described, after the defeat, as dark and tedious.

The Berghof did not become an alpine Versailles, nor did it reproduce the conditions in little castles like Marly where French kings went to escape the oppressive demands of etiquette. At the Berghof, the representative function remained important. However, the setting created an atmosphere of intimacy favourable to *rapprochement*. Hitler used it as a machine for creating solidarities and exchanging disingenuous confessions. During rambles in the mountains or during a tea party, he set forth his views and pretended to give personal attention to his interlocutors. He thereby compensated for his difficulty in sharing the passion for action shown by high officials who would have preferred that he invite them, like

Louis XIV, to go hunting. These old soldiers retained their love of tracking and the excitement of pursuing game through the woods.

Hunting as a Rite of Integration

The Rominten forest is located in northern Germany, about twenty kilometres from Tilsit. It had been part of the state's domains since the Prussian monarchy, which had a castle there. On the morning of 27 September 1936, traces of ice still covered the countryside, but the sun was shining when Marshal Göring's guests arrived by car at 11:30 a.m.[75] Five men had been invited to join this exceptional hunting party: von Neurath, the foreign minister; von Papen, the former chancellor who felt more comfortable as a diplomat; Milch, Göring's state secretary at the air ministry and a major-general in the army; Körner, Göring's adjutant at the president of Prussia's office, where he was a state secretary; and Ernst Udet, who was in charge of pursuit aviation at the air ministry. The objective was to flush and hunt down stags, animals that stood high on the international point-scale.

According to Göring's hunting diary, the beaters brought in by the head huntsman, Menthe, and the head forester, Schade, flushed a few animals. Suddenly one of the marshal's collaborators, Ulrich Scherping, spotted a stag that had stopped at the edge of a cliff. Sensing the arrival of the hunters, the animal rose up and belled. He tried to escape his pursuers by going down the slope. The hunters had a hard time following him. Göring shot first, at a distance of about eighty paces, and hit the animal in the liver. The second shot missed the target, which collapsed further on and was finished off. So far as anyone could remember, it was the largest specimen ever seen in the woods, a trophy of great value both in Germany and abroad. Its antlers were huge and its coat a beautiful dark colour. The stag's data sheet was filled out; he was worth 217.6 points. Several storm troopers and foresters were needed to drag the body off and put it on a truck.

The following day two new guests, von Lipski and von Kedell, joined the hunting party. Von Neurath, von Papen, Milch, Körner, and von Lipski all racked up good scores. During the hunt, a male and his females were flushed. One of the animals was hit by a shot but continued to run. It was found much later. The others went to ground deep in the bushes. That afternoon, it began to rain. No animal showed itself. The perimeter of the hunt was expanded. Hunting dogs had to be brought in to flush the game. Three other animals were shot. The bad weather continued on 29 September, but the men killed a fine specimen. On 1 October, new officials helped with the tracking and the trophy animals fell one after the other. Finally, on 2 October, the hunt was coming to an end when numerous young stags were spotted, and Scherping was able to kill an old male with towering antlers. Other guests had come to join the group: 'Colonel Thomas, Lieutenant Colonel Warlimont, General Wilberg, State Councillor Neumann, Consul Tröger, Bernhard (of Spain), Herbert Göring and Hanke [Karl]'. They all wished Körner happy birthday and the hunting horns were sounded for him. In all, twenty-two stags had been killed during this hunt; one animal had been hit but the body was not found.

Göring, who was also the Third Reich's Master of the Hunt, was equal to his office and his reputation: he got the highest score, killing six stags, including the gigantic one. The perfect host, he had allowed everyone to have his moment in the limelight and to enjoy the extraordinary conditions provided by the forest administration for pursuing this sport. What the marshal loved about hunting was the physical effort, the performance. He also enjoyed the decorum and the disciplined mobilization of groups in the service of this task for true lords as part of a great noble tradition.

Göring was not a utilitarian hunter seeking food; he hunted out of a sense of competition and tactics. On the one hand, he wanted to show off the result of his hunts and did not hesitate to employ taxidermists to adorn the walls of his home; this was one way of drawing attention to his role as a leader and his sense of traditions. On the other hand, he allowed high German officials and foreigners to benefit from his position in order to win their support. Thus he maintained an ancient tradition for which he had provided unprecedented possibilities for development through new laws adopted in 1934.

Thanks to Göring, Germany had very generous hunting laws that were the envy of the French and members of the International Hunting Committee, which asked him to be its honorary chairman. The law created a veritable administration whose role was to watch over game populations and to act in concert with hunting societies to provide choice specimens.[76] Göring made a unilateral decision to extend the game population to include Nordic species, in order to strengthen the myth of the Germanic nature of the forests. Thus between 1934 and 1938 he had herds of elk brought from Sweden, at great cost. In addition, he continued the protection of small birds, which traditionally are not much eaten in Germany because of a superstitious belief that they are forest spirits. According to Backe, the marshal's passion for hunting made him close to rural people and allowed him to understand the problems of the German peasant world.[77]

Behind this taste for tracking down game we can glimpse a certain conception of virility, no doubt shaped by the First World War. Hunting, like mountain climbing, is an activity practised chiefly by men, who, challenging nature, arrange adventures that allow them to surpass and even to realize themselves – as war transforms men through the experience of death. The cult of virility and the influence of fashion explain the unprecedented success of hunting under Nazism. This passion sometimes led great personages to travel long distances in order to hunt a rare animal.

This was notably the case for Himmler.

The Reichsführer SS liked this physical exercise. Himmler, who was described by his personal masseur as rather clumsy and awkward, sought to compensate for his physical weakness by forcing himself to walk for hours and sometimes take part in athletic activities to show that he was not as feeble as he appeared to be.[78] Hunting was thus an opportunity for him to prove that he had fairly good endurance and was a good shot. These motives were not, however, the only ones that explain the way he used hunting.

Himmler also used hunting to reward the best groups and attributed game according to rank. Starting in 1938, he seems to have increasingly proceeded in this way. The method became permanent when the war began, to the point that those fortunate enough to be chosen received printed invitations. On 3 November 1938, thirteen guests arrived at Joachimshof for a hunt. Among them were both present and former close collaborators of Himmler's, such as August Heissmeyer, who had worked in the SS's central office and specialized in training, Reinhard Heydrich, the head of the Reich's secret police and criminal police, and Karl Wolff, the head of Himmler's Adjudantur. They were accompanied by Sepp Dietrich, the head of Hitler's personal guard, Ludwig Steeg, who was preparing to take office as mayor of greater Berlin, Wiegel, a ministerial director, and a series of high-level adjutants. In addition to Himmler, four persons in the group held the highest rank in the SS. This kind of encounter might resemble a work meeting. The list of game killed suggests otherwise: rabbits, hares, foxes, buzzards, birds of prey, and all the other wild animals that had been flushed by the beaters, including in particular female deer. In September 1942,[79] in the middle of the war, the distribution of the animals was determined in advance. The invitation was henceforth merely a symbolic reward, because rationing had made eating game a luxury. Himmler combined a sort of prefiguration of the executive retreat with the awarding of a bonus in kind depending on rank.

The logic of integration and promotion is also seen in Himmler's personal practice. His passion for hunting was known to people in high society, and his mailbox was full of missives courting his favour. For instance, one of his relatives in Gmund wrote because he had learned that Himmler regularly came to hunt in that region. He asked the Reichsführer to let him know when he was coming so that he could leave abundant game by hunting on another reserve.[80] The two men obviously knew each other well, since at the end of his letter this correspondent gave Himmler news about his father, who was ill. On the other hand, some letter writers were not known to Himmler. They nonetheless proposed unusual hunting expeditions in order to enter into personal contact with him. The officer responsible for occupied Norway, for instance, invited Himmler to come and hunt elk, because the herds had grown immensely, and a hunt to reduce them had been organized between 20 September and 20 October.[81]

For his part, Kurt Daluege, who had become chief of police for Bohemia-Moravia and was one of those who called Himmler by his first name, sent him a list of hunting dates in his region and asked him to tell him when he expected to come.[82] Still better, the director of the German Museum of Hunting proposed that he take part in an expedition to Romania to hunt bears and birds. Himmler was not available at that time and wondered if such an operation might not have political effects.[83] He ultimately recommended that the museum director ask Hitler's advice regarding the appropriateness of such a trip.

On the other hand, Himmler very willingly accepted invitations he received from Göring, who had let him benefit from the advantages accompanying his office as Master of the Hunt. The two men met once or twice a year, and must have used the occasion to compare points of view apart from the influence of a third party, in particular Hitler. Göring asked small favours, and Himmler did the same. The advantage of hunting was it that it left time to talk, have fun, and eat, as well as for moments of silence. There was plenty of time to negotiate calmly and thoughtfully.

An examination of Himmler's appointment book and his correspondence relative to hunting shows that he far preferred this activity to theatre or the opera. Similarly, his home seems not to have been the site of an important social life. On the other hand, he invited his acquaintances to Schorfheide or Gmund in order to entertain them and establish a close relation with them in the course of a long hunting expedition. His penchant for outdoor activities was shared by other leaders, such as Albert Speer, Hans Lammers (in Schorfheide), and Walther Funk, who moved from the propaganda ministry to the economics ministry in 1938. Funk had a hunting lodge and invited Hitler there to enjoy the pleasures of walking. Obtaining a hunting lodge or reserve became fashionable during the Second World War.[84] Leaders took advantage of the occupation of Poland in order to receive from the Führer fine lands on which they could practise the art of hunting.

It would be anachronistic to consider this passion as a simple leisure activity. Under the Third Reich, hunting was far more than that. First of all, it was part of the policy of undertaking major public works, because the forestry sector flourished, doubling the number of its employees in three years. The regulation of hunting in the collective interest was also presented as an application of corporatist ideology. Finally, modes of greeting specific to hunters passed into general usage. Thus letters always ended with a 'Waldmannsheil' ('Woodsmen's Greeting') before the classic 'Heil Hitler'. These codes were smoothly adopted by those who became addicted to this activity. To gain esteem in this milieu, one had to hunt ever larger or more dangerous animals and carry out increasingly complicated hunts. For that reason, the size of the animals killed was not left to chance, and neither were positions in hunting blinds. Göring knew all that and navigated this world of references with great ease. He had his men control the rituals of releasing and stopping game. He knew how to sound a hunting horn and he had a very accurate gun equipped with a telescopic sight.

This relationship to instruments, this ceremonial and solidarity going beyond old and new social circles, brings to mind a kind of Freemasonry. Was it to compensate for the prohibition of that organization that helped mix different social groups that Nazism was led to make hunting an area where elites and popular milieus could come together around a common experience of taking control of the territory and surpassing oneself? The fact that it was still being pursued during the war years, when human beings had become a more common prey, would tend to support that hypothesis. In the contact with wild animals and the earth, the ideologists of Aryanness thought they found a confirmation of their prejudices regarding natural selection, the race of supermen, and strength. 'These days, a man who obtains a hunting licence is certified to think and act as a National Socialist,'[85] wrote a zealous supporter of the regime. This belief was so widespread in German society that in images the hunter's attitude was soon conflated with that of Nazi soldiers.[86]

7

The Splendours of Diplomacy

On 29 September 1934, a young Englishwoman, Christabel Bielenberg, went to the German embassy in London to exchange her British passport for a German one bearing the eagle and swastika. Her marriage that morning had given her the right to German citizenship. 'You've not made a very good swop I'm afraid,'[1] the embassy official said, to her great surprise (he was a friend of Christabel's and her husband's). Never mind, Christabel was passionately in love with her husband, Peter. She liked German culture, and she had no particular doubts regarding the value of the new Germany. She knew about the change in the regime, which had been going on for two years – that is, since she had met her husband – but she was not aware of its deeper impact. Moreover, a friend who was sympathetic to the NSDAP had persuaded her to go to a meeting to see for herself in the autumn of 1932. She returned from it puzzled, astonished by the ambient enthusiasm and finding it hard to take the whole thing seriously. Like many foreigners in the early 1930s her perception of the historical reality of Nazism was limited.

In diplomatic milieus the rise of National Socialism was given sporadic attention. Hitler was able seduce certain observers during meetings and confidential interviews. Eager to gain the support of the Fascists, in the mid-1920s he was already forging links with Italy. Like any party head, he conducted an embryonic diplomacy. To be sure, his obsession with European issues led him to ignore the importance of the United States, as Ernst Hanfstaengl was bitterly to complain,[2] but much of his aura in Germany came precisely from the fact that he was capable of taking radical positions regarding international problems. During the occupation of the Ruhr, he made one ferocious declaration after another against France. His violent hostility to the Versailles treaty made him a *bête noire* for diplomats who defended the League of Nations and humanistic pacifism. Thus during his rise to power, Hitler knew that entire states and the democratic governments that had created the principles of collective security were strongly opposed to him. He knew that he was going to have to make a special effort to seduce these adversaries and bring them around to a point of view that would serve his interests. This strategy went even further. Like a good politician, he sought to mask his intentions and to keep people wondering about his objectives. In addition, the actual level of German power had to be not known. To pursue this strategy, Hitler had to influence news circulating around Germany and create sympathetic channels that could spread his message and dupe the public.

Life in high society was one of the channels for influencing the way foreigners looked on Germany. First, because it brought together the major actors in international relations – heads of state and government, diplomats, journalists, and businessmen – in a regular, pleasant context that allowed a climate of confidence to be created. Second, because travellers who belonged to what already formed an international high society caused fashions and prejudices to circulate among countries. They could also occasionally exercise influence. Finally, because diplomatic life was broadly covered in newspapers and newsreels around the world; it could produce a fascination with Nazi ideology and aesthetics, a political illusion that was all the more attractive because, for the second time, a government claiming to be fascist had come to power.[3] The Third Reich's racial utopia and its imperial designs thus wove links with persons and countries that would soon dream of imitating its appearance and its actions.

The Führer's First, Reassuring Steps

In 1933, diplomatic activity in Germany was concentrated in Berlin, even though consulates and cultural missions had been opened in large cities such as Hamburg, Frankfurt, and Munich. In the German capital, about two hundred persons from more than forty countries were engaged in diplomatic activity. There were the diplomats proper – ambassadors, envoys, chargés d'affaires, and advisors – whose task was to monitor national and international politics. Then came the military advisers and attachés, who sometimes had a technical function of monitoring international conventions, and sometimes acted as spies. In addition, there were maritime and commercial attachés as well as consular employees, for at that time many countries required entry visas. All of them were generally accompanied by their families. Their children went to German schools or to foreign schools like the Collège français, which still exists. The young people met at parties organized for them, such as the one the French ambassador, François-Poncet, gave annually at his residence, or the one given by their mothers in the Mon-Bijou park in June. As for the diplomats' wives, they went to the same balls, the same shows, and the same dressmakers. They sometimes established true friendships with native Germans.

Ambassadors were generally posted for periods of between four and ten years, depending on the country. Some did not want to leave Germany, like Hassan Nachat Pasha, the Egyptian ambassador, who was having a love affair with the widow of a German prince.[4] On 11 October 1932, Hassan gave a party for four hundred guests; entertainment was provided by a belly dancer – the charm of the Orient was only for the elites. German was the language most commonly spoken in the embassies, even by representatives of countries on other continents, such as China, Japan, and Brazil. Many also knew French and English, which they had often learned while on post in countries where those languages were spoken. The diplomatic world was used to luxury. The heads of diplomatic missions had several servants, including a chauffeur, and the staff often wore livery and even wigs at old-fashioned receptions. And then there was decorum: a great chandelier on the ceiling, old master paintings on the walls, and valuable carpets on the floors. The music was of good quality; the cuisine was refined and not limited to the specialities of the country of origin. The international format of a cocktail party and cold buffet was very frequent. At the Italian embassy, fine marbles adorned the interior of the building and golden plates were used at great dinners. The French preferred porcelain and Gobelins tapestries. The Soviet Union remodelled its building and provided its representatives with dinner jackets in order to make a good impression. The rules of propriety were thus observed, even if the Russians made timid efforts to change the protocol of their receptions by experimenting with unprecedented schedules and reception procedures. In this comfortable world, people were wondering if the change that had occurred on 30 January 1933 was going to alter their pleasant way of life in Berlin.

Adolf Hitler's first official foray into the diplomatic world took place on 10 February 1933. Along with the heads of foreign missions, he was responding to a dinner invitation issued by President Hindenburg. Konstantin von Neurath, the foreign minister, was also invited. An old diplomatic hand, he had begun his career in 1901. He had already been a minister in the von Papen and von Schleicher governments. His continuation in office under Hitler was intended to indicate that nothing had really changed with the accession of the new chancellor. Similarly, within his ministry State Secretary Bernhard Wilhelm von Bülow, then forty-eight years old, was the type of noble who naturally moved in diplomatic circles. Since 1923, he had been serving German interests at the highest level; the son of a major general in the army and the nephew of the chancellor of the same name, he belonged to a great family of public servants. The head of protocol, Rudolf von Bassewitz, was four years older than von Bülow and had a similar profile: having entered the diplomatic service in 1906, he had long worked in consulates and embassies before occupying his current strategic post, which consisted in putting the state's political objectives in the proper form.[5] In choosing continuity at the foreign ministry, Hitler was following the advice of a diplomat who was a member of the NSDAP, Viktor, Prince zu Wied.[6] For the latter, it was imperative to reassure foreign chancelleries in order to avoid weakening the Reich's position on the international scene. Germany had to pretend to be following the same principles of action that had guided it in the time of Stresemann and Rathenau.

Von Papen, von Neurath, von Bülow, and von Bassewitz tempered Germany's sudden withdrawal from the Geneva conference on disarmament and then from the League of Nations in 1933 by putting blame solely on the unequal treatment accorded their country. They also minimized the importance of the few excesses that diplomats had been able to observe, such as the SA's untimely appearances at elegant parties or attacks on foreigners carried out by rowdies.[7] Von Neurath explained that the government was taking extremists in hand, and would not hesitate to use force to ensure the safety of foreigners. The following year, the concerns elicited by the liquidation of Röhm and von Schleicher on 30 June 1934 were also quickly damped down by the impression that routine functioning had been restored in official intercourse. On 2 January 1934, German and foreign officials eagerly attended the annual reception held by the Reich's president, and a month later they joined in a magnificent celebration of von Neurath's sixty-first birthday at his Berlin apartment.

International tensions soon attracted people's attention. The issue of Austria brought to light a disagreement between Germany and Italy that impeded Göring's attempts to arrive at a *rapprochement* with Italy, a *rapprochement* that Hitler seems also to have desired. In addition, it blocked the Duce's plan to arrange a four-power directorship with France and the United Kingdom.

The sudden rebellion by Austrian Nazis and the assassination of Chancellor Dollfuss on 25 July 1934 led Italy to mobilize its armed forces. Hitler had to have Austrian Nazis arrested and their organization dismantled. This was a setback for him. He had to send von Papen to Vienna as a special ambassador to calm the strong feelings aroused by this event, and he had to undertake a massive diplomatic offensive. For Hitler, the death of President Hindenburg in early August 1934 provided a unique opportunity to change the course of events, to assert himself on the international scene, and to make people forget his mistake. Here emerged the way Hitler's official services sought to influence international public life by ensuring that diplomats were well received and were kept happy, and also by using the resources of etiquette to channel tensions between states.

The correspondence between protocol offices shows the care taken to respect the traditional ways of taking up a position in the Great Game. On 1 August, the foreign ministry informed all the world's chancelleries of the emergency law adopted to ensure the transfer of sovereignty to Adolf Hitler by uniting the functions of the chancellor and the president of the Reich in the event of the head of state's death. The reaction was swift; the new regime was recognized. Italy was the only state to express astonishment,[8] a sign of its relative ill will toward Germany because of the Austrian affair. Ambassador Cerruti wrote a note indicating that diplomats did not know what title should be used in designating the chancellor-president, because article 1 of the law adopted on 1 August did not specify it: was he to be addressed as Führer, chancellor, or president? Thus protocol required the distribution of a document clarifying the proper international title: 'The German chancellor of the Reich'.[9]

Detailed preparations for Hitler's assumption of office followed. The care taken by the foreign ministry to respect etiquette and try to establish the regime's legitimacy required careful study to show that German diplomats were fully aware of the relevant historical precedents. The ceremony foreseen was modelled on that for the inauguration of Hindenburg as president in 1925.[10] Here again, continuity was emphasized down to the smallest detail. The proceedings show that the bureaucracy taken over by the new regime served it loyally, without any apparent opposition whatever. This zeal is indicative of the willing participation of the central administrative departments in the Nazification of the country. In 1934, many officials in the foreign ministry, such as Dörnberg, chose to join the NSDAP. Three of the seven bureau directors were members of the NSDAP before 1937.[11] In addition, Ribbentrop's influence strengthened the SS's role at every level.

The ceremonial reception of the diplomatic corps on 12 September 1934 was thus a key event, both because it situated Hitler as an omnipotent interlocutor with respect to the diplomatic corps and because it exported abroad an image of the Führer as solemn, legitimate, reassuring, and faithful to the traditional protocol.[12] At the foreign ministry, the essential figure in this strategy of appeasement was none other than Rudolf von Bassewitz. The head of protocol's task was to maintain routine relationships with the embassies. He sent out invitations, proposed formulas, and vetted speeches that were to be given at the ceremony. Bassewitz, as the defender of respect for formalities, urged that an official message be sent to all heads of state to announce the transfer of sovereignty. It is a sign of the persistence of a classical style that these letters were divided into two categories: those addressed to monarchs, and those addressed to republics.[13] Of course, the objective was to ease the work of the secretariat in choosing formulas of politeness and address, but the historian can also see to what extent the ministry's staff was attached to a conservative political apparatus, while at the same time they were leading their country down the path to totalitarianism. For them, the world was divided not into dictatorships and democracies, but rather into states that retained a nobility and a monarch, and those that leaned toward a republicanism from which communism threatened to emerge.

Once these declarations were sent out, the real preparation for the meeting began. Two points required special attention: persuading as many guests as possible to attend and seeing to it that the Führer's speech was widely reported. Whence a particular emphasis on the ceremonial and on the positions occupied by the various officiants. The framework thought up by the bureaucrats on the model of receptions held under the Weimar Republic constrained the behaviour of the ambassadors. Such a transfer of traditional forms calmed foreign guests, some of whom had, however, been recently appointed and were not familiar with earlier rituals. In addition, on the same day the ambassador of the Soviet Union and envoys from Uruguay and Haiti had to submit their credentials to Hitler, between 11 and 12 p.m., in order to receive their accreditation.[14] Around noon, all the other representatives arrived at the chancellery, at no. 73 Wilhelmstrasse.

At 12:20, von Bassewitz asked the papal nuncio and dean of the diplomatic corps, Mgr Cesare Orsenigo, to follow him into the reception room.[15] The forty-seven members of the diplomatic corps who had arrived since noon fell in behind them. They entered a vast rectangular room along the sides of which SS guards in dress uniforms, servants, and high officials of the foreign ministry were already standing. Foreign minister von Neurath and the state secretaries stood before the guests. From left to right, the hierarchy was respected. First came the nuncio, then the ambassadors, the envoys, and the chargés d'affaires, forming a semi-circle. In the anteroom, guests had been given cards indicating where they were to stand.

At 12:30, the Führer entered by a door at the end of the room facing the audience and walked to the middle of the room, where he stood somewhat stiffly. The nuncio stepped forward and congratulated him: 'Herr Chancellor of the German Reich, the diplomatic corps is delighted to assemble around you to offer our most sincere congratulations and best wishes to the immediate successor of the venerable president of the Reich, Marshal von Hindenburg, whose memory will live forever in our hearts.'[16] The nuncio then expressed his confidence that German authorities would do their best to help diplomats carry out their work, and recalled that only justice and charity could improve matters in this world.

Hitler's voice then resounded in the corridors of power. He thanked the nuncio and the diplomats present, and then stated the Reich's official position: 'The irreducible objective of my policy is to make Germany a centre of peace.'[17] Next, he related the interior transformation of his country to international stability. This was enough to make people smile after the series of violent events in June and Nazi agitation in Austria.

When Hitler had completed his speech, von Bassewitz approached and led Hitler to the nuncio. Hitler shook the latter's hand. Afterward he went around the hall and shook everyone's hand. The hierarchy among ambassadors, envoys, and chargés d'affaires was respected. They all received a few minutes' conversation. Once this had been accomplished, the Führer left the room with his entourage, not without taking his leave of the nuncio. The latter, accompanied by the head of protocol and followed by the diplomats, left the room and bid his German hosts farewell on the steps of the building. The official order was respected in the departure of private cars.

In this ceremony, Hitler donned the garments of a head of state in the eyes of the world. The ritual made his power incontestable with respect to international law, as was soon confirmed by exchanges of letters with foreign heads of state congratulating him and recognizing his new role.

How to Make a Good Impression

On the whole, this ceremony left a favourable impression on diplomats. Hitler had been able to rub them the right way, especially the ambassadors, since the various regional offices of the foreign ministry had prepared precise 'conversation topics'[18] that had been individualized and put on file cards. For the American ambassador, William E. Dodd, for instance, the topics included both public news and private life. The first point concerned President Roosevelt's vacation; he had just completed a cruise on a warship. The other three points were directly concerned with the ambassador and his family.

> 2. Recently, the ambassador attended the Passion Play in Oberammergau. The performance made a deep impression on him.
> 3. This summer, Mrs. Dodd took a car trip in southern Germany, accompanied by her two adult children (a son and a daughter). They came back enthusiastic. – Autobahns!
> 4. Dodd's son is studying history at the University of Berlin under the direction of Professor Friedrich Meinecke and Professor Hermann Oncken; he plans to take his doctorate here, and pursue an academic career in the United States. The ambassador is a professor at the University of Chicago in the same field; he too took his doctorate in Germany (Leipzig). – Foreign students, and especially Americans, are welcome in German universities.

With the French ambassador, André François-Poncet, who had communicated French criticisms of Germany policy and been sceptical of the Führer's claims to have peaceful intentions, the office of the Western European sector suggested bringing up the trip taken by a few members of the French parliament, including a former war minister, Senator Messiny, who had come to Germany the preceding week and had been very impressed by the country. 'Such visits are highly desirable,' the note concludes. However, a parenthesis explains that for the moment, no face-to-face interview must be granted the French ambassador, and that any conversation conducted with him must be on completely apolitical subjects. The protocol office removed this recommendation and the final version is striking in its brevity. François-Poncet was thus put under observation while awaiting a more propitious moment to influence him.

Discussions with the Italian ambassador seem to have been programmed in a similar way, in order to avoid subjects that might give rise to conflicts. It would be better to take up with his Excellency Ambassador Cerruti the change in the Germano-Italian Society. The German foreign ministry proposed as its president Winterfeld, the head of the Siemens corporation. The ambassador's support would be desirable.

We can understand the state of diplomacy in 1934, when Italy remained suspicious with regard to a Germany it considered too enterprising in Austria. Mussolini intended to support the Austro-Fascist government in Vienna against pan-Germanist aims. As for France, it still relied on its military power to direct European affairs without suspecting that Hitler was surreptitiously encouraging an ambitious military programme.

Britain, which was playing a more autonomous role, was courted more assiduously. Like Dodd, the British ambassador, Sir Eric Phipps, was allowed a longer moment of conversation with the Führer and, as a sign of confidence, the talk turned on more personally engaging subjects. First the king's health had to be inquired into; the newspapers said he was ill. Then his majesty was to be congratulated on the engagement of his fourth son, Prince George, to marry Princess Marina of Greece. Finally, it is noted that it was Sir Eric who had represented Britain at Hindenburg's funeral; it would be appropriate to thank him for his participation in the ceremony.

The formulas provided for conversation with the nuncio were just as warm. One had to ask about the health of the pope, who had fallen ill, and that of the nuncio himself, 'who despite a resurgence of his old bile problem took an important part in the funeral ceremonies held in Berlin for the president and was forced immediately thereafter to enter a clinic, where he remained for several weeks'. The diplomatic services added that the nuncio was still ill at the time of the ceremony. The second point on the card concerns the pope's vacation at Castel Gandolfo, recently renovated with German help. The writer adds: 'The pope's particular interest in technology – radio.' The closeness to the Church is presumably in line with the concordat signed the preceding year.[19] But the special attention given to the nuncio is no doubt connected with his essential role in the structure of Berlin high society. As the dean of the diplomatic corps, he was invited to all receptions. His influence had to be courted in order that he maintain the image of a Germany that had fallen into line. In addition, the Führer visited him the next day, going to the Nunciature in the company of State Secretary Otto Meissner and his personal adjutant, Brückner.

These notes, preserved in the diplomatic archives in Berlin, give us an idea of the strategy adopted for the semi-official conversations that characterized society life in high diplomatic circles. They show one of the ways Hitler seduced people, by being well informed about his interlocutors thanks to the efficiency of his ministerial departments. In the background we can discern the Third Reich's political objectives and its duplicity. How can we fail to be struck by the way Göring was used to seduce Mussolini in 1934, at the very time when the Austrian Nazis were preparing a *coup d'état* with the active support of German propaganda? Similarly in these notes the enthusiastic affability with regard to the Japanese ambassador prefigures the shift in alliances in Asia and the ongoing *rapprochement* with Japan. A few weeks earlier the Japanese crown prince had sung Germany's praises after making a European tour, and the press in Tokyo had commented favourably on the transfer of power from Hindenburg to Hitler.

Later on, preparation for conversations was further improved. At the beginning of a year that was crucial for the Third Reich's diplomacy, the file preparatory to the reception held on 11 January 1937 shows that the technique of individual interviews with the diplomatic corps had been refined.[20] The content of the conversations foreseen shows more subtlety in its information and more confidence in the subjects taken up. This is further evidence that the foreign ministry was fully aware of the political objectives. The cards for discussions with Dodd suggest that Roosevelt should carry out a *rapprochement* with Germany during his second term. In discussions with François-Poncet, the German pavilion at the Paris World's Fair, certain to be a success, was to be brought up. For the Brazilian ambassador, the subjects to be dealt with were the next flight of the *Hindenburg* and the necessity of opening regular flights between the two countries. Still following the logic of *rapprochement* outlined in this question of transportation, the Norwegian ambassador was to be informed of the development of a direct rail link between Berlin and Oslo.

Biographical sketches were henceforth included in the preparatory materials. They provided information about all the participants. The Führer could choose private or public subjects, as he wished. Special attention was given to the aesthetics of the ceremony, since the descriptive materials emphasized the presence in the courtyard of the chancellery, where the reception took place, of an SS honour guard in dress uniforms that would line the way for the ambassadors' cars as they arrived and departed. One has to imagine these tall soldiers, dressed in black with dark, shining helmets, with white gloves and facings, standing at attention and presenting arms. They were also in each corner of the reception room.

This very routine event never ceased to be secretly refined in order to impress people and further Germany's strategic aims. In 1937, the compliments addressed to the Japanese ambassador, like the question asked the representative of Italy regarding his impressions of the new direction taken by relations between the two countries, show that the preparation of the anti-Comintern pact was well advanced. Henceforth the tactics of sudden coups was to be replaced by military enterprises, for the Third Reich knew it had supporters. Its geopolitical analysis fully coincided with its ideological interpretation and its belief in the struggle and hierarchy of races so often mentioned during the NSDAP congresses in Nuremberg.

Forging Ideological Support

Attending the Nuremberg congress was one of the ways Hitler and von Neurath thought foreign perceptions of Nazi ideology could be changed. For this reason, the foreign ministry reserved places for diplomats from 1933 on. Their attendance was not emphasized in Leni Riefenstahl's film about the event, *Sieg des Glaubens* (The Victory of Belief), to the official projection of which high society was invited a year later, on 1 December 1934. The seven boxes on the left side of the UFA Palast in Berlin were reserved for plenipotentiaries.[21] Several of them expressed dissatisfaction with the sorry role they played in the film. A similar complaint made on the occasion of the international car show in March 1934 led the head of protocol to say it would be necessary to do a better job of preparing for the year's major events.[22]

This explains why a ministry official, Herbert Mumm, the assistant head of protocol, wrote to the NSDAP chancellery in preparation for the 1934 party congress. This document explains what was essential for the diplomats and thus gives an idea of the standard of life expected by socialites. First of all, the diplomats had to be filmed and told that they would be filmed, so that they could prepare themselves. Next, 'We must surprise the diplomats by awarding them the party's medal of honour. It is desirable that the SS men accompanying them be the same as last year, if possible, and that they receive the same medal.'[23] We understand the goal of forging enduring personal connections and thus a sort of fraternity centred on the party, but we can also see here a way of quickly awarding decorations to friends in the SS. The writer adds that it would be desirable to arrange a visit to an SS camp at night and to entertain the group under a marquee, serving them large quantities of beer and Nuremberg sausage. After that, details multiply. Good seats near the platform had to be found for these guests of honour and these must not be (as they had been the preceding year) simple wooden benches uncomfortable to sit on for five hours. The group also had to be taken to typical restaurants. It was very important that the diplomats be able to bathe and wash without having to mix with the ordinary people coming to Nuremberg. Telephones must be provided for them. Finally, they should be taken to Berchtesgaden to see the Haus-am-Wachenfeld. This last point concludes the letter, from which emanates a deep desire to create a kind of Nazi pilgrimage for foreigners.

Clearly, the party registered these requests and the ministry put together a complete programme that was carried out despite President Hindenburg's death. The latter may even have favoured the enterprise, since the last invitations were sent out at the end of August. On 24 August, Mumm wrote to reserve forty seats intended for his guests, emphasizing that the seats must be comfortable and that their placement mattered. These diplomats represented governments and had to be seated near high state officials, and certainly not near people who had no official function, as had already happened, otherwise 'their expectations will not be met'.[24] Incidentally, the letter pointed out that an ambassador had the rank of a head of state, and an envoy that of a minister. A copy of this letter was sent to the Reich chancellery, to the minister of propaganda, and to the minister of Prussia.

Several eminent figures in the diplomatic corps did not attend the party congresses in 1933 and 1934, such as François-Poncet, Phipps, and Dodd. But the representatives of Egypt and Portugal accepted the invitation. The total number of participants, about twenty, was less than the forty-two diplomats present at the inauguration of the German hunting show held on 4 May 1934. Moreover, this latter event, sponsored by Göring in his capacity as Master of the Hunt, had to compete with the opening of a week of equestrian sports that took place from 4 to 13 May and also offered diplomats complimentary invitations.

The programme for the trip to the NSDAP congress in September 1934 was perfectly worked out. The cost was entirely paid by the foreign ministry, which arranged a special night train: first class for diplomats, and a third-class car for their servants, which was added in the Nuremberg station.[25] Breakfast cost two marks and other meals four marks. The convoy included a dining car that served beer, water, and wine. As for the wine, the supplier, the Mitropa firm, had ordered an 'Oppenheimer Goldberg 1929' and a Pfälzer (a sweet wine) as well as fine Moselle wines (less sweet). The train was to remain in the station during the congress and would serve as housing for the diplomats. Baths were available in the station. Mitropa undertook to provide a high-quality staff to maintain the cars and guaranteed special care. The cost would be about nine hundred marks, to which a 10 per cent service charge would have to be added.

These political tourists left Berlin on 6 September 1934 at 8:05 p.m. and arrived in Berchtesgaden the following day. After a brief stop at the Grand Hotel, they went for a walk guided by Fritz Todt (the head of the Reich's autobahn programme), who told them about the condition of the roads. Then they passed in front of the Führer's house.[26] That evening, they all dined in the train, which was on its way to Nuremberg, where they were expected at 8 o'clock the following morning. After being greeted by a group of party members from the Hitler Jugend, the diplomats met with the Führer just after lunch, in a saloon car. A walk. Return to the railway car, and departure for the SS camp, unfortunately without Hitler (who had initially been expected to go along). The next day, 9 September, at 8 a.m., the ceremonies at Luitpoldhain began; they ended with a parade on the Adolf-Hitler Platz, followed by lunch in the Rathskeller restaurant. The afternoon was devoted to cultural activities, such as visiting Albrecht Dürer's house, the Germanic Museum, and Nuremberg's churches. At 10 a.m. there was a parade by the Reichswehr and then, at 6 p.m., the party congress. Finally at 11.15 p.m. the special train left for Berlin, where it was scheduled to arrive at 9:15 a.m. on 11 September. In five days, the diplomats actually spent no more than five hours at the congress! An implicit message emerges from these visits and the series of meetings: Nazism is an accord with German tradition and magnifies it through its organizational ability, its sense of order and discipline. The guests were provided with a friendly and comfortable experience. Well supervised and escorted, the foreign witnesses were influenced by National Socialist ideas and aesthetics more than by partisan speeches at the congress itself.

Aesthetics was in fact at the heart of the NSDAP congresses: the setting was carefully prepared, with its neo-classical architecture and immense party symbols; everywhere flags and pennants lent colour; units of party members composed a tableau vivant that was sometimes immobile, sometimes undulating; at nightfall, light shows were added; the music was intoxicating; the songs and cheers resounded and made the air tremble. The event was also given impressive coverage in the press, newsreels, and propaganda.

On this point, the head of protocol, Bassewitz, thought that full use was not being made of his department.[27] A few days after the congress, the reception at the chancellery, and the international conference on highway networks, three events during which the presence of diplomats was required, Bassewitz wrote to the propaganda minister to point out that the press had made numerous errors in the names and titles of diplomats, and suggested that this damaged Germany's relations with their countries. Because of insufficient cooperation, he said, it had not been possible to organize full press coverage of the diplomats' stay in Nuremberg. Hence Bassewitz recommended that this impression be corrected in the film that the party was currently producing.

Bassewitz knew that the film about the 1934 congress was one of Hitler's projects, and was of greater scope than the ones previously produced. Hitler had personally entrusted this film to his friend Leni Riefenstahl (as he had the preceding one) and gave it the name of the congress, *Triumph des Willens* (The Triumph of the Will). The film, for which Albert Speer designed the architectural setting and Benno von Arendt provided the scenography, was launched during the cinema festival held from 26 April to 1 May 1935. Protocol had reserved fifty-five seats for diplomats. About twenty of them, most accompanied by their wives, went to see the film at 8:30 p.m., 28 April, at the UFA Palast at the Berlin Zoo. The British ambassador was there, but neither François-Poncet nor Dodd attended. No doubt their defection was explained by the fact that the Americans and French had not attended the party congress. In addition, we should certainly see this failure to respond to the NSDAP's invitation as a sign of the democracies' rejection of fascism. After the war, François-Poncet attributed his refusal and Dodd's to their desire not to lend approval to a place where German politicians were indulging in verbal excesses and glorifying a xenophobia insulting to their guests.[28]

Spreading the Party's Ideas and the Cult of the Führer

Attending the party congress eventually became almost obligatory for foreign diplomats. This event played too important a role in the life of the country to ignore it. Above all, international figures attended in order to understand the anomalous phenomenon of Nazism. Evidence of the expanding influence of the congresses is shown by the exemplary presence of great British families at the 1935 session, at which the racial laws were announced. For instance, Lord Mitford, whose elder daughter Diana was the wife of the leader of Britain's extreme right wing, Oswald Mosley, was given a place of honour, along with his wife and children; they were prominent guests at following congresses as well.[29] Unity, Lord Mitford's second daughter, was introduced to the Führer and is said to have had an affair with him. When the affair ended, she is supposed to have made a suicide attempt that left her handicapped. Other prominent Britons went to the Nuremberg congress; among them were Lord Rothermere, a newspaper baron who admired Hitler's courtly manners and exchanged greetings with him every year, and Lord Londonderry, on whom Ian Kershaw has written a book.[30]

In 1937, Sir Neville Henderson, the newly appointed British ambassador replacing Phipps (who had been transferred to Paris), decided to break ranks with the democracies by attending the party congress. In order to avoid creating the impression that he was abandoning his ally, François-Poncet attended as well. As the senior ambassador in the absence of the nuncio, François-Poncet even had to give an address thanking the party. He took advantage of this to slip in a criticism of Goebbels. The day before, Goebbels had made a speech in which he said that the democracies were a herd of stupid calves awaiting the butcher. The French ambassador declared that the Führer's invitation to the congress had reassured him that the chancellor did not share his minister's opinion. Hitler laughed along with the audience, while Goebbels blushed. Only the American ambassador, Dodd, continued to refuse to participate in the party congress.

The foreign press initially gave only grudging coverage to this event, but it was soon caught up in the frenzy. It should be noted that the ministries of propaganda and foreign affairs sent out an increasing number of invitations and attractive offers. The number of newspapers in each country allowed to send representatives ultimately had to be limited, so great was the demand. In 1938, the only Italian papers whose representatives were invited were the *Corriere della Sera*, the *Giornale d'Italia*, and *La Stampa*. For France, reporters for *Le Matin*, *Le Figaro*, *Le Journal*, and *Le Temps* were authorized to attend.

These channels were considered insufficient to shape public opinion, and political figures were also invited to the party congresses. On the recommendation of Ribbentrop's man at the German embassy in Paris, Otto

Abetz, certain Frenchmen were selected.[31] For the 1938 congress, Abetz recommended two extreme right-wing members of 'Doriot's party', Claude Jeantet and Florimond Dussart.[32] Other French writers established direct relationships with Hitler's Adjudantur in order to be received at the Berghof, such as Alphonse de Châteaubriant, who declined to participate in the 1937 party congress.

Journalists were among Germany's honoured guests at the congress. As such, all their expenses were paid by the Reich and the NSDAP. They were given special favours, invited to festivities in company, with high party dignitaries and provided with cars. However, according to the ministry's lists, less than a third of the Frenchmen invited in 1937 and 1938 accepted. This shows that few Frenchmen were unaware of Hitler's true feelings about their country, while those who accepted the invitations often knew his feelings and shared them. However, the list for 1937 proposed by Ribbentrop, and thus by Abetz, seemed to reward those who were already involved in bilateral relations: Fernand de Brinon, the vice-president of the France–Germany Committee; Charles Pomaret, a non-Marxist socialist member of the French parliament; Ernest Fourneau, a professor at the Pasteur Institute and a member of the Academy of Medicine, and also a vice-president of the France–Germany Committee.[33] This group moved in high society, because both work relationships and family life were pursued during the trip. This is also suggested by the presence of Mme Boisel, the wife of the editor of the *Réveil du peuple*; he was a 'well-known anti-Semite', according to the file card on him, which also noted that she was accompanied by her two sons.[34] These five or six French guests of honour are far from counterbalancing the large contingents of British, Japanese, and Italian journalists. The French delegation was about the same size as Afghanistan's.

These privileged guests came in addition to visitors who were recruited chiefly among anti-Semitic journalists. It seems that their expenses were also paid in large part by Germany. Thus at the 1937 congress, Lucien Rebatet, Robert Brasillach, Georges Blond and his wife from *Je suis partout* were lodged at the same Bamberg hotel as their friends Pierre-Antoine Cousteau (the brother of Jacques Cousteau, the famed naval officer and ecologist), Paul Creyssel, a former member of the Croix-de-Feu and his wife, and Senator Maurice Fabre and his family. These right-wing sympathizers, who were violently anti-Communist, were given special attention, since Otto Abetz accompanied them during their stay and lodged at the same hotel. Collaboration under the German occupation of France was already being prepared before the war by 'a drift toward Fascism'.[35]

In addition, Hitler received large numbers of foreigners who came to Germany for meetings or trade fairs. The economy was thus a constant priority. On 27 April 1937, the Italian delegation of the Confederation of Fascist Industrialists, led by Alberto Pirelli, the rubber products magnate, was received at the chancellery. On 16 June the same year, Austrian industrialists were allowed only a fifteen-minute audience. On 20 June, members of the International Chamber of Commerce went to the palace for tea. They also met with Göring to discuss the Reich's economic planning. These examples show that not only the milieus of politics and the press but all areas of social life were targeted for seduction.

By means of constant efforts to manipulate diplomats posted in Berlin, Germany succeeded in dividing its adversaries, breaking their habits, and focusing most of their activity around events orchestrated by the state and by the party. In a sense, the diplomatic corps found itself being mobilized along with all Germans by the activist spirit. The rate of invitations steadily increased: state receptions, memorial services, party congresses, inaugurations of international fairs and expositions, state visits, premières at the theatre or the Opera, not to mention events organized by specific organs such as the Labour Front, the KdF ('Strength through Joy'), associations for bilateral exchanges, and so on. In addition, there were the private requests made by dignitaries seeking to establish their reputations. Certainly, no one was unaware that behind the smiles an aggressive strategy was being pursued. But the human and generous face put on it tempered the concerns aroused by National Socialist ideology and encouraged good will.

The foreign ministry supported this effort to promote the party abroad in collaboration with other authorities that were involved in international politics. The NSDAP had an organization that established connections in numerous foreign countries in order to facilitate German emigrants' participation in the public life of their homeland. These organs were instruments of propaganda, centres in which good will toward National Socialism was forged. In addition, the foreign desk in the party's press office sold articles favourable to Germany and helped arrange trips and investigations for reporters from all over the world. Journalists themselves aided in these seductive enterprises: The Berlin foreign press centre, for instance, held an annual ball to which high officials and Nazi news services were invited.

Before becoming foreign minister, Ribbentrop had created, with Hitler's authorization, his own organization to conduct delicate negotiations. This organization remained relatively autonomous even after Ribbentrop was named ambassador to Britain in 1936 and became foreign minister in 1938, replacing von Neurath, whom Hitler had found incapable of following the new political line.

The cumulative action of all these groups produced an important effect abroad: greater influence for the Third Reich and especially greater popularity for Hitler. One indication of this was the flood of mail the Führer received on his birthdays and on the anniversaries of his becoming chancellor, his great successes, and so on. These documents were archived and a tally of them was kept, though it provides more details about foreigners than about Germans. These lists suggest that the number of messages coming in from abroad constantly increased until 1938. From France, there is less mail, and sometimes none. The old adversary kept its distance. More active, obviously, were countries that had large German minorities, such as Austria before the Anschluss in 1938. The Austrian Nazis, despite the prohibition of their party and the imprisonment of some of them after Dollfuss's assassination, worshipped Hitler. In Czechoslovakia the Sudeten minority and in Poland the German population in Danzig influenced the volume of correspondence.[36] However, the list of names for the United States shows that German roots were not the only source of this popularity abroad. It reflected the efficacious work of the German–American Bund, which enthusiastically thanked Hitler for the hospitality received at the 1938 Nuremberg congress.[37]

Great Britain had always had a small group of faithful supporters of Germany – specialists in German culture, university professors, and teachers who were occasionally invited to NSDAP congresses. The letters sent by Britons mixed praise for the new Germany with exhortations to keep the peace.

Latin American countries like Brazil and Argentina had been infiltrated by pro-German groups and by the Colonial Society.[38] Thus they always had a contingent of supporters who wrote letters. Let us add that at the chancellery in Berlin, foreigners passing through wrote their compliments in the guest book.[39]

In accord with the Nazi version of the personality cult, starting in 1935 German embassies and consulates organized festivities in most foreign capitals. In April 1935, the consul gave a reception in honour of the Führer in Seattle.[40] Pompous poems were declaimed in his honour, the most remarkable of which was published in a German newspaper. In 1936, a hundred guests celebrated the Führer's birthday at the home of the German consul in Durban, South Africa; among the guests were the captain and crew of a German ship that was passing through.[41] Thus Hitler had become a pretext for high-society events, for he was to be worshipped with a glass in one's hand.

Between Prestige, Influence, and Intelligence-Gathering

The celebration of Hitler's birthday led exceptional personages to come to Germany. His fiftieth birthday in 1939 was celebrated with unparalleled pomp. If Bassewitz had been in charge, he would no doubt have complained that the newsreel did not accord more attention to diplomats and international visitors. But he had retired three years earlier. Vico von Bülow-Schwandte replaced him for one year; he in turn was succeeded by Alexander Freiherr von Dörnberg zu Hausen. Like Ribbentrop, Dörnberg was a die-hard Nazi and belonged to the SS. He did all he could to see to it that the celebration provided useful support for Germany's foreign policy.

Some twenty foreign delegations had accepted his invitation. The point was to seduce and persuade them, and also to supervise and direct them. The foreign ministry sought to seduce them by providing a warm welcome. Their rooms were specially decorated for the occasion. One of Hitler's favourites, the architect Benno von Arendt, conceived the floral compositions (he also decorated the Führer's entry hall and reception room for this occasion). The suites assigned to the heads of diplomatic missions were given particular attention: the décor was more expensive than that in the accommodations for their subordinates. Additional amenities were provided. The delegations could reach their embassies by telephone from their rooms directly, without passing through an operator. A post office was set up in the hotel lobby. The festivities themselves were designed to weaken the guests' defences. Luncheons, dinners, visits, shows, operettas, receptions. . . Ribbentrop gave a dinner in their honour on the terrace of the Hotel Adlon, at the ministry's expense. An orchestra played mood music (for twenty-seven hundred marks). In addition, there were meals for seven hundred and fifty guests at ten marks each, and beverages in quantity: three hundred and four bottles of Henkell sparkling wine (produced by Frau Ribbentrop's family); a hundred and thirty litres of Pilsener beer; forty bottles of white wine; a few bottles of champagne (Hennessy), whisky, liqueurs (Chartreuse, eaux de vie), two glasses of sherry, and a vermouth.[42] Did the guests allow themselves to get drunk?

Two key events were supposed to finish winning them over. The first was a reception at the chancellery. Clearly, Ribbentrop's men were convinced that Hitler would make a deep impression on his visitors, and this reflects their faith in his charisma. The second was a military parade. The foreign delegations included military men whose objective was to gauge the Reich's ability to make war. In 1939, its military potential was enormous. All observers noted this fact. The goal was to make guests feel the strength offered by such an ally, and the negative consequences to which the adverse camp exposed itself.

Every effort was made to supervise and orient opinion. A reliable man was assigned to each delegation. These official companions were chosen from the main bodies: the army, the air force, the NSDAP, and the foreign ministry. Usually they spoke the language of the delegation to which they were assigned. Two days before the delegation's arrival, they met to receive their final instructions.[43] First of all, they were to carry out a classic mission of providing hospitality and anticipating the desires of the guests of honour. They were to ensure the delegation's security, see to it that convoys of cars were not interrupted when passing through the city, and guarantee punctuality. They also served as protocol agents during official dinners and the reception at the Führer's residence, so that the predetermined seating plan was respected. They were to ensure that the initial programme was carried out. But these men were also expected to note the reactions of members of their delegations and their opinions regarding Germany and especially the Reich's policies.

In fact, these men were intelligence agents, and submitted reports at the end of their visit. Most of these reports show that the Germans' efforts were not made in vain. For example, the British delegation, which consisted of General Fuller and Lord Brocket, said they enjoyed the parade.[44] They found particularly impressive the meeting with the Führer, which was for them the highpoint of their visit.

The Spaniards and the Portuguese, who were accompanied by Count of Moulin, were more eloquent in their approval. Although most of them were monarchists, the Spanish delegates stated that under the current circumstances they opposed a restoration. The continuation of Franco's regime was 'the only solution', a Falangist accompanying them declared. Franco's supporters explained their armament needs for the coming war: more than two thousand aeroplanes. They would like their Italian allies to provide half of these, and the German firm of Heinkel to produce the other half in the Iberian Peninsula. The Spaniards expressed 'hatred for France and to a lesser extent for Britain',[45] because of their role during the Civil War. Germany could count on their friendship. But the Count of Moulin noted that Spain was asking for a respite of at least a year in order to reconstruct its forces before entering a war on Germany's side. The Portuguese delegation also found much to admire; one member thought the military parade far superior to those in France and Britain.

Other delegations were still more won over. The report on the Slovaks emphasized the representatives' pleasure on hearing their president greeted with the cry 'Heil Tiso'. The Yugoslavs kept repeating a remark with which the Führer had favoured them: 'We came to appreciate each other as adversaries during the war.'[46]

The information thus provided did not concern solely positive aspects. For the Scandinavian countries, the parade showed German 'Prussianism', an innate sense of discipline and brute force. The Norwegians looked at the German tanks and thought that some of them had been built with financial aid their government had provided the Czech Skoda factories. The Swedish delegate deemed it in bad taste to choose Franz Lehar's *The Merry Widow* to celebrate the birthday of a head of state. Didn't he know that it was Hitler's favourite work? It is more likely that he was aware that his remark would be reported to the Nazi leaders, as was Stoycho Moshanov, the president of the Bulgarian national assembly, who cried, 'We can only hope that we won't have to fight this army!'[47] The last word was left to a perplexed Norwegian: 'What future is all this preparing for us?'

The official hosts prudently expressed themselves with a sense of tactics. In 1939, the world knew that the Nazi regime had vast networks of informers and subversives that were already being called 'the fifth column'. But François-Poncet's memoirs show how naïve he could be at the beginning of Hitler's regime.[48] Once a month, he met with representatives of the countries of the Little Entente at Berlin's Horcher restaurant. Although the atmosphere was at first frank, these meetings were deserted by Poland and then lost their meaning. No doubt we should see in this the result of German diplomacy's effort to produce dissociation on the European scale, as François-Poncet thought. But it was certainly also the result of espionage. One rumour suggests that Horcher, who was in good odour among Nazi leaders, allowed microphones to be placed in his restaurants, and particularly in the one in London.[49] Was François-Poncet unaware of this? Did he learn that a confidential report provided Hitler with information about his departure for Paris only when he left his post in October 1938? Was he also unaware that German security services had long employed servants to obtain confidential information?

For her part, Bella Fromm mentions what she calls 'salon spies'.[50] Some of these were operating even before the Nazis came to power, like Wilhelm Starr, who had the advantage of writing newspaper columns on high society. Fromm thought there was a system of high-society espionage.[51] She cites Edit von Coler, a figure in Berlin theatre, who is supposed to have been assigned to monitor François-Poncet's invitations. Fromm also mentions Baroness von der Heyden-Rynsch, whom she nicknames 'the plague of teas'. According to the Austrian representative in Germany, Walli von Richtofen, a widow who regularly invited socialites to her elegant home in Potsdam, was in the pay of the foreign ministry and the Gestapo. She did indeed play a prominent role in all the ministry's social events.

Everyone knew that the leaders' wives were involved in public life and that they reported what they heard. People were concerned about being denounced to the authorities if they made inappropriate remarks, unless they had diplomatic immunity. But other figures acted in a more covert way.

In the archives of Hitler's Adjudantur there are letters from informers who belonged to high society, and especially British high society.[52] They report on the evolution of opinion and mention a few potential sympathizers. One of these informants who used her relations to help the Third Reich was Stephanie von Hohenlohe. As a figure in international high society, she is particularly interesting because of her unusual career and the role of salon spy that she undertook. The daughter of an Austrian physician, she met Prince von Hohenlohe and married him. It seems that her family was of Jewish origin, even if, according to her biographer, Martha Schad, she always denied it.[53] Was this fact known at the time? Probably not. A wealthy widow who enjoyed the very respectable title of princess, she led an idle existence, frequenting the conservatives and soon the Nazis. Hitler called her his 'favourite princess'. She took advantage of her close ties in high society to promote National Socialist ideas and when she travelled she submitted regular reports on the opinions of influential persons she met. She played this role of an agent for Hitler and for

Göring.[54] Fritz Wiedemann, Hitler's adjutant and his former officer during the Great War, established an intimate relationship with her. That is why when she was looking for a quiet residence in 1938, Wiedemann, surely with Hitler's permission, had the Leopoldskron Castle in Austria restored at the chancellery's expense and put it at her disposal. The modernization of the castle and the installation of a heating system cost no less than nine thousand, four hundred and seventy marks, at a time when a worker earned about two hundred marks a month.[55] The princess spent several months at the castle with her son Franz, who used the attached tennis court. A payment of sixty thousand marks made by the chancellery in November 1938 amply covered her expenses. Wiedemann indeed gave her the official title of 'social adviser'.[56] In 1939, the princess left for the United States, probably to gather intelligence, rejoining there Wiedemann, who had been named consul. She ended up opposing the Nazi regime, but the American government had doubts about her, and after the Japanese attack on Pearl Harbor she was incarcerated as a spy.

The use of domestic servants and socialites as informers did not, however, suffice to provide information regarding international strategy. Thus the security and intelligence services did not hesitate to open mail and listen in on telephone conversations. The American ambassador, Dodd, stated as early as 1934 that not one of his letters crossed the German border without censorship.[57] This concern about espionage also affected the regime's great figures, to the point that even Himmler was convinced that Hitler was having him spied upon. Ribbentrop, his state secretary, and his protocol chief all demanded confidentiality, especially when the war was being launched: no conversations were to be held in the corridors, and office doors were to be closed during work sessions.[58] Constant suspicion spread in the salons, and conversations henceforth focused on subjects that were anodyne or at least did not contradict the official line. In addition, starting in 1938 the foreign ministry's guests were not such as might lead foreign diplomats to make great geopolitical statements. They were all figures well integrated into the regime.

The Little World of the Foreign Ministry and Its Rules of Conduct

The ministry of foreign affairs did not limit itself to inviting the heads of other countries' diplomatic missions and their wives. It invited to its receptions and great social events representatives of the major sectors of activity. All of them might serve Germany's interests in dealing with the diplomats. This ordinary practice took on a peculiar coloration in a regime that tended to try to guarantee that those close to it enjoyed the greatest influence, and that did not hesitate to concentrate resources around selected clienteles. One of the protocol office's dossiers dating from the late

1930s describes with precision the range of guests and allows us to form an image of the diplomatic world of the time.[59]

This dossier was a set of individual profiles classified by milieus, organizations, or specialities. Each of these indicated the individual's name, address, family status, children, if any, and sometimes also contained personal remarks, especially concerning their relationships. Nothing truly intimate, but the whole thing indicates that the protocol services were concerned about clan links within high society, accorded an unequal role to political groups by privileging the SA and the SS, and inserted guests, including private guests, into the ministry's ongoing activities. This very bureaucratic dossier ignores central figures such as Hitler and his adjutants. Was that because the addresses of the men in the top echelon were known by heart or because that elite was contacted only by the minister in person?

The mixture of names and private and public groups is characteristic of these official events, which sought to provide an opportunity for establishing friendly and familial relations. Marriages occurred within this little world. Ribbentrop, his wife, and his daughter regularly invited members of their family, such as Annelies von Ribbentrop's mother, brother-in-law, and uncle, as well as an uncle of the minister. It is more amusing to see the category of 'friends of Fräulein Bettina von Ribbentrop', the minister's daughter, explicitly appear – no doubt to help her avoid the boredom of spending the evening among elderly bigwigs. Among her friends were the daughter of the Italian commercial attaché and the daughter of a great banker. The category of 'private circle' was not limited to the family. The people in it were not all Ribbentrop's friends or intimates, far from it. For instance, it included Brandt, Hitler's physician, whose address is given as 'the Führer's apartment'; his role perhaps explains his presence in this category. Great names with prestigious addresses also appear, such as the Princes zu Schaumberg-Lippe, Hohenlohe-Langeburg, Hessen, and Reuss, and among the nobles Dönhoff, Richtofen, Stülpnagel, and others. The family of Count von Toerring-Jettenbach was rather dazzling: his wife Elisabeth was Princess of Greece and Denmark and the sister of Princess Paul of Yugoslavia and the Duchess of Kent.

A few familiar friends of Nazism also appear: Viktoria von Dirksen, Walli von Richtofen, and Ilse Göring. The list of 'single women and girls' is a sort of concentrate of widows and debutantes, including Editha von Schröder, called Dia, the daughter of Kurt Schröder, the banker who supported Hitler's rise to power and lent his house for the meeting with von Papen; Luise Schwerin von Krosigk, the daughter of the finance minister; and Felicitas von Tschammer und Osten, the daughter of the national head for sports. Regular guests of the Führer like Viktoria von Dirksen's niece, Sigrid von Laffert, are also on the list. Sigrid was soon to marry a rising young official at the foreign ministry. The presence of Vera Lammers, the daughter of a state secretary at the chancellery, allows us to date the document between 1938 and 1940, because Vera then got married and Hitler gave her a painting.[60]

Businessmen were well represented in the specialized groups. This was probably because economic problems remained urgent and the ministry supported efforts to increase exports and the regular quest for foreign currency to finance rearmament and avoid food shortages. The group that emerges is no different from the one Hitler convened each year to launch the winter aid campaign. Krupp was a member, as were the heads of Siemens, Heinrich von Buol and Oskar Henschell, of IG Farben, Max Ilgner, of the Dresdner Bank, Hans Pilder, and, of course, of the Hermann Göring factories, Wilhelm Voss. Let there be no mistake: the ministry was not just an annexe of the business world. It merely sought to facilitate entrepreneurs' activity in order to obtain their political support – in short, an exchange of courtesies.

The approximately forty files on artists and scholars are in agreement with what we know from other sources. In them we find the little world of the arts and sciences that ardently supported National Socialism: Benno von Arendt, Woldemar Brinkmann, Heinrich George, Gustav Gründgens, Heinrich Hoffmann, Fritz Klintsch (sculptor), Ferdinand Sauerbruch (surgeon), Heinz Tietjen (general superintendent of the Prussian theatre), Wilhelm Furtwängler, Lothar Kreuz (rector of the University of Berlin). Some of them, like Clemens Scharschmidt, were clearly mentioned for their particular competence: a specialist on Japan at the University of Berlin or a specialist on Hungary, Julius von Farkas.

In the area of the press, we find the usual names: Gustav Albrecht, the representative of the official press agency, the DNB; Gunther d'Alquem, editor of the SS magazine *Das Schwarze Korps*; Max Amann, the NSDAP's publisher; Theodor Boetticher of the *Völkischer Beobachter*; and also Thea von Puttkammer, who was related to Hitler's adjutant for the navy.

The reasons for inviting a person are evident, ranging from the need to do business to the desire to defend ideological values and to create reliable relationships. Wasn't the point basically to cement the alliance between all these elites that intersected in a vast set of dominant people masked by the caricatural name of 'Prominenten'? This practice was in line with the tradition perpetuated by the nobility through the season of balls and the festivities that were sometimes reserved for young people so that they could find spouses. The difference lay in the mixture of the groups encouraged to melt into an unprecedented aristocracy.

The apparently heterogeneous character of this society makes us wonder about the possibility of harmony between old noble families like the Schaumburg-Lippes or the Stülpnagels and wealthy parvenus like Ribbentrop, vulgar men reputed to be drunkards like Robert Ley, the head of the KdF, young, dynamic officials like Arthur Axmann of the HJ, or Lorenz, Otto Dietrich's assistant at Hitler's press office. The protocol maintained by the Third Reich did much to facilitate these encounters.

Etiquette played a fundamental role and was based on a hierarchy of politeness. Since the Weimar Republic, etiquette had no longer been determined by noble titles but by an individual's rank in the state apparatus. Nazism adopted this principle and was even able to extend it after 1933 through the new political and administrative relationships, while at the same time reintegrating the nobility. It established an official hierarchy and a set of titles that removed much of the ambiguity in high society, where everything was ultimately based on power. In the late 1930s, disputes regarding precedence were over. The highest dignity resided at the summit of the state, and then spread out to its provincial margins. Etiquette thus maintained civility in the sense defined by Norbert Elias on the basis of the court society of the *ancien régime*.[61] It channelled the potential violence engendered by a regime that stimulated competition while at the same time subjecting decisions to forms of debate and compromises that favoured the most powerful and energetic.

One indication that Nazi politeness did not abandon civility is the gestures the leaders used in greeting one another. We may be tempted to think that extending one's arm and crying 'Heil Hitler!' was enough to greet an interlocutor. That was not the case. Usually the German salute, which had been made official in the administration since 1934 and then among the public after 1935, was only one element in introducing oneself. It was followed by a classic handshake. Newsreels show that Hitler himself forced his interlocutors to engage in a complicated series of gestures. He approached them, made an initial salute, shook men's hands or kissed ladies' hands, and then stepped slightly backward and saluted again. This maintained old customs while inserting them into the new ideological framework.

The protocol services incorporated these practices and stressed politeness and etiquette by applying strict rules regarding the placement of guests at receptions, dinners, or shows. Their skill in placement went back to the period of the Prussian royalty (the former *Marschallamt*), and the other ministries, and even the Reich chancellery, consulted them when foreign guests were invited. In the process, subtle borderlines between categories of guests emerged. It was possible to meet people without associating with them and without risking confusion among social groups.

The invisible but very real barriers between the traditional elites and those promoted by National Socialism are revealed by the example of Göring's famous party on the evening of 11 January 1936, when he received at the Opera everyone who was anyone in Berlin.[62] Priority was given to official power. Thus ambassadors were seated in the boxes of honour alongside important ministers (Neurath, Blomberg, Frick, Seldte, Darré). We are struck by one anomaly at the beginning of this list and thus at the pinnacle of this implicit hierarchy: Göring himself was surrounded by his family and close friends, notably the Prince and Princess of Hesse. Was this to show that the highest German authority present had no equivalent abroad? The second series of seats, situated on the left, was occupied by lower-ranking ministers and the heads of major Nazi organisations (Ley, Lutze), along with envoys, that is, intermediate-level diplomats. There were also seated the imperial family, its entourage, King Ferdinand and Queen Eudoxie, and the princes, including Christophe of Hesse. The mixture was limited because the members of the crown prince's entourage separated the imperial family from the Nazi dignitaries, in this case Lutze and his wife. Farther down in the hierarchy the placement became less respectful of these invisible borderlines. For instance, one box shows a confusion of types: Ribbentrop, who was then an ambassador, was seated with his wife next to Prince August-Wilhelm, who was a general in the SA. The other guests were seated at tables on the wooden floor adjoining the stage. Here the rules were still less strict, to the point that for some tables the plan showed only indications such as 'two major industrialists', a tangible sign that the world of economics served to fill out the tables and did not have the commanding function that an orthodox Marxist interpretation would suggest.

This kind of arrangement shows that despite the theoretical abolition of titles under the Weimar Republic, birth was still important in governmental offices. However, as Stephan Malinowski has pointed out, the nobility as such was no longer a political force.[63] It had fused with the regime and shared leadership with other elites. For this reason, it still served as an official reference point on great occasions. Its way of life was perfectly well understood by the regime, which, far from hindering it, adopted its essential characteristics, notably its sense of hospitality.

Munificence in the Service of International Relations

Official visits to Germany became more frequent during the second half of the 1930s. Representatives of Yugoslavia, Hungary, Bulgaria, Italy, Spain, and other countries came on official visits, and unofficial, almost recreational visits were also made, for instance by the King of Denmark. Each time, the chancellery and the foreign ministry were called upon to organize the programme for the visit, and they included major social events, always seeking new amusements that their guests might remember and talk about after their departure or when making other trips. However, a typical itinerary with certain obligatory elements gradually emerged. A gala dinner at the chancellery and a visit to Göring's residence at Karinhall could scarcely be omitted. In addition, there was an evening show, usually at the Opera, cultural activities (museums, exhibits, schools), and a tour of military or industrial sites.

This itinerary included meetings with German high society in both public and more intimate contexts. Even during a crisis as serious as the Munich Conference, the foreign guests, Chamberlain, Daladier, and

Mussolini, were treated by their hosts in accord with the etiquette for prestigious visitors, with several occasions for conversation and sit-down luncheons and dinners. A kind of modesty related to the danger of the time explains the absence of a full-scale state reception. On the other hand, when Admiral Horthy, the regent of the Kingdom of Hungary, came on an official visit with his wife in August 1938, the Nazi regime gave him a sumptuous welcome.[64] We can sense the desire to create a durable relationship that would favour the Third Reich's policies in Central Europe and the Balkans.

To ensure the comfort of their Hungarian guests, the foreign ministry and chancellery as usual designated ladies of honour who were to see to it that everything took place in accord with the programme. Acting as veritable companions, they made conversation during the rather frequent periods of waiting. State secretary Ernst von Weizsäcker's wife undertook this task for Horthy's wife, accompanying her on her journeys in Germany. The Horthys' visit was punctuated by the classical obligations: dinners, galas, receptions, visits, inaugurations. But to mark the solemnity of these days, a cruise on the North Sea on two separate boats was arranged. The flotilla met on the high seas and the *Grille* and the *Patria*, carrying Horthy and his wife, sailed up alongside each other. A happy group (two hundred persons) took part in this event and witnessed a maritime parade. Contemporary photos taken on the *Patria* show Frau Horthy and Frau von Weizsäcker talking with Frau Lorenz, the wife of a German diplomat, and Signora Attolico, the wife of the Italian ambassador; they are sitting in comfortable armchairs, their hats pinned to their head to keep them from blowing away. At the same time, on the deck, Goebbels, Tschammer und Osten, and Funk are seated behind beautiful girls wearing sunglasses who are sunbathing on deckchairs. The men are smiling.

The leaders were familiar with pleasure cruises. From 31 March to 4 April 1939 they took a maiden cruise on the *Robert Ley*, the KdF's ship, which was fitted out with bedrooms, an orchestra, and all the staff necessary for long cruises, for the idea was soon to put this vessel in the service of German workers.[65] In the case of foreign guests, the cruises were usually limited to a trip on one of the rivers, usually the Rhine, to allow them to laze about while being told about local traditions and legends.

A cruise on a large vessel was more expensive. It required arranging transportation from Berlin or Munich. Special trains were chartered and convoys of cars organized. For example, the nine-day voyage taken by the king and queen of Siam in June 1934 cost the foreign ministry alone forty thousand marks for a chartered train and other expenses. The chancellery's share was four times greater. The German taxpayer did not know about these expenditures, which the foreign ministry did not always record because these trips were financed by the head of state's budget, which was itself only partly recorded. Moreover, for his guests' journeys through Germany, Hitler sometimes lent his own car in order to ensure the best lodging and transportation. Thus when Edda Ciano, the wife of the Italian foreign minister and Mussolini's daughter, made an unofficial trip in 1936, she used the Führer's personal car, which he had had specially decorated with flowers.[66] She went to visit him at the Berghof. This allows us to see how friendly relations were created among states without general politics being an issue. After this episode, Edda Mussolini-Ciano became an ardent supporter of an entente between Italy and Germany. She thereby confirmed the choices made by her husband, who wanted to persuade the Duce to reverse his alliances once and for all.

Such gestures were interpreted as signs of generosity and attentiveness. The proof of this is that at a more tragic moment, Hitler authorized the Princess of Piedmont to cross Germany on her way to visit her brother, the King of Belgium, in 1940, when the country was under German occupation.[67] The princess also went to the Berghof to thank Hitler. Relationships with European sovereigns, and even with politicians, were thus not limited to the diplomatic arena alone.[68] They gave Hitler an additional way of asserting his grandeur as well as regular and intimate contacts with these interlocutors that were praised in the news and propaganda produced by the Reich. The Mussolini–Hitler pair thus became a kind of icon after 1936.

Hitler had gone to Italy shortly before he came to power. In June 1934 he visited Venice, but had not been very happy with the way he was received there. On the other hand, his second trip in May 1938 was a triumph. For his part, Mussolini first came to Berlin in September 1937. His journey was immortalized by Chaplin's *The Great Dictator*, which distorts reality only slightly. But at the time the Italian and German news services saw in this event the combination of two great powers. The characters in Ettore Scola's film *A Special Day* probably give us a better sense of its meaning at the time. The heroine's Fascist husband comes home dazzled by the sumptuousness of Hitler's reception in the spring of 1938. He concludes: 'If we make a baby tonight, we'll name him Adolf.'

On each of these occasions, the statesmen were accompanied by large entourages. The embassies received Hitler and Mussolini, organized entertainment, and facilitated the creation of links between the two countries. Fraternization between Fascist and Nazi high societies resulted from this *rapprochement*. Diplomatic officials travelled back and forth more frequently and even went on vacation in their new ally's country. When they were in Rome, Ribbentrop and Dörnberg were not merely taken under Ambassador Mackensen's wing, as we can see in the albums of photographs made by the head of protocol;[69] they also spent a few hours relaxing at the Golf Club with Italian countesses and in the company of Ciano, who, during his visits to Germany, was invited by high dignitaries to take part in fine hunting parties. Ribbentrop received him on the domains that were at his ministry's disposal, inviting Himmler and Schwerin-Krosigk for the occasion. Together, the hunters lunched in the forest on tables set up outside but provided with hotplates and silver. Göring used his domain at Karinhall to satisfy the taste for luxury shown by prestigious guests such as Ciano, Balbo, Horthy, or the Duke of Windsor. Hitler played a similar card by receiving them lavishly at the Berghof and taking them on the ritual walk to the tea house or the Eagle's Nest.

In order to strengthen these ties, guests in Germany were usually given presents that were not always purely utilitarian, far from it. They received art objects or historical artefacts: paintings, sculptures, local products, SS china. The practice of giving state gifts is universal, but the Nazi administration expanded, rationalized, and systematized it. Foreign friends received more expensive presents than those given by France or Great Britain: Mercedes costing between twenty and thirty-five thousand marks for Paul of Yugoslavia, Farouk of Egypt, Zog I of Albania, and General Franco.[70] The foreign ministry also used decorations to establish ties. A report on Germany's competition with France and Britain in Brazil recommended that decorations, distinctions, and presents be given to prominent figures in order to counterbalance the growing influence of countries opposed to Germany.[71] This project, which was conceived before Hitler's accession to power, was carried out. The Reich pursued a rather broad policy of symbolic rewards.

A system of gifts and counter-gifts emerged whose objective was to secure support among regular partners. It reflected the extension of the courtly game to the global scale. In order to prevent the creation within the Führer's staff of a clientele that might escape his control, foreign decorations could be awarded to members of his entourage only with his personal approval. Proposals to grant such medals and honours came most often after an official visit abroad. Members of the Adjudantur were the first to benefit. This shows that no one doubted that these honours influenced Hitler. Thus Brückner, Schaub, Bormann, et al. were decorated by Bulgaria, Yugoslavia, and of course Italy.[72] The Italians did not hesitate to add substantial material gifts to these signs of recognition.

Obviously, these exchanges were significant only in relation to the Reich's strategic goals. They strengthened the latter's orientation and established alliances for the time that complicity prevailed. When war came, these exchanges could strengthen solidarity between leaders and ties within the elites. The method became all the more efficacious for Germany when its diplomatic network was extended by the absorption of Austria's embassies and consulates after 1938 and by the appropriation of those of Czechoslovakia.

Farewell to Routine

When the war started, life in the diplomatic world took on a singular appearance. For a time, carefree travel and hunting continued, but more often in uniform than in civilian clothing. The official costume worn by German diplomats had been redesigned by the Third Reich, because Hitler wanted to unify officials' garb in order to establish their authority.[73] As the war continued, it increasingly forced diplomats to adopt military modes of behaviour: wearing uniforms all the time, changing work schedules to include long periods of standing guard, carrying weapons, travelling in vehicles and in combat aeroplanes, and so on. When bombardments of Berlin became more frequent, the ministry's men hesitated to go home for fear of not being able to get back to work on time. Very high officials like Dörnberg, the protocol chief, and Rühle, another office head, took refuge in the Adlon Hotel with their secretaries in order to be closer to the ministry in case of an emergency, they said.[74]

At the beginning of the war, diplomats from countries opposing Germany who had not left were arrested. They had to entrust the management of their property to the embassies of neutral countries. Until 1941, the United States performed this function for France and for Britain.[75] For its part, Germany entrusted its interests to Switzerland. In North and South America, German officials were interned in 1941. Socialites who had been accustomed to prestigious hotels and grand receptions found themselves reduced to modest conditions. There were a little more than five hundred foreigners waiting for an agreement with the Reich that would allow them to go home.[76] A thousand Germans were in an analogous situation. It is revealing that in January 1942 these men preferred to return to Nazi Germany rather than stay where they were. Didn't their colleagues in the central administration, who were aware of the extensive massacres in the Soviet Union in the autumn of 1941, tip them off as to what German policy really amounted to? Were they actually unaware that they were serving a criminal regime?

Foreigners who were not protected by diplomatic status found themselves in a difficult situation, but those who moved in the upper strata of society must have considered themselves fortunate when the great deportations began. Most of them remained discreet when they disapproved of the Third Reich. For instance, Christabel Bielenberg tried to speak an unaccented German in order to conceal her English origin.[77]

On the other hand, a small minority exulted in the victories, as did Colin Ross, a rich American who had resided in Berlin since the 1930s and was a friend of the Schirachs and of Hitler. After his attempts at mediation with the United States failed, he chose to remain with his National Socialist comrades right up to the end.[78] He and his wife committed suicide in April 1945. Others experienced a strange disgrace, like Princess Mafalda, the daughter of the King of Italy and the wife of Prince Philipp von Hessen. After the Italian monarchy ended its alliance with Germany in September 1943, she was interned along with her husband. However, the prince had been a Gauleiter and had close ties to Hitler and to Göring. They were detained under harsh conditions. Mafalda fell ill in the Nazi jails and died.

Suspected of crimes against humanity, in 1945 her husband was transferred directly from a Nazi camp to an Allied detention camp.

Several diplomats were prosecuted in trials connected with the
Nuremberg Trials and known as 'the Wilhelmstrasse Trials' (the foreign
ministry had been in the Wilhelmstrasse). State Secretary Luther, interned
by Ribbentrop and Hitler after being involved in an attempted conspiracy
in 1943, was liberated by the Red Army, but died of illness in May 1945.
Ribbentrop had already been sentenced to death at the Nuremberg Trials
and was executed on 1 October 1946. There remained State Secretary
Weizsäcker. He denied any knowledge of the Holocaust. In the absence of
conclusive documentation, the court accepted his claim of ignorance. He
was sentenced for having written 'raise no objection' on orders to deport
six thousand Jews from France. Not until 1987 did a German historian,
Hans-Jürgen Dörscher, prove what had been suspected all along: starting
in the autumn of 1941, official memos regularly informed high officials in
the ministry as to what was going on.[79] As early as the spring of 1942, all
the departments, including the protocol department, knew about the massacres and the Final Solution. These deceitful diplomats had misled everyone before 1939. They repeated the same deceits after the war. The foreign
ministry was one of the least purged, whereas it was one of those that had
the highest rates of membership in the SS and continued to pay discreet
homage to these amazing hypocrites who suddenly discovered the charms
of democracy after the war.

In contrast, the story of a career diplomat like Fritz Kolbe astonishes us.
His biographer, Lucas Delattre, has shown how this austere man spied
on the Nazis because he became convinced that only a military defeat
could restore freedom to his country.[80] Although jovial, he was shy and no
socialite. He frequented only one of the groups around Professor
Sauerbruch, the head of the La Charité Hospital. He did not appear at the
ministry's great evening parties, no doubt being thought too obscure or
unreliable. Although he refused to join the NSDAP or the SS during the
war, Kolbe nonetheless functioned as liaison with the Army General Staff.
This allowed him to duplicate documents for American intelligence. He
was unable to continue his career after the defeat; his former colleagues
considered him a traitor. This anti-socialite and heroic anti-Nazi ended his
days in Australia. In 2004 he was finally rehabilitated by the German
foreign minister, Joschka Fischer, who also removed from the gallery of
former officials the portrait of Alexander von Dörnberg that had remained
hanging there after his death in 1983 at the age of eighty-two.

8

The Second Worldly War

Mein Führer

Your brilliant conduct of the war, the incomparable courage of our troops and their first-class weaponry have been able, in the inconceivably short space of five weeks, to force Holland and Belgium to capitulate, to throw the remains of the British expeditionary force into the sea, and to defeat, in a series of great, destructive battles, the courageous defence offered by the French army. Today, the fighting is dying down in the West and the way is open for a definitive settlement of accounts with perfidious Albion. At this hour of historic importance, I wish to shake your hand with all my admiration as an old soldier and a German. May God protect you and our German fatherland. Sieg Heil. Wilhelm, Crown Prince.[1]

The German imperial prince is exultant. He has his revenge for the war lost in 1918, that shameful defeat that led his family to abdicate and go into exile. His praise for Hitler was repeated by all the elites. Grand Duke Friedrich Franz von Mecklenburg sent Hitler a telegram in the same register on 14 June 1940.[2] He was enthusiastic about the taking of Paris, and also mentions the brilliance that made this victory possible. Everyone found a way to distinguish himself in courteously expressing his joy. For example, von Neurath, the former foreign minister, writing from Bohemia-Moravia, which he governed, also praised 'the brilliance' of the way the war was conducted. Brilliance. A whole people believed it had definitively buried the 'Diktat' of Versailles. This idea of revenge was expressed by Irmengard von Brockhausen, née Hindenburg, the daughter of the former president, when she wrote:

On this day of immense historical importance, your day of glory, I beg you to allow me to tell you something that has long moved me: how much my beloved father would be grateful to you and how happy and proud he would be to experience these events. My best wishes and my thoughts accompany you, my Führer, and I am proud that my three sons are serving under our flag.[3]

The archbishop of Trier, Dr Bornewasser, added to this chorus of praise the prayers and hymns of his flock.[4] Outside Germany, some of the conquered joined in this communion.[5]

This illusion of triumphal power imbued German society at a time when its armies were spreading over Europe. Rarely had the popularity of the government been so great. Even members of the opposition began to wonder whether it would ever be possible to halt this tornado. High society more than other social sectors bathed in this glorious and brutal dream. It profited greatly from the benefits that accompanied the conquest and partly forgot the sadness of the first deaths. Secretary of State Weizsäcker, for instance, lost a son during the attack on Poland. Everyone adapted to the strengthening of social supervision, restrictions, and the allocation of additional resources. For this reason the Second World War, like the First, appeared to be a socialites' project, the progeny of a vision in which the strong can make use of the weak and the vanquished and blithely pillage them. This vision also appears in the crudeness of the ideological programme: killing people to create a new world. Life in high society reflected these developments. First, it espoused the strategy of accumulation and enjoyment imposed by Hitler's government. Then it narrowed as death approached and defeat loomed.

Prospering in Difficult Times

At the beginning of the war, the German bureaucracy strengthened its grip on society. Prices were strictly controlled and salaries frozen. The propaganda ministry was assigned to supervise salaries in show business: the cinema, theatre, orchestras, singers.

To this end, Goebbels had drawn up a restricted list of artists and their levels of remuneration. This document is instructive in many respects, since it identifies the darlings of German show business. Issued in 1939, the list indicates by incremental categories corresponding to 10,000 marks the wages received by an artist.[6] The top category concerns actresses and actors receiving salaries in excess of 50,000 marks a year. The best-paid was Zarah Leander, a Swedish actress who had made her debut in Stockholm in the 1920s. She had known some stars of that period in Berlin, such as Fritzi Massary, the operetta singer. In October 1936, after a successful experiment on the Viennese stage, she met Hans Jacob Weismann, the president of the Berlin Chamber of Cinema, who was in the middle of a recruitment campaign for the Third Reich. By offering her financial advantages (a high salary and payment of half her wages in Swedish Kroner),

Weismann persuaded her to sign a contract with the UFA. She moved with her children to Berlin in January 1937 and began making *La Habanera* under the direction of Detlef Sierck. The film was an immense success, but Sierck, whose wife was Jewish, was not well regarded by those in power and left Germany for Hollywood shortly afterward. Zarah Leander pursued her career in Germany. Under the direction of Carl Froelich, the following year she made *Heimat*, starring opposite Heinrich George. Again, the film was a great success and Froelich wanted to give her further leading roles. She had become the best-known foreign actress under contract in Germany. Henceforth she was perfectly integrated into the Nazi upper crust, frequenting cinema circles in Berlin and Munich, and meeting Goebbels and even Hitler – while her annual salary reached 150,000 marks. Despite the outbreak of war, she remained in Germany and worked there until 1943. The destruction of her large home in Grunewald in 1943 led her to return to Sweden, discreetly, while her last films continued to be shown in the Reich.

The Swedish actress Ingrid Bergman also appears on the list of salaries in excess of 50,000 marks, but she chose to leave for Hollywood in 1939. The young actress had come to work in Germany the preceding year, and she too was under contract for three films with the UFA: the blondeness of these Nordic Venuses and their legendary beauty conformed well to Nazi criteria. Bergman made only one film, a rather banal comedy of manners called *Die Vier Gesellen* (*The Four Companions*). She was on the list for 1939 only because of her contract, which was still valid at the time the war began. Perhaps the Germans also hoped that she would return, although she had already obtained new engagements in Hollywood.

Other stars listed in the highest category of remuneration are less surprising. They were already among the beneficiaries of tax exemptions, such as Hans Albers (120,000 marks), Emil Jannings (120,000 marks), Gustav Gründgens (80,000 marks), and Paula Wessely (120,000 marks). Among the well-paid foreign artists was Beniamino Gigli (132,000 marks). Gigli was one of the greatest tenors of his age, which explains the special attention he enjoyed in Germany at a time when singing had become part of the state religion. Pola Negri (75,000 marks) is also on the list; her real name was Barbara Apollonia Chalipec. Born in Poland, she had made films in Germany in the 1920s before becoming a star of the American silent film, but the advent of sound films ended her Hollywood career. In Germany, however, she regained popularity in the 1930s and made about one film annually for the UFA during the Hitler years. Nonetheless, in 1941 she returned to the United States, fleeing the increasing rigidity of the Nazi regime. Lilian Harvey (120,000 marks) was on her way into exile when the list was drawn up. This half-English actress had returned to Germany in 1935, but troubles with the Gestapo. because she had helped the homosexual choreographer Jens Keith get out of prison and emigrate in 1937, had put her in a delicate situation. Goebbels' support on this occasion did not prevent her from being suspect in the eyes of the regime.

The level of remuneration thus did not depend solely on proximity to the regime. Celebrity and the salaries received abroad were also taken into account. The government hoped to export its ideas and encourage support through the distribution of its mass culture. The cinema was also a way of bringing in foreign currency and compensating for imports, particularly food imports. Hence the regime sought to use high salaries to attract international stars.

Fundamentally, the function of this 1939 list was to define a salary scale for the war that was beginning. The government wanted to avoid salary increases that would ultimately contribute to inflation and encourage competition among German public institutions. The salary freeze thus had a general significance and was part of a legal mechanism. However, there again the bureaucrats saw exemptions proliferating. Two basic motives were involved. The first was political, because it was a matter of supporting a propaganda effort. Thus when in February 1940 Ferdinand Marian asked for 50,000 marks to play in *The Jew Süss*, whereas up to that point he had received no more than 25,000 marks, Goebbels was asked to authorize the payment.[7] Goebbels agreed, citing the significance of this film and the importance of having quality actors to ensure its success. The second motive involved human relations and affection. In the preceding example, Goebbels personally knew Marian, who was a great party-goer and a heavy drinker.

This way of according advantages and privileges to certain persons, and even to a few groups, was characteristic of Nazi management as a whole. For instance, when the war began, generals, marshals, and admirals obtained a special bonus amounting to between 2,000 and 4,000 marks a month, depending on their rank. Göring's bonus was 20,000 marks a month. This practice, which might be justified as a way of motivating the troops, had no equivalent at other echelons. The most zealous officers obtained in addition estates in the areas newly conquered in the east, or gifts of money: Marshal von Rundstedt received a cheque for 250,000 marks in December 1941; Marshal von Kluge received a like amount in October 1942; Keitel was given the same sum in September 1942, and then an estate valued at 739,340.76 marks on 13 July 1944; for General Guderian, the amount was 1,240,000 marks in October 1942,[8] and so on. This advantageous treatment for high-ranking officers constituted both a motivating bonus and a recognition of their membership in a new landed aristocracy. Nonetheless, as the war went on, the practice of giving gifts became so systematic and regular that it resembled the divvying up of loot among thieves convinced that they are working in the same direction.

By receiving these gifts, military men accepted the symbolism that accompanied them and the system that made them possible.[9] They accepted, sometimes implicitly, sometimes officially, anti-Semitism, the institutional conception of racism, anti-communism, and the design of creating a Greater Germany. Their strategic reservations concerned less the meaning and objectives of the war than the way it was conducted.

The ministers were no less generously endowed. They received a monthly bonus equivalent to that of the military officers. Additional payments were made on the occasion of a family event or a birthday. Thus sums exceeding 100,000 marks were received by a whole cohort of dignitaries, including Otto Meissner, Wilhelm Ohnesorge, Franz Schlegelberger, Konstantin Freiherr von Neurath, Joachim von Ribbentrop, and others. Hans Heinrich Lammers distributed these sums, which were paid from the chancellery budget. This position allowed him to evaluate what Hitler's friends and servants received. As a reward for his discretion, he received in turn an exceptional endowment of 600,000 marks on his birthday, 7 May 1944. Other, more modest gifts had preceded this one. The private aspect of these gifts emerges from the way in which Lammers suggested to certain beneficiaries that they remain silent about having received them. Testifying before the Nuremberg prosecutors, he tried to camouflage the sums received.[10] Obviously he feared that repayment would be demanded, even though it was the German government that had distributed them.

Hitler had refined this practice of state gifts accompanied by tax exemptions before the war, thanks to his artist friends. Vollbehr, Thierack, Speer, Troost, and many actors benefited from them. Architects had received them: for instance, Gablonsky, who was given 50,000 marks in April 1939, as were three of Speer's assistants.[11] The Führer continued his generosity during the war. He even increased it as difficulties piled up, as if he wanted to make the situation less bitter for those close to him and convince the sceptics.

Was this corruption pure and simple, as Frank Bajohr thinks?[12] The absence of any visible and immediate service done in return for these gifts might make us wonder. The beneficiaries were well aware that this practice implicated them in the system, but no case of restitution has been actually proven, according to Ueberschär and Vogel, who were the first to undertake a precise study of this practice.[13] Moreover, a single minister, the minister of finance, Count Schwerin von Krosigk, declared after the war that he had been forced to receive these gifts (250,000 marks).[14] Nothing confirms this statement. In reality, it was more a matter of sharing the booty than of corruption as a strategy to advance certain policies. From the practice of gift giving there emerges a picture of a very high Nazi society that shared passions and interests in a clan-like way. This is shown by the payment of large sums and the support given to widows of dead comrades. Thus Hans Tschammer und Osten's widow benefited from exceptional gifts that helped her pay her debts and preserve her level of resources. Lina Heydrich was also generously supported after the death of her husband, the former head of the police who had been appointed governor of Bohemia-Moravia. Thus what was at stake was a way of life based on luxury and the assertion of distinctive elitist signs: an abundance of goods, luxurious buildings, loads of artworks, and discussions about the grandeur of the Aryan race.

The war largely benefited the pinnacle of high society, the men who controlled culture, politics, the administration, and especially the army. For that reason they were slow to recognize the bloody nature of the conflict. Similarly, the relative opulence that reigned in high society until 1943 masked how hard it was for the poorest people to get basic products, which were nonetheless generously subsidized. For socialites, the war was at first a time of plenty.

Eating Well Despite Rationing

The diplomat Walther Hewel, Hitler's personal friend and a supporter of National Socialism from the outset, was one of the regime's great hedonists. During the war years he continued to enjoy his sybaritic pleasures and even increased them. His task was to represent the interests of the foreign ministry at Hitler's Adjudantur and the General Staff. This made it possible for him to draw on the chancellor's resources and abundant supplies, and to receive his generous invitations. Starting in the mid-1930s, Hewel kept the menus for the main dinners to which he was invited: the continuity of the way the meals were put together and the choice of meats is striking. Thus at a dinner given in Wilhelmshaven on 1 April 1939, soup and fish were followed by a goose. On 4 June 1939, at a dinner given by the foreign ministry in honour of the regents of Yugoslavia, lobster and soup were followed by veal and duck chaudfroid. Afterward, melon farci and a chester gratinee were served.[15] At a private supper for the Führer and his friend Maria Holst at the Imperial Hotel in Vienna on 20 November 1940, a herb soup preceded paprika chicken and a homemade cake. On 28 November 1941, for a dinner with the Queen of Romania, fowl followed the soup that was the standard first course on the official menus during the war.

Fowl, and especially goose, became a luxury item at this time. Beef remained rare, but traditional German cuisine was less attached to it than to fowl: autumn was the season for duck, and it was customary to prepare a goose for Christmas Day. In 1940, demand exceeded supply; a report on the consumption and production of fowl shows that in 1941 the level was very inadequate, and the situation did not improve in 1942–3:[16] prices shot up.

The meals eaten by high officials and the wealthy were not affected by rationing, as is shown by the items ordered for the leaders' meals. For example, in 1940 a simple dinner was planned for a meeting of regional economic advisers at Rudolf Hess's ministry and food for it was ordered from the supply ministry. The latter recommended the following quantities for ninety guests: 20 kg of meat, 4.5 kg of butter, 2.5 kg of lard, 6 kg of cheese, 5 kg of sugar, 1 kg of oil, 30 kg of bread, and fifty eggs.[17] That is, an average of 222 grams of meat per person for a single meal. At that time the ration allotment for a labourer was at most 74 grams of meat per meal.[18] If we compare the amounts of cheese, the difference is even greater: 66 grams vs 4 grams. The labourer's ration of bread was 271 grams per meal, whereas each guest at this dinner received 330 grams. The gap increased as time went on. In 1943, when meat rations had been reduced to 250 grams per week, luxury restaurants continued to offer meals without ration coupons that were equivalent to a week's food consumption.

In Berlin, wild game and fowl were still to be found at the Neva Grill, Pelzer's, the Atelier, and the Tusculum, off the Kurfürstendamm.[19] The best food had long been found at Horcher's, Göring's favourite restaurant. Göring had his own stock of wines in the restaurant's cellars. Horcher was such a favourite that he was able to buy the Three Hussars restaurant in Prague, work at Maxim's in Paris, and open branches of his restaurant in Oslo and Belgrade. However, Goebbels was finally able to have Horcher's restaurant in Berlin closed because its excesses were incompatible with war propaganda. Other establishments such as the Adlon Hotel relied on special cocktails to allow their wealthy customers to entertain the illusion of undiminished prosperity.[20]

At the top of the administrative hierarchy, the supply ministry also tried to put controls on food consumption. It managed the rationing system set up in 1939. To preserve its authority, Hitler assigned it the task of checking meals and shipments of foodstuffs paid for with both public and private funds. The letter explaining his position nonetheless implies that his adjutants must not be starved; far from it.[21]

Officials at the agriculture ministry also tried to see to it that the people did not lack food; a sense that there were shortages could give rise to envy. They paid special attention to the price of pork, which was eaten in all households. Ham imported from Brazil was certainly not so good as German ham, but it was a worthy addition to the shopping basket and was reasonably priced.[22] Price checks were carried out every week by experts. The price of potatoes also remained reasonable at the beginning of the war, in the order of twenty-four pfennigs a kilogram, when a worker earned more than two hundred marks. Along with cabbage, they constituted the basis of family food supply.

German calorie intake decreased only slightly when the war began.[23] In 1938–9, it averaged 3,239 calories per capita per day. In 1939–40, it fell to 3,165, then rose to 3,295 in 1940–1, reaching 3,620 in 1942–3, remaining at 3,520 in 1943–4, before finally falling to 2,828 in 1944–5. We should note that at the time an ordinary individual was supposed to consume an average of 2,334 calories per day and a labourer 4,226. Consumption in conquered or occupied countries was far lower, reflecting Germany's appropriation of foreign food supplies during the war. The initial strategy was based on the idea that the 20 per cent deficit in German food production could be made up by levies carried out in countries that in theory had surplus calories – such as Poland and Romania! But it soon appeared that the systematic levies of food supplies were made for other reasons.[24] The SS worked out a plan to buy on the black market in order to divert a little more food and at the same time weaken the conquered peoples' ability to resist.[25] This plan was set in motion but not fully carried out.

To gauge the difference in access to food, we have only to look at the official statistics on the disparate consumption of meat in the following countries in the autumn of 1943, when agricultural production was in serious difficulty: 250 grams per capita per week in Germany; 140 grams in Belgium; 125 grams in Holland; 120 grams in France; 100 grams in Poland. Moreover, this alimentary hierarchy reflects the Third Reich's racial beliefs, because it is in accord with the supposed degree of Aryan blood. The Nazis considered the Dutch to be pure Aryans, whereas French blood had been corrupted. Belgium's position is explained by its mixed population and the presence of a Germanic minority on its territory. The Slavs in Poland, on the other hand, were seen as subhumans.

Propaganda sought to conceal these disparities, and within Germany itself, the gap between rich and poor. It constantly showed Hitler as a humble soldier, eating his soup standing up at a makeshift table, as he did when he visited the troops. Newsreels and photographs in the Hoffmann archive thus reinforce the legend of an ascetic Hitler, whereas his intimates and his physicians tell us that like Göring, the Führer gained weight.[26] The contrast is symptomatic of the regime's hypocrisy.

From Civilian Clothes to Uniforms

Controls on consumer goods gradually took hold. On 28 August 1939, before the war began, only certain basic products were controlled: soap, coal for domestic use, a few fabrics, and shoes.[27] A month later, rationing began to look like sumptuary laws and the repositioning of the regime with regard to luxury began. At the end of September 1939 fashionable footwear such as patent-leather shoes was forbidden, whereas certain athletic shoes (such as those for ice-skating) had to be produced using only recycled materials. The use of fabric to make certain things that were considered useless was forbidden. This spelled the end of umbrellas, whose elegance had already declined in Germany since the end of the Great War.

In November, a ration card was introduced for clothing. Its function was similar to the one already in use for food supplies. The card was divided into 100 points. When needed, the buyer had to provide points along with a cash payment. This amounted to a way of managing consumption. Clothing worn for work cost only 20 points, whereas suits and evening dresses required between 45 and 60 points. The system assumed that everyday clothing could be replaced about every six months.

Initially, this posed no great difficulty for high society, but it became more of a problem as wardrobes aged and the quality of products decreased. As elsewhere in wartime Europe, the range of colours, for instance, shrank. In 1944, there was only one colour of stockings for sale in Germany: grey. Women who cared about their appearance soon had to draw a line down the backs of their legs and put walnut stain on them to simulate stockings. However, at the beginning of the war, newspapers and newsreels offered many hints about how to remain fashionable. In the spring of 1940, a fashion week was organized in Vienna to maintain morale and spread the idea that in the area of clothing things were going on more or less as usual.[28] Unfortunately, the rise in prices made it difficult to buy clothing from fashion design houses; the result was a flood of complaints that this sector was controlled by Jews, despite the Aryanization that had been going on since 1938! Leather clothing and fur coats were hard to find during the first winter of the war. German production of rabbit and mouton coats was able to satisfy part of the internal demand. Fox or mink coats became an unheard-of luxury. Nevertheless the regime's great ladies had several of them: Eva Braun, for instance, had three.

The long overcoats in dark leather that were fashionable for military officers from the mid-1930s on should therefore be seen as a form of luxury. It was surely accompanied by the idea that this noble material showed man's superiority – as the stronger – over animals. This symbolic dimension explains dignitaries' desire to wear leather. Hitler and his adjutants launched this style by buying their coats from the same supplier, Herpich.[29] They also favoured made-to-measure uniforms in fabric.

The wearing of uniforms did not correspond solely to a kind of standardization attributable to the outbreak of the war or to a desire to break down differences in appearance and to regiment society. To be sure, uniforms maintained esprit de corps not only in the armed forces but also in the police, major administrations such as the ministries of foreign affairs, the postal service, and even propaganda, as well as in institutions derived from the NSDAP, such as the SS, the SA, the HJ, and the BDM.[30] But it also reproduced hierarchies, because there were more or less expensive versions, with accessories reserved for officers, such as caps and daggers, capes for high-ranking dignitaries, and gold ornaments for generals. The uniform's prestige differed depending mainly on the social importance and power of the organizations concerned, and varied individually in the decorations, chevrons, ribbons, and medals that were worn. However, all these uniforms increased an individual's prestige; they had been the object of a cult in Germany since the end of the nineteenth century.[31]

High society took this into account. Invitations to galas and programmes for official visits frequently indicated whether civilian garb or uniforms were to be worn. Protocol required that at official parties men wore dress uniforms with facings, braids, epaulettes, stripes, and top-stitching. Göring was watched with particular care, because the long list of his titles allowed him to have special clothes designed that lent him a visual advantage over his peers. He was fond of his marshal's costume accented with red bands, which justified him in carrying his ceremonial baton. Evening dress was generally dark in colour: SS wore black, ministers wore navy blue or black, and the SA wore brown. Officers wore differing trousers, most preferring riding breeches and high boots. Party members liked these as well, because it made them look like cavalrymen and lent them the prestige of the equestrian nobility.

Uniforms were prized not only as a matter of taste. They also had practical advantages. They were generally provided by administrations and sold to be worn at work. At a time when raw materials were in short supply, uniforms were thus easier to replace than civilian clothes. The foreign ministry, for example, had a special budget for providing new uniforms for its agents every year. Important officials had them adjusted or made to measure in fine fabrics at their own expense.

Officials who had access to forced labour were able to have their clothing tailored free of charge. Thus the concentration camps were turned into fitting rooms for Nazis. Rudolf Höss, the head of the Auschwitz camp, set up a workshop staffed by some thirty seamstresses who worked for his men and ensured that they felt comfortable in their adjusted uniforms.[32] His wife had two seamstresses who worked exclusively for her, taking care of her wardrobe and that of her children. The Sachsenhausen camp had a similar arrangement.

This system was also used outside Germany. In Paris, starting in 1943, camps were set up for Jews married to Aryans and people with one Jewish parent. One of these camps, opened in 1944, bore the name of the street where it was located, Bassano.[33] It was a private mansion that had been converted into a centre of *haute couture* for Nazi dignitaries and officers. There, customers were received, their measures taken, and clothes tailored. Paris fashions and the skill of these specialists thus fell directly under the control of the Third Reich. One department made clothing for women, and great German ladies travelled to Paris to build up their wardrobes or had their husbands buy clothes for them when they went there. The beneficiaries of these services could thus go to the theatre in brand-new clothes.

Restricted Shows or Immoderate Pleasures?

After 1940, people were still talking about Berlin's Bar-Frasquita cabaret. It was more closely monitored. At first, on 30 January 1941, a favourable report was submitted. The nude dances were, according to one observer, 'impeccable', whereas the audience's behaviour was less satisfactory.

Moreover, 'according to my informant, the Führer's portrait is placed in such a way that it has no relationship with the stage where the nude dances are performed'.[34] However, new complaints flowed into the propaganda ministry. First, it appeared that the Frasquita had two 'artistic' programmes, one in the afternoon and the other in the evening. The afternoon programme was more 'aesthetic': the dancer 'wears gloves and a pointed hat, and her private parts are covered by a narrow strip of cloth attached to her hips. She also carries an umbrella. The spectator has the impression that this is not really about art, the goal being rather to display her nudity.'[35] An entrance fee of two marks was charged, while a bottle of wine worth a mark and a half cost six marks, noted a report less indulgent than the first one.

The propaganda ministry opened further investigations, notably in April 1941, because it did not want soldiers to visit establishments that might stain their military honour. An inspector went to the cabaret and submitted a report that denounced the show's obscenity: he was disturbed by the proximity of the spectators to the stage and wondered whether he ought to negotiate with the Wehrmacht command in order to avoid a prohibition.[36] In September, the cabaret's owner tried to defend himself, noting that the show had already been presented and that the dancers were known and were engaged in an artistic activity. He argued that since Berlin was an international metropolis, it should attract strangers with shows that they knew in order not to be surpassed by Paris or Vienna, in accord with the Führer's wishes.[37] His efforts were in vain; soldiers in uniform were forbidden to go to the Frasquita after 1 October 1941.

The war accentuated the old contradictions of Nazism in power. On the one hand, its goal was improve morality and put the nation back on its feet spiritually in order to found the 'thousand-year Reich'; on the other, it had to make people move in its ideological direction no matter what concessions and misappropriations this might require. Fashionable cabarets offering strip-teases felt the full force of this contradiction.

We find a similar tension in the attitude toward jazz. The ideological battle led the ministry of propaganda to scold local radios that broadcast too 'jazzy' versions of 'German melodies'.[38] At the same time, the regime's dignitaries and their wives went to the Wintergarten or the Zoo-Palast to see American-style revues with girls and musicians playing jazz. Hitler himself went to the fiftieth-anniversary celebration at the Wintergarten, a major music hall.[39]

On the other hand, those who played swing or decided to dance it were treated very severely. Behind the mass arrests and imprisonment of nearly a hundred thousand young people in this connection between 1939 and 1945, we can discern a kind of social gap and protest. Swingers were considered asocial and imprisoned alongside political activists, especially communists, and petty delinquents. The scope of these arrests shows that a clandestine milieu had formed around music and through it celebrated a society that escaped Nazi morality.

Coco Schumann, a young man who had become passionate about swing after having heard it during the Olympic Games, left us an astonishing description of this marginal milieu. Heinz Schumann ('Coco' was his nickname) was born in 1924 to a bourgeois family.[40] He was half-Jewish according to the classification of the time. His father was a war veteran. He suffered rejections but took advantage of a moment of calm in 1936 to go to some concerts. There he discovered swing. He learned to play the guitar and at sixteen he was already playing under borrowed, Americanized names in nightclubs around the Kurfürstendamm. He met one of the glories of German jazz, Helmut Zaccharias. His group often moved from German jazz to swing, which led to him being prohibited from time to time. The band had to change its name and venue frequently, because infractions were sometimes sanctioned by closing down the establishment. Despite this habit of clandestinity, Coco Schumann was denounced as a swinger and deported to Theresienstadt in 1943. At that time this camp was said to be a model. There Schumann created a new jazz band used in the propaganda film *The Führer Gives the Jews a City*, whose goal was to deceive people about the real conditions under which prisoners were detained.[41] Schumann escaped extermination, probably because of his status as half-Jewish and because the Aryan part of his family intervened on his behalf, and ended up in Auschwitz with a band assigned to entertain German soldiers. In his memoirs, he recounts how the guards asked them to play 'La Paloma' while they were taking prisoners to the gas chambers.

For the SS, the concentration camps were linked with another function that connects them with high society. They were the production site of a whole industry whose revenues flowed into the organization's coffers and helped pay for the salaries and all the advantages in kind that were granted superior officers on active duty. In this way the elite organization strengthened its internal cohesion.

Himmler was the first to use products issuing from the exploitation of workers in the camp. The lists of his gifts to friends and collaborators frequently mention high-quality porcelain cups, vases, and plates. These objects were bought at preferential prices from the Allach firm which was located in the Dachau camp and was run, like the others, by the SS.[42] The value of these gifts was not negligible and frequently represented the equivalent of several months' salary for a factory worker. On 24 December 1942, for instance, the Reichsführer SS gave the Italian ambassador, Alfieri, a Christmas gift of two large porcelain plates, a statuette, a large vase, and a basket of flowers, the whole worth several hundred marks.[43] In this case, a porter took the objects from SS headquarters to the ambassador's home.

Routine gifts were delivered directly by the manufacturer. This was the case for the candlesticks given when children were born to SS men. On the base were engraved the child's first name and date of birth. Appropriate candles were included. This gift was also given to deserving children.[44] Many beneficiaries sent the SS leadership thank-you notes, sometimes written in a grandiloquent style. In January 1943 a high-ranking police official in Duisberg, Robert Runne, warmly thanked Himmler for this gift, which had been given him on the occasion of the birth of his seventh child.[45] It was the second time he had received a present from the NSDAP; in 1927 he had been given the second volume of *Mein Kampf* with the Führer's personal dedication. At the end of his letter, Runne mentioned his desire to be assigned in the East, if possible on the Baltic. Himmler's departments gave his request all the more attention because the head of the SS had agreed to be the newborn's godfather. He had moreover sent the family the other standard SS gift: a case of vitamins (Vitaborn). The SS thus connected both the concentration camps and the police with this astonishing gift-economy based on material advantages both small and large.

Himmler's organization went further in establishing practices that had to do with this paternalistic conception of high society. In 1938 it set up a system of marriage for the production of pure-blooded Aryan children. Young German women agreed to marry members of the SS in order to produce a genetically perfect stock. Himmler himself is said to have had an adulterous relationship that resulted in a child who was placed in this programme (Lebensborn). Despite their statements regarding the moral recovery of Germany, many Nazi leaders violated the rules of common morality. Himmler led a double and even triple life with his wife, his secretary, and occasional lovers.

The Bormanns went still further in challenging traditional social rules. Martin Bormann became Hitler's main assistant for party matters after Rudolf Hess's strange flight to Scotland in 1941. Bormann's wife Gerda, born in 1909, was the daughter of Walter Buch, a career officer who came from a family of pharmacists and joined the National Socialist movement early on, becoming its supreme judge in the 1930s.[46] He thus belonged to the highest elite of the NSDAP and got along particularly well with Richard Darré, the supply minister during the war. In September 1929, Gerda Buch married Bormann, a promising young SA member whom she had met at an NSDAP meeting a year earlier. Hitler was a witness at the wedding. The couple had nine children. Gerda said that her husband's Aryan quality deserved to be reproduced. After having lived in Munich, where he had entertained a small group associated with the party, received visits from Hitler, and had the honour of inviting the four participants to the Munich Conference in 1938, Bormann and his wife set up housekeeping in the Obersalzberg in 1940; from there he directed the NSDAP's administration. The Bormanns might seem like a conventional family, especially when Martin Bormann took as his mistress a young actress, Manja Behrens, in October 1943. The break with the traditional ménage à trois came when Gerda Bormann encouraged her husband to take other mistresses in order to have still more children in the interests of the race. She even proposed a system with several wives and concubines so that the children would be properly brought up and so that her husband (so attractive, she said) could make other women happy. In fact, Bormann did add a few more mistresses to his list of conquests. Gerda expressed her disappointment that of her husband's mistresses only Manja Behrens bore him a child. Bormann was flattered that his wife encouraged him to be polygamous and imposed this situation on the Nazi elite who frequented the Obersalzberg, from his neighbours the Görings (Emmy liked Gerda) to the Speers. His wife and his mistress were both frequently at the Berghof, even when the Führer was there; Hitler saw nothing scandalous in this situation because it reflected his ideal of male domination.

Moreover, Hitler did not complain about the existence of a strange building only a few dozen metres away from his residence, 'Barracks B'.[47] In this building French, Polish, and Russian women prostituted themselves under the supervision of doctors who provided them with work certificates. They were supposed to meet the needs of forced labourers, including a largely French contingent that was in the Obersalzberg to carry out earthworks. It seems that these women chose to perform this task rather than go to a concentration camp. Other prostitutes served German soldiers. Not very conspicuous in Germany, where the network of traditional brothels continued to function in the usual way, this system of prostitution was extended to the whole of occupied Europe in order to limit fraternization with subject peoples.

Officially, racial separation was strict. A German soldier or officer must not soil the race by siring a child on a Jewess or non-Aryan. This rule held for the concentration camps, where the SS had brothels provided with Aryan prostitutes, and also for the army, which organized almost a state department for this purpose.[48] The French example shows that the military high command did not leave this matter to chance. Very quickly after occupying a territory, it Aryanized houses of prostitution and organized a network of brothels under German sanitary supervision where soldiers could go to indulge in a warrior's rest.[49] Officers were not forgotten, and had their own special pleasure sites in order to keep them from fraternizing with the occupied peoples. Thus references to the little women of Paris did not allude to Parisian chic but rather to the delicious opportunities afforded by a stay in France.

All this is evidence of a change in the private life of the elites during the war. Hannah Arendt pointed out the way private life was crushed in totalitarian regimes by recalling what Robert Ley said: 'The only person who is still a private individual in Germany is somebody who is asleep.'[50] This intrusion on private life, perceptible in the 1930s in laws regarding the family, changes to the penal code, and the regimentation of mass organizations, was reinforced after 1939 to meet the needs of civil defence (curfews, blackouts, evacuation plans, supervision of passive defence, etc.) and to ensure that the whole population was mobilized. Thus sexual relations, already regulated, were henceforth oriented and channelled, and birth, marriage, and soon death were reinterpreted in the regime's bellicose and productivist perspective. A socialite had a duty to devote all his time to public life and had to continue to act in conformity with this duty when he was alone – or at least when he thought he was alone, since the system of wiretapping, espionage, and mutual surveillance was steadily expanded.[51] For a time, the cult of the dead and war victims promoted a spiritual fusion of the elites that was finally threatened by the prospect of defeat.

Watching Death Approach with Thunderous Steps

> During night attacks, British aeroplanes drop their bombs on German cities randomly. Only points without military significance are hit. A hospital in Weimar, Bismarck's tomb in the Friedrichsruh forest, a historic sixteenth-century church in . . . ; in Berlin as well, English bombs struck only residential quarters.[52]

Despite Göring's promises, starting in September 1940 German cities were bombed, as noted by the commentator on the newsreel, or rather the propaganda film, just cited. The commentator fails to mention that the bombardments were a direct response to earlier German attacks, and that Churchill had ordered Berlin bombed after several bombs struck parts of London. At this time, light subjects regarding life far from the front still dominated the news. The same newsreel also praised German tennis players who had just won a narrow victory over the Hungarian team during a tournament in Munich. The uniforms seen in public were the only sign of the mobilization.

However, death was already there. It entered Germany surreptitiously, along with the hundreds of victims of the attack on Poland. People had not yet got used to the frequency of deaths that meant that condolences had to be sent as soon as possible in order to avoid overlapping expressions of solicitude. The campaign in France, which cost more lives, did not dissipate the illusion that death was being kept at a distance from German civilians. The latter experienced bereavement chiefly though the deaths of combatants. But news about this subject did not yet fill the announcement columns in daily papers or conversations in salons. The moment when death really began to gnaw at socialites' minds came later.

One useful clue is provided by the aristocracy's newspaper. It continued to publish social announcements, but they took an increasingly morbid turn: births and marriages were overwhelmed by death notices. In 1939, there was no rubric for war deaths. Starting in 1941, however, special notices about soldiers who had fallen on the field of honour increased in number. In the January 1942 issue, under a new rubric on pages two and three appeared photographic portraits accompanied by brief captions giving the individual's name and regiment, sometimes followed by a short text written by a relative or friend. Nine young men with often serious faces are listed: 'From the ranks of the German nobility, they gave their lives for the Führer and the Fatherland.'[53] The father of one of them, Jürgen von Oerken, dedicated a poem to his son:

> Before the gates of Riga
> They are in a long line
> Calm in their pose
> Dead, dead, the soldiers
> And my son among them.

These efforts to sublimate death and assuage the pain of bereavement often take a tone more characteristic of high society. The announcement of the death of General von Reichenau mentions that eulogies were delivered by Marshal von Rundstedt and by Göring. This practice became more common starting in March 1942. Henceforth there were four pages illustrated with portraits, or about twenty noble soldiers whose faces haunted the newspaper. But nationalism did not flag. With bravado, some even rejected the notion of mourning, as did Arnold von Weiss und Wickert, who wrote in the number for 1 May 1942: 'Don't be sorry, be proud.'[54] The profusion of images and texts is explained by the fact that portraits of men who had died in combat were published free.[55] It is true that there continued to be many pages of advertising, probably compensating for the additional expenses involved. At the beginning of 1943 we find the same stoicism and the same articles expressing unstinting praise for the regime. But the situation was getting more serious. After April 1943, the paper published thirty photographs per issue. Women now wrote to eulogize members of their families, as did Winfried von Wedel-Parlow, whose contribution is entitled 'The Comrade'. The final verse rings like the refrain of a song: 'One word is confirmed in action, in life, in death: your comrade.'[56]

By this time, death truly occupied an enormous space in the mental landscape. This change, which began slowly in 1942 and accelerated in the spring of 1943, is also discernible in private diaries and memoirs. High society had largely learned to live with the situation and reshaped its practices to meet the challenge.

Letters announcing deaths became a sort of forced writing, almost an ideological genre. Friends, of course, expressed their feelings through them, but there were many relationships in which such announcements were more social and less personal. These letters sought to revive faith in the regime and institutions, in the necessity of the war. To console families, the army generally wrote that soldiers had died courageously in a particularly important battle and that they died in the Christian faith. Ursula von Kardoff has described the feelings that this multiplication of death announcements elicited. She explains how a new sense of panic spread, feeding on rumours and worries. For example, in the spring of 1943 a rumour circulated among journalists to the effect that an allied attack was planned to hinder the celebration of the Führer's birthday on 20 April.[57] An ambient depression sent people to their jobs with a feeling of the emptiness and futility of their work.[58] Ursula von Kardoff describes her editorial office as a cackling henhouse or, worse, a laboratory of robots going through the motions without thinking.

The same shift is found in institutional archives. Between early 1942 and spring 1943 the question of death in fact came to play a new role that worried the regime and led it to make more ample use of techniques for mobilizing public opinion. The goal was to generalize the habits of bourgeois mourning. Reasons that are more human than ideological explain why people did not revolt when faced with the sacrifice of a generation: mourning was made part of a process of social recognition and mutual aid.

In order to understand this process, we must recall that the Nazis had early on established a cult of the dead that entered into traditional sensibilities. The commemoration of men killed during the 1923 Putsch, parades in memory of Horst Wessel, and homage paid to comrades who died during the 1930s all constituted preludes demonstrating the doctrinal powers of funerals. The ceremonies in honour of Gauleiter Wilhelm Friedrich Loeper, who 'died after a long illness' on 26 October 1935, are a good example of the adaptation of the political religion to high-society life.[59] They took place in Dessau at the old Friedrich theatre. Seven hundred guests were expected. A hundred seats were reserved for state officials, a hundred for the province of Brunswick, and four hundred for the district. Hitler sent a telegram celebrating the movement's 'combatant' and 'servant'.[60] He repeated the main arguments in the speech he delivered after the period of reverential silence in the theatre. The guests had arrived at precisely 11 a.m. so that the ceremony, scheduled like a military parade, would not be delayed. At 11:15, the orchestra began to play the overture to *Parsifal*. The choir sang 'Keep the Faith Even unto Death'.[61] Finally the speeches began. Freyberg, state minister, spoke first, followed by Klagges, as the minister president of Brunswick, and then Hitler. At 12:15, the funeral cortège left the theatre to go to the Mildensee for the interment, preceded by a sermon by Mgr Peter and a few words by Councillor Eggeling. The invitation recommended that gentlemen wear a uniform or dark suit with an overcoat.[62] The following year, a similar ceremony was held on 25 June 1936 in honour of Secretary of State von Bülow.[63] Homage paid to the dead was already being transformed into a public representation.

After the war began, this way of dramatically setting the scene for photographers and cameramen – and, through invitations, selecting an elite that gathered long enough to demonstrate that it shared values – was accentuated. Reinhardt Heydrich's funeral shows this very amply. He had died from a wound received in an attack by the Czech resistance on 27 May 1942. On 4 June Himmler noted Heydrich's death in his diary simply by writing the name of his former subordinate who had remained his friend.[64] He went to the funeral along with other leaders of the regime. Lina Heydrich, who had been born into a noble family, the von Ostens, collapsed. Her family saw to the details of the ceremony, which was performed with great pomp in Prague.[65] Three hundred official guests had travelled to Prague to attend. They lunched at Heydrich's country estate near Prague, a castle that had been Aryanized in 1939. Himmler took Heydrich's four children to the ceremony, holding them by the hand. Hitler, despite his anger at such a stupid death – Heydrich had been travelling in an unarmoured car – laid a wreath on the tomb and eulogized the deceased. Wagner's music once again accompanied the ceremony. This time a passage from the *Götterdämmerung* was chosen. The next day, Heydrich's body was brought back to Berlin, to the Prinz Albrechtstrasse. Himmler took the opportunity to congratulate, among those present, the General SS Ohnesorge, who was celebrating his seventieth birthday. SS men were probably over-represented in this group. In fact their organization also transformed them into a community that was welded together especially around death.

Himmler, a veritable social strategist, soon established relationships with families. Births were one opportunity to do so. For marriages, the relationship was marked by a pin bearing the SS symbol. The head of the SS had letters and telegrams of condolence sent to the wives of men who had fallen in combat. His personal archives contain documents that testify to this effort to produce a solidarity that could be put to ideological uses. A few letters from women involved in the Lebensborn programme who had given birth shortly before their husbands were killed show the ample confidence placed in the SS.[66] The help and financial aid they received, along with the belief that this support would continue, indicate that solidarity with the regime was not affected by the impact of death. These letters remind us of what Victor Klemperer wrote in Dresden, towards the end of the war, when he noted the return of superstition and blind faith, even among people who had long been sceptical.[67]

In this correspondence, certain expressions show to what extent the idea of death was not completely repressed by adherence to the party. One example is provided by a letter written by Ursel Dietrich, the wife of Sepp Dietrich, the former head of Hitler's bodyguard who had become a divisional general in the Waffen SS, to Himmler, thanking him for his gifts.[68] She explains that she misses her husband and conceals her fear of becoming a widow behind emphatic praise for her husband's military valour. Other women find the strength to express gratitude for help received after their husbands' deaths, as if refusing to see that the primary cause of those deaths was the National Socialists' mad imperialist desire.

Repression, multiple forms of denial, and entrenchment grew more intense as the war went on. Strange expressions of despair turned into political statements. For instance, during a bombardment of Berlin in 1944, a man, beside himself, cried out 'Democracy, democracy', as one might howl at death. The journalist Ursula von Kardoff notes that the regime's terror apparatus worked less well in the context of defeat and aerial attacks.[69] Some people ended up lacking the strength to take shelter during an attack and remained at home. Alarm grew on reading the notices of death after death in the press. In December 1943, after having read in a daily paper that ten members of a family had died in a single aerial attack, Ruth Andreas-Friedrich wrote in her diary: 'Death, death, death, everywhere one looks. . . . Truly, we have sealed our bond of brotherhood with the Grim Reaper.'[70]

From East to West: Journeys, Meetings, Transfers

Despite all the deaths, German society continued to exist in a territorial framework expanded by conquest. It acquired the habit of thinking in terms of a Europe that stretched from the Atlantic to the Black Sea. In practice, this meant that part of the elite, and not solely military men, henceforth travelled over larger distances to carry out a task or to enjoy a good time. Economic actors were particularly affected by this geographical expansion. They were thinking about how to organize production and distribution in relation to centres of cheap labour, such as concentration camps, or pursuing the logic of industrial specialization. SS businessmen such as Oswald Pohl created enterprises like Osti to circulate throughout Europe the currencies acquired by spoliation.[71] Still more often, they hurried to places where there were opportunities to purchase raw materials or finished products at ridiculously low prices.

German journalists and propaganda ministry officials also travelled widely. They henceforth provided a vast information network that their country nearly monopolized through its news agencies, such as the Deutscher Nachtrichten Büro. Some, like Eberhardt von der Heyden, who died in Corinth, Greece, while covering a parachutist operation, were killed while working for Goebbels' PK-Stiftung. To assuage their parents' grief, the PK gave them a special allowance of five hundred marks so that they could take vacations outside Berlin.[72] Others, like a propaganda official appointed to assist the general in charge of the army in Norway, needed help to move themselves and their families to a new location.[73]

In order to provide its officials with good working conditions, the German state requisitioned prestigious establishments in conquered countries. In Paris, the great hotels were a favourite prey. The Lutetia (the Abwehr, the secret service), the Majestic (central command for greater Paris), the Crillon (lodging for the General Staff in France), and the Astoria (economic cooperation) are good examples. The hotel's services were changed and financial compensation generally paid to the owners.[74]

The elites in the occupied countries discovered in their turn that National Socialism did not place the same constraints on every part of the population. They saw that accommodation, and even collaboration, with the occupier had definite advantages.

The Germans modified sociabilities and customary relationships in the countries they invaded. Paris under the occupation provides a revealing example of this. A significant number of socialites spread a message in conformity with National Socialist interests that they had acquired by frequenting German officials concerned with culture and censorship. Thanks to these new-found friends, it was possible to improve one's everyday life and pursue a career. A writer like Drieu la Rochelle came to dominate the *Nouvelle Revue Française* because of his friendship with a German. Cocteau continued to work relatively undisturbed because he was close to Becker and protected by Speer.

My goal here is not to rewrite the history of the occupation, but rather to point out that Paris became part of a new European high society. Thus the German embassy in Paris, where Otto Abetz worked, was no longer merely the site of infrequent receptions spread out through the year; it became the centre of an extremely active social life whose function was to seduce the French elites. In this game, Abetz had a major advantage: he was able to serve a quality and an abundance of food that many great Parisian restaurants could only envy. The list of his guests grew between 1940 and 1944, and included everyone who counted in France, from old celebrities of the defunct Third Republic, who were eager to find a new role, to young anti-Semites who felt right at home.[75] The ambassador knew how to vary the categories, because he was a Francophile who had been working Parisian circles since his first meetings with friends in the 1920s.

Abetz also received major German dignitaries who were visiting Paris, including the Führer, just after Paris was taken, and Göring, who visited at the beginning of May 1942. Göring travelled frequently between headquarters on the Eastern Front and the west, stopping over several times in Paris.[76] This time, his attention was focused chiefly on the Jeu de Paume museum, which he visited twice. Paintings that had been seized were kept there. Evidently, Göring had come to choose items for his gigantic private collection. He seems even to have found a supplier who brought him works by Fragonard, a painter of whom he was fond. Some of the works stored at Karinhall must have been moved because it was feared that they would be destroyed in aerial attacks. Göring's companions and Hitler himself did the same, appropriating more and more masterworks in the countries they occupied.

Life in occupied Europe was more difficult than it was in Berlin. But not for everyone. Collaborators enjoyed far better conditions than did their peers, while the great families enjoyed another advantage, their fortunes.

The synthesis of these two worlds can be seen in the person of Josée de Chambrun. The only daughter of Pierre Laval, she married a lawyer from a great family of soldiers and political dignitaries whose fortune had been built through industry and commerce. Her diaries show that it was possible to lead a delicious, idle life in occupied Paris.[77] This childless woman divided her time between buying luxurious clothing and going to balls and dinners where one met such charming persons, some of whom, like Arletty, were infatuated with German officers. She also had a little vice: she gambled large sums at the racetrack, and mentioned it when she won. She still accompanied her father on his official travels and sometimes served as his messenger. A few of her friends who had been arrested asked her to intervene on their behalf. She protected a few Jewish friends, but was not upset by the anti-Semitic laws of 1940, or by the decision made by her father and his friend René Bousquet to round up Jews in July 1942.[78] She often went to the theatre, where she forgot the violence of the conflict; she did not understand the hostility directed against her father. She also took care of her little dog. She ate well; her in-laws supplied her with food from their estates in Champagne and her mother sent her sumptuous parcels prepared in the kitchen at Châteldon, her father's residence.

Ernst Jünger's diary complements this Francocentric viewpoint.[79] In it we see how a German officer sojourning in France tried to frequent the local intelligentsia – Guitry, Morand, Benoist-Méchin, Cocteau, Bonnard, and even Picasso – and shared with it a common aesthetic experience. He also enjoyed its gustatory pleasures, going to tea at the home of Ladurée, lunching with Drouant, dining at the Coq Hardi, and reading Guégan's *Le cuisinier français*, which appeared in 1934: 'Cut up a live rock lobster and cook until bright red in an earthenware pan with a quarter-pound of very fresh butter.'[80]

The German occupiers succeeded in producing a semblance of society life everywhere, all the more easily because they were able to receive eminent Berliners whose influence attracted the local courtiers. In Holland, the governor Seyss-Inquart, who had come from Austria, hosted Himmler several times to discuss the deportation of Jews and security matters. During a visit between 16 and 20 May 1942,[81] he tried to seduce the Reichsführer SS and his imposing entourage by organizing a kind of tourist trip. It began with a tea and a dinner for a select few at Seyss-Inquart's home. Felix Kersten reported on the atmosphere at these meals, at which there was a muted competition among guests seeking to obtain privileges or additional power.[82] The next day, after a late breakfast, Himmler and Seyss-Inquart played tennis. That evening, Himmler dined with another of his subordinates, the Gruppenführer SS Hans Rauter, head of the police. On 18 May, the little court went to Haarlem to admire the tulip fields, and then visited Amsterdam in the late morning. There, lunch was provided by Meinout Rost Van Tonningen, a Dutch collaborator. In the afternoon they discussed police issues, and in the evening

Seyss-Inquart arranged another dinner, this time with a large circle of guests. On 19 May, they left for Utrecht, where they held further discussions and lunched at the home of Aadrian Mussert, the Nazi Führer in Holland, who accompanied Himmler and had him to tea. They also visited a castle where it was planned to install a Napola, a school for training future SS men. On 20 May, finally, after another tennis match with Seyss-Inquart, Himmler left for Munich. On arrival, he immediately went by car to his residence in Gmund. The objective of these visits seems to have been to perfect the police system in Holland. In addition, it allowed Himmler, who was also a collector, to locate a few paintings.

Himmler's journeys did not stop there. In 1942, he travelled from Friedrichsruh to Berlin, to Prague (several times), to Munich, Gmund, and again Berlin. A two-day inspection tour, return to Berlin, Paderborn, Wewelsburg, Rothenburg, Fallingbostel, Munich, Rastenburg, back to Friedrichsruh to see the Führer, then on to Berlin. And Himmler was not even the one who travelled most. Some Nazi leaders, such as Ribbentrop and Göring, wanted to be everywhere, keeping watch on the fronts, defending their interests, courting Hitler, doing favours for their friends, seeing to it that their subordinates carried out their orders, and so on.

In 1941, Göring's appointment book clearly shows his movements back and forth between headquarters in the east and in the west, sojourns in Berlin to take care of ongoing affairs at the ministry, trips to Karinhall, where his wife preferred to live with their daughter, and trips to the Obersalzberg that allowed him to remain close to Hitler. Other major Nazi leaders like Ribbentrop did much the same. They spent many days following the Führer around.

The headquarters in East Prussia, the Wolfsschanze, was also a place for meetings and very masculine high-society activities, because the head of state stayed there for long periods. While there, he received superior officers and dignitaries at his table, which continued to be well supplied. It was especially at the Wolfsschanze that he delivered the long monologues that are collected in his 'table-talk'.[83] In the evening, everyone got back into his special train. Of all means of transportation, the train best expressed a certain sociability of the regime's organic elites, a desire for luxury and an art of filtering and hierarchizing human relationships.

Hitler was aware of the advantages provide by this mode of transportation. In 1933 he took over the chancellor's old railway carriages, and in 1934 those of the head of state. He even ordered new carriages, which were delivered in 1936 and allowed him to lend the old ones to other prominent figures. The railways, in fact, chartered the carriages on request and made them available with the authorization of the main beneficiary. Himmler and Ribbentrop had whole trains at their disposal. Other ministers' budgets allowed them only specially equipped carriages that could be added to regular trains. Military men and high-ranking SS men had special trains assigned to their organizations and were also equipped with comfortable carriages paid for by the state. They were fitted out in such a way as to allow them to be lived in for several days. Thus trains provided lodging for Himmler's and Göring's entourages, whereas they themselves often slept in requisitioned rooms.

Hitler's train, which was the best equipped, had a bathtub, a reception room, and a bedroom. Particular care was taken with the chairs and the décor. One or two other carriages were generally reserved for special guests, each of whom had his own compartment. There were about ten of them, guests or members of the Führer's immediate entourage, such as his physicians, Morell and Brandt, or the civilian and military adjutants Julius Schaub and von Below. The rest of the Adjudantur was lodged in a less elegant carriage. Next came the Führer's personal guard, policemen, and even a carriage equipped with heavy weapons in the event of aerial attack. The rest of the train consisted of a kitchen carriage and the locomotive.

Travel is tiring, but this kind of transportation remained one of the most reliable. It was normally so punctual that the railway minister felt obliged to write a detailed letter of excuse when the Führer's train was late. Hitler's guard also made sure his journeys during the war remained confidential, in order to avoid an assassination attempt.[84] Instructions were given to avoid untimely shows of support and to limit noise in stations when the Führer's special train passed through at night.

According to the reconstitution of Hitler's schedule attempted by Christa Schröder, his secretary for almost ten years, he nonetheless spent more and more time at his mountain residence.[85] There, the large network of bunkers and shelters located higher up provided protection against any attack. Even the great feared air raids.

Ruth Andreas-Friedrich reports that one day in 1943 when Göring was on special leave in Karinhall, he became anxious about a raid and ordered all pursuit planes into the air.[86] More than a hundred fighters are supposed to have taken off, sometimes attacking each other as a result of inadequate coordination, while anti-aircraft guns, suddenly put into action, took them as targets, leading to several useless deaths. The fear of bombardments thus crossed all social strata.

In Berlin, behaviour in high society changed under the impact of the military pressure and the shortages that were beginning to make themselves felt. Von Studnitz, a diplomat, mentions this phenomenon in connection with a party held in February 1943 at the home of a friend, Count Hans Coudenhove-Kalergi, a great Bohemian aristocrat, the son of an Austrian ambassador and a Japanese mother. The count gave a cocktail party with German beer and vermouth imported from Italy. Suddenly he stepped forward with a valise under his arm and placed it in the middle of his guests.

> He had prepared it as a surprise for the ladies, filling it with Paris perfumes, American stockings, and English soap. Crying 'take what you need', he

opened the valise. Instantly, the salon turned into a battlefield. Officials' wives, daughters of high-ranking ministers, and the ambassador's wife fell all over each other trying to seize a coveted treasure. Women with mink coats rushed to pick things up from the floor. Handbags made of crocodile skin were used as weapons, Parisian hats were torn, stockings run. The veil was ripped away: greed, belligerence, and tears of rage were open to view. Meanwhile, the count enjoyed witnessing this diabolical spectacle.[87]

As the war came to an end, parties at the Croatian embassy became still more bitter and decadent; the imminence of defeat produced an even more serious breakdown of codes of conduct.

Von Studnitz felt immense relief when he left the stony atmosphere in Berlin for Vienna in the summer of 1943. 'Living in the protectorate is like being in heaven.' The bombardments were ignored in conversations in Vienna, which had thus far been spared. Von Studnitz envied people like the governor Baldur von Schirach, who enjoyed this idyllic city where culture still reigned. However, for artists Vienna was far from being a paradise.

Aryanization had been carried out, but Goebbels continued to try to reform the Viennese art scene to make it conform to National Socialist imperatives. In particular, he reproached the director of the Opera for continuing to allow performances of a decadent musical style: atonality.[88] He set traps and had clandestine recordings made in order to confound the impudent director, who still dared to produce a work by Rudolf Wagner-Regeny, *Johanna Balk*, with accents worthy of Weill's *Threepenny Opera*. The composer's work was forbidden in Germany but could still be produced in Vienna. There more than elsewhere, high society had rallied to the support of those who were carrying out the unification of Germany. Young musicians like Werner Egk, the author of *Joan von Zarissa*, annoyed Richard Strauss, who left during the interval at its première, taking Gerhart Hauptmann with him to discuss the editing of his trilogy on Iphigeneia. Some Austrian writers were well regarded by Germanic cultural institutions, such as Heinrich Ritter von Srbik, who won a seat in the new Reichstag in 1938 and obtained prestigious literary prizes through his political activity. A little cultural court emerged around Baldur von Schirach, who organized numerous receptions and used Vienna's traditional institutions to curry favour with Hitler. His position was made easier by his family relations and his marriage with Henriette Hoffmann. The latter's father, Heinrich Hoffmann, the NSDAP's official photographer, took advantage of this windfall to open a branch in Austria. Schirach organized evenings at the Opera, supported the two philharmonic orchestras, and tried to limit the influence of the Czechs, of whom there were many in the region. He also toyed with a certain kind of liberalism, allowing two exhibits of works by Käthe Kollwitz and Egon Schiele, very decadent artists.[89] One of Schirach's fiercest critics was the former superintendent of the Vienna Opera, who published his memoirs under a pseudonym after the war.[90] In these memoirs, he describes the meticulous princely entourage of servants that surrounded Schirach, who was extremely demanding concerning the details of his everyday life, which seems to have been empty and indolent. The author concludes that it was basically a harmful way of life, marked by a kind of dangerous deceitfulness. No doubt this view was influenced by the author's friendship with Richard Strauss, whose disgrace and prudent return at the beginning of the war he had witnessed. Although he was not a native of Vienna, he was also aware of the Aryanization of Viennese society. There as elsewhere, the police monitored the activities of enemies of the state.

The city was caught up in the war. Soon it was hit by aerial bombardments. The diary of Marie Wassiltschikow, a former propaganda ministry employee who had followed her physician husband to Vienna, where she worked as a nurse in a Luftwaffe hospital from January to March 1945, throws light on this new period.[91] Her description shows that Viennese high society suffered during this last phase of the war. The Jockey Club building was destroyed. The Opera was hit by bombs and burned for several days. Many theatres were no more than crumbling façades. The great establishments, such as the Bristol Hotel, were also hit: not a single window remained unbroken.[92] Socialites met for elegant dinners in the private saloons of the Sacher Hotel, but entertainments were now lacking. Only the Philharmonic pursued its programme; in mid-February it was still offering a concert every day despite the bombing, which also came every day.[93] Moreover, it was following the example of the great German orchestras, which also continued to work right to the end, and whose concerts were broadcast over the radio and recorded. German technology gave them a magnificent stereophonic sound whose quality explains why some of these performances are still regarded as classics. The conductor who stood out at this time was Herbert von Karajan, whose energy was inexhaustible. The affection and admiration in which he later basked probably had their origin in his work at a time when music was the only remaining distraction that allowed people to forget their troubles and communicate without having to take into account some people's errors and other people's foolishness. Although Karajan was an Austrian, he reflected the Germany that had embraced Nazism out of an inclination to conform. As a young orchestra conductor, he joined the NSDAP in April 1933 and was involved in the intrigues that sought to supplant Furtwängler in Berlin.

In Germany, people still went to shows and concerts, despite the mourning and the bombardments. The SD's reports for Berlin express surprise at attendance figures that did not flag all through the conflict, though free shows experienced occasional off-days and people's eagerness to return to the theatre immediately after an attack waned as the war advanced.[94] The police interpreted this passion for distractions as a way of keeping up morale and not focusing on death.

A Whole Little World

Because of security requirements and his shaky health, Hitler went much less often to the theatre and concert hall after 1942. His world shrank, and with it his courtly entourage. This resulted in part from the filtering inherent in his despotism. But the war accentuated this penchant: he feared an assassination attempt, an attack.

In 1939, security measures were strengthened. An exhaustive list of those who were allowed to approach the Führer was drawn up. On it we find adjutants, guards, servants, and personal friends like 'Fräulein Braun', who is mentioned without specification. Any change had to be reported immediately. If a repairman came to check the heating system, he was obliged to obtain three different authorizations to ensure that he would be admitted. Authorizations were so carefully examined that if one was lost, a new, numbered document was created. Filtering was ensured by an enlarged corps of guards and by sentinels patrolling the Voßstrasse, Wilhelmstrasse, and Hermann-Göring Strasse.[95] These precautions were backed up by specific measures regarding gifts. A circular explains that they must be put in a room far from the Führer's apartment in order to avoid an assassination attempt. Only presents given by known personages could be delivered directly to the Führer's adjutants.[96] Others were to be inspected by security agents. In reality, presents from unknown persons were distributed among the staff, which ended up considering them a sort of bonus added to the gifts given them by the chancellery. These presents did not consist solely of embroidered cushions, a gift often sent to the head of state, but also included food and decorative objects. Moreover, at Christmas time the distribution of these gifts led to conflicts between the household staff and the security personnel.[97]

In the Obersalzberg, security was increased by the network of bunkers that protected against aerial attack and by the installation of a veritable SS barracks. Suspicion was spreading even to the Führer's entourage. Concern about security probably explains the perceptible tensions that arose when access to certain zones was forbidden. For instance, Hitler's personal guard was no longer authorized to enter the kitchen at night. Was that to avoid an attempt to poison the Führer or to prevent the guards from pinching food? However that may be, the pressure was increasing in this little world. Albert Bormann undertook an investigation of the personnel to determine whether all their parents and grandparents were Aryans and whether their families were members of the NSDAP. Discovering that one of the chambermaids, Anna Plaim, belonged to a Catholic family and that her father was a churchgoer (*Kirchengänger*), he immediately had her fired.[98] Eva Braun tried to intervene by appealing to Hitler, but he asked her to accept Bormann's decision. Döhring also tried to help Plaim. In vain. And yet she had been the Führer's and Eva Braun's servant for more than three years.

The slightest ideological deviation being likely to prove very costly, conversations were gradually emptied of all political meaning when unknown persons were present. Christabel Bielenberg described this rapid evaluation of interlocutors in order to avoid stumbling and getting in trouble.[99] While having coffee at the home of some friends in Grunewald, she noticed a particularly zealous woman but was unable to warn one of her friends who was of English origin and who said something critical about the regime. Afterward, they worried about the consequences. Christabel's husband Peter, a friend of Carl Langbehn, one of the figures in the eleventh-hour resistance, was thrown into one of the Gestapo's prisons because of his opinions. Nonetheless, the clear prospect of defeat led some groups to talk secretly about the actual situation. In a sense, just as a fraction of high society had helped Nazism take power, the attempt on Hitler's life in 1944 emanated from a similar group. These high dignitaries were not rebelling against Nazism so much as against the leadership of the regime that had led Germany to defeat.

With the assassination attempt on 20 July 1944, part of the old group of leaders disappeared; it was composed of diplomats, military men, and high officials. The conspirators were sentenced to death by a People's Court presided over by Judge Roland Freissler, who had proved his mettle by condemning to death members of the White Rose resistance group, Christoph Probst and Sophie and Hans Scholl, in 1943. The severity of these judgments, executions that were sometimes carried out immediately after sentencing, and summary liquidations struck public opinion. Friends of those less deeply involved, such as Helmuth von Moltke, tried to obtain clemency for them.[100] We can see how the logic of clientelism now came into play in an attempt to attenuate the judgments. To this end, intermediaries were sought. Did anyone know one of the valets or servants of a powerful man who might be able to pass a message? Hopes were focused on Himmler, whose adjutant agreed to transmit the request. But the ploy didn't work. Count von Moltke was executed on 25 January 1945.

The narrowing of the elite strengthened the relational dimension and concentrated Hitler's last devotees around a few central points. The Führer's court henceforth included only intimate associates and those whose services were required. The Braun family visited more frequently than at the beginning of the war. Gretl, Eva's sister, often came to the Obersalzberg to see her sister; there she met the SS's representative on the Führer's staff, Hermann Fegelein. She married him in June 1944. Their wedding in Hitler's mountain residence was attended by a few bigwigs such as Himmler and Bormann. Fegelein, it was rumoured, was marrying only because he thought it would ensure that he enjoyed the Führer's favour. This group met again on New Year's Eve, 1945. A ball was organized at the Berghof with cotillions and confetti. People drank and danced until dawn. It was as if the war had been forgotten for a few hours and the execution of opponents was a mere detail.

However, the war immediately reasserted its rights. The competition among leaders continued. Göring lost ground in Hitler's esteem because the Luftwaffe was incapable of defending the country against aerial attack. The bombing of Dresden during the nights of 13 and 14 February 1945, which resulted in thirty-five thousand victims, seemed to prove Göring's failure and that of his anti-aircraft defence.[101] For his part, Himmler was discredited by the errors he made in commanding the Waffen SS and the front. Goebbels continued his propaganda work. However, he lacked the stature of a warrior. Martin Bormann, the head of the NSDAP, who had urged the continuation of the war and, like Hitler and Nazi propaganda, constantly used 'fanatical' as a term of praise,[102] emerged as the winner in this competition.

According to post-war testimony, after January 1945 Bormann succeeded in isolating the Führer and limiting personal access to him. He knew that only his regular visits influenced Hitler's choices. He slyly denounced the incompetence of all those who could not meet with the Führer for military reasons. He even tried to make Hitler believe that some of his friends were ill so that he could keep them away. This was the case for Heinrich Hoffmann; Bormann gave Hitler to understand that the photographer had typhus.[103] Hoffmann had to ask Eva Braun to come to his aid and sent her medical certificates attesting to his good health in order to regain the Führer's graces. However, it is not true that Bormann alone exercised a kind of dictatorship during the final months. Even with the shrinkage of the elite, several persons remained continuously around Hitler, notably the officers on his staff, who counterbalanced Bormann's influence.

What better symbol could there be to express this withering away and the retrospective illusion it created than the bunker situated below the Berlin chancellery?[104] The final group that spent the last days of the Third Reich around its founder ultimately does not accurately reflect what Nazism was. It gives a distorted image that is too often projected *a posteriori* on the days of grandeur and omnipotence. However, certain enduring characteristics of the regime are particularly clear in this image. Official morality remained quite strict; it was composed of obedience, discipline, partisan passion, indestructible loyalty, devotion, zeal, and sacrifice. Hitler's marriage to Eva Braun is part of this moralistic farce. Nonetheless, the regime's other face was everywhere visible: violence, prostitution, preferential treatment, looting, alcohol, and opulence. The bunker was well provided with food and even with champagne. Bormann, Schaub, and Hewel now stayed drunk all the time. The SS men put obscene graffiti on the walls of their quarters and let themselves go. During the last days, however, this underground refuge was cut off from Germany, able to communicate only with difficulty using a defective civilian radio.

At this point, most of the true socialites were preparing to switch sides and had already bid farewell to a world that was on its way out. Starting in December 1944, high society left Berlin and tried to find shelter in regions where it thought there would be less violence. Everyone who was in the east therefore began to rush towards the west and the south to escape the Red Army's reprisals, which they imagined would be terrible. They also had to leave Berlin, which was too exposed to bombardments. Going away was not easy. Those who left didn't know when or even if they would come back. These last meetings left an impression of concern and irrevocable separation. Houses that were sometimes in pitiable condition after a bombardment also had to be abandoned, and objects that could not be carried left behind. Socialites counted on the aid given to refugees and victims of the bombardments; propaganda was still telling them that they would automatically receive the furniture seized from the Reich's enemies, i.e. from Jews. That is the meaning of the 'furniture operation' entrusted to Alfred Rosenberg's office.[105]

After 20 April 1945, certain dignitaries took leave of Hitler and went to hide out in Bavaria or Austria, whose countryside they imagined to be less threatened. Speer left with his family; Göring also fled to the Obersalzberg; Himmler went north after a final conversation with Kersten, his masseur, to whom he had given a sumptuous Christmas gift, more expensive than those he had given his own family. Kersten the confidant left for Sweden. Lammers, Meissner, Ribbentrop, all dispersed. The last little group in the bunker consisted of a narrow core of First World War veterans who identified with the Führer's battle as an existential (or rather a morbid) quest and a few young fanatics who, like Traudl Junge, remained armed until they were captured by the Soviets and attempted, right up to the end, to carry out a mission in the service of the Third Reich – in Traudl's case, by transmitting confidential documents to Admiral Dönitz.

At that time, as during the last weeks of the Reich's collapse, the expression 'high society' seems inappropriate to describe groups that were imprisoned in an extremist logic of war but were getting drunk on liquor, tranquillizers, and music in a sombre dance of death. Life in this world was no longer quite that of a man of the world, a gentleman. It reflected the sparks of pleasure thrown off by the last banquets while the industrialized massacres were being completed. Even the least well informed of these socialites were fully aware of the massacres by March 1945, according to von Studnitz, or as early as 1943, if we accept the rumours that were mentioned by Ernst Jünger, for instance, even though at that time he was posted in Paris – unless, like the men at the foreign ministry, they had followed their development since the autumn of 1941, or, like Göring and Bouhler, organized them.[106] The fear of reprisals led a few leaders to prefer suicide to capture or the uncertainty of a confrontation with Russian soldiers, those mad devils or 'Asiatic barbarians', as the propaganda called them. Others, like Goebbels and his wife, who killed their children before committing suicide themselves, thought they had made their act a symbol of the grandeur of the National Socialist conception, imitating the distant

Punic example of Hasdrubal's widow, who strangled her children before sacrificing them to the god Baal during the siege of Carthage.

Distinction Overthrown

The story does not stop with these last hours of a Nazi high society that was in fact still dominant in certain isolated areas. The capitulation, the captures, and arrests opened a new phase during which the old world found itself faced with new institutions that harshly judged its way of functioning. The Nazi world, in its camps and prisons, continued to manage itself and maintain discipline and respect for the men who had nonetheless inexorably led their country to defeat and destruction.

The wives of Nazi dignitaries also experienced regroupings and the taste of poorly cooked soups. Emmy Göring, arrested and separated from her husband, found herself in Fishhorn, Austria, with her daughter Edda and a little suite composed of her niece, her nephew, a chambermaid, and a nurse. On 31 May Hedi Bouhler, the widow of the deceased Reichsleiter Philipp Bouhler, arrived in Fishhorn. Depressed, Hedi committed suicide two days later, terrifying the little community living under American surveillance. Emmy Göring, her daughter, her sister, her niece, and the servant and the nurse who cared for Edda were then imprisoned in the Straubing camp before finally being freed in February 1946. In May, Frau Göring was arrested, this time alone. She was interned with old acquaintances: Henriette von Schirach, Frau Kaltenbrunner (the wife of the head of the SD), and Frau Funk. They exchanged information regarding their husbands and encouraged each other. It was their lot to experience the strange link between the accused at the Nuremberg Trials and their friends and relatives. There were hurried meetings in the corridors of the tribunal while waiting for the sessions to begin. They lowered their voices to continue their conversations while being watched by the guards and the other accused. In her memoirs, Henriette von Schirach mentions Frau Göring's blindness in still believing her husband innocent of crimes against humanity.[107] A few photographs show these former princes reduced to the condition of prisoners eating soup at makeshift tables. Hermann Göring jokingly told his wife that he had finally found a good way to lose weight.

In this penal context, they went back over their past lives. Robert Kempner, the prosecutor who interrogated them, acquired a fairly accurate view of the matter by working through the archives and taking testimony from witnesses.[108] He also watched films to find proofs of the presence of this or that leader in certain essential places where the genocide was committed. Kempner was not a historian. His goal was not to reconstitute social relationships within an elite, the function that this group might have fulfilled, and still less its social life. More simply, he was trying to find responsibilities and proofs. He wanted to know who had

initiated and carried out the genocide, and who, through their compla-
cency, had made themselves its accomplices. He listened – looking by
turns ironic, furious, or calm – to Lammers telling him that he was only a
humble official, Meissner declaring that he knew nothing about it, Schaub
flaunting his admiration for Hitler, Göring explaining how the four-year
plan worked, and Darré expressing his disillusionment.

Surreptitiously, imperceptibly, the world of yesterday emerged again,
with its wealth, its fortune, its pleasures, and, behind everything, its
crimes. The frightening thing about these interrogations is the almost universal absence of remorse. All the accused claimed that their consciences
were clear, and lied shamelessly. They failed to mention the gifts they had
received and acknowledged them only when forced to do so by irrefutable
evidence. They falsified their schedules. During the sessions, they tacked
about to take shelter behind an order given by someone now dead or the
responsibility of someone who had disappeared. However, the judicial
apparatus had what was needed to confound them. Many of the documents it assembled are still used by scholars. But the questions have
changed. What now matters is the reconstitution of an atmosphere, a
period, watching it live, and understanding. And then it is a question of
restituting, making known.

This reservoir of high society, the vast, broad third circle of sociability
that so well served the first phases of Nazism, was never really purged in
the Federal Republic. As Norbert Frei has shown, the rates of dismissal
fluctuated depending on the profession and the needs of the new state.[109]
Konrad Adenauer, the first chancellor of the Federal Republic, complained
in 1949 that the purge had been so poorly carried out.[110] The old elite kept
its head above water and transmitted its patrimony, often augmented by
the Third Reich, to the following generation. The old illusions had a
tremendous hold on some of them. Concluding his diary on the pre-war
years in 1976, Carl Vincent Krogmann, the mayor of Hamburg during the
Nazi era, repeated the claims of his former idols. Hitler didn't want war,
he didn't want to kill the Jews but only to drive them out of Germany. He
had no worldwide ambitions. It was Roosevelt and those who hid behind
him, the Jews, who had sealed Germany's fate as early as 1933–4 and
finally destroyed it. The old man wondered nostalgically if the Third Reich
might one day rise again. He placed his hope in the young, and dedicated
his book to his grandchildren. Decidedly, the Federal Republic had a hard
time opening the eyes of many of its elderly citizens who nurtured in their
hearts a secret love for Hitler's world, for that easy life spent gorging on
pleasures at the price of a field of ruins and desolation. Military men,
diplomats, bankers, insurers, merchants, aristocrats or commoners, bourgeois or proletarians, all refused to see the crime and their share in the
responsibility for it. According to them, the war excused everything. They
laid a burden of guilt on future generations that was not the latter's own.

Conclusion

Writing to Martin Bormann in 1941, Joseph Goebbels fulminates: how do women dare wake at noon and lie in bed while the war is in full swing? How can these privileged females wallow in the idle delights of a spa or the terrace of a café, staying there for hours, chattering? The very thought is unbearable for him. Shouldn't these nonchalant people be taught what life is about by sending them to work in munitions factories? Goebbels had already mentioned this to Hitler, who agreed with him and wondered whether radical steps ought to be taken. Patience, austerity is coming. There is something illogical about this note when one reflects that the women in question belonged to good society and must have occasionally frequented leadership circles.[1] Who were Goebbels and Bormann talking about, if not the mothers, wives, and daughters of many of their friends and collaborators? Pressed by the constraints of exhausting schedules and the hazards of the military situation, the 'Prominenten' rewrote their official conception of the art of living. No more praise for pleasant German hospitality. Now their propaganda constantly emphasized effort.

Social life evolved along with this mutation of Nazism. In 1933, it more or less coincided with the elegant life that Balzac had described a century earlier (in thinking about dandies). It presupposed a relative idleness and material wealth that limited its practice to a very small fraction of the elites. The opening of good society, of the world of the court, of the world of elegance and fashion to a wider group of patricians, industrialists, and financiers during the Belle Époque and just after the Great War modified the ideal of *farniente*. High society learned the qualifying value of professional activity. Having a job became an element of distinction that allowed excellence to be demonstrated without resorting to the criteria of birth and fortune alone. Personal value and celebrity were indubitably the keys to the society world of the 1920s, and this trend became stronger after 1933. Even participation in parties and politics was professionalized, becoming a full-time job for the political bureaucracy and raising those involved in the social hierarchy by allocating wealth and notoriety to them. Working thus became a means of acquiring signs of recognition that impressed everyone. Nazism was convinced of this to the point that activism was the only way of being in the world at the end of twelve years of dictatorship. It was only then that the divorce between a large part of high society and the power that had federated them came to light.

High society was thus not a comfortable refuge for disabused men of the world or melancholy dowagers. On the contrary, its intensity and density under the Third Reich show that its mechanisms of sociability performed a primordial function for those in power: bringing the leading elites into conformity. First, by modifying the old channels of functioning and reducing the role played by salons, it weakened the traditional relays of conservatism and liberalism. Next, by destroying the political parties, labour unions, and organizations connected with foreign countries, like the Masonic lodges or the Rotary Club, it promoted the development of meetings organized around the NSDAP and encouraged local elites to seek greater influence on the leaders in the capital. Hitler's programme of centralization also led to a greater concentration of major social events in Berlin. To be sure, cities like Munich or Nuremberg automatically received benefits from the NSDAP's increased influence: monumental structures, congresses, festivals, and games. Hamburg and Frankfurt tried to resist the trend towards centralization by connecting their traditions to the new practices. But other large cities generally suffered from this development. A city like Weimar or a regional metropolis like Dresden seemed dull in comparison to the lustre they had had a few years earlier.

The expansion of the Reich increased the distortions between the centre and the periphery because local celebratory policies were far from coordinated. With the conquests, Vienna, Paris, and Rome entered into this complicity and into these networks while at the same time preserving their particularism. Local officials appointed by the Nazis tried to emulate the practices they had seen around leaders in Berlin, but quickly learned that rushing things in their own countries could prove very disadvantageous for them.

The elites' support for the National Socialist movement was therefore not exclusively ideological. It proceeded largely from conformism. The latter should not be understood as a simple product of the laws of imitation[2] or the natural tendency of bourgeois societies, but rather as a subtle form of alienation. Analysed on the basis of the Nazis' seizure and exercise of power, it seems to result from micro-solidarities that by small adjustments and repetition finally create a feeling that an idea or situation is normal. Conformism was thus largely constructed by the interplay of encounters and interactions within good society and influenced the Nazi leaders as much as it did their hosts.

This bringing into conformity thus helped reinforce and disseminate the principal components of National Socialism's conception of high society: the adaptation of politeness to the new politico-social hierarchies, the personalization of power relationships, and the aestheticization of collective actions. The first was based on a revived etiquette. Precedence was granted to the most powerful in the state and in the party. Nonetheless, the role played by the nobility as a crucial ideological institution helped soften this pragmatic hierarchy through reverence for those who held ancient dignities or brilliant titles. Whence the relative incoherence of the system of civility at the beginning of the Third Reich, because depending on the circumstances, the organizers sometimes gave priority to the parameter of power and sometimes to that of antiquity. Over time, this apparent contradiction was resolved as the NSDAP's and the SS's sociabilities developed and gained influence. The second element, personalization, had the effect of favouring cabals and mafias within local and national institutions, further accentuating the National Socialist regime's disorders but helping give them a lustre peculiar to high society, because leaders both great and small multiplied social events in order to prove that they had a reason for being. The last element, aestheticization, made it possible to anchor everywhere in Europe a symbolism whose effects were long felt: the liturgies of the extreme right were associated with fantasies of success, opulence, and force.

In this sense, the project of fusing the elites that we mentioned at the outset was only partially realized. There was in fact a sociability common to the diverse social and professional elites, including the most corrupt of them, and these social ties transformed support for the Third Reich into an act in accord with common morality. Nevertheless, the relative segregation of old elites, people whose social status had declined, organic elites, and new elites persisted. In the same place, invisible threads created tiny distinctions that hampered the fusion of all the individuals into a coherent, dominant group. If there was a high society, it was composed of several groups sharing common times, practices, and passions but refusing to be reduced to the simple expression of a single, unique power elite. The vast reservoir of high society in the 1930s, with its three to four million potential participants, was obviously not unambiguous. It was not a matter of four million individuals acting like robots in perfect harmony. Even very high Nazi society, with a few hundred members, did not function like a monozygotic organism. The strong internal competition and the awareness of certain people's privileges resulted in the creation of numerous sub-groups struggling to monopolize collective resources.

The reader will have understood that members of good society, *die feine Gesellschaft*, followed fashion and gave free rein to their prejudices, but also looked to the future in the event that the Nazi solution failed. For this reason, they did not really adopt strategies of clan and family alliances with the current leaders. They willingly proclaimed the value of the *Volksgemeinschaft*, but they were too concerned about their own excellence to agree to be shaped in the mould of a vulgar uniformity. Goebbels' and Bormann's diatribes and even the tone of Hitler's testament show how far courtly behaviour was based on the ambiguity of a servility that was willingly accepted out of a desire for distinction. On 31 August 1942, the high nobility still gathered at Sigmaringen castle to celebrate the marriage of Princess Maria Adelgrunde von Hohenzollern and His Royal Highness Prince Konstantin von Bayern. Out of conformism, the men wore their uniforms covered with decorations, sometimes using uniforms that went back to 1914–18, and the dancing was brief because of the war.[3] The ladies also gave up their tiaras for the occasion. There was no criticism of the regime and no expectation that the leaders would be grateful. Only Pope Pius XII's telegram was read at the wedding. Essentially, the old aristocracy felt at ease under a regime that respected it, preserved its dignity, and drew it into an ideological adventure whose bases it shared. In this group, only the defeat changed people's minds and led some of those present at the wedding, such as Ulrich von Hassel, to join the eleventh-hour opposition that resulted in the 1944 assassination attempt.

A sort of mental screed was imposed on people's minds and helped unify the way they imagined membership in good society as a complementarity and the common pursuit of a collective interest. This state of mind was especially characteristic of the years when the regime was at its apogee, between 1936 and 1940. The first effect of this ideological adherence was to make permanent the hierarchical, authoritarian, and disciplinary model of which Prussia had been the symbol and that Weimar had threatened. This image, so convenient for Nazi leaders, should not prevent us from seeing all the discontinuities that persisted in the social fabric and that compose the portrait, not of one but of several elites that undertook a common ideological project without completely abandoning their specific characteristics. This phenomenon is, moreover, not a monopoly of the Third Reich.

The Nazi social practices of opening up to new strata and promoting celebrity as a mode of access to respectable elites could be found throughout Europe and in the United States at the same period. Nevertheless, the Nazi regime made these human relationships part of a long-term strategy. Its system of hidden rewards and compensations had as its objective to involve as many people as possible and to create a social hierarchy that was closely dependent on proximity to those in power: under Nazism; getting rich and rising in society were not a matter of chance. Nazi court life was based on an opacity that favoured obedience. It masked interactions and mutual influences to present the ideal form of a pyramid of vassalage and obligations. In reality, power relationships and *de facto* situations left room for individual initiative and rapid promotions obtained by means of demonstrated favour, servility, activity, and efficiency. Here, as elsewhere, Nazism is distinguished by a difference of degree in the loyalty demanded and in the means used to advance its policies.

It was not the personal gifts, tax exemptions, multiple forms of corruption, distribution of social advantages, or nepotism that distinguished the

Nazi regime, but rather the fact that it integrated these elements into its bureaucratic work and tried to rationalize them in the service of the new kind of state that it imagined. These phenomena thus took on a peculiar amplitude and aesthetics.

Deep-rooted expectations regarding behaviour explain the extreme attention Nazism gave to cultural life and forms of civility. It was not simply a question of restoring the German culture celebrated by Herder and Fichte, but rather one of laying the foundations for a genuinely fascist civilization. The word 'civilization' was strongly disparaged by Hitler and his followers. However, their whole politics was situated on the level of human relationships and had as its objective the creation of a new man. This idea was so firmly anchored in the leaders' minds that each of them tried to incarnate it in his own way, creating for public consumption a false private life in which he appeared in a flattering light as a star worthy of his official position. The ideologizing of the private sphere thus was not simply a way of intruding upon ordinary households; it was also imposed on leaders who were constantly nurturing the fiction of their perfection while at the same time committing in their everyday lives repeated transgressions against their own morality and their theoretical codes of conduct. This practice of duplicity and a taste for general, permanent secrecy insinuated themselves into every one of the National Socialist leaders' acts. They were the necessary condition for giving material form to the utopia of a better world that was supposed to mobilize the collectivity behind its elites.

Thus examination of this way of life leads us to the disturbing problem of the kind of civilization that National Socialism and its major allies wanted to create. When Japan, Italy, and Germany entered an alliance in 1937, the three governments had more than an international relations agreement in mind. They believed that they were inaugurating an era during which the three countries would divide up the globe among themselves and promote an unprecedented way of being in the world by creating social relationships that transcended traditional powers and that would provide peoples with a virile energy. This fascist civilization never got beyond its initial stages, whose ambiguities and structural violence are demonstrated by the example of social life under the Third Reich. It would certainly have resulted in the destruction of immense areas of culture and would have oriented behaviours towards artificial forms of relationship duly codified to promote obedience and a certain dehumanization of social relations. Here, the questions of how to manage the human stock and how to domesticate the species would have meant being able to shape life directly, and genetics would have been raised to the level of a technology of social control.[4] Such a development would have contradicted the process of civilization as conceived by Norbert Elias, who imagined the future as involving states of steadily increasing size in which individuals would enjoy ever more extensive rights.[5] In planetary fascism, the state would have been huge, to be sure, but rights would have been denied. This catastrophic utopia had, however, a terrifying power to mobilize people, and its seductive echoes still enchant the nostalgic and ignorant. A comparative study of this transcontinental project, its implementation, and the fascination it still exercises would show what our societies have inherited from this depressing attempt at globalization.

Notes

Introduction

1 *My Life in Germany before and after the 29th January 1933* (Max Reiner), Widener Library, Harvard University, pp. 169–70.

2 Ibid. (Sybil Peech), pp. 85–6.

3 Joachim Fest, *Hitler*, trans. Richard and Clara Winston, New York, Harcourt Brace Jovanovich, 1974; Ian Kershaw, *Hitler*, London, Longman, 1991; Harald Peuschel, *Die Männer um Hitler: braune Biographien, Martin Bormann, Joseph Goebbels, Hermann Göring, Reinhard Heydrich, Heinrich Himmler und andere*, Düsseldorf, Droste, 1982; Stefan Martens, *Hermann Göring. ' Erster Paladin des Führers' und 'Zweiter Mann im Reich'*, Paderborn, Schoningh, 1985; Ralf Georg Reuth, *Goebbels – Eine Biographie*, Munich, Piper, 1995; Heinrich Fraenkel and Roger Manvell, *Himmler. Kleinbürger und Massenmörder*, Herrsching, Pawlak, 1981; Peter Padfield, *Himmler Reichsführer SS*, London, Papermac, 1991. Cf. Reinhard Vogelsang, *Der Freundeskreis Himmler*, Göttingen, Musterschmidt, 1972.

4 For example, Michael Wildt, *Generation des Unbedingten – Das Führungskorps des Reichssicherungshauptamtes*, Hamburg, HIS Verlag, 2002; Gerd R. Ueberschär, ed., *Hitlers militarische Elite*, Darmstadt, 1998, 2 vols; Bernd Wegner, *Hitlers politische Soldaten: die Waffen SS 1939–1945*, Paderborn, Schönig, 1988. See also Ulrich Herbert Best, *Biografische Studie über Radikalismus, Weltanschauung und Vernunft, 1903–1989*, Bonn, Dietz, 2001; Hans-Jürgen Dorscher, *Das Auswärtiges Amt im dritten Reich*, Berlin, Siedler, 1987; Paul Gerhard and Klaus-Michael Mallmann, eds, *Die Gestapo im Zweiten Weltkrieg. 'Heimatfront' und besetzes Europa*, Darmstadt, Primus Verlag, 2000.

5 For a documentary approach, Wolfgang Schneider, *Frauen unterm Hakenkreuz*, Hamburg, Hoffmann und Campe, 2001; a social analysis, Rita Thalmann, *Être femme sous le IIIe Reich*, Paris, Laffont, 1982; fashion and style, Irene Guenther, *Nazi Chic – Fashioning Women in the Third Reich*, New York, Berg, 2004; for biographies, Erich Schaake, *Hitlers Frauen*, Munich, Ullstein, 2000; Anna-Maria Sigmund, *Die Frauen der Nazis*, Vienna, Heyne, 1998–2002, 3 vols; Anja

Klabunde, *Magda Goebbels*, Munich, Bertelsmann, 1999; François Delpla, *Les tentatrices du diable – Hitler, la part des femmes*, Paris, L'Archipel, 2005.

6 On the historiography of Nazism, Pierre Ayçoberry, *La question nazie*, Paris, Le Seuil, 1979; Jean Solchany, *Comprendre le nazisme dans l'Allemagne des années Zéro*, Paris, PUF, 1997; Ian Kershaw, *The Nazi Dictatorship: Problems and Perspectives of Interpretation*, London, Edward Arnold, 1985; Edouard Husson, *Comprendre Hitler et la Shoah – les historiens de la République fédérale d'Allemagne depuis 1949*, Paris, PUF, 2000.

7 Nicolas Berg, *Der Holocaust und die westdeutschen Historiker. Erforschung und Erinnerung*, Göttingen, Wallstein, 2003.

8 Stephan Malinowski, *Vom König zum Führer – Sozialer Niedergang und politische Radikalisierung im deutschen Adel zwischen Kaiserreich und NS-Staat*, Berlin, Akademie Verlag, 2003.

9 Winifried Schulze, *Sozialgeschichte, Alltagsgeschichte, Mikro-Historie*, Göttingen, Vandenhoeck & Ruprecht, 1994; Thomas Lindenberger, ' "Alltagsgeschichte" oder: als um die zünftigen Grenzen der Geschichtswissenschaft noch gestritten wurden', in Martin Sabrow, Ralph Jessen, and Klaus Große Kracht eds, *Zeitgeschichte als Streitgeschichte – Grosse Kontroversen seit 1945*, Munich, Beck, 2003, pp. 74–91. On German writing on social history, see Jürgen Kocka, *Sozialgeschichte Begriff, Entwicklung, Probleme*, Göttingen, Vandenhoeck & Ruprecht, 1986.

10 Peter Reichel, *Der schöne Schein des Dritten Reichs. Gewalt und Faszination des deutschen Fachismus*, Munich, Carl Hanser Verlag, 1991.

11 George L. Mosse, *The Nationalization of the Masses: Political Symbolism and Mass Movements in Germany from the Napoleonic Wars through the Third Reich*, New York, Fertig, 1975. Cf. Emilio Gentile, *Politics as Religion*, trans. George Staunton, Princeton, Princeton University Press, 2006.

12 Frank Bajohr, *Parvenüs und Profiteure – Korruption in der NS-Zeit*, Frankfurt, Fischer, 2001; Götz Aly, *Hitlers Volksstaat – Raub, Rassenkrieg und Nationaler Sozialismus*, Frankfurt, Fischer, 2005; Jonathan Petropoulos, *Kunstraub und Sammelwahn – Kunst und Politik im Dritten Reich*, Hamburg, Propyläen, 1999.

13 Norbert Elias, *The Germans: Power Struggles and the Development of Habitus in the Nineteenth and Twentieth Centuries*, trans. Eric Dunning and Stephen Mennell, Cambridge, Polity, 1996.

14 Hartmut Kaelble, *Der historische Vergleich – Eine Einführung zum 19. und 20. Jahrundert*, Frankfurt, Campus, 1999. Cf. Christophe Charle, *Les intellectuels en Europe au XIXe siècle – Essai d'histoire comparée*, Paris, Le Seuil, 1996; Bénédicte Zimmermann and Michael Werner, eds, *De la comparaison à l'histoire croisée*, Paris, Le Seuil, 2004.

15 Annette Becker, Stéphane Audoin-Rouzeau, Christian Ingrao, and Henry Rousso, eds, *La violence de guerre – Approche comparée des deux conflits mondiaux*, Brussels, Complexe, 2002; Anne Duménil, Nicolas Beaupré, and Christian Ingrao, eds, *1914–1945, L'ère de la guerre*, Paris, Agnès Vienot, 2004, 2 vols; Christopher Browning, *Ordinary Men: Reserve Police Battalion 101 and the Final Solution in Poland*, London, Penguin, 2001; Christian Gerlach, *Krieg,*

Ernährung, Volkermord–Forschungen zur deutsche Vernichtungspolitik, Hamburg, HIS, 1998; Florent Brayard, *La solution finale de la question juive*, Paris, Fayard, 2004; Sven Reichardt, *Faschistische Kampfbünde. Gewalt und Gemeinschaft im italienischen Squadrismus und in der deutschen SA*, Cologne–Weimar–Vienna, Böhlau Verlag, 2002.

16 Norbert Elias, *The Civilizing Process*, trans. Edmund Jephcott, New York, Pantheon Books, 1982.

17 Maurice Agulhon, *La République au village*, Paris, Le Seuil, 1979.

18 Anne Martin-Fugier, *La vie élégante ou la formation du Tout-Paris 1815–1848*, Paris, Fayard, 1990; idem., *Les salons sous la IIIe République – Art, culture, politique*, Paris, Perrin, 2003; Myriam Chimenes, *Mécènes et Musiciens – Du salon au concert à Paris sous la IIIe République*, Paris, Fayard, 2004.

19 Pierre Bourdieu, *Distinction: A Social Critique of the Judgement of Taste*, trans. Richard Nice, Cambridge, Mass., Harvard University Press, 2007. Cf. Jean-Claude Kaufmann, *La trame conjugale – Analyse du couple par son linge*, Paris, Nathan, 1992.

20 Mark Mazower, *Dark Continent. Europe's Twentieth Century*, London, Penguin Books, 1999.

21 Philippe Ariès and Georges Duby, eds, *A History of Private Life*, Cambridge, Mass., Harvard University Press, 1992–8, 5 vols. Cf. Pierre Nora, ed., *Les lieux de mémoire*, Paris, Gallimard, 1984–1992, 7 vols. On Germany, Étienne François and Hagen Schulze, eds, *Deutsche Erinnerungsorte*, Munich, Beck, 2001, 3 vols.

22 Gerd R. Ueberschär and Winfried Vogel, *Dienen und Verdienen – Hitlers Geschenke an seine Elite*, Frankfurt, Fischer, 2001.

23 François Furet, *Le passé d'une illusion – Essai sur l'idée communiste au XXe siècle*, Paris, Laffont, 1995.

24 Emilio Gentile, *Politics as Religion*.

25 Paul Ekman, ed., *Emotion in the Human Face*, Cambridge, Cambridge University Press, 1982.

26 I follow the definition of charisma offered by Luc de Heusch, *Rois nés d'un coeur de vache*, Paris, Gallimard, 1982.

27 Giovanni Levi, 'Il piccolo, il grande e il piccolo', *Meridiana*, no 10, 1990, pp. 211ff.

28 François Laplantine, *De tout petits liens*, Paris, Mille et Une Nuits, 2003, pp. 48 ff. Cf. Marc Abélès, 'Pour une anthropologie de la platitude. Le politique et les sociétés modernes', *Anthropologie et Sociétés*, vol. 13, no. 3, 1989, pp. 13–24.

29 Daniel Arrasse, *On n'y voit rien – Descriptions*, Paris, Denoël, 2000.

30 Clifford Geertz, 'Thick Description: Toward an Interpretive Theory of Culture', in *The Interpretation of Cultures: Selected Essays*, New York, Basic Books, 1973, pp. 3–30.

31 Vilfredo Pareto, *The Mind and Society: A Treatise on General Sociology*, trans. Andrew Bongiorno and Arthur Livingston, New York, Dover, 1963; cf. idem, *I Sistemi socialisti*, Milan, Istituto editoriale italiano, [1902], 7 vols.

32 Cornelia Essner and Edouard Conte, *La quête de la race – Une anthropologie du nazisme*, Paris, Hachette, 1995 ; Cornelia Essner, *Die 'Nürnberger Gesetze' oder*

Die Verwaltung des Rassenwahns 1933–1945, Paderborn, Schöningh, 2002; Christian Ingrao, 'Une anthropologie historique du massacre: le cas des *Einsatzgruppen* en Russie', in David El Kenz, ed., *Le massacre objet d'histoire*, Paris, Gallimard, 2005, pp. 351–69.

33 Hannah Arendt, *The Origins of Totalitarianism*, New York, Harcourt Brace, 1951.

34 Maurice Bloch, *La violence du religieux*, Paris, Odile Jacob, 1997; Marcel Détienne and Jean-Pierre Vernant, *La cuisine du sacrifice en pays grec*, Paris, Gallimard, 1979.

35 On Himmler's father, see Alfred Andersch, *Der Vater eines Mörders*, Zurich, Diogenes, 1980.

36 Philippe Burrin, *Ressentiment et Apocalypse. Essai sur l'antisémitisme nazi*, Paris, Le Seuil, 2004.

37 Mary Douglas, *Purity and Danger: An Analysis of the Concepts of Pollution and Taboo*, 2nd edn, London and New York, Routledge, 2000.

Chapter 1 The Birth of Nazi High Society

1 David Clay Large, *Where Ghosts Walked: Munich's Road to the Third Reich*, New York, Norton, 1997.

2 Ian Kershaw, *Hitler*.

3 Heinz Reif, 'Hauptstadtentwicklung und Elitenbildung: "Tout Berlin" 1871–1918', in *Geschichte und Emanzipation. Festschrift Reinhard Rürup*, Berlin and New York, 1999, pp. 679–99.

4 David Clay Large, *Where Ghosts Walked*, p. 29.

5 Robert Bouchez, *Hitler que j'ai vu naître*, Paris, ed. Jacques Melot, [1946], p. 45.

6 Ernst Hanfstaengel, *Hitler: The Missing Years*, New York, Arcade, 1994, p. 39.

7 Ian Kershaw, *Hitler*.

8 Joachim Fest, *Hitler*.

9 Cf. Fabrice d'Almeida, 'Postures d'orateurs et jeux de mains dans la France de l'entre-deux-guerres', in Michèle Ménard and Annie Duprat, eds, *Histoire, images, imaginaires*, Le Mans, Presses Universitaires du Maine, 1998, pp. 451–61.

10 *Verleger J. F. Lehmann – Ein Leben im Kampf für Deutschland*, Munich, Lehmann, 1935.

11 Stephan Malinowski, *Vom König zum Führer*, pp. 184–5.

12 Anton Joachimsthaler, *Hitlers Liste*, Munich, Herbig, 2003, p. 62.

13 Anna-Maria Sigmund, *Die Frauen der Nazis*, vol. 1, p. 11, based on Hitler's *Tischgespräche*.

14 Ernst Hanfstaengl, *Hitler: The Missing Years*, pp. 39, 42.

15 Ibid., p. 43.

16 Brigitte Hamann, *Winifred Wagner oder Hitlers Bayreuth*, Munich, Piper, 2002.

17 Idem, *Hitlers Wien – Lehrjahre eines Diktators*, Munich, Piper, 1996, pp. 39 ff.

18 Ibid., p. 514.

19 Hannah Arendt, *The Origins of Totalitarianism*, p. 87.

20 *Verleger J. F. Lehmann.*
21 Erich Grissbach, *Hermann Göring – Werk und Mensch*, Munich, Zentral Verlag der NSDAP, 1938, p. 183.
22 Quoted by Anna Maria Sigmund, *Die Frauen der Nazis*, vol. 1, p. 42.
23 Ernst Hanfstaengl, *Hitler: The Missing Years*, p. 72.
24 Ibid., pp. 110ff.
25 Anton Joachimsthaler, *Hitlers Liste*, p. 19.
26 Ian Kershaw, *Hitler.*
27 BAB, NS 10/123, fols 7–12.
28 Ibid., fol. 8.
29 Ibid., fol. 9.
30 Ibid., fol. 12.
31 Ernst Hanfstaengl, *Hitler: The Missing Years*, p. 22.
32 Cf. Joachim Fest, *Hitler.*
33 Ibid.
34 Ernst Hanfstaengl, *Hitler: The Missing Years*, pp. 65–6.
35 See Ian Kershaw, *Hitler*; Hermann Weiss, *Personen Lexikon 1933–1945*, Vienna, Tosa, 2003, p. 218.
36 Anja Klabunde, *Magda Goebbels.*
37 Anna-Maria Sigmund, *Die Frauen der Nazis*, vol. 1, pp. 105–143.
38 Sven Reichardt, *Faschistische Kampfbünde.*
39 Stephan Malinowski, *Vom König zum Führer*, pp. 422ff. Cf. Christa Schröder, *12 ans auprès d'Hitler, 1933–1945: la secrétaire privée d'Hitler témoigne*, Paris, Pages après pages, 2004, pp. 435ff.
40 BAB, NS 10/1283.
41 Büro des Reichspräsidenten, Abt. B/III, Bd. 47, Bl. 259/260, quoted in Renzo Vespignani, *Über den Faschismus*, Berlin, Neue Gesellschaft für Bildende Kunst und das Kunstamt Kreuzberg, 1976, p. 11.
42 Karl Dietrich Bracher, *Die Auflösung der Weimarer Republik*, Düsseldorf, Droste, 2004.
43 Hannah Arendt, *The Origins of Totalitarianism.*

Chapter 2 The Great Pleasures and Small Benefits of Nazi High Society

1 Anton Joachimsthaler, *Hitlers Liste*, p. 204.
2 Bella Fromm, *Als Hitler mir die Hand küsste*, Berlin, Rowohlt, 1993, p. 112.
3 BAB, Filmarchiv, K178469, 'Hitler und Hindenburg'.
4 BAB, NS 10 and Hitler's personal documents in NS 26.
5 Antonio Gramsci, *Gli intellettuali*, Rome, Editori Riuniti, 1971, pp. 13–16.
6 Ibid.
7 Peter Reichel, *Der schöne Schein des Dritten Reichs.*
8 Emmy Göring, *An der Seite Meines Mannes: Begentheiten und Bekenntnisse*, Göttingen, Schütz, 1967 (in English as *My Life with Goering*, London, David Bruce and Watson Ltd, 1972).
9 Film of the ceremony, K177394, 'Ereignisse der Jahre 1935–36 mit Göring'.

10 Carl Vincent Krogmann, *Es ging um Deutschlands Zukunft 1932–1939*, Landsberg, Druffel, 1976, pp. 185–6.

11 BAB, NS 10/42, fols 128–30.

12 BAB, NS 10/42, letter of 15 August 1936, c. fol. 140.

13 BAB, NS 10/43, fols 27–33.

14 Lida Baarova, *Die süße Bitterkeit meines Lebens*, Koblenz, Kettermann-Schmidt, 2001.

15 Olga Chekhova worked for Soviet intelligence. See Antony Beevor, *The Mystery of Olga Chekhova*, London, Penguin, 2005.

16 BAB, R 43 II/789, fols 177–88.

17 Ibid., letter to Lammers, 21 May 1938.

18 Ibid., fol. 176.

19 Ibid., fol. 177.

20 Ibid., fol. 189.

21 Josef Goebbels, *Tagebücher*, p. 646, 22 July 1936: 'Furtwängler hat sich sehr geändert. Er ist jetzt ein richtig netter Mensch'; p. 648, 27 July 1936 : 'Er hat viel gelernt und ist ganz bei uns.'

22 BAB, R 43 II/1244, fols 142ff.

23 BAB, R 43 II/791, fol. 131.

24 Hans Martin, *Darf ich mir erlauben. . . ?*, Stuttgart, Süddeutsches Verlagshaus, 1935, p. 74.

25 Wulf C. Schwarzwäller, *Hitlers Geld*, Vienna, Ueberreuter, 1998, pp. 112ff.

26 Anton Joachimstahler, *Hitlers Liste*, p. 11.

27 Ibid., pp. 10–11; the list for 1935–6 is on pp. 12–15.

28 BAB, NS 10/124, fols 217–c. 279.

29 Béatrice Durand, *Cousins par alliance – Les Allemands en notre miroir*, Paris, Autrement, 2002.

30 Henriette von Schirach, *Der Preis der Herrlichkeit*, Munich, Herbig, 1975, p. 40.

31 BAB, NS 19/3535, fols 9ff.

32 BAB, NS 10/12, fols 140ff.

33 Marcel Mauss, *The Gift: Form and Reason for Exchange in Archaic Societies*, trans. W.D. Halls, London, Routledge, 2008.

34 Emmy Göring, *An der Seite Meines Mannes*.

Chapter 3 Managing Hitler's Court

1 BAB, NS 10/123, fol. 44, letter of 25 April 1934.

2 V BAB, NS 10/123.

3 BAB, NS 10/123, fols 45–6.

4 BAB, NS 10/122, fols 18, 21, 22, 27, 28–31.

5 BAB, R 601.

6 BAB, R 601/99.

7 BAB, R 601/118.

8 See Emilio Gentile, *Politics as Religion*.

9 Martha Schad, *Hitlers Spionin – Das Leben von Stephanie von Hohenlohe*, Munich, Heyne, 2002, pp. 144ff.
10 IFZ, ZS 137, Schaub.
11 Christa Schröder, *12 ans auprès d'Hitler, 1933–1945*; Traudl Junge, *Until the Final Hour: Hitler's Last Secretary*, ed. Melissa Müller, New York, Arcade Publishing, 2004.
12 IFZ, ZS 137, Schaub.
13 Helmut Ulshöfer, ed., *Liebesbriefe an Adolf Hitler – Briefe in der Tod*, Frankfurt, VAS, 1994.
14 BAB, NS 10/10, fol. 112.
15 BAB, NS 10/10.
16 BAB, NS 10/125, fol. 144.
17 BAB, NS 10/110, fols 86, 88, 89, 106–15.
18 Ibid., fol. 108.
19 BAB, NS 10/110, fol. 98.
20 Letter from Italian embassy, 9 June 1934, BAB, NS 10/119.
21 BAB, NS 10/122, fols 77 and 196–7.
22 Nicolaus von Below, *At Hitler's Side: The Memoirs of Hitler's Luftwaffe Adjutant, 1937–1945*, trans. Geoffrey Brooks, London, Greenhill Books, 2001.
23 BAB, NS 19/3666, fols 30–2.
24 Ibid., fol. 38.
25 BAB, NS 19/3938, NS 19/603.
26 Jacques Gandouly, 'Hans Grimm et la Révolution conservatrice: les ambiguïtés du néo-conservatisme agraire', in Barbara Koehn, ed., *La révolution conservatrice et les élites intellectuelles*, Rennes, PUR, 2003, pp. 63–79.
27 Ernst Jünger, *Second journal parisien*, Paris, Christian Bourgois, 1980, p. 107.
28 Bundesarchiv, Filmarchiv, k 1843, 'Goebbels Geburtstag'.
29 Bundesarchiv, Filmarchiv, k 174633, 29 October 1942.
30 Leni Riefenstahl, *The Sieve of Memory: Memoirs of Leni Riefenstahl*, London, Quartet, 1999.
31 BAB, NS 10/110, fol. 12, letter from Wünsche, 26 June 1940.
32 Gerd R. Ueberschär and Winfried Vogel, *Dienen und Verdienen*, pp. 118–23.
33 BAB, NS 10/110, fol. 7.
34 Stefan Zweig, *The World of Yesterday: An Autobiography*, introduction by Harry Zohn, New York, Viking, 1964.
35 BAB, NS 10/111, fol. 141, letter of 1 July 1935.
36 BAB, NS 10/111, fols 142–3, letter of 17 June 1935.
37 Ibid., fols 146–7, letter of 13 July 1935.

Chapter 4 The Destruction of Jewish High Society

1 Janin Reif, Horst Schumacher, and Lothar Uebel, *Schwannenwerder – Ein Inselparadies in Berlin*, Berlin, Nicolai, 2000.
2 Stephan Malinowski, 'Politische Skandale als Zerrspiegel der Demokratie. Die

Fälle Barmat und Sklarek im Kalkül der Weimarer Rechten', in *Jahrbuch für Antisemitismusforschung*, no. 5, 1996, pp. 46–65.

3 Saul Friedländer, *L'Allemagne nazie et les Juifs*, Paris, Le Seuil, vol. 1, 1997, pp. 96ff.

4 Klaus Mann, *Mephisto* [1936], trans. Robin Smyth, Harmondsworth, Penguin, 1995, p. 157.

5 Cornelia Essner and Edouard Conte, *La quête de la race*. For cultural racism, see Arthur Gobineau, *Essai sur l'inégalité des races humaines*, Paris, Nouvel Office d'Édition, 1963.

6 Klaus Mann, *Mephisto*, p. 143.

7 Nicolaus Sombart, *Jugend in Berlin, 1933–1943: ein Bericht*, Munich, Hanser, 1984.

8 Richard von Weizsäcker, *Vier Zeiten*, Berlin, Taschen Verlag, 2002, pp. 59ff.

9 Wolfgang Benz, ed., *Die Juden in Deutschland*, Hamburg, Beck, 1988; idem, *Bilder vom Juden. Studien zum alltäglichen Antisemitismus*, Munich, Beck, 2001.

10 Bella Fromm, *Als Hitler mir die Hand küsste*, p. 159.

11 *My life in Germany* (Max Reiner).

12 Ibid., p. 37.

13 Saul Friedländer, *L'Allemagne nazie et les Juifs*, vol. 1.

14 *My Life in Germany* (Moses), p. 16.

15 Ibid., p. 5.

16 Michael H. Kater, *Doctors under Hitler*, Durham, University of North Carolina Press, 1989.

17 Frank Bajohr, *Unser Hotel ist Judenfrei – Bäder-Antisemitismus im 19. und 20. Jahrhundert*, Frankfurt, Fischer, 2003.

18 'Laßt keinen Jud' in Eure Mitte, Borkum soll frei von Juden sein!'

19 Bella Fromm, *Als Hitler mir die Hand küsste*, p. 212, during a visit to Liebermann, 20 December 1934.

20 Ursula von Kardoff, *Berliner Aufzeichnungen 1942 bis 1945*, Munich, DTV, 1997, p. 71, note to 3 March 1943.

21 *My Life in Germany* (Hildegarde Bollmann).

22 See Rosenberg's note for propagandists, 8 April 1935, BAB, NS 8/128, fols 14–20.

23 Hartmut Jäckel, *Menschen in Berlin – Das letzte Telefonbuch der alten Reichshauptstadt 1941*, Stuttgart, DVA, 2000, pp. 159–61.

24 Bella Fromm, *Als Hitler mir die Hand küsste*, p. 158.

25 David Clay Large, *Where Ghosts Walked*, p. 247.

26 IFZ, ZS 618, Grimm, fols 45ff.

27 Rita Thalmann, *La nuit de cristal*, Paris, Robert Laffont, 1972.

28 See David Clay Large, *Where Ghosts Walked*.

29 Ruth Andreas-Friedrich, *Der Schattenmann*, Berlin, Suhrkamp, 1986, p. 29.

30 Saul Friedländer, *L'Allemagne nazie et les Juifs*, vol 1.

31 Henriette von Schirach, *Der Preis der Herrlichkeit*, pp. 6ff.

32 Lothar Steinbach, *Ein Volk, ein Reich, ein Glaube?* Bonn, Dietz, pp. 61ff.

33 IFZ, ZS 137, Schaub, fol. 45.

34 Richard von Weizsäcker, *Vier Zeiten*, pp. 74–6; cf. Bernd Freytag von Loringhoven, *In the Bunker with Hitler*, New York, Pegasus, 2007.
35 IFZ, ZS 317/1 Wolff, fols 12ff. Cf. IFZ, ZS 191 Wiedemann, fols 10ff.
36 *Den Nürnberger Prozess gegen die Hauptkriegsverbrecher vom 14 november 1945–1. Oktober 1946*, Nürnberg, 1947, vol. IX.
37 Ibid., p. 603.
38 Ibid., p. 601.
39 Ibid., p. 597.
40 Ibid., p. 591.
41 Wolfram Wette, *Gustav Noske – Eine politische biographie*, Düsseldorf, Droste, 1987; Gustav Noske, *Erlebtes aus Aufstieg und Niedergang einer Demokratie*, Offenbach, 1947, p. 27.
42 *Adlige Jugend*, no. 2, 21 January 1933, supplement to the *Deutsches Adelsblatt*.
43 *Deutsches Adelsblatt*, 1 April 1933.
44 Ibid., February 1936, p. 171.
45 BAB, R58/1066.
46 Ibid., fol. 183.
47 *Der Rotarier*, February 1937, no. 2, p. 1. 'Die Kunst des Lesens wie des Lernens ist auch hier : Wesentliches behalten, Unwesentliches vergessen.'
48 BAB, R 43 II/922 O, fols 151ff.
49 Ibid., fol. 143.
50 Ibid., fol. 134.
51 Charlotte Beradt, *Das Dritte Reich des Traums*, Munich, Nymphenburger Verlagshandlung, 1966.
52 *My Life in Germany* (Barbara de Sevin), p. 158.

Chapter 5 Was There a Nazi Luxury?

1 Cf. Alain Ehrenberg, *Le culte de la performance*, Paris, Pluriel, 1995. On virility, George L. Mosse, *The Image of Man: The Creation of Modern Masculinity*, New York, Oxford University Press, 1996.
2 BAB, NS 10/119, fols 54, 57.
3 BAB, NS 10/127, fol. 256.
4 BAB, NS 10/121, fols 49–51.
5 André Gunthert, 'La voiture du peuple des seigneurs. Naissance de la Volkswagen', *Vingtième siècle*, no. 15, July–September 1987, pp. 29–42.
6 Elly Beinhorn-Rosemeyer, *Mein Mann, der Rennfahrer*, Berlin, Deutscher Verlag, 1938.
7 *Arbeitmaiden am Werk*, Leipzig, Seemann, 1940. Work as a gift to girls; p. 22, camp leaders must do in their camps what the Führer has done in Germany.
8 *Hausbuch für die deutsche Familie*, Berlin, Verlag für Standesamtwesen, 1938 edn.
9 On the politics of German fashions, see Irene Guenther, *Nazi Chic*.
10 *Früjahrs und Sommermodelle des deutschen Modeinstituts*, Berlin, DMI, 1934.
11 Cf. Gloria Sultano, *Wie geistiges Kokain – Mode unter Hakenkreuz*, Vienna, Verlag

für Gesellschaftskritik, 1995.

12 BAB, NS 10/38, fols 138–42. The project is dated 3 October 1940.

13 Ibid., fol. 142.

14 Irene Guenther, *Nazi Chic*, pp. 3–4.

15 Ibid., pp. 109ff.

16 *Die Dame*, 1938, no. 16, pp. 30–1.

17 Irene Guenther, *Nazi Chic*, p. 120.

18 *12 Uhr Blatt*, 12 April 1934.

19 Ibid., 14 April 1934.

20 Ibid., 20 October 1939.

21 *Die Dame*, 1938, no. 14, p. 1.

22 Ibid., 1938, no. 19, pp. 8–9.

23 On men's fashions, see Ingrid Loschek, *Mode im 20 Jahrhundert – Eine Kulturgeschichte unserer Zeit*, Munich, Bruckmann, 1978, pp. 108ff.

24 *Die Dame*, 1938, no. 15, pp. 28–9, 'Sommerliche für den Herrn'.

25 Cf. Marie-Anne Matard-Bonucci and Pierre Milza, eds, *L'homme nouveau dans l'Europe fasciste (1922–1945). Entre dictature et totalitarisme*, Paris, Fayard, 2004.

26 Tschammer und Ostens gives a good example in *Die Bedeutung von Vollblutzucht und Rennsport für Staats und Wehrmacht*, 1936.

27 *My Life in Germany* (Haynes), fols 8–26.

28 On the history of the Union Klub, see Generalsekretariat des Union-Klubs, *Der Klassische Sport*, Berlin, Deutscher Archiv Verlag, 1942. Cf. Bella Fromm, *Als Hitler mir die Hand küsste*, pp. 94–5.

29 Generalsekretariat des Union-Klubs, *Der Klassische Sport*.

30 Bella Fromm, *Als Hitler mir die Hand küsste*, p. 34.

31 BVB, Hoffmann collection, Modenschau 1935–8 series.

32 Carl Vincent Krogmann, *Es ging um Deutschlands Zukunft 1932–1939*, p. 209.

33 Jonathan Petropoulos, *Kunstraub und Sammelwahn*.

34 Katharina Lepper, *Moderne Kunst im Nationalsozialismus: die Kampagne 'Entartete Kunst' und die Sammlung des Wilhelm-Lehmbruck-Museums Duisburg 1933–1945*, Duisburg, Wilhelm-Lehmbruck-Museum, 1992; Peter-Klaus Schuster, *Nationalsozialismus und 'Entartete Kunst': d. 'Kunststadt' München 1937*, Munich, Prestel, 1988.

35 Jonathan Petropoulos, *Kunstraub und Sammelwahn*, p. 73.

36 According to Hanfstaengl, he never missed a chance to belittle the work of his distant predecessor. Cf. Ernst Hanfstaengl, *Hitler: The Missing Years*, p. 220.

37 Regarding the attractiveness of a collection, he writes: 'The goal is to provide a diversity of perspectives organized around the invisible centre of creative energy. That is also the meaning of gardens, and the meaning, ultimately, of the road to life in general.' Ernst Jünger, *Premier journal parisien*, Paris, Bourgois, 1980, p. 185.

38 Eric Michaud, *Un art de l'éternité – l'image et le temps du national-socialisme*, Paris, Gallimard, 1996.

39 George L. Mosse, *The Nationalization of the Masses*. On civic religions, see

Emilio Gentile, *Politics as Religion*.
40 Jonathan Petropoulos, *Kunstraub und Sammelwahn*.
41 The title of Frank Bajohr's book *Parvenüs und Profiteure*.
42 Cf. the Hoffmann collection in the BSB (Munich) or the USHMM collection, as well as the media collection of the Library of Congress in Washington, DC.
43 Klaus Scholder, ed., *Die Mittwochsgesellschaft – Protokolle aus dem geistigen Deutschland 1932 bis 1944*, Berlin, Severin und Sieler, 1982.
44 BAB, NS 10/117, fols 6–11.
45 Ibid., fol. 37.
46 Traudl Junge, *Until the Final Hour*.
47 André François-Poncet, *Souvenirs d'une ambassade à Berlin*, Paris, Flammarion, 1946, pp. 276–7.
48 IFZ, ED 100, vol. 209, Henriette Hoffmann, pp. 5–6.
49 Ibid., vol. 259, Darré.
50 Emmy Göring, *An der Seite Meines Mannes*, pp. 143–4.
51 Victor Klemperer, *The Language of the Third Reich. LTI – Lingua Tertii Imperii. A Philologist's Notebook*, trans. Martin Brody, London and New Brunswick, NJ, Athlone Press, 2000, p. 68.
52 Franz Tepel, *Gastlichkeit im neuen Deutschland*, Düsseldorf, Grosse Verlag und Dückerei, 1937, p. 7.
53 Ibid., p 98. Josef Goebbels, *Vom Kayserhof zur Reichskanzlei*, Munich, 1934.
54 Franz Tepel, *Gastlichkeit im neuen Deutschland*, p. 104.
55 Ibid., p. 105.
56 For a concrete example, see *My Life in Germany* (Franziska Schubert), pp. 68ff.
57 BAB, NS 10/124, fols 200ff.
58 Ibid., fol.160.
59 Karl Wilhelm Krause, *Kammerdiener bei Hitler 10 Jahre Tag und Nacht*, Hamburg, Hermann Laatzen Verlag, 1949, p. 11.
60 Ibid.
61 Heinz Linge, *Bis zum Untergang*, Munich and Berlin, Herbig, 1980.
62 Kurt Kuch and Anna Plaim, *Bei Hitlers – Zimmermädchen Annas Erinnnerungen*, Tulbing, Kleindienst, 2003, pp. 19–21.
63 IFZ, ZS 3135.
64 Cf. Emmy Göring, *An der Seite Meines Mannes*, pp. 234–5.
65 Kurt Kuch and Anna Plaim, *Bei Hitlers*, p. 91.
66 Karl Wilhelm Krause, *Kammerdiener bei Hitler*, pp. 37, 71–2.
67 Heinz Linge, *Bis zum Untergang*, p. 14.

Chapter 6 Sociabilities in a Totalitarian State

1 Nicolaus Sombart, *Jugend in Berlin, 1933–1943*.
2 Ibid., p. 122.
3 *My Life in Germany* (Barbara de Sevin), fol. 357.
4 Ibid., fol. 115.
5 *My Life in Germany* (Franziska Schubert).

6 Ibid., p. 51. The expression 'Salondame' could be ambiguous.

7 Ibid., p. 55.

8 Cf. Stephan Malinowski, *Vom König zum Führer*.

9 *Deutsches Adelsblatt*, 1 January 1933, p. 9.

10 Ibid., 21 March 1936, p. 403.

11 Ibid., 28 January 1939, p. 153.

12 Ibid., 14 March 1936, p. 369.

13 Ibid., 28 March 1936, p. 435.

14 Isabelle, Countess of Paris, *Tout m'est bonheur*, Paris, France-Loisirs, 1979.

15 BAB, NS 10/19, fol. 3, letter of 19 August 1940.

16 *Berliner Illustrierte Zeitung*, no. 3, 20 January 1938, for the marriage of 'Paul von Griechenland und Prinzessin Friederike-Luise vom Braunschweig und Lüneburg'. For the telegrams between Hitler and the Brunswick family, BAB, NS 10/5, fols 178ff.

17 BAB, NS 10/1, fol. 187.

18 BAB, NS 10/1a, fol. 117.

19 On the disagreement between Himmler and Röhm, IFZ, ZS 317/1, fol. 3.

20 On banks and the SS, Peter-Ferdinand Koch, *Die Geldgeschäfte der SS – Wie die deutsche Banken den schwarzen Terror finanzieren*, Hamburg, Hoffmann und Campe, 2000, esp. pp. 32ff on Kurt von Schröder.

21 BAB (ex-BDC), PK/K 0223, fol. 136, letter of 26 August 1938.

22 BAB (ex-BDC), PK/EO 306, fol. 584, letter of 23 September 1938.

23 BAB (ex-BDC), PK/B 91 for Else and Hugo.

24 For Liselotte and Helene, BAB (ex BDC), PK/A 237, fols 2052, 2054; 2064 on Bouhler; 2090 on the exemption.

25 BAB (ex-BDC), PK/B 91.

26 BAB (ex-BDC), PK/A0437, fol. 1345.

27 BAB (ex-BDC), PK/K0223, born 12 December 1908.

28 Ibid., fols 1398ff.

29 NS 19/2828, fols 1–4.

30 For an overview, Wolfgang de Boor, *Hitler – Mensch, Übermensch, Untermensch*, Munich, Fischer, 1985.

31 Wilhelm Reich, *The Mass Psychology of Fascism*, trans. Vincent R. Carfagno, New York, Farrar, Straus & Giroux, 1970.

32 Magnus Hirschfeld, ed., *Sittengeschichte des 20. Jahrhunderts*, vol. 2: *Zwischen zwei Katastrophen*, Hanau/Main, Schustek, 1967; vol. 3: *Zweiten Weltkrieg*, Hanau/Main, Müller & Kiepenheuer, 1978.

33 Ernst Günther Schenck, *Patient Hitler. Eine medizinische Biographie*, Düsseldorf, Droste, 1989.

34 Hans-Ulrich Wehler, 'Psychoanalysis and History', *Social Research*, no. 47, Autumn 1980, pp. 519–36.

35 Ernst Günther Schenck, *Patient Hitler*.

36 In his *Jugend in Berlin, 1933–1943* Nicolaus Sombart makes this one of the essential aspects of the German tragedy. Cf. Ulfried Geuter, *Homosexualität in der deutschen Jugendbewegung – Jugendfreundschaft und Sexualität im Diskurs von*

Jugendbewegung – Psychanalyse und Jugendpsychologie am Beginn des 20. Jahrhunderts, Frankfurt, Suhrkamp, 1994; Gisela Völger and Karin von Welck, eds, *Männerbande, Männerbünde. Zur Rolle des Mannes im Kulturvergleich*, Cologne, Museumsdienst Köln und Rautenstrauch Joest Museum, 1990, 2 vols, esp. the essay by Klaus Theweleit, 'Homosexuelle Aspeckte von Männerbünden unter besonderer Berücksichtigung des Faschismus', vol. 1, pp. 59–63.

37 Lothar Machtan, *The Hidden Hitler*, trans. John Brownjohn, New York, Basic Books, 2001.

38 On Hitler's alleged sado-masochism and coprophagy, see Vincent Jauvert, 'Hitler, le sexe et l'OSS', *Le Nouvel Observateur*, no. 1966, 11 July 2002, and Walter Langer, *The Mind of Adolf Hitler*, New York, Basic Books, 1972.

39 Florence Tamagne, *Histoire de l'homosexualité en Europe – Berlin, Londres, Paris 1919–1939*, Paris, Le Seuil, 2000.

40 Maggie Koreen, *Immer feste druff – Das freche Leben der KabarettKönigin Claire Waldoff*, Düsseldorf, Droste, 1997, p. 192.

41 Ibid.

42 Cf. Hannah Arendt, *The Origins of Totalitarianism*.

43 Herbert Hoffmann, *Gaststätten*, Stuttgart, Julius Hoffmann Verlag, 1939, p. 168.

44 BAB, R 55/20239a, fols 424 and 460–1 re. the complaint of 9 May 1940.

45 Ibid., fols 428, 429.

46 Ibid., fol. 351.

47 On music under Nazism, Pascal Huynh, ed., *Le IIIe Reich et la musique*, Paris, Fayard/Musée de la musique, 2004 ; idem, *La musique sous la république de Weimar*, Paris, Fayard, 1998.

48 Laure Guilbert, *Danser avec le IIIe Reich – Les danseurs modernes sous le nazisme*, Brussels, Complexe, 2000.

49 BAB, R 55/20239a, fol. 356 (363). The dance troupe led by 'the Jew Geissler' was denounced and threatened with being forbidden to participate in the Munich festival; letter of 19 May 1937, ibid., fols 82–6.

50 Ibid., fol. 350, 1 March 1939.

51 Ibid., fols 307–9.

52 Ibid., fol. 323.

53 Ibid., fol. 333, letter from the head of the Gestapo, 15 December 1938.

54 Ibid., fol. 331, letter of 3 January 1939.

55 Ibid., fol. 326.

56 BAB, R 58/740, fols 2–6.

57 Peter Laregh, *Heinrich George – Komödiant seiner Zeit*, Berlin, Ullstein, 1992.

58 Max Schmeling, *Erinnerungen*, Berlin, Ullstein, 1995.

59 Ibid., p. 98.

60 BAB, NS 10/124, for the birthday letter.

61 BAB, NS 10/9, fol. 148, for the award ceremony.

62 For the complete list, BAB, NS 10/5, fols 1–21.

63 BAB, NS10/126, fol. 80, 'Programm für Tag der deutschen Kunst'.

64 Ibid., fols 127–34 for 1939.
65 David Clay Large, *Where Ghosts Walked*, p. 274.
66 Ibid., p. 275.
67 Filmarchiv, no. 2790, *Münchner Oktoberfest*, 1939.
68 Ulrich Chaussy and Christoph Püschner, *Nachbar Hitler – Führerkult und Heimatzerstörung am Obersalzberg*, Berlin, Link, 1995.
69 BAB, NS 10/119, fols 63–71.
70 Ulrich Chaussy and Christoph Püschner, *Nachbar Hitler*, p. 75.
71 See, for example, the Baedeker for 1938.
72 BAB, NS 26/16.
73 IFZ, ZS 3135.
74 IFZ, ED 100/209, 5.
75 Hermann Göring, *Jagdkalender*, typescript in IFZ, original in Library of Congress (Washington), pp. 5ff.
76 Erich Grissbach, *Hermann Göring*, pp. 99ff.
77 IFZ, Ms 577, Backe.
78 The testimony of his masseur, Félix Kersten, suggests that his physical condition was mediocre. Joseph Kessel, *Les mains du miracle*, Paris, Gallimard, 1960.
79 BAB, NS 19/3371, fol. 4ff.
80 Ibid., fol. 209, letter from Karl Adolf Schmitt, 7 July 1938.
81 Ibid., fols 50ff.
82 Ibid., fol. 49, letter from Daluege to Himmler, 24 August 1942.
83 BAB, NS 19/3289, letter of 16 March 1939 and reply of 8 April.
84 Frank Bajohr, *Parvenüs und Profiteure*, pp. 62ff; Gerd Ueberschär and Winfried Vogel, *Dienen und Verdienen*, pp. 71ff.
85 Erich Grissbach, *Hermann Göring*, p. 107.
86 Cf. Christian Ingrao, 'Une anthropologie historique du massacre'.

Chapter 7 The Splendours of Diplomacy

1 Christabel Bielenberg, *When I Was a German, 1934–1945: An Englishwoman in Nazi Germany*, Lincoln, University of Nebraska Press, 1998, p. 16.
2 Ernst Hanfstaengl, *Hitler: The Missing Years*, p. 41.
3 François Furet, *Le passé d'une illusion*. Cf. Sophie Coeuré, *La grande lueur à l'Est*, Paris, Le Seuil, 2000.
4 Bella Fromm, *Als Hitler mir die Hand küsste*, pp. 40, 65, 72.
5 Cf. Claudine Haroche, Olivier Ihl, and Yves Déloye, eds, *Le protocole ou la mise en forme de l'ordre politique*, Paris, L'Harmattan, 1996.
6 Hans-Jürgen Dörscher, *Das Auswärtiges Amt im dritten Reich*, pp. 59–60.
7 Bella Fromm, *Als Hitler mir die Hand küsste*, pp. 97ff.
8 AA PA, R 118946, prot., 5027, letter of 9 August 1934.
9 Ibid., André François-Poncet's letter of 14 August 1934.
10 Ibid., note of 9 August 1925 (prot. 5015).
11 Hans-Jürgen Dörscher, *Das Auswärtiges Amt im dritten Reich*, p. 192.
12 AA PA, R 118946, draft of the letter of 21 August 1934 and Hitler's manuscript

version.

13 Ibid., undated list of addresses (prot. 4985 III).

14 Ibid., prot. 5015.

15 Ibid., R 118947.

16 AA PA, R 118947.

17 Ibid.

18 AA PA, R 118946, for drafts and final versions.

19 On relations between the Vatican and the Nazis, Michael Phayer, *The Catholic Church and the Holocaust, 1930–1965*, Bloomington, Indiana University Press, 2001.

20 BAB, NS 10/2, fols 2–39.

21 AA PA, R 118839, invitations and guest list for 1 December1934 at 9 p.m.

22 Ibid., Bassewitz's report of 9 March 1934.

23 Ibid., letter from Mumm to Stenger, 23 June 1934.

24 Ibid., letter from Mumm to the official responsible for the Reichsparteitag, 24 August 1934.

25 Ibid., letter from the Mitropa company to the foreign ministry, 27 August 1934.

26 Ibid., 'Vorläufige Programm für die Teilnahme der Diplomaten an Nürnberger Parteitag', 4 pp.

27 AA PA, R 118840, Bassewitz's letter, 22 September 1934.

28 André François-Poncet, *Souvenirs d'une ambassade à Berlin*, p. 270 : 'Our absence implied disapproval.'

29 BAB, NS 10/130.

30 Ian Kershaw, *Making Friends with Hitler: Lord Londonderry, the Nazis, and the Road to War*, London, Penguin, 2004.

31 On this protohistory of collaboration, see Barbara Lambauer, *Otto Abetz et les Français ou l'envers de la Collaboration*, Paris, Fayard, 2001.

32 BAB, NS 10/130, letter of 11 August 1938.

33 See AA PA, R 99141 and R99142 for the complete file on foreigners at the 1937 Nuremberg congress. R99142 gives lists of guests by country and their lodging arrangements.

34 AA PA, R 99141, table of honorary guests (July 1937?) and specific requirements.

35 Cf. Philipe Burrin, *La dérive fasciste – Doriot, Déat, Bergery*, Paris, Le Seuil, 1986.

36 Cf. AA PA, R 118949 which contains several summaries for 1935; see also BAB, NS 10/3, fol. 125; BAB, NS 10/9, fols 272ff, BAB, NS 10/21.

37 BAB, NS 10/7, fol. 51, letter of 19 September 1938.

38 AA PA, R 128728.

39 Cf. IFZ, Hoffmann, F 155, Gastbuch, 1940.

40 AA PA, R 118950, report of 25 May 1935.

41 Ibid., report of 23 April 1936.

42 AA PA, R 118952.

43 Ibid.

44 AA PA, R 118952.

45 Ibid., Count of Moulin's report, p. 1.

46 AA PA, report of 25 April 1939.

47 Ibid., report on the Bulgarian delegation.

48 André François-Poncet, *Souvenirs d'une ambassade à Berlin*, pp. 161–4.

49 Bella Fromm, *Als Hitler mir die Hand küsste*, p. 289.

50 Ibid., p. 74.

51 Ibid., p. 137.

52 For example, BAB, NS 10/36, fol. 372, letter accompanying a report on the state of English salons, submitted by Fritz Wiedemann to Oberleutnant Oster of the Abwehr, with a copy for Göring's adjutant. Wiedemann concludes: "The writer of this report is well known to you.' Was it Princess von Hohenlohe?

53 Martha Schad, *Hitlers Spionin*.

54 BAB, NS 10/118, letter from the chancellery to Göring, 15 October 1938.

55 Ibid., letter of 2 December 1938. For his emoluments, see letter of 4 November 1938.

56 BAB, NS 10/118, letter from Wiedemann to Göring's office, 15 October 1938.

57 Bella Fromm, *Als Hitler mir die Hand küsste*, p. 212.

58 AA PA, 119154, Dörnberg's note of 18 January 1940 ; repeated by Ribbentrop in 1942, in the same file.

59 AA PA, R 119238.

60 BAB, NS 10/124, fol. 154 v.

61 Norbert Elias, *The Civilizing Process*.

62 AA PA, R 118841, note on 11 January 1936 produced by the protocol office.

63 Stephan Malinowski, *Vom König zum Führer*, pp. 45–6.

64 BAB, NS 10/127, fols 271ff; cf. NS 10/129, fols 19 and 21; the complete programme for the visit from 21 to 26 August is found in fols 3–18.

65 BAB, NS 10/127, fols 129ff.

66 BAB, NS 10/1a, trip in June 1936, fols 18–19, fol. 51.

67 BAB, NS 10/15, fol. 99.

68 See the exchange of telegrams between Hitler and Stalin on the occasion of birthdays, BAB, NS 10/11, fol.?55. Cf. Ernst Nolte, *Der europäische Bürgerkrieg, 1917–1945*, Berlin, Propyläen, 1987.

69 AA PA, Nachlass Dörnberg, 12 vols.

70 Gerd R. Ueberschär and Winfried Vogel, *Dienen und Verdienen*, pp. 85–6.

71 AA PA, R 118815, report of 15 August 1932.

72 BAB, NS 10/7, fol. 68 on the Yugoslav medals, fol. 134 for the King of Italy's declarations, and NS 10/11, fols 7–9, for the same. BAB, NS 10/8 fol. 154, Schaub and two SS, decorated by Boris of Bulgaria. Robert Ley complains about the delay in receiving his decoration from General Franco in 1939, AA PA, R 98965.

73 AA PA, R 119154.

74 Ibid., letter of 11 October 1944, asking for reimbursement.

75 AA PA, R 119122, documents for May and June 1940.

76 The file is in AA PA, R 119154.

77 Christabel Bielenberg, *When I Was a German, 1934–1945*.

78 Henriette von Schirach, *Der Preis der Herrlichkeit*, pp. 13ff.

79 Hans-Jürgen Dörscher, *Das Auswärtiges Amt im dritten Reich*, pp. 243ff.
80 Lucas Delattre, *Fritz Kolbe*, Paris, Denoël, 2003.

Chapter 8 The Second Worldly War

1 BAB, NS 10/18, fol. 3, telegram from Hitler to the General Staff, 25 June 1940.
2 Ibid., fol. 45.
3 BAB, NS 10/19, fol. 53.
4 Ibid., fol. 41.
5 Ibid., fol. 81.
6 BAB, R 55/949, fols 60–2.
7 R 55/949, fols 141–2, exchange of letters, February–March 1940
8 Cf. Gerd R. Ueberschär and Winfried Vogel, *Dienen und Verdienen*, pp. 218ff.
9 From the point of view of the analyses of Marcel Mauss, *The Gift*.
10 IFZ, ZS 353, interrogation of Lammers conducted by Robert Kempner : 'You were a murderer, we know that, how much did they pay you ?' Kempner asked (fol. 53). After replying that his salary was 3,000 marks per month, Lammers acknowledge that he had received raises and ended up receiving 8,000 marks per month, in addition to the allocation of 600,000 marks. Who says crime doesn't pay?
11 BAB, NS 10/37, fol.?158, 25 April 1939.
12 Bajohr, *Parvenüs und Profiteure*.
13 Gerd R. Ueberschär and Winfried Vogel, *Dienen und Verdienen*.
14 Ibid., pp. 128, 133.
15 IFZ, Ms Hewel, 79 vol. 2, fol. 45.
16 Revealing report by the SD, 27 December 1943, BAB, R 55/191, fols 123ff.
17 BAB, NS 10/37, fol.?136.
18 BAB, NS 10/107, fols 35ff.
19 Hans-Georg von Studnitz, *Als Berlin brannte – Diarium der Jahre 1943–1945*, Stuttgart, Kohlhammer, pp. 9–10.
20 Marie Wassiltischkow, *Die Berliner Tagebücher 1940–1945*, Munich, BTP, 1996, p. 205, for a description dating from April 1944.
21 BAB, NS 10/107, fols 33ff.
22 Ibid., fols 96–107.
23 Jürgen Kuczynski, *Geschichte des Alltags des deutschen Volkes 1918–1945*, Pahl-Rugenstein Verlag, 1982, pp. 70–1.
24 BAB, NS 10/107, fols 2ff.
25 According to Félix Kersten, this plan was put partly into effect, cf. Joseph Kessel, *Les mains du miracle*, pp. 177–82.
26 BSB, Hoffmann collection, now available on-line: *http://www.bsb-muenchen.de/Image_Archive.591+M57d0acf4f16.0.html*.
27 Gloria Sultano, *Wie geistiges Kokain*, pp. 30ff.
28 Ibid.
29 BAB, NS 10/38, fol?202 ; for the bills for the overcoats, and also for Frau Troost,

see S 10/119. The bills date from 1934.

30 For the changes, see Jill Halcomb, *Uniforms and Insignia of the German Foreign Office and Government Ministries 1938–1945*, Columbia, SC, Crown / Agincourt, 1984.

31 Christian von Krockow, *Les Allemands dans leur* XXe *siècle*, Paris, Hachette, 1990.

32 Irene Guenther, *Nazi Chic*, pp. 4–5.

33 Sophie Gensburger and Jean-Marc Dreyfus, *Des camps dans Paris*, Fayard, 2004, pp. 157–9.

34 BAB, R 55/20239a, fol.? 464.

35 Ibid., fol. 468.

36 Ibid., fol. 469, Theaterabteilung report, 26 April 1941.

37 Ibid., fol. 474, letter from Geiger, 11 September 1941.

38 BAB, R 58/191, fol. 62, in an SD report, 27 December 1943.

39 BAB, NS 10/37, fols 210–11.

40 Coco Schumann, *Der Ghettoswinger*, Hamburg, DTV, 1997.

41 BAB, Filmarchiv, documentaire, 3372, 'Der Führer schenkt den Juden eine Stadt', 1944–5.

42 BAB, NS 19/1121, fol. 2, letter from the SS's management department to Wolff, 9 February 1939, proposing a discount of 40 per cent for purchases in Allach, this discount to be extended to other high dignitaries in the SS.

43 BAB, NS 19/3666, fol. 15.

44 BAB, NS 19/424, fol. 2, letter of 9 January 1945, for a group of children in the Nationalpolitische Erziehungsanstalt (National Political Education Institute).

45 BAB, NS 19/1337, fols 3–7.

46 Anna-Maria Sigmund, *Die Frauen der Nazis*, vol. 1, pp. 7ff.

47 Horst Möller, Volker Dahm, Hartmut Mehringer, and Albert A. Feiber, *Die tödliche Utopie*, Munich, IFZ, 1999, pp. 73ff.

48 Stefan Maiwald and Gerd Mischler, *Sexualität unter dem Hakenkreuz*, Munich, Ullstein, 1999, pp. 194–205.

49 Jean-Marc Dreyfus, 'L'aryanisation économique des maisons de prostitution: un éclairage sur quelques proxénètes juifs en France occupée, 1940–1944', *Revue des études juives*, January–June 2003, vol. 162, pp. 219–46. Cf. Insa Meinen, *Wehrmacht und Prostitution im besetzten Frankreich*, Bremen, Temmen, 2002.

50 Hannah Arendt, *The Origins of Totalitarianism*, p. 331.

51 Ibid.

52 INA, newsreel, 18 September 1940.

53 *Deutsches Adelsblatt*, January 1942, pp. 2–3.

54 pp. 114–15.

55 *Deutsches Adelsblatt*, no. 11, June, p. 130.

56 Ibid., no. 9, June 1943, p. 90 : 'Nur das Wort ist gemeinsam erhätert durch Tat, Im Leben, im Sterben: dein Kamarad.'

57 Ursula von Kardoff, *Berliner Aufzeichnungen 1942 bis 1945*, p. 77.

58 Ibid., p. 288.

59 Cf. Emilio Gentile, *Il Culto del littorio*, Bari and Rome, Laterza, 1998.
60 BAB, NS 10/39, fol. 6, copy of a telegram sent on 23 October 1935.
61 'Sei getreu bis in den Tod.'
62 BAB, NS 10/39, fol. 4.
63 BAB, NS 10/1a, fol. 21.
64 *Der Dienstkalender Heinrich Himmlers 1941/42*, Hamburg, Christians, pp. 448ff.
65 Anna-Maria Sigmund, *Die Frauen der Nazis*, vol. 2, pp. 103ff.
66 BAB, NS 19/3359, fol. 7,
67 Victor Klemperer, *The Language of the Third Reich*.
68 BAB, NS 19/3359, fol. 2, letter of 25 October 1942.
69 Ursula von Kardoff, *Berliner Aufzeichnungen 1942 bis 1945*, pp. 262–3.
70 Ruth Andreas-Friedrich, *Der Schattenmann*, p. 124.
71 Peter Ferdinand Koch, *Die Geldgeschäfte der SS*, pp. 152ff.; cf. Constantin Goschler and Philipp Ther, eds, *Raub und Restitution*, Frankfurt, Fischer, 2003.
72 BAB, R 55/239, fol. 50.
73 Ibid., fol. 48.
74 Pierre Assouline, *Lutetia*, Paris, Gallimard, 2005.
75 AA PA, Paris 1.101 A.
76 IFZ, ED 180, Terminkalender Göring, 1942.
77 Yves Pourcher, *Pierre Laval vu par sa fille, d'après ses carnets intimes*, Paris, Cherche Midi, 2002.
78 Ibid., p. 264.
79 Ernst Jünger, *Second journal parisien*.
80 Ibid., p. 91, 26 June 1943.
81 Regarding Himmler's schedule in 1942, BAB, NS 10/1443. Cf. NS 19/1449, fols 33ff. For complete information on Himmler in 1942, see *Der Dienstkalender Heinrich Himmlers 1941/42*, Hamburg, Christian, pp. 248ff. for the trip to Holland.
82 Joseph Kessel, *Les mains du miracle*, p. 148, esp. for the trip to Holland, pp. 210–18.
83 Henry Picker, *Hitlers Tischgespräch in Führerhauptquartier 1941–1942*, Stuttgart, Seewald, 1963.
84 BAB, NS 10/37.
85 BAB, NS 26/16 (film 71943).
86 Ruth Andreas-Friedrich, *Der Schattenmann*, pp. 126–7.
87 Hans Georg von Studnitz, *Als Berlin brannte – Diarium der Jahre 1943-1945*, Stuttgart, Kohlhammer, 1963, p. 10.
88 W. Th. Andermann (pseud.), *Bis der Vorhang fiel*, Dortmund, Schwalvenberg, 1947, p. 120.
89 Ibid., p. 216.
90 Ibid., pp. 174–201.
91 Marie Wassiltschikow, *Die Berliner Tagebücher 1940–1945*.
92 Ibid., p. 312.
93 Ibid., p. 301.
94 BAB, R 58/191, fols 44–47, a report from December 1943.

95 On general security intructions, BAB, NS 10/36, fols 158ff., 'Sicherung der Reichskanzlei'.

96 BAB, NS 10/138, fol. 3, instructions for 31 December 1940, for 77 Wilhelmstrasse, and the Obersalzberg.

97 Ibid., fols 1ff.

98 Kurt Kuch and Anna Plaim, *Bei Hitlers*, pp. 130–3.

99 Christabel Bielenberg, *When I Was a German, 1934–1945*, pp. 91–2.

100 Ruth Andreas-Friedrich, *Der Schattenmann*, pp. 186–92.

101 I adopt here the only figure officially recognized by a state, the former East Germany.

102 Victor Klemperer, *The Language of the Third Reich*, pp. 52–6.

103 IFZ, ZS 71, Heinrich Hoffmann, p. 3.

104 Joachim Fest, *Inside Hitler's Bunker: The Last Days of the Third Reich*, trans. Margot Dembo, London, Picador, 2005.

105 Sophie Gensburger and Jean-Marc Dreyfus, *Des camps dans Paris*.

106 Cf. Stéphane Courtois and Adam Rayski, *Qui savait quoi? L'extermination des Juifs 1941–1945*, Paris, La Découverte, 1987.

107 Henriette von Schirach, *Der Preis der Herrlichkeit*, pp. 99–100.

108 Robert Kempner, *Ankläger einer Epoche – Lebenserinnerungen*, Berlin, Ullstein, 1986.

109 Norbert Frei, ed., *Karrieren im Zwielicht – Hitlers Eliten nach 1945*, Frankfurt, Campus, 2001.

110 Ibid., p. 310.

Conclusion

1 These texts are published in Wolfgang Schneider, *Frauen unterm Hakenkreuz*, pp. 118–19.

2 Gabriel Tarde, *La logique sociale*, Paris, Alcan, 1895, p. 33.

3 Marie Wassiltschikow, *Die Berliner Tagebücher 1940–1945*, pp. 90ff.

4 Peter Sloterdijk, *La domestication de l'être*, Paris, Mille et Une Nuits, 2000.

5 Norbert Elias, *The Civilizing Process*.

Sources

Archives: Bundesarchiv Berlin (BAB), Lichterfelde

Series R, State Archives (Reich)
R 43: Reichskanzlei
R 53: Reichsministerium für Volkserklärung und Propaganda
R 58: RSHA
R 61: Greetings and good wishes

NS Series on the National Socialist Movement
NS 8: Kanzlei Rosenberg
NS 10: Personaladjundantur von Hitler
NS 15: Amt Rosenberg
NS 18: Reichspropaganda Leiter der NSDAP
NS 19: The SS and the Reichsführer SS with his personal Adjudantur
NS 26: Hitler personally

PK series (ex-Berlin Document Center), Personnal Kartei der NSDAP (party correspondence).
Biographical notes and personal files of the Chancellery and the NSDAP.

Ministry of Foreign Affairs (Auswärtiges Amt/Politisches Archiv), AA PA
Inland
Partei
Manuscripts
Dörnberg Collection

Institut für Zeitgeschichte (IFZ, Munich)
Harvard University, Widener Library, collection *My Life in Germany before and after the 29th January 1933*.

Memoirs used include: Abraham, Georg; Albert, Henry; Altmann, Eugen; Andermann, Martin; Arrington, Miriam; Axelrath, Elsie; Baerwald, Alice; Bluhm, Arthur; Bollmann, Hildegarde; Breusch, Robert; de Sevin, Barbara; Diel, Paul; Dienemann, Max; Frank, Ernest; Freudenheim, Martin; Gyssling, Walter; Hallgarten, Constance; Haynes, Edna; Jaray, Stephen; Kahle, Maria; Kastan, Benno; Klugmann, Hermann; Koch, Hilde; Kretschmer, Julian; Meissner, Kurt; Menzel, Rudolfine; Mibberlin, Rafael; Moses, Hugo; Neumann, Siegfried; Paeschke, Samuel Arthur; Schalom, Ben Charin; Schloss, Oscar; Schreier, Fritz; Schubert, Franziska; Schwabe, Karl; Schwartzert, Ernest; Spiegel, Margot; Wickerhauser-Lederer, Gertrud; Wilhelm, Theodor; Wolf-Arndt, Philippine; Yourgrau, Wolfgang.

Iconographic Sources

Photographic Agencies: DPA, Corbis, Image Forum
Bayerische Staatsbibliothek (Munich), Bild Datenbank, Heinrich Hoffman collection.
Bundesarchiv, Filmarchiv (Berlin)

Printed Sources

Press

Daily newspapers

Berliner illustrierte (Nachtausgabe), 1938, 1939, 1943
Berliner illustrierte Zeitung, 1938
Das 12 Uhr Blatt, 1934, 1936, 1939
Hamburger Fremdenblatt, 1933, 1934, 1939, 1943
Illustrierte Zeitung (Leipzig), 1938
Völkischer Beobachter, 1932, 1935, 1936, 1939

Weeklies

Deutsche illustrierte, 1934, 1935, 1936, 1938
Funk Woche, 1934, 1936, 1938, 1940
Illustrierte Film-Kurier, 1933–44
Deutsches Adelsblatt, 1932–44
Die Dame, 1936, 1938, 1939

Periodicals

Deutsches Adelsblatt, 1932–44
Die Dame, 1936, 1938, 1939

260 *Sources*

Testimonies and Memoirs of Actors

Andermann, W.T. (pseud.), *Bis der Vorhang fiel*, Dortmund, Schwalvenberg, 1947.

Andersch Alfred, *Der Vater eines Mörders*, Zurich, Diogenes, ed. 1980.

Andreas-Friedrich, Ruth, *Der Schattenmann*, Berlin, Suhrkamp, 1986.

Baarova, Lida, *Die süße Bitterkeit meines Lebens*, Koblenz, Kettermann-Schmidt, 2001.

Beinhorn-Rosemeyer, Elly, *Mein Mann, der Rennfahrer*, Berlin, Deutscher Verlag, 1938.

Below, Nicolaus von, *At Hitler's Side: The Memoirs of Hitler's Luftwaffe Adjutant, 1937–1945*, trans. Geoffrey Brooks, London, Greenhill Books, 2001.

Beradt, Charlotte, *Das Dritte Reich des Traums*, Munich, Nymphenburger Verlagshandlung, 1966.

Bouchez, Robert, *Hitler que j'ai vu naître*, Paris, Jacques Melot [1946].

Den Nürnberger Prozess gegen die Hauptkriegsverbrecher vom 14 november 1945– 1 Oktober 1946, Nuremberg, 1947, 20 vols.

Der Dienstkalender Heinrich Himmlers 1941/42, Hamburg, Christians, 1999.

François-Poncet, André, *Souvenirs d'une ambassade à Berlin*, Paris, Flammarion, 1946.

Freytag von Loringhoven, Bernd, *In the Bunker with Hitler*, New York, Pegasus, 2007.

Fromm, Bella, *Als Hitler mir die Hand küsste*, Berlin, Rowohlt, 1993.

Goebbels, Josef, *Vom Kayserhof zur Reichskanzlei*, Munich, 1934.

Göring, Emmy, *An der Seite Meines Mannes: Begentheiten und Bekenntnisse*, Göttingen, Schütz, 1967 (in English as *My Life with Goering*, London, David Bruce and Watson Ltd, 1972).

Got, Ambroise, *L'Allemagne après la débâcle*, Strasburg, Imprimeries strasbourgeoises, 1919.

Grissbach, Erich, *Hermann Göring – Werk und Mensch*, Munich, Zentral Verlag der NSDAP, 1938.

Hanfstaengel, Ernst, *Hitler: The Missing Years*, New York, Arcade, 1994.

Hassell, Ulrich von, *Die Hassell-Tagebücher 1938–1944*, Berlin, Siedler Verlag, 1988.

Hoffmann, Heinrich, *Hitler wie ich ihn sah*, Munich, Herbig, 1974.

Junge, Traudl, *Until the Final Hour: Hitler's Last Secretary*, ed. Melissa Müller, New York, Arcade Publishing, 2004.

Jünger, Ernst, *Premier journal parisien*, Paris, Bourgois, 1980.

Jünger, Ernst, *Second journal parisien*, Paris, Bourgois, 1980.

Kardoff, Ursula von, *Berliner Aufzeichnungen 1942 bis 1945*, Munich, DTV, 1997.

Kempner, Robert, *Ankläger einer Epoche – Lebenserinnerungen*, Berlin, Ullstein, 1986.

Klemperer, Victor, *The Language of the Third Reich. LTI – Lingua Tertii Imperii. A Philologist's Notebook*, trans. Martin Brody, London and New Brunswick, NJ, Athlone Press, 2000.

Krämer, Willi, *Vom Stab Heß zu Dr. Goebbels*, Vlotho, Verlag für Volkstum und Zeitgeschichteforschung, 1979.

Krause, Karl Wilhelm, *Kammerdiener bei Hitler 10 Jahre Tag und Nacht*, Hamburg, Hermann Laatzen Verlag, 1949.

Krogmann, Carl Vincent, *Es ging und Deutschlands Zukunft 1932–1939*, Landsberg, Druffel, 1976.

Kuch, Kurt and Plaim, Anna, *Bei Hitlers – Zimmermädchen Annas Erinnerungen*, Tülbing, Kleindienst, 2003.

Langer, Walter, *The Mind of Adolf Hitler*, New York, Basic Books, 1972.

Lanzmann, Claude, *Un vivant qui passe: Auschwitz 1943–Theresienstadt 1944*, Paris, Mille et Une Nuits, 1997.

Mann, Klaus, *Mephisto* [1936], trans. Robin Smyth, Harmondsworth, Penguin, 1995.

Moczarski, Kazimierz, *Entretiens avec le bourreau*, Paris, Gallimard, 1979.

Noske, Gustav, *Erlebtes aus Aufstieg und Niedergang einer Demokratie*, Offenbach, 1947.

Perroux, François, *Des mythes hitlériens à l'Europe allemande*, Paris, LGDJ, 2nd edn, 1940.

Picker, Henry, *Hitlers Tischgespräche in Führerhauptquartier 1941–1942*, Stuttgart, Seewald, 1963.

Riefenstahl, Leni, *The Sieve of Memory: Memoirs of Leni Riefenstahl*, London, Quartet, 1999.

Schacht, Hjalmar, *76 Jahre meines Lebens*, Bad Wörischen, K & S, 1953.

Schmeling, Max, *Erinnerungen*, Berlin, Ullstein, 1995.

Schröder, Christa, *12 ans auprès d'Hitler, 1933–1945: la secrétaire privée d'Hitler témoigne*, Paris, Pages après pages, 2004.

Schumann, Coco, *Der Ghettoswinger*, Hamburg, DTV, 1997.

Sombart, Nicolaus, *Jugend in Berlin, 1933–1943: ein Bericht*, Munich, Hanser, 1984.

Speer, Albert, *Spandauer Tagebücher*, Frankfurt, Propyläen, 1975.

Stresemann, Wolfgang, *Wie konnte es geschechen? Hitlers Aufstieg in der Erinnerung eines Zeitzeugen*, 2nd edn, Berlin, Ullstein, 1987.

Studnitz, Hans-Georg von, *Als Berlin brannte – Diarium der Jahre 1943–1945*, Stuttgart, Kohlhammer, 1963.

Verleger J. F. Lehmann – Ein Leben im Kampf für Deutschland, Munich, Lehmann, 1935.

Vogel, Georg, *Diplomat unter Hitler und Adenauer*, Düsseldorf, Econ, 1969.

Wassiltschikow, Marie, *Die Berliner Tagebücher 1940–1945*, Munich, BTP, 1996.

Weizsäcker, Ernst von, *Erinnerungen*, Munich, List, 1950.

Weizsäcker, Richard von, *Vier Zeiten*, Berlin, Taschen Verlag, 2002.

Books Published under the Third Reich

Adolf Hitler – Bilder aus dem Leben des Führers, Altona, Cigaretten Bilderdiens, 1936.

Arbeitsmaiden am Werk, Leipzig, Seemann, 1940.

Baedeckers Autoführer Deutsches Reich, Leipzig, 1938.

Deutscher Hotelfürher 1933, Düsseldorf, 1933.

Franken, Konstanze von, *Der gute Ton: Handbuch des guten Tones*, Berlin, 1938.

Franken-Kalender 1938, Nuremberg, Verlag der Stürmer, 1938.

Franken-Kalender 1939, Nuremberg, Verlag der Fränkischen Landeszeitung, 1939.

Frühjahr und Sommer Modelle des deutschen Modeinstitut, Berlin, DMI, 1934.

Generalsekretariat des Union-Klubs, *Der Klassische Sport*, Berlin, Deutscher Archiv Verlag, 1942.

Martin, Hans, *Darf ich mir erlauben. . . ?*, Stuttgart, Süddeutsches Verlagshaus, 1935.

Hausbuch für die deutsche Familie, Berlin, Standesamtwesen, 1939.

Heimeran, Ernst, *Glückwunschbuch für alle Gelegenheiten*, Munich, Heimeran, 1935.

Hoffmann, Heinrich, *Hitler abseits vom Alltag. 100 Bilddokumente aus der Umgebung des Führers*, preface by Wilhelm Brückner, Berlin, Zeitgeschichte-Verlag, 1940.

Hitler wie ihn keiner kennt – Bilddokumentation, Munich, Verlag Heinrich Hoffmann, 1934.

Hoffmann, Herbert, *Gaststätten*, Stuttgart, Julius Hoffmann Verlag, 1939.

Hoffmann, Moritz and Reichelt, W.O., *Reiseverkehr und Gastlichkeit im neuen Deutschland*, Hamburg, Hotel-Nachrichten, 1939.

Klipper, *Regenkleidung*, Rosenheim, 1938.

Rauers, Friedrich, *Kulturgeschichte der Gaststätte*, Schriftenreihe der Hermann Esser Forschungsgemeinschaft für Fremdenverkehr, Berlin, Alfred Metzner Verlag, 1942.

Soldan, Georg, *Zeitgeschichte in Wort und Bild*, Odenburg, Stalling Verlag, 1933.

Tepel, Franz, *Gastlichkeit im neuen Deutschland*, Dusseldorf, Grosse Verlag und Drückerei, 1937.

Unser Führer zum 50 Geburtstag 20 April 1939, Munich, Eher Verlag, 1939.

Weech, Sigmund von, *Textil und Mode Schule der Reichshauptstadt*, Berlin, 1942.

Wir benehmen uns – Ein fröhlich Buch für fähnrich Gent und kleines Fräulein, Berlin, Scherl, 1936.

Selective Bibliography

Historiography and Historical Methods

Agulhon, Maurice, *La République au village*, Paris, Le Seuil, 1979.

Ayçoberry, Pierre, *La question nazie*, Paris, Le Seuil, 1979.

Berg, Nicolas, *Der Holocaust und die westdeutschen Historiker. Erforschung und Erinnerung*, Göttingen, Wallstein, 2003.

Charle, Christophe, *Les intellectuels en Europe au XIXe siècle – Essai d'histoire comparée*, Paris, Le Seuil, 1996.

De Felice, Renzo, *Le Interpretazioni del Fascismo*, Bari, Laterza, 1969.

Deutsche Gesellschaftsgeschichte 1914–1949, Munich, Beck, 2003.

El Kenz, David, ed., *Le massacre objet d'histoire*, Paris, Gallimard, 2005.

François, Étienne, Siegrist, Hannes, and Vogel, Jakob, eds, *Nation und Emotion – Deutschland und Frankreich im Vergleich – 19. und 20. Jahrhundert*, Göttingen, Vandenhoeck & Ruprecht, 1995.

Haupt, Heinz-Gerhard and Kocka, Jürgen, eds, *Geschichte und Vergleich*, Frankfurt, Campus, 1996.

Husson, Edouard, *Comprendre Hitler et la Shoah – Les historiens de la République fédérale d'Allemagne depuis 1949*, Paris, PUF, 2000.

Kaelble, Hartmut, Kocka, Jürgen, and Siegrist, Hannes, eds, *Europäische Konsumgeschischte. Zur Gesellschaft und Kulturgeschichte des Konsums (18. bis 20. Jahrhundert)*, Frankfurt am Main / New York, Campus, 1997.

Kaelble, Hartmut, *Der historische Vergleich – Eine Einführung zum 19. und 20. Jahrundert*, Frankfurt, Campus, 1999.

Kaelble, Hartmut and Schriewer, Jürgen, eds, *Diskurse und Entwicklungspfade. Der Gesellschaftsvergleich in den Geschichts- und Sozialwissenschaften*, Frankfurt, Campus, 1999.

Kershaw, Ian, *The Nazi Dictatorship: Problems and Perspectives of Interpretation*, 2nd edn, London, Edward Arnold, 1989.

Kocka, Jürgen, *Sozialgeschichte Begriff, Entwicklung, Probleme*, Göttingen, Vandenhoeck & Ruprecht, 1986.

Kocka, Jürgen and Conrad, Christoph, eds, *Staatsbürgerschaft in Europa: Historische*

Erfahrungen und aktuelle Debatten, Hamburg, Körber-Stiftung, 2001.

Levi, Giovanni, 'Il piccolo, il grande e il piccolo,' *Meridiana*, no. 10, 1990.

Lindenberger, Thomas, ' "Alltagsgeschichte" oder: als um die zünftigen Grenzen der Geschichtswissenschaft noch gestritten wurden', in Martin Sabrow, Ralph Jessen, and Klaus Große Kracht, eds, *Zeitgeschichte als Streitgeschichte – Grosse Kontroversen seit 1945*, Munich, Beck, 2003, pp. 74–91.

Möller, Horst, *Europa zwischen den Weltkriegen*, Munich, Oldenburg, 1998.

Rousso, Henry and Petit, Philippe, *La hantise du passé. Entretiens*, Paris, Textuel, 1998.

Sabrow, Martin, Jessen, Ralph, and Große Kracht, Klaus, eds, *Zeitgeschichte als Streitgeschichte – Grosse Kontroversen seit 1945*, Munich, Beck, 2003.

Schulze, Winifried, *Sozialgeschichte, Alltagsgeschichte, Mikro-Historie*, Göttingen, Vandenhoeck & Ruprecht, 1994.

Solchany, Jean, *Comprendre le nazisme dans l'Allemagne des années Zéro*, Paris, PUF, 1997.

Solchany, Jean, *L'Allemagne au XXe siècle*, Paris, PUF, 2003.

Wehler, Hans-Ulrich, 'Psychoanalysis and History', *Social Research*, no. 47, Autumn 1980, pp. 519–36.

Zimmermann, Bénédicte and Werner, Michael, eds, *De la comparaison à l'histoire croisée*, Paris, Le Seuil, 2004.

Detailed Analysis and Approaches in the Human and Social Sciences

Abélès Marc, 'Pour une anthropologie de la platitude. Le politique et les sociétés modernes,' *Anthropologie et Sociétés*, 1989, vol. 13, no. 3, pp. 13–24.

Arendt, Hannah, *The origins of totalitarianism*, New York, Harcourt Brace, 1951.

Arrasse, Daniel, *On n'y voit rien – Descriptions*, Paris, Denoël, 2000.

Bloch, Maurice, *La violence du religieux*, Paris, Odile Jacob, 1997.

Pierre Bourdieu, *Distinction: A Social Critique of the Judgement of Taste*, trans. Richard Nice, Cambridge, Mass., Harvard University Press, 2007.

Détienne, Marcel and Vernant, Jean-Pierre, *La cuisine du sacrifice en pays grec*, Paris, Gallimard, 1979.

Douglas, Mary, *Purity and Danger: An Analysis of the Concepts of Pollution and Taboo*, 2nd edn, London and New York, Routledge, 2000.

Durand, Béatrice, *Cousins par alliance – Les Allemands en notre miroir*, Paris, Autrement, 2002.

Ehrenberg, Alain, *Le culte de la performance*, Paris, Pluriel, 1995.

Ekman, Paul, ed., *Emotion in the Human Face*, Paris, Maison des Sciences de l'homme / Cambridge, Cambridge University Press, 1982.

Elias, Norbert, *The Civilizing Process*, trans. Edmund Jephcott, New York, Pantheon Books, 1982.

Essner, Cornelia and Conte, Edouard, *La Quête de la race – Une anthropologie du nazisme*, Paris, Hachette, 1995.

Foucault, Michel, *Discipline and Punish: The Birth of the Prison*, trans. Alan Sheridan, Harmondsworth, Penguin, 1991.

Furet, François, *Le passé d'une illusion – Essai sur l'idée communiste au xxe siècle*, Paris, Laffont, 1995.

Geertz, Clifford, 'Thick Description: Toward an Interpretive Theory of Culture', in *The Interpretation of Cultures: Selected Essays*, New York, Basic Books, 1973, pp. 3–30.

Goffman Erving, *The Presentation of Self in Everyday Life*, New York, Anchor, 1959.

Gramsci, Antonio, *Gli intellectuali*, Rome, Editori Riuniti, 1971.

Heusch, Luc de, *Rois nés d'un coeur de vache*, Paris, Gallimard, 1982.

Kaufmann, Jean-Claude, *La trame conjugale – Analyse du couple par son linge*, Paris, Nathan, 1992.

Laplantine, François, *De tout petits liens*, Paris, Mille et Une Nuits, 2003.

Mauss, Marcel, *The Gift: Form and Reason for Exchange in Archaic Societies*, trans. W.D. Halls, London, Routledge, 2008.

Pareto, Vilfredo, *I Sistemi socialisti*, Milan, Istituto editoriale italiano, [1902], 7 vols.

Pareto, Vilfredo, *The Mind and Society: A Treatise on General Sociology*, trans. Andrew Bongiorno and Arthur Livingston, New York, Dover, 1963.

Reich, Wilhelm, *The Mass Psychology of Fascism*, trans. Vincent R. Carfagno, New York, Farrar Straus & Giroux, 1970.

Sloterdijk, Peter, *La domestication de l'être*, Paris, Mille et Une Nuits, 2000.

Tarde, Gabriel, *La logique sociale*, Paris, Alcan, 1895.

Weber, Max, *Le savant et le politique*, Paris, Plon, 1959.

Individual and Collective Biographies

Beevor, Antony, *The Mystery of Olga Chekhova*, London, Penguin, 2005.

Browning, Christopher, *Ordinary Men; Reserve Police Battalion 101 and the Final Solution in Poland*, London, Penguin, 2001.

Burrin, Philippe, *La dérive fasciste – Doriot, Déat, Bergery*, Paris, Le Seuil, 1986.

De Boor, Wolfgang, *Hitler – Mensch, Übermensch, Untermensch*, Munich, Fischer, 1985.

Delattre, Lucas, *Fritz Kolbe*, Paris, Denoël, 2003.

Delpla, François, *Les tentatrices du diable – Hitler, la part des femmes*, Paris, L'Archipel, 2005.

Ferro, Marc, *Les individus face aux crises du XXe siècle – L'histoire anonyme*, Paris, Odile Jacob, 2005.

Fest, Joachim, *Hitler*, trans. Richard and Clara Winston, New York, Harcourt Brace Jovanovich, 1974.

Fest, Joachim, *Inside Hitler's Bunker: The Last Days of the Third Reich*, trans. Margot Dembo, London, Picador, 2005.

Fraenkel, Heinrich and Manvell, Roger, *Himmler. Kleinbürger und Massenmörder*, Herrsching, Pawlak, 1981.

Frei, Norbert, ed., *Karrieren im Zwielicht – Hitlers Eliten nach 1945*, Frankfurt, Campus, 2001.

Guilbert, Laure, *Danser avec le IIIe Reich – Les danseurs modernes sous le nazisme*, Brussels, Complexe, 2000.

Hamann, Brigitte, *Hitlers Wien – Lehrjahre eines Diktators*, Munich, Piper, 1996.

Hamann, Brigitte, *Winifred Wagner oder Hitlers Bayreuth*, Munich, Piper, 2002.

Herbert, Ulrich, *Best. Biografische Studie über Radikalismus, Weltanschauung und Vernunft 1903–1989*, Bonn, Dietz, 2001.

Jäckel, Hartmut, *Menschen in Berlin – Das letzte Telefonbuch der alten Reichshauptstadt 1941*, Stuttgart, DVA, 2000.

Jauvert, Vincent, 'Hitler, le sexe et l'OSS', *Le Nouvel Observateur*, no. 1966, 11 July 2002.

Joachimsthaler, Anton, *Hitlers Liste*, Munich, Herbig, 2003.

Kater, Michael H., *Doctors under Hitler*, Durham, University of North Carolina Press, 1989.

Kershaw, Ian, *The 'Hitler Myth': Image and Reality in the Third Reich*, Oxford, Clarendon Press, 1987.

Kershaw, Ian, *Hitler*, London and New York, Longman, 1991.

Kershaw, Ian, *Making Friends With Hitler: Lord Londonderry, the Nazis, and the Road to War*, London, Penguin, 2004.

Klabunde, Anja, *Magda Goebbels*, Munich, Bertelsmann, 1999.

Lambauer, Barbara, *Otto Abetz et les Français ou l'envers de la Collaboration*, Paris, Fayard, 2001.

Laregh, Peter, *Heinrich George – Komödiant seiner Zeit*, Berlin, Ullstein, 1992.

Machtan, Lothar, *The Hidden Hitler*, trans. John Brownjohn, New York, Basic Books, 2001.

Martens, Stefan, *Hermann Göring. 'Erster paladin des Führers' und ' Zweiter Mann im Reich'*, Paderborn, Schoningh, 1985.

Meyer, Beate and Simon, Hermann, eds, *Juden in Berlin*, Berlin, Zentrum Judaïcum, 2000.

Padfield, Peter, *Himmler Reichsführer SS*, London, Papermac, 1991.

Peuschel, Harald, *Die Männer um Hitler: braune Biographien, Martin Bormann, Joseph Goebbels, Hermann Göring, Reinhard Heydrich, Heinrich Himmler und andere*, Düsseldorf, Droste, 1982.

Pourcher, Yves, *Pierre Laval vu par sa fille, d'après ses carnets intimes*, Paris, Cherche-Midi, 2002.

Remaud, Olivier, 'Norbert Elias et l'effondrement de la civilisation: les *Studien über die Deutschen*', *Working Paper*, no. 8, Centre Marc-Bloch, Berlin, September 2002.

Reuth, Ralf Georg, *Goebbels – Eine Biographie*, Munich, Piper, 1995.

Schaake, Erich, *Hitlers Frauen*, Munich, Ullstein, 2000.

Schad, Martha, *Hitlers Spionin – Das Leben von Stephanie von Hohenlohe*, Munich, Heyne, 2002.

Schenck, Ernst Günther, *Patient Hitler. Eine medizinische Biographie*, Düsseldorf, Droste, 1989.

Schmölders, Claudia, *Hitlers Gesicht – Eine physiognomistische Biographie*, Munich, Beck, 2000.

Schwarzwäller, Wulf C., *Hitlers Geld*, Vienna, Ueberreuter, 1998.

Sigmund, Anna-Maria, *Die Frauen der Nazis*, Vienna, Heyne, 1998–2002, 3 vols.

Ueberschär, Gerd R., ed., *Hitlers militarische Elite*, Darmstadt, 1998, 2 vols.

Ulshöfer, Helmut, ed., *Liebesbrief an Adolf Hitler – Briefe in der Tod*, Frankfurt, VAS, 1994.

Vogelsang, Reinhard, *Der Freunderskreis Himmler*, Göttingen, Musterschmidt, 1972.

Waller, John H., *The Devil's Doctor: Felix Kersten and the Secret Plot to Turn Himmler against Hitler*, New York, John Wiley & Sons, 2002.

Wehler, Hans-Ulrich, ed., *Mediziner im Dritten Reich*, Göttingen, Vandenhoeck & Ruprecht, 1990.

Weiss, Hermann, *Personen Lexikon 1933–1945*, Vienna, Tosa, 2003.

Wette, Wolfram, *Gustav Noske – Eine politische Biographie*, Düsseldorf, Droste, 1987.

Wildt, Michael, *Generation des Unbedingten – Das Führungskorps des Reichssicherheitshauptamtes*, Hamburg, HIS Verlag, 2002.

Lifestyles, Social Practices, and Aesthetics

Almeida, Fabrice d', 'Postures d'orateurs et jeux de mains dans la France de l'entre-deux-guerres', in Michèle Ménard and Annie Duprat, eds, *Histoire, images, imaginaires*, Le Mans, Presses universitaires du Maine, 1998, pp. 451–61.

Aly, Götz, *Hitlers Volksstaat – Raub, Rassenkrieg und Nationaler Sozialismus*, Frankfurt, Fischer, 2005.

Ariès, Philippe and Duby, Georges, eds, *A History of Private Life*, Cambridge, Mass., Harvard University Press, 1992–8, 5 vols

Assouline, Pierre, *Lutetia*, Paris, Gallimard, 2005.

Bajohr, Frank, *Parvenüs und Profiteure – Korruption in der NS-Zeit*, Frankfurt, Fischer, 2001.

Breuer, Stefan, *Grundpositionen der deutschen Rechten 1871–1945*, Tübingen, Diskord, 1999.

Broszat, Martin, *The Hitler State*, Harlow, Longman, 1981.

Chaussy, Ulrich and Püschner, Christoph, *Nachbar Hitler – Führerkult und Heimatzerstörung am Obersalzberg*, Berlin, Link, 1995.

Chimenes, Myriam, *Mécènes et musiciens – Du salon au concert à Paris sous la IIIe République*, Paris, Fayard, 2004.

Dahrendorf, Ralf, *Society and Democracy in Germany*, New York, Anchor, 1969.

Ehrenfreund, Jacques, *Les Juifs de Berlin à la Belle Époque*, Paris, PUF, 2000.

Elias, Norbert, *The Germans: Power Struggles and the Development of Habitus in the Nineteenth and Twentieth Centuries*, trans. Eric Dunning and Stephen Mennell, Cambridge, Polity, 1996.

François, Etienne and Schulze, Hagen, eds, *Deutsche Erinnerungsorte*, Munich, Beck, 2001, 3 vols.

Funk, Marcus and Malinowski, Stephan, ' "Character ist alles!" Erziehungsideale und Erziehungspraktiken in deutschen Adelsfamilien des 19. und 20. Jahrhunderts', *Jahrbuch für historische Bildungsforschung*, vol. 6, Bad Heilbrunn, 2000, pp. 71–92.

Gentile, Emilio, *Il Culto del littorio*, Bari/Rome, Laterza, 1998.

Gentile, Emilio, *Politics as Religion*, trans. George Staunton, Princeton, Princeton University Press, 2006.

Guenther, Irene, *Nazi Chic – Fashioning Women in the Third Reich*, New York, Berg, 2004.

Geuter, Ulfried, *Homosexualität in der deutschen Jugendbewegung – Jugendfreundschaft und Sexualität im Diskurs von Jugendbewegung – Psychanalyse und Jugendpsychologie am Beginn des 20. Jahrhunderts*, Frankfurt, Suhrkamp, 1994.

Gunthert, André, 'La voiture du peuple des seigneurs. Naissance de la Volkswagen', *Vingtième siècle*, no. 15, July–September 1987, pp. 29–42.

Haroche, Claudine, Ihl, Olivier, and Deloye, Yves, eds, *Le protocole ou la mise en forme de l'ordre politique*, Paris, L'Harmattan, 1996.

Hirschfeld, Magnus, ed., *Sittengeschichte des 20. Jahrhunderts*, Hanau/Main, Schustek, 1967, 3 vols.

Huynh, Pascal, *La musique sous la république de Weimar*, Paris, Fayard, 1998.

Huynh, Pascal, ed., *Le IIIe Reich et la musique*, Paris, Fayard/Musée de la musique, 2004.

Kessel, Joseph, *Les mains du miracle*, Paris, Gallimard, 1960.

Koch, Peter-Ferdinand, *Die Geldgeschäfte der SS – Wie die deutsche Banken den schwarzen Terror finanzieren*, Hamburg, Hoffmann und Campe, 2000.

Koehn, Barbara, ed., *La révolution conservatrice et les élites intellectuelles*, Rennes, PUR, 2003.

Koreen, Maggie, *Immer feste druff – Das freche Leben der KabarettKönigin Claire Waldoff*, Düsseldorf, Droste, 1997.

Krockow, Christian von, *Les Allemands dans leur XXe siècle*, Paris, Hachette, 1990.

Krogmann, Carl Vincent, *Bellevue – Die Welt von Damals*, Hamburg, Hollstein Verlag, n.d.

Kuczynski, Jürgen, *Geschichte des Alltags des deutschen Volkes 1918–1945*, Cologne, Pahl-Rugenstein Verlag, 1982.

Large, David Clay, *Where Ghosts Walked: Munich's Road to the Third Reich*, New York, Norton, 1997.

Lepper, Katharina, *Moderne Kunst im Nationalsozialismus: die Kampagne 'Entartete Kunst' und die Sammlung des Wilhelm-Lehmbruck-Museums Duisburg 1933–1945*, Duisburg, Wilhelm-Lehmbruck-Museum, 1992.

Loschek, Ingrid, *Mode im 20-Jahrhundert – Eine Kulturgeschichte unserer Zeit*, Munich, Bruckmann, 1978.

Lottman, Herbert, *La Rive gauche. Du Front populaire à la guerre froide*, Paris, Le Seuil, 1981.

Maiwald, Stefan and Mischler, Gerd, *Sexualität unter dem Hakenkreuz*, Munich, Ullstein, 1999.

Malinowski, Stephan, *Vom König zum Führer – Sozialer Niedergang und politische Radikalisierung im deutschen Adel zwischen Kaiserreich und NS-Staat*, Berlin, Akademie Verlag, 2003.

Martin-Fugier, Anne, *La vie élégante ou la formation du Tout-Paris 1815–1848*, Paris, Fayard, 1990.

Martin-Fugier, Anne, *Les salons sous la IIIe République – Art, culture, politique*, Paris, Perrin, 2003.

Matard-Bonucci, Marie-Anne and Milza, Pierre, eds, *L'homme nouveau dans l'Europe fasciste (1922–1945). Entre dictature et totalitarisme*, Paris, Fayard, 2004.

Michaud, Eric, *Un art de l'éternité – L'image et le temps du nationalsocialisme*, Paris, Gallimard, 1996.

Mosse, George L., *The Nationalization of the Masses – Political Symbolism and Mass Movements in Germany from the Napoleonic Wars through the Third Reich*, New York, Fertig, 1975.

Mosse, George L., *The Image of Man : The Creation of Modern Masculinity*, New York, Oxford University Press, 1996.

Nora, Pierre, ed., *Les lieux de mémoires*, Paris, Gallimard, 1984–92, 7 vols.

Petropoulos, Jonathan, *Kunstraub und Sammelwahn – Kunst und Politik im Dritten Reich*, Hamburg, Propyläen, 1999.

Phayer, Michael, *The Catholic Church and the Holocaust, 1930–1965*, Bloomington, Indiana University Press, 2001.

Reichel, Peter, *Der schöne Schein des Dritten Reichs, Gewalt und Faszination des deutschen Fachismus*, Munich, Carl Hanser Verlag, 1991.

Reif, Heinz, 'Hauptstadtentwicklung und Elitenbildung : "Tout Berlin" 1871–1918', in *Geschichte und Emanzipation. Festschrift Reinhard Rürup*, Berlin / New York, 1999, pp. 679–99.

Reif, Heinz, *Adel im 19 und 20 Jahrhundert*, Munich, Oldenbourg, 1999.

Reif, Heinz, *Adel und Bürgertum in Deutschland*, Berlin, Akademie-Verlag, 2000, 2 vols.

Reif, Janin, Schumacher, Horst, and Uebel, Lothar, *Schwanenwerder – Ein Inselparadies in Berlin*, Berlin, Nicolai, 2000.

Schneider, Wolfgang, *Frauen unterm Hakenkreuz*, Hamburg, Hoffmann und Campe, 2001.

Scholder, Klaus, ed., *Die Mittwochsgesellschaft – Protokolle aus dem geistigen Deutschland 1932 bis 1944*, Berlin, Severin und Sieler, 1982.

Schuster, Peter-Klaus, *Nationalsozialismus und 'Entartete Kunst': die 'Kunststadt' München 1937*, Munich, Prestel, 1988.

Schwabe, Klaus, ed., *Das diplomatische Korps 1871–1945*, Boppard / Rhein, Boldt, 1985.

Sultano, Gloria, *Wie geistiges Kokain – Mode unterm Hakenkreuz*, Vienna, Verlag für Gesellschaftskritik, 1995.

Tamagne, Florence, *Histoire de l'homosexualité en Europe – Berlin, Londres, Paris 1919–1939*, Paris, Le Seuil, 2000.

Teuteberg, Hans J. and Wischermann, Clemens, *Wohnalltag in Deutschland 1850–1914*, Münster, F. Coppenrath Verlag, 1985.

Thalmann, Rita, *Etre femme sous le IIIe Reich*, Paris, Laffont, 1982.

Ueberschär, Gerd R. and Vogel, Winfried, *Dienen und Verdienen – Hitlers Geschenke an seine Elite*, Frankfurt, Fischer, 2001.

Völger, Gisela and Welck, Karin von, eds, *Männerbande, Männerbünde. Zur Rolle des Mannes im Kulturvergleich*, Cologne, Museumsdienst Köln und Rautenstrauch Joest Museum, 1990, 2 vols.

Winkler, Heinrich-August, *Die deutsche Staatskrise 1930–1933*, Munich, Oldenburg, 1992.

Violence, War, and Anti-Semitism

Bajohr, Frank, *Unser Hotel ist Judenfrei – Bäder-Antisemitismus im 19. und 20. Jahrhundert*, Frankfurt, Fischer, 2003.

Becker, Annette, Audoin-Rouzeau, Stéphane, Ingrao, Christian, and Rousso, Henry, eds, *La violence de guerre – Approche comparée des deux conflits mondiaux*, Brussels, Complexe, 2002.

Benz, Wolfgang, ed., *Die Juden in Deutschland*, Hamburg, Beck, 1988.

Benz, Wolfgang, *Bilder vom Juden. Studien zum alltäglichen Antisemitismus*, Munich, Beck, 2001.

Bracher, Karl-Dietrich, *Die Auflösung der Weimarer Republik*, Düsseldorf, Droste, 2004.

Bracher, Karl Dietrich, Funke, Manfred, and Jacobsen, Hans-Adolf, eds, *Neue Studien zur nationalsozialistischen Herrschaft – Deutschland 1933–1945*, Bonn, Bundeszentrale für Politische Bildung, 1993.

Brayard, Florent, *La solution finale de la question juive*, Paris, Fayard, 2004.

Broszat, Martin and Frohlich, Elke, *Alltag und Widerstand. Bayern im Nationalsozialismus*, Munich, Piper, 1987.

Burrin, Philippe, *Ressentiment et apocalypse. Essai sur l'antisémitisme nazi*, Paris, Le Seuil, 2004.

Courtois, Stéphane and Rayski, Adam, *Qui savait quoi? L'extermination des Juifs 1941–1945*, Paris, La Découverte, 1987.

Dorscher, Hans-Jürgen, *Das Auswärtiges Amt im dritten Reich*, Berlin, Siedler, 1987.

Dreyfus, Jean-Marc, 'L'aryanisation économique des maisons de prostitution: un éclairage sur quelques proxénètes juifs en France occupée, 1940–1944', *Revue des études juives*, vol. 162, January–June 2003, pp. 219–46.

Duménil, Anne, Beaupré, Nicolas, and Ingrao, Christian, eds, *1914–1915, L'ère de la guerre*, Paris, Agnès Vienot, 2004, 2 vols.

Essner, Cornelia, *Die 'Nürnberger Gesetze' oder die Verwaltung des Rassenwahns 1933–1945*, Paderborn, Schöningh, 2002.

Friedländer, Saul, *L'Allemagne nazie et les Juifs*, Paris, Le Seuil, 1997, 2 vols.

Gensburger, Sophie and Dreyfus, Jean-Marc, *Des camps dans Paris*, Fayard, 2004.

Gerhard, Paul and Mallmann Klaus-Michael, eds, *Die Gestapo im Zweiten Weltkrieg. 'Heimatfront' und besetzes Europa*, Darmstadt, Primus Verlag, 2002.

Gerlach, Christian, *Krieg, Ernährung, Volkermord – Forschungen zur deutsche Vernichtungspolitik*, Hamburg, HIS, 1998.

Gobineau, Arthur de, *Essai sur l'inégalité des races humaines*, Paris, Nouvel Office d'Edition, 1963.

Goschler, Constantin and Ther, Philipp, eds, *Raub und Restitution*, Frankfurt, Fischer, 2003.

Halcomb, Jill, *Uniforms and Insignia of the German Foreign Office and Government Ministries 1938–1945*, Columbus, SC, Crown / Agincourt, 1984.

Ingrao, Christian, 'Une anthropologie historique du massacre: le cas des *Einsatzgruppen* en Russie', in David El Kenz, ed., *Le massacre objet d'histoire*, Paris, Gallimard, 2005, pp. 351–69.

Lüdtke, Alf, *Herrschaft als soziale Praxis. Historische und sozial-anthropologische Studien*, Göttingen, Vandenhoeck & Ruprecht, 1991.

Malinowski, Stephan, 'Politische Skandale als Zerrspiegel der Demokratie. Die Fälle Barmat und Sklarek im Kalkül der Weimarer Rechten', in *Jahrbuch für Antisemitismusforschung*, no. 5, 1996, pp. 46–65.

Mazower, Mark, *Dark Continent. Europe's Twentieth Century*, London, Penguin, 1999.

Meinen, Insa, *Wehrmacht und Prostitution im besetzten Frankreich*, Bremen, Edition Temmen, 2002.

Möller, Horst, Dahm, Volker, Mehringer, Hartmut, and Feiber, Albert A., *Die tödliche Utopie*, Munich, IFZ, 1999.

Mosse, George L., *Fallen Soldiers: Reshaping the Memory of the World Wars*, Oxford, Oxford University Press, 1990.

Reichardt, Sven, *Faschistische Kampfbunde. Gewalt und Gemeinschaft im italienischen Squadrismus und in der deutschen SA*, Cologne/Weimar/Vienna, Böhlau Verlag, 2002.

Sabrow, Martin, *Der Rathenaumord – Rekonstruktion einer Verschwörung gegen die Republik von Weimar*, Munich, Oldenburg, 1994.

Schieder, Wolfgang, ed., *Faschismus als soziale Bewegung: Deutschland und Italien im Vergleich*, Hamburg, Hoffmann und Campe, 1976.

Tatar, Maria, *Lustmord – Sexual Murder in Weimar Germany*, Princeton, Princeton University Press, 1995.

Thalmann, Rita, *La nuit de cristal*, Paris, Robert Laffont, 1972.

Vogel, Jakob, *Nationen im Gleichschritt. Der Kult der 'Nation in Waffen' in Deutschland und Frankreich (1871–1914)*, Göttingen, Vandenhoeck & Ruprecht, 1997.

Wegner, Bernd, *Hitlers politische Soldaten: die Waffen SS 1939–1945*, Paderborn, Schöningh, 1988.

Index